Northwestern University

STUDIES IN *Phenomenology &*

Existential Philosophy

Phenomenology and
the Natural Sciences

Joseph J. Kockelmans
Theodore J. Kisiel

Phenomenology and the Natural Sciences

Essays and Translations

NORTHWESTERN UNIVERSITY PRESS

1970   EVANSTON

Copyright © 1970 by Northwestern University Press
All rights reserved
Library of Congress Catalog Card Number: 74–116052
ISBN 0–8101–0314–1
Manufactured in the United States of America

Joseph J. Kockelmans is Professor of Philosophy
at The Pennsylvania State University.
Theodore J. Kisiel is Associate Professor of
Philosophy at Northern Illinois University.

235249

Contents

Preface

THE GOAL OF THIS ANTHOLOGY is to give the English-speaking reader a first impression of the contributions made by phenomenology to the vast domain of the philosophy of the natural sciences. In order to avoid misunderstanding about what is involved in this aim, a brief explanation seems to be in order.

Over the past forty years the term "phenomenology" has been used to refer to a great variety of basic philosophical conceptions. Although almost all contemporary phenomenologists claim that they take their point of departure from Husserl's phenomenology, it is nonetheless very difficult to specify the basic philosophical views which these phenomenologists share. Speaking of the various and often conflicting claims made by contemporary phenomenologists, Merleau-Ponty rightly remarked that the attitude of the responsible philosopher must be that phenomenology can be practiced and identified as a manner or style of thinking, that it existed as a movement, before arriving at complete awareness of itself as a philosophy.[1] It is not our intention in this introduction to specify precisely what phenomenology is for the authors represented in this anthology. Nor do we conceive of it as our task to formulate a kind of definition clearly outlining the basic ideas which all contemporary phenomenologists have in common. We may say, however, that almost all of the philosophers mentioned in this book agree with Husserl on the following theses:

1. Maurice Merleau-Ponty, *Phenomenology of Perception*, trans. Colin Smith (New York: Humanities Press, 1962), p. viii.

[xi]

1. There is a radical difference between philosophy and science. Notwithstanding this radical difference, there is a necessity of cooperation between the two. Within the context of this cooperation philosophy has in some sense a foundational task in regard to the sciences, whereas science offers to philosophy at least a substantial part of its typically philosophical problems.

2. In order to achieve its own goal philosophy must return from the realm of "objectified meaning" as found in the sciences to the realm of immediate experience (lifeworld).

3. In order to be authentically philosophical phenomenology must transcend the ontical in the direction of the ontological, "being" in the direction of "meaning." As Husserl and Heidegger have briefly formulated it: Philosophy's main interest is in "the meaning and Being of being." [2]

In the essays which follow the question of what is to be understood by phenomenology is sometimes explicitly touched upon by the authors themselves, and the reader will undoubtedly be able in each case to evaluate what exactly is meant by the phenomenological approach and more specifically by the phenomenological methods about which the authors speak. Where the authors do not explicitly specify in what sense their conception is meant to be phenomenological, the editors have tried briefly to delineate the authors' views and to explicitly relate them to Husserl's phenomenology.

As far as the expression "philosophy of natural science" is concerned, it is a well-known fact that this expression refers to a complex and multiform body of doctrines and conceptions. Under the general heading "philosophy of natural science" one can encounter investigations concerning the natural sciences which are methodological, logical, epistemological, or "ontological" in character. Since the meaning of the first three terms is sufficiently clear, it suffices to indicate here that by the term "ontological" in this connection is meant any philosophical in-

2. Edmund Husserl, *Formale und transzendentale Logik: Versuch einer Kritik der logischen Vernunft* (Halle a.d.S.: Niemeyer, 1929), pp. 13, 148 (hereafter cited as *FTL*); Martin Heidegger, *Being and Time*, trans. John Macquarrie and Edward Robinson (London: SCM, 1962), pp. 21–31, 188–95, 244–56, and *passim*. See also Alwin Diemer, *Edmund Husserl: Versuch einer systematischen Darstellung seiner Phänomenologie* (Meisenheim a.d. Gl.: Hain, 1965), pp. 9–42 *passim*.

vestigation the purpose of which is to show the function which the realm of meaning constituted by the natural sciences (the world of natural science) plays within the totality of meaning (*the* world), and to describe the relationships which (within this totality of meaning, world, or Being) exist between the domain of meaning constituted by natural science and other limited realms of meaning constituted by other forms of man's experience, such as religion, art, social practice, and so on.[3]

In the essays brought together in this anthology the stress is very seldom on methodological and logical issues. The explanation of this is *not* to be found in the widespread idea that phenomenology adopts a merely negative attitude in regard to the methodology and logic of science. Nor is it the case that phenomenologists have never paid attention to this aspect of science (we need only mention the names of Weyl, Becker, Gaston Bachelard, Suzanne Bachelard, Jean Cavaillès, Jean Ladrière, among others). The explanation of this fact should be found rather in the deliberate choice of the editors. The reason why we, after long reflection and discussion, have finally decided not to include methodological and logical analyses is that as far as methodological and logical issues are concerned phenomenologists are in fundamental agreement with philosophers of other trends and schools. Adding analyses of that nature to the selections chosen would have amounted merely to a repetition of well-known and generally accepted views and by no means would have contributed to clarifying the rather unique position of phenomenology within philosophy of science as a whole. In order to be able to show as clearly as possible the contributions to the philosophy of the natural sciences made by phenomenologists, we have chosen those essays which focus mainly on epistemological and especially on "ontological" issues, the latter term understood in the sense briefly indicated above.

In the light of this decision one may wonder about the inclusion of several essays which are either overtly or covertly a reflection on mathematics. But ever since Husserl struck the theme of the mathematization of nature, the mutual relations between mathematical formalization and the data of experience

3. The interpretation of the term *ontological* is Heideggerian in origin. For a further explanation and justification of this interpretation, see Joseph J. Kockelmans, *The World in Science and Philosophy* (Milwaukee, Wis.: Bruce Publishing Co., 1969), chap. 1.

have been a central issue in the phenomenology of natural science. Such an inquiry calls for, among other things, a study of mathematics' formalism in its own right. An evaluation of its positive scope as well as its limitations is all the more necessary since Husserl's concern over the depletion of the lifeworld's meaning that formalization necessarily brings about puts mathematics in a somewhat negative light. The works of Cavaillès, Suzanne Bachelard, and Ladrière especially serve as a much-needed antidote to the "denigrating" tendency which this theme initiated among phenomenologists, or better among those who are more concerned with "existential" matters. These authors join hands with the earlier Husserl in their concern that the ideal objects of formal ontology be investigated for their own sake, in order to be in a better position to evaluate the ontological status of these objects the moment it becomes clear that they constitute an integral part of the network of ideas (*Ideenkleid*) which natural science has thrown over the lifeworld. The amazing capacity of mathematics to address itself to nature and to open up dimensions hitherto unexpected continues to be the core of, the secret of, and the gateway to the essence of mathematical physics. Any reflection which aims, as phenomenology does, at situating natural science in the larger context of science as such must come to terms with the peculiar life that the fertility of mathematics bestows upon natural science.

The reasons why we have limited the scope of this book to the realm of the *natural* sciences are the following. First of all, a relatively large number of books have already been dedicated to showing phenomenology's contribution to the "human sciences." Furthermore, the contributions made by phenomenology to the realm of the "human sciences" are so great in number and so varied in goal and scope that we thought it impossible to include this very important aspect of philosophy of science in this anthology.[4] Finally, we felt justified in this decision by the fact that

4. Edmund Husserl, *Phänomenologische Psychologie* (1925), *Husserliana* IX, ed. Walter Biemel (The Hague: Nijhoff, 1962) (hereafter cited as *H* IX). Hermann Drüe, *Edmund Husserls System der phänomenologischen Psychologie* (Berlin: de Gruyter, 1963). Joseph J. Kockelmans, *Edmund Husserl's Phenomenological Psychology* (Pittsburgh, Pa.: Duquesne University Press, 1967). Jean-Paul Sartre, *The Emotions: Outline of a Theory*, trans. Bernard Frechtman (New York: Philosophical Library, 1948); *L'Imaginaire: Psychologie*

it is a generally accepted practice in treatises on philosophy of science to focus mainly on the natural sciences.

However, two brief remarks are in order here. First of all, in making this merely practical decision, it is not our intention to suggest that we believe there is an *essential* difference between the natural sciences and the *empirical* sciences of man. Although there are certainly phenomenologists who have defended such a view, this view is definitely not shared by the leading phenomenologists (Husserl, Heidegger, Sartre, Merleau-Ponty), and personally we have many reasons to prefer the latter view over the former. On the other hand, we are deeply aware of the fact that the "human sciences" indeed confront the philosopher with a great number of problems which do not occur in the realm of the natural sciences. Such problems, as we understand them, do not immediately pertain to the methodology and logic of the *empirical* sciences, but in almost all cases belong to the realm of epistemological and specifically ontological problems.

As far as the choice of selections is concerned, it has been very difficult in many instances to come to a final decision. We are fully aware of the fact that other reasonable choices could have been made from the abundance of available material. We

----

phénoménologique de l'imagination (Paris: Gallimard, 1940). Maurice Merleau-Ponty, *The Structure of Behavior,* trans. Alden L. Fisher (Boston: Beacon Press, 1963); *Signs,* trans. Richard C. McCleary (Evanston, Ill.: Northwestern University Press, 1964); *The Primacy of Perception and Other Essays,* ed. James M. Edie (Evanston, Ill.: Northwestern University Press, 1964). Alfred Schutz, *Collected Papers,* 3 vols. (The Hague: Nijhoff, 1964–66). Erwin Straus, *Phenomenological Psychology: Selected Papers* (New York: Basic Books, 1966). Aron Gurwitsch, *Studies in Phenomenology and Psychology* (Evanston, Ill.: Northwestern University Press, 1966). *Existence: A New Dimension in Psychiatry and Psychology,* ed. Rollo May, Ernest Angel, and Henri F. Ellenberger (New York: Basic Books, 1960). *Being-in-the-World: Selected Papers of Ludwig Binswanger,* trans. Jacob Needleman (New York: Basic Books, 1963). Ludwig Binswanger, "On the Relationship between Husserl's Phenomenology and Psychological Insight," *Philosophy and Phenomenological Research,* II (1941–42), 199–210. S. Strasser, *Phenomenology and the Human Sciences* (Pittsburgh, Pa.: Duquesne University Press, 1963). *Phenomenology: The Philosophy of Edmund Husserl and Its Interpretation,* ed. Joseph J. Kockelmans (New York: Doubleday, 1967), pt. III. *Philosophy of the Social Sciences: A Reader,* ed. Maurice Natanson (New York: Random House, 1963).

also know that it would be very difficult in each case to give a convincing justification for the choice made. Nevertheless we believe that the anthology as it stands gives a rather objective idea of the great variety of contributions phenomenology has made to the philosophy of natural science.

A glance through the table of contents reveals immediately the heterogeneous character of the book: in addition to translations of original essays the book also contains a number of studies written by the editors. We have included these studies because we were not able to select passages from the works of Husserl, Heidegger, and Merleau-Ponty which we felt would in themselves give a really clear idea of the contributions these authors have made to the realm of philosophy of natural science. To the best of our knowledge Merleau-Ponty never wrote an essay explicitly dealing with the natural sciences as such, although throughout his works there are a great number of ideas which are immediately relevant to the philosophy of natural science. It is these ideas which we have tried to present in a systematic way to the reader. The situation is similar for Heidegger, although among his writings there are a few essays which deal directly with the natural sciences. In Heidegger's major works there are many short passages which are of great importance for philosophy of natural science and which in our view can be taken full advantage of only if they are presented in a somewhat systematic form. The few essays in which Heidegger explicitly deals with the natural sciences form parts of books (namely, *Vorträge und Aufsätze* and *Holzwege*) which are not yet translated but will be available in English before long. Furthermore, the language and content of these essays is so complicated that a kind of paraphrase of them seemed to be preferable to an attempt at literal translation. Finally, it is Husserl's last work *Die Krisis der europäischen Wissenschaften* which for our purposes contains the most interesting material. Although this book has recently been translated, we felt that presenting a brief paraphrase of the most interesting passages would be an appropriate approach.[5] In order to compensate for what could not be included in this way we have added a few essays focusing on two aspects of Husserl's philosophy which are indispensable for an adequate understanding of his major concern in *Krisis*.

5. The *Crisis of the European Sciences*, trans. David Carr (Evanston, Ill.: Northwestern University Press, 1970).

In our introductory remarks, which are mainly biographical and bibliographical in character, we have limited ourselves to a reasonable minimum in order to be able to use as much of the available space as possible to reach our main goal. In the Selected Bibliography we have listed only those books and articles immediately relevant to the scope of our work here. The quotations we have used in the text have been translated by us unless otherwise indicated.

Grateful acknowledgments are made to the authors, publishers, and translators represented here for their generosity in granting permission to reprint or translate selections from copyright material and for their kind cooperation. Thanks are due to Fred H. deOliveria, Jr., for his help in compiling the indexes. The editors are especially indebted to Northwestern University Press for its support and enthusiasm for the project and for its unremitting cooperation in bringing it to this final form.

Joseph J. Kockelmans
The Pennsylvania State University

Theodore J. Kisiel
Northern Illinois University

Acknowledgments

Some of the articles collected in this volume have already appeared in print. The following material is reprinted with permission of the publishers:

Hermann Weyl, *Raum, Zeit, Materie: Vorlesungen über Allgemeine Relativitätstheorie*, 5th rev. ed. (Berlin: Springer, 1923), Introduction.

Hermann Weyl, *Philosophy of Mathematics and Natural Science* (Princeton, N.J.: Princeton University Press, 1949; 2d ed., 1966; paperback ed., New York: Atheneum, 1963), reprinted with permission of Princeton University Press.

Oskar Becker, "Beiträge zur phänomenologischen Begründung der Geometrie und ihrer physikalischen Anwendungen," *Jahrbuch für Philosophie und phänomenologische Forschung* (Halle a.d.S.: Niemeyer, 1923), VI, 493–507, 536–37, 547–60.

Wilhelm Szilasi, "Erfahrung und Wahrheit in den Naturwissenschaften," *Philosophie und Naturwissenschaft* (Bern: Francke, 1961), pp. 25–51.

Eugène Minkowski, *Vers une cosmologie* (Paris: Aubier, 1936), pp. 163–72.

Gaston Bachelard, *L'Activité rationaliste de la physique contemporaine* (Paris: Presses Universitaires de France, 1951), pp. 21–49.

Jean Cavaillès, *Sur la logique et la théorie de la science*, 2d ed. (Paris: Presses Universitaires de France, 1960), pp. 1–78.

Suzanne Bachelard, *La Conscience de rationalité: Etude phénoménologique sur la physique mathématique* (Paris: Presses Universitaires de France, 1958), pp. 1–28.

Jean Ladrière, "La Philosophie des mathématiques et le problème du formalisme," *Revue philosophique de Louvain*, LVII (1959), 600–22.

Jean Ladrière, "Mathématiques et formalisme," *Revue des questions scientifiques* (Louvain), October 20, 1955, pp. 538–74.

List of Abbreviations

EU	*Erfahrung und Urteil*
FD	*Die Frage nach dem Ding*
FTL	*Formale und transzendentale Logik*
H III	*Husserliana III, Ideen, Vol. I, Allgemeine Einführung in die reine Phänomenologie*
H IV	*Husserliana IV, Ideen, Vol. II, Phänomenologische Untersuchungen zur Konstitution*
H V	*Husserliana V, Ideen, Vol. III, Die Phänomenologie und die Fundamente der Wissenschaften*
H VI	*Husserliana VI, Die Krisis der europäischen Wissenschaften*
H VII	*Husserliana VII, Erste Philosophie, Vol. I, Kritische Ideengeschichte*
H VIII	*Husserliana VIII, Erste Philosophie, Vol. II, Theorie der phänomenologischen Reduktion*
H IX	*Husserliana IX, Phänomenologische Psychologie*
HW	*Holzwege*
Ideas I	*Ideas: General Introduction to Pure Phenomenology*
LU	*Logische Untersuchungen*
PP	*Phenomenology of Perception*
PrP	*The Primacy of Perception*
SB	*The Structure of Behavior*
US	*Unterwegs zur Sprache*
VA	*Vorträge und Aufsätze*
VI	*Le Visible et l'invisible*

See Selected Bibliography for full citations of these works.

PART I

Phenomenology and Science in Germany

Edmund Husserl

EDMUND GUSTAVE ALBRECHT HUSSERL was born in Prossnitz, Moravia, on April 8, 1859. After receiving his secondary education in Vienna, he studied mathematics and physics at the University of Leipzig from 1876 to 1878, and later at the University of Berlin from 1878 to 1881. He received his degree in 1883 at the University of Vienna where he had studied under Königsberger from 1881 to 1883. His dissertation was entitled *Beiträge zur Theorie der Variationsrechnung*. After working as Weierstrass' assistant in Berlin, Husserl returned to Vienna where he devoted himself to the study of philosophy. He received his first introduction to the subject from W. Wundt in Leipzig and from Paulsen at Berlin. In Vienna he attended the lectures of Brentano for about two years. In 1886 Brentano advised Husserl to go to the University of Halle as Stumpf's assistant. There Husserl became *Privatdozent* in 1887, teaching philosophy from that time until 1901. From 1901 until 1916 Husserl taught philosophy at Göttingen, and from 1916 until 1928 he taught in Freiburg. He died there on April 27, 1938.

The phenomenological method which Husserl discovered around 1896 was originally conceived of as a new philosophical approach to define the essences of conscious phenomena. This method was employed for the first time in his *Logische Untersuchungen*, 2 vols., (1900–1901), where it was applied to the realm of meaning constituted by formal logic. In the first volume of his second major work, *Ideen zu einer reinen Phänomenologie* (1913), phenomenology is presented as the necessary propaedeutic method to be used in every authentically philosophical

[3]

investigation concerning the meaning of all being. Systematic application of this method in Husserl's view necessarily leads to transcendental phenomenology as the metaphysical theory of the universal constitution of all meaning by the transcendental ego. Although Husserl's transcendental phenomenology, as far as its basic insights are concerned, comes very close to the metaphysical position defended by Kant, it differs from Kant's philosophy radically because of the completely different way in which this basic conception is arrived at.

Husserl, who came to philosophy from mathematics and physics and who also had a relatively solid knowledge of empirical psychology, has always shown a great interest in philosophy of science. It is to this aspect of his philosophy that the three essays which follow are dedicated. The first tries to explain the relationship which, in Husserl's view, exists between philosophy and science. In this essay a special effort is made to give the reader a founded insight into Husserl's phenomenology as a whole and its function in regard to the realms of meaning constituted by the various empirical sciences in particular. The second essay is devoted to Husserl's quite original conception of the meaning of Galileo's mathematization of nature. The last essay deals with Husserl's interpretation of the history of science and its relevance for philosophy of science.

1 / Phenomenology as the Science of Science

Theodore J. Kisiel

IN RETROSPECT, from the vantage point of the 1920's, after over thirty years of philosophical effort, Husserl sought to unravel the several interwoven paths which had led him to the central insight of his transcendental phenomenology. The shortest of these routes is the Cartesian way that dominates the works published during his lifetime. But the first historically was the course generally entitled as the "way through the critique of the positive sciences," [1] which laboriously wends its way from the empirical to the existing a priori sciences, mathematics and logic, to the a priori but still positive ontologies, both formal and material, culminating in the ontology of the lifeworld, all of which were born and developed in the course of these critiques, before converging on their common Archimedean point in transcendental subjectivity. It is in this long way through the objectivity of the positive sciences that phenomenology is best seen as the endeavor to be the science *of science*.

The critique is at once the clarification of the foundations of the positive sciences. And it is in the radical clarity of its presuppositions that a science is truly a science, and therefore rigorous. But what nowadays is commonly called a scientific foundation is already an end product, a first in theory but not in knowledge. Husserl's thirst for radicality could be satisfied with nothing less than the most ultimate evidences, so that, before the full clarifi-

---

1. Edmund Husserl, *Erste Philosophie* (1923–24), Vol. II: *Theorie der phänomenologischen Reduktion*, *Husserliana* VIII, ed. R. Boehm (The Hague: Nijhoff, 1959), p. 259. (Hereafter cited as *H* VIII.)

cation of the sciences is reached, his critique of science expands into a critique of experience which becomes one with the critique of reason itself. That all sciences have their ultimate ground in the evidence from experience is a commonplace. But that there is more to evidence than facts taxes common parlance. That evidence and experience always involve the subject and that therefore all sciences are ultimately grounded in the "productive intentionality" of subjectivity are consequences that many would prefer not to face. There is no objectivity in the positive sciences which is not at once subjective through and through. On the other hand, Husserl's lifelong battle with objectivism and his consequent espousal of the Cartesian way should not blind us to the other side of the paradox of intentionality, namely, that the transcendental subjectivity is itself oriented to objectivity through and through. Consequently, as the investigation becomes more radically subjective, it becomes *eo ipso* that much more objective. This is what the longer road through the positive sciences constantly keeps before us. The sciences, which historically and necessarily precede phenomenology, serve as the "guiding clues" which are to lead us men of the twentieth century to the "heart of the matter" which sustains them. "But this is precisely what is new about phenomenology which, having emerged from the concern for a clarification and deepening of traditional logic, has placed these most universal and ultimate problems of science and of knowledge in general on their true intuitive grounds and thus has been the first to grasp them in their concrete fullness." [2]

NATURALISM AND A SCIENTIFIC PHILOSOPHY

PHILOSOPHY HAS LONG FELT the need to be scientific, but this exigency became particularly intense with the emergence of modern natural science. In Husserl's day, the most powerful movement toward the construction of a scientific philosophy was that of naturalism, which sought to model philosophy after natural science. As a critique of cognition, naturalistic philosophy then assumed the form of psychologism, which considered cognition as a psychological fact to be investigated in

2. *H* VIII, p. 250.

terms of its natural causes and the natural laws of its development and occurrence, in short, a "physics of thought." [3] Hence logic as the art of scientific cognition was to be founded in empirical psychology, as chemical engineering is founded in chemistry and the art of surveying in geometry.[4] And empirical psychology was to explore the causal genesis of thought in terms of the inductive laws of the coexistence and succession of psychic facts.

But inductive generalizations from facts can only be probable and never exact. Are we then to presume that the principle of noncontradiction, *modus Barbara, modus ponens,* etc., and all of the pure mathematical principles as well, are only probable approximations? Husserl insists that these laws at the very heart of logic and mathematics are "absolutely exact" and apodictically evident, hence supra-empirical.[5] As necessary laws, they transcend the contingency of facts. This is not to deny that the cognitive acts of representation, judgment, proof, etc., have a psychological origin, but there are more than psychic events involved here. Terms such as "knowledge," "thought," "judgment," etc., are equivocal, referring as they do to both the subjective and objective poles of the process. And the identity of the logical laws of thought with the psychological laws of "thought" serves to perpetuate this confusion. But inasmuch as, for example, the logical form "Barbara" is identically the same ideal object in any number of empirical subjective acts, the distinction is essential. Without it, it would not be possible to speak of the same category in factually different events occurring at different times in different places. This distinction is then a first step toward overcoming the skeptical consequences of psychologism.[6] For true objectivity is not a factual but an ideal objectivity, which Husserl will eventually correlate with acts of a higher order, not of the reactive subject of psychologism but of the productive life of a transcendental subjectivity, in the order of pure rationality and meaning.

The psychologizing of even logic, "an exemplary index of all

3. *Logische Untersuchungen,* 5th ed. (Tübingen: Niemeyer, 1968), Vol. I, § 19, p. 55, quoting Theodor Lipps. (Hereafter cited as *LU.*)

4. *LU,* Vol. I, § 17, p. 51.

5. *LU,* Vol. I, § 21, pp. 62–64.

6. *LU,* Vol. I, § 46, 170–73.

ideality," [7] measures the extreme to which the naturalizing of consciousness was being executed, whereby reason is relativized and made dependent on a nonrational source. But "the spell of inborn naturalism" [8] is an all-pervasive one that has its roots in the natural attitude of daily life. The natural attitude assumes a factual world of existing beings given in advance as "really there" to such a degree that it literally overlooks the active constituting processes of the consciousness by which these objects are brought to awareness. In such an attitude, even the human ego is considered to be *in* this existentially posited world and not the subject *for* which this world has being insofar as it appears to me. [9] Not only the natural sciences but also the human sciences, and even logic, as they have developed historically, even if they can justify their theoretical steps, do not carry their self-criticism to the original productions of consciousness, and to that extent, like the daily attitudes, remain "naïve," i.e., lack the complete clairvoyance necessary for full scientific sophistication. [10] They are positive sciences without being positing sciences through and through. They accept nature as given without considering the sources of this givenness. And so the clarity of their relative rationality is shadowed by a dark side of "complete irrationality as its necessary inverse," [11] on the side of the submerged beginnings of their foundations. It is phenomenology which purports to supply this depth dimension to the positive sciences through the methodical exposure of the hidden presuppositions expressed in their subjective performances.

As "naïvetés of a higher order," the natural sciences do represent a step beyond the natural attitude, and when naturalism uses these sciences as models for the construction of a scientific philosophy, the search for scientific rigor and evidence that it endeavors to transplant to a philosophical level is to be commended. Even if naturalism is discredited because it attempts to

7. "Philosophy as Rigorous Science," in *Phenomenology and the Crisis of Philosophy*, trans. Quentin Lauer (New York: Harper Torchbook, 1965), p. 80.
8. *Ibid.*, p. 110.
9. *Ideas: General Introduction to Pure Phenomenology*, trans. W. R. Boyce Gibson (New York: Collier, 1962), p. 8. (Hereafter cited as *Ideas I.*)
10. *Cartesian Meditations: An Introduction to Phenomenology*, trans. Dorion Cairns (The Hague: Nijhoff, 1960), § 64, p. 152.
11. *FTL*, p. 15.

EDMUND HUSSERL / 9

apply a uniform method to both nature and spirit, its ultimate aim of a scientific philosophy should not be discounted.[12] But since philosophy has a different "object" than natural science, it demands a different method to achieve its rigor. Since its objects are fundamentally not real but ideal, it cannot use the methods employed by the sciences of the real world but one that penetrates to the ideal realm of consciousness. Since its concern is not with contingent facts but with necessary essences, it must develop a method for "observing" essences. Since its ultimate task takes it to the active constituting subject, it must find a way to seize its vital intentions without turning them into dead letters.

And so philosophy as a strict science cannot be an empirical science but an ideal science, a scientific knowledge of ideal objects. Not the least of these ideal objects is science itself. Since science itself is a product of "spirit," it cannot be investigated by a science of nature. A science of science is necessarily a science of spirit (*Geisteswissenschaft*). Science as a human activity is to be clarified by the methods of the humanities rather than by the methods of natural science. For natural science is natural science, but to speak about natural science is not a natural science. In this sense, phenomenology involves a movement counter to the historically developed sciences, moving toward an original knowledge that precedes and founds them. For phenomenology, natural science and philosophy are sharply separated in method and object.

And yet, in spite of this sharp dichotomy, positive science and phenomenology are profoundly intertwined in their scientific intentionality through the course of the history of reason, as Husserl affirms in his famous letter of March 11, 1935, to Lévy-Bruhl. For positive science is necessarily the first science in relation to which phenomenology, as the "last science," discovers its unique transcendental dimension in the process of bringing the positive sciences to their full clairvoyance. But since the sciences have grown, sometimes surprisingly rapidly, without this self-clarity, it apparently is not necessary for a working scientist to possess this intrinsic rationality. It is even a fortunate situation that not essential insight but a certain "scientific instinct"[13] coupled with method is what makes scientific re-

12. "Philosophy as Rigorous Science," p. 82.
13. *LU*, Vol. I, § 71, p. 253.

search possible. The typical working scientist is like an artist who creates without being particularly aware of the theory behind his performances.[14] This one-sided brilliance is even to a certain extent necessary for the advance of science. He who goes forward cannot look over his shoulder for long. But without intrinsic rationality and clarity in its foundations, a working science is just that, i.e., a technology whose "theoretical techniques" permit the prediction of future events and the technical control and domination of nature, which makes the world more useful but not more understandable. This even applies to a priori sciences like logic and mathematics. The mathematician who constructs his theories to solve particular problems, the logician who programs a computer, are but "ingenious technicians."[15] The technical rationality thus developed is comparable to the rationality, satisfying because useful, of the crafts of a prescientific people, even though on a much higher level.[16] But it is precisely this brilliant "century of technology"[17] which has also generated the crises in the foundations of the "dogmatic" sciences to which phenomenology is the ultimate response. In times of crisis, the scientist turns philosopher to the extent necessary to restore his presuppositions back to working order, but it belongs to the philosopher to assume the work of clarification of presuppositions as a continuing and never-ending task. And quite naturally, the felt need for such a labor is most intense when the progress of science has obscured its origins with a technical superstructure which no longer answers to the self-evident.

The demand for absolute clarity in presuppositions is one indication of the strongly Cartesian vein in Husserl's thought. Like Descartes, Husserl sees the particular sciences as members of the all-inclusive science of philosophy which provides them as well as itself with an absolute foundation through radical insights into evidence behind which one can go no further. But Descartes introduces "a fateful prejudice"[18] by assuming the

14. *LU*, Vol. I, § 4, p. 9.
15. *LU*, Vol. I, § 71, p. 253.
16. *H* IX, p. 249.
17. *Ideen zu einer reinen Phänomenologie und phänomenologischen Philosophie*, Vol. III: *Die Phänomenologie und die Fundamente der Wissenschaften, Husserliana* V, ed. Marly Biemel (The Hague: Nijhoff, 1952), p. 95. (Hereafter cited as *H* V.)
18. *Cartesian Meditations*, § 3, p. 7.

ideal of science to be a deductive mathesis of the order approximated by geometry and mathematical physics, for which the ego's absolute certainty of itself and its innate principles are to supply the axiomatic foundation. Likewise naturalism, in restricting evidence to the empirical intuition of individuals, relies heavily on the mediate modes of inference to win its general propositions and to construct its elementary concepts through increasingly more skillful technical artifices. Already in the *Philosophy of Arithmetic*,[19] where he rejects Frege's attempt to found arithmetic by an exhaustive formal-logical definition of its most elementary concepts and calls rather for a *description* of how we come to the intrinsically indefinable concepts of number, plurality, unity, etc., Husserl locates the ideal of knowledge in an immediate intuition of the ideational order rather than in any mediate inference. Instead of a deduction from the ego, Husserl proposes a description of the life of the ego in its intuitive correlation with the field of categorial and eidetic objectivities which constitute the elementary concepts and presuppositions of the sciences. The demands for a scientific philosophy are thus to be satisfied by a return to evidence in its total context as evidence, and not just to the one kind of evidence that naturalism has glorified into the "superstition of the fact." [20] Its rigor lies entirely in the apodictic clarity of direct seeing rather than in deductive exactness, although a similarity persists in the a priori and eidetic character of both. But where the "object" is flowing, as in the life of consciousness, one cannot insist on exactness and still claim to have the rigor which comes from a regard for the subject matter. It is this sort of refusal to go beyond the data of consciousness, the "phenomena," which constitutes phenomenology.

THE SCIENCE OF SCIENCE

HUSSERL'S INITIAL EFFORTS were directed toward the philosophical clarification of mathematics and logic. Against the psychologistic trend of his day, he defends the possibility of a pure logic, an a priori science of pure theoretical forms independ-

19. *Philosophie der Arithmetik: Psychologische und logische Untersuchungen* (Halle a.d.S.: Pfeffer, 1891), p. 130–31.
20. "Philosophy as Rigorous Science," p. 141.

ent of the applied a posteriori art of methodological techniques. Such a logic would be an ideal rather than a real science, directed toward ideal meanings and forms and culminating in a theory of all possible theories, a science of science. But since any science is a movement from evidence to its ideal systems of meaning, a science of science must eventually include an elucidation not only of the concepts and laws that confer theoretical unity upon knowledge but also of the sources of evidence for such ideal unities. For the systematization which is proper to a science is not invented by us but discovered in the "things themselves." [21] Such was the task initially conceived for phenomenology. "Phenomenology reveals the 'sources' from which the fundamental concepts and the ideal laws of pure logic 'arise,' and to which they must be traced back again in order to provide the 'clarity and distinction' necessary for a critical comprehension of pure logic." [22] Thus at first phenomenology was conceived as a "philosophical supplement to the pure mathesis." [23] But since it executes the doubling return of reflection on the foundations of pure logic itself, it is phenomenology which is more fundamentally the science of science, the *mathesis universalissima* [24] or transcendental logic, as it is later called.

Moreover, even in its inception, it was intimated that phenomenology could be directed toward founding the fundamental concepts of not only pure formal logic but of all the other sciences. "Pure phenomenology represents a sphere of neutral investigations in which various sciences have their roots." [25] For one thing, each science constitutes its theories according to the general norms of formal logic, which in turn is founded by phenomenology. But more properly, each science is determined by the character of its unique domain, so that the system of a priori disciplines under phenomenology is gradually expanded to include the eidetics of the various regions of matter, life, mind, society, etc., which Husserl calls material ontologies and even at times logics, insofar as they aim at the logos of the structure of various domains.[26] The problems of the constitution

21. *LU*, Vol. I, § 6, p. 15.
22. *LU*, Vol. II, pt. 1, § 1, p. 3.
23. *LU*, Vol. II, pt. 1, § 7, p. 21.
24. *H* VIII, p. 249.
25. *LU*, Vol. II, pt. 1, § 1, pp. 2–3.
26. *H* VIII, p. 213; *H* IX, p. 43.

of these various material domains are finally united into the problem of the "lifeworld" as their integrated field. Even the ideal unities of pure logic which constitute a formal ontology are to have their genealogy traced back to the invariant structures of the lifeworld.

But the felt need to clarify the hidden foundations of science drives Husserl to take the more radical step of a transcendental critique, which establishes science and all human knowledge on the foundation of an intentional subjectivity. Accordingly, all the ontological structures, formal, material, and world-comprehensive, are to be investigated in correlation with the kind of categorial intuition peculiar to each, whose final integration is attained in the unity of the transcendental ego, in which the previous phases find their culmination in an absolutely apodictic foundation beyond which presuppositions are no longer tenable. "A genuine ontology, a universal and all-sided logic, at once analytic and regional, is nothing but the actual execution of transcendental idealism as an a priori science." [27]

In summary, Husserl provides three bases for the unity of the sciences, each one more fundamental and encompassing than what comes before: initially the formal logical level of theory, then the pretheoretical material level of their domains in the lifeworld, and finally the transcendental level of subjectivity. It should be noted that even though on the one hand the movement runs counter to the empirical sciences by being placed from the start in the historically available a priori sciences and then remaining on the a priori level, on the other hand it is a movement which returns to the world of experience. But this is still the world of the natural attitude, and the ontology of the lifeworld is still a positive science, and not until the transcendental attitude is assumed does the complete clairvoyance of rationality become possible. The critique of science finds its center of gravity only when it attains the pure rationality of the transcendental subjectivity.

PURE LOGIC AND FORMAL ONTOLOGY

EVERY SCIENCE, in seeking to know the objects of its domain, makes judgments about these objects. And ordinarily in

27. *H* VIII, pp. 215–16.

judging, we find ourselves directed toward the objects rather than toward the judgments through which we know them. But science, unlike ordinary knowledge, wants its judgments to be well-founded, so that in one of its moments it develops a critical attitude toward its judgments, hence provisionally turning away from its objects. Science moves in "zigzag"[28] fashion, now turned toward its objects, now toward its judgments. For the critical movement of the scientific profession is not occasional, as in everyday life where, when problems arise, we are easily satisfied even by feelings of evidence. Committed to the acquisition of authentic knowledge, science continually authenticates its judgments in an ongoing and permanent critique. Critical truth is a concept native to the scientific ambience. This movement might even be considered an *epochē in ovo,* insofar as it counters the naïve and dogmatic acceptance of immediate certitudes which is characteristic of the natural attitude.[29] The scientific critique is by essence a "modalization" of the immediate certitude unbroken by doubt. The scientific method interjects a doubt between judgment and object in order to attain tested and confirmed certainty. Toward this goal, each science develops procedures of verification to assure well-founded judgments based on evidence and thus true. Such procedures are designed to solve the problems of adequation between judgment and object, hence to bridge the gap opened up by the critical exigence.

But the goal of any particular science is still the knowledge of its domain, its ever-present "substrate objects," for which its critique of judgment plays only a mediating role.[30] Traditionally, it is logic which has taken over the thematic of judgment as such. As a theory of apophansis, logic is the science of the critique of science in its judicative efforts. It thus continues and thematically fixes the teleology of science in its critical function. Since in the first movements of critique, the judgment is separated from its objects, logic at first considers the judgment apart from the problems of adequation, without regard to its truth or falsity and therefore formally, as an "empty" judgment unful-

28. *FTL,* p. 111.
29. Suzanne Bachelard, *La Logique de Husserl* (Paris: Presses Universitaires de France, 1957), p. 136. A translation of this text is now available: *A Study of Husserl's Formal and Transcendental Logic,* trans. Lester E. Embree (Evanston, Ill.: Northwestern University Press, 1968). See p. 75.
30. *FTL,* p. 115.

filled by the intuition of evidence. The judgment is considered purely and simply as meant, as an intention, an "opinion," placed in quotation marks, as Husserl sometimes expressed the *epochē*.

Now "judgment" is an ambiguous word. If we exclude its physical assertion in order to get beyond the confusions of psychologism and penetrate into the realm of meaning, "judgment" includes both the noetic act of bestowing judicative meaning and the noematic content of meaning in this act. Furthermore, if we now nominalize the judgment *S is p* into, e.g., "the fact that *S is p* indicates otherwise," we find that the judgment objectively considered is not only an intention of meaning, but a "state of affairs" (*Sachverhalt*) to which the judicative meaning refers. Thus, according to Husserl, objective formal logic must concern itself not only with the forms of meaning (formal apophantic) but also with the forms of the meant object (formal ontology). The possibility of a formal ontology, overlooked by traditional logic, is more evident in formal mathematics, in its concern with form-objects like number, set, and relation. Mathematics and logic fuse even further when it is noted that operations like colligation are comparable to predicative copulation. The very notion of operation, transferred from mathematics to logic, has been shown to be quite fruitful, suggesting that further interchanges between the two formal sciences might be possible. But overarching both traditional disciplines is the reciprocal relation between formal apophansis and formal ontology, which consider the judgment from two intimately intertwined orientations, that of the meant object *as meant* and that of the formally considered object *toward which* this intention tends. Note that this is not the object *about which*, the substrate-object, i.e., the subject of the proposition, although the object-in-general is sometimes defined as anything which *can be* the subject of a proposition, a possibility made actual simply by the operation of nominalization. The categorial objectivities, the pure something or object-in-general and its modifications, like state-of-affairs, property, genus, species, unity, plurality, number, set, and relation, emerge nowhere else but in the judgment,[31] while the ultimate substrate-object is the perceived individual. The categorial activi-

31. *Erfahrung und Urteil: Untersuchungen zur Genealogie der Logik,* ed. Ludwig Landgrebe, 3d ed. (Hamburg: Classen, 1964), p. 2. (Hereafter cited as *EU.*)

ties generate ideal objects which form a superstructure or "cladding" of logical meaning over the logically indeterminate substrate-objects of the domain under consideration,[32] like the garment of ideas laid over nature by the idealizations of mathematical physics. But on the strictly logical level, the categorial judgment and categorial object in their inner unity simply represent two themes of one and the same domain, that of the scientific system. It is in this sense that "we can say that logic as the science of *science* has an ontological orientation, and as the *science* of science has an apophantic orientation."[33]

Traditional logic classified its propositions into simple and compound: under the simple were the singular, particular, and universal judgments; under the compound, the hypothetical, conjunctive, disjunctive, and causal. To this list could be added the modal propositions. But what are the scope and limits of the possible forms of judicative signification, and what are the laws which govern their formation? These are the questions to be answered by the most germinal branch of formal apophantic, variously called the pure doctrine of signification, the pure morphology of judgments, or the pure logical grammar, a division unique to Husserl and indicative of his radical intentions. In anticipating a later discussion, we might even call it an eidetic of judgment, inasmuch as it attempts to delineate the realm of the conceivable judgment and to articulate the conditions without which a judgment would not be possible. Since it is a matter of determining the internal structure of possible judgments, without regard to their consistency or truth, the first task is to establish the simplest elements of meaning which enter into the constituents of a proposition. Beneath the simple proposition S *is* p and its syntactical subject-form and predicate-form is a stratum of nuclear forms such as substantivity and adjectivity, with rules which govern their permissible movements to the syntactical stratum and their ordered composition into meaningful propositions.[34] Even though it is contradictory, "The circle is square" is a proposition with meaning, whereas "The square if either" is a meaningless sequence. Inasmuch as adjectives and other nuclear forms can always be substantified or nominalized (e.g.,

32. *EU*, pp. 278, 284.
33. Bachelard, *La Logique de Husserl*, p. 132. (Eng. trans., p. 72.)
34. *EU*, p. 248.

"red" to "redness"), whereas the reverse is not always possible, substantivity is the most universal of nuclear forms, which is based on the universality of "object-in-general," the basic concept of formal ontology.[35] It is possible to backtrack even further and expose beneath the nuclear forms a stratum of nuclear material which remains the same while being subjected to the forming operations of substantifying and adjectifying, as in "red" and "redness." That this nuclear core of sameness still has a bearing on logic is evident from syllogisms like "all men are mortal, all mortals are transient, etc.," where the sameness of the middle *term* in fact *terminates* in this nuclear stuff underlying the adjectival and substantive forms.[36] But to push further into this stratum of nuclear meaning would be to leave the problematic of a pure logical grammar and to enter the problems of a "genealogy of logic," that of the prejudicative experience upon which logic is based. Moving in the other direction into the more complex strata of a pure logical grammar, we find that not only the elements but the propositions themselves can be operated on. The primitive meaningful proposition S is p can be nominalized (*That S is p indicates* . . .), modified (*If S is p*), modalized (*Is S p?; S may be p*), and conjoined into an endless series (*Sp is q etc.*). There is some question though, perhaps even for Husserl, on how to unite such diverse operations under a single comprehensive notion.[37] Be that as it may, the shift in emphasis from static form to dynamic operation is indicative of the shift toward genetic phenomenology in the later Husserl. And the law of iteration that he finds to be basic for all operations prefigures the open-ended character to be discovered in the upper reaches of science itself.

Husserl adds two additional levels to his formal apophantic. While pure logical grammar deals with judgments in general, the logic of noncontradiction is concerned with distinct judgments, and the logic of possible truth handles clear judgments. The progression of strata is such that the higher depends upon the lower for its possibility. Thus the distinct judgment, freed from the vagueness and confusion of contradiction, provides the

35. *EU*, p. 263; *FTL*, pp. 272–73.
36. *FTL*, p. 274.
37. Bachelard, *La Logique de Husserl*, p. 65. (Eng. trans., pp. 12–13.) Cf. below, Jean Cavaillès, "On Logic and the Theory of Science," p. 387.

possibility for the clear judgment, with its possibility for truth through potential adequation in the clarity of evidence. Since pure logic is on the level of the formal a priori, the adequation here is not with actual objects but with the possible objects of formal ontology, in which pure logic as a theory of science, whose goal is always truth, finds its natural conclusion. For formal ontology provides "the possible categorial forms, in which substrate objectivities must be able to truly be." [38]

Up to this point, the formal apophantic has been concerned largely with individual judgments. But science consists of theories, groups of judgments organized systematically. Accordingly, the highest task of formal logic is the development of a theory of possible forms of theories, a theory of formal deductive systems. This apophantic par excellence evokes a development of its correlative formal ontology, a theory of "manifolds," i.e., a theory of the possible forms of region in general. The vocabulary of metamathematics and mathematical logic here points to the seminal historical milieu in which Husserl worked. As early as the preparatory period leading up to the *Logical Investigations* (1900), at a time when the problem of the foundations of mathematics was just beginning to take shape, Husserl saw in the developments of formal mathematics a partial realization of the goals of a science of science, a theory of theories. But even on the level of the "theory of foundations," the typical mathematician constructs his theoretical forms more through "scientific instinct," without the knowledge or the need to know what makes a theory as such possible, and other similar questions which belong to philosophical investigation and can be approached only by the "essential insight" of philosophical methods.[39]

Theoretical and exact sciences like arithmetic, geometry, analytical mechanics, mathematical astronomy, theoretical optics, and theoretical physics in general provide examples of theories in the strictest sense, which are the ones to be investigated here. What is most significant in such theories is not their ability to explain particular facts, e.g., mathematical astronomy accounting for the facts of gravitation, but their character as closed systems of ideal laws in which one or several are fundamental and from which all the others are deducible. It is really

38. *FTL*, p. 129.
39. *LU*, Vol. I, § 71, pp. 253–54.

this nomological character of these systems which provides the basis for the a priori account of the possible facts included within them and gives them their explanatory power. Indeed, rather than beginning with particular instances, as descriptive sciences like history and geography do, the nomological sciences begin at once on the categorial level. Geometry, for example, rather than describing the countless shapes available through sensory intuition, begins with a few fundamental constructs like body, surface, point, and angle, from which it formulates its axioms or "primitive laws of essence," [40] from which are then deduced laws and essences that in general are foreign to our direct intuition.

It is perhaps most difficult, here on the level where the problems of totality are drawn into pure logic, to maintain the formal viewpoint. At this level, Euclidean geometry is considered not as a regional (material) ontology of the objective domain of space, but as an "exemplary system-form" [41] with a definite group of axiom-forms which define a theory-form of a manifold, i.e., the form of a region belonging to the formal genus of manifolds with the categorial form: n-dimensional space. The same applies to discrete as well as continuous manifolds, in which, e.g., "+" refers no longer to the addition of numbers but to a formal operation determined by the properties of commutativity and associativity, where the ideal objects need not be numbers but anything which is capable of being submitted to this operation-form.[42] The full power of the formal viewpoint now becomes manifest, in being able to establish structural kinships between theories whose similarity was at first obscured by the heterogeneity of their concrete contents. The overview now made possible of families of theories, and indeed of entire sciences, gives pure logic its measure of justification to the title of science of science, a *mathesis universalis* which constructs the complete system of a priori possible forms of deductive systems, a system of systems, "a realm of universal construction on a priori grounds . . . through and through a realm of operative transformations, and nevertheless capable of being dominated a priori in their infinity." [43]

For according to Husserl, these deductive systems have the

40. *Ideas I*, § 72, p. 187. Translation altered.
41. *FTL*, p. 81.
42. *LU*, Vol. I, § 70, p. 249.
43. *FTL*, pp. 90–91.

remarkable logical property of being "complete" or "saturated," which constitutes its correlative domain into a "definite" manifold. A mathematical manifold, which contains an open infinity of objects, is definite when a finite number of concepts and propositions completely and univocally determine all the possible configurations of that domain "according to a purely analytical necessity." [44] When the system is unequivocally complete, then there is no question with regard to the logical status of any proposition conceivable in the language of the system. It is either a logical consequence or a logical contradiction of the axioms: *Tertium non datur*. Accordingly, a decision can be made with regard to every possible proposition of the system. The system is closed, its propositions are decidable, and its manifold is exhaustively defined.

But in the light of recent developments in mathematical logic, the formal problems that accrue to the conceptions of completeness and definiteness are considerable. Husserl's conception parallels that of his mathematician colleague Hilbert, who believed that he could justify what was actually infinite in mathematics, and hence the whole of classical mathematics, through finite considerations, utilizing actually realizable operations like the iterations of mathematical induction in order to show that all mathematical problems are soluble, i.e., decidable. But this thesis of the finitist school was shown to be untenable by Gödel's theorem (1931), which demonstrated that any system of at least the power of ordinary arithmetic will always contain undecidable propositions. The noncontradiction of such a system can only be demonstrated by a more powerful theory. At this level of mathematics, there are no closed systems, let alone a system to close all lesser systems. Rather, the theories ramify into a network of theories, and the entire network opens onto an indeterminate horizon. The idea of a perfectly closed system which dominates its propositions is a limit idea which can never be actually reached. [45]

Though this result of metamathematics calls for the modification of Husserl's remarks on definite manifolds, it does not

44. *Ideas I*, § 72, p. 187. Translation altered.
45. Jean Ladrière, *Les Limitations internes des formalismes* (Louvain: Nauwelaerts, 1957), p. 410. Cf. below, Cavaillès, "On Logic and the Theory of Science," p. 405. See also Bachelard, *La Logique de Husserl*, p. 111 (Eng. trans., pp. 52–53).

violate the general spirit of phenomenology. As Husserl progressed, he became more and more appreciative of the open
horizon which characterizes the teleology of science. If he was
carried away by the claims of the axiomatics prevalent in his
milieu, it is indicative of his respect for the power of the formal
approach. But this power which manifests itself in the mobility
and liberty of its constructions equally evokes the pervasive
tendency of turning formalism into a mere playing with symbols, threatening to empty it of its meaning, what Husserl called
Sinnentleerung. And his antidote for this, a return to the intuitive ground from which the acts which originate a formal system
receive their sustenance, might also reveal the hidden source of
the limitations which formalism has found within itself. For its
liberty is a bound freedom still regulated by its archeology, even
if in a highly mediated form and through a multiplicity of strata.
Every formal system, no matter how remote it may seem to be
from these roots, is still a possible form of real theories. For even
though a formal-ontological manifold lives only in its theoretical
forms, it still bears its relationship with the ontology of the
world from which it draws its "self-evident" axioms and first
premises. A formal manifold is only a "quasi-region" [46] which
still bears the marks of its rough draft in the real region.

THE REGIONAL EIDETICS

BUT SUCH ASSERTIONS evoke the need for an ontological
investigation of the original regions of which formal ontology
studies only the forms. There are also the questions in reverse to
be answered, such as those pertaining to the conditions necessary for a material region to be considered as a "definite" manifold, for example, the condition that the concepts formed from
this domain be exact, through the process of concept formation
called idealization or mathematization. Whether a material region can be mathematized depends throughout on the peculiar
character of the region itself.[47] It is only after this ideal substructure is established that the issue becomes purely formal. Even
the nomological sciences need an ontology of the world.

46. *Erste Philosophie* (1923–24), Vol. I: *Kritische Ideen-
geschichte, Husserliana* VII, ed. R. Boehm (The Hague: Nijhoff,
1956), p. 187. (Hereafter cited as *H* VII.)
47. *Ideas I,* § 73, p. 189.

Moreover, there are further questions which confront a science of the sciences. For if the principle of unity in the nomological sciences is the law from which all others are deduced, what of the less exact and more descriptive sciences, like history, geography, psychology, indeed phenomenology itself? Their principle of unity flows directly from the domains which they study, and so can be investigated only by means which exceed the analytical-logical form of knowledge.[48] From the very beginning, the tasks assigned to a theory of science in the *Prolegomena toward a Pure Logic* were of such diversity that they exceeded the competence of a pure logic alone. The sciences were to be treated as systematic unities not only with regard to their forms but also with regard to their "intrinsic articulation into domains," [49] in a systematization which is not invented by us but which "resides in the 'things' themselves, where we simply find it, discover it." [50] This dimension of the problem gradually evolves into a systematization of the sciences on the basis of the diversity of the evidence presented to them, in which each type of evidence is to be studied by its own material a priori discipline, its regional ontology.

The ordinary descriptive science stays close to the facts and is therefore based on the empirical intuition of individual objects. But so does ordinary everyday prescientific experience. How does this natural confused experience become scientific experience? How is an empirical science initiated and set on its way? By means of an intuition into the meaning or essence of the manifold of experiences of a certain kind, which institutes an order in the confusion and suggests the "fact-finding" methods necessary to secure this order. It was Galileo's pioneering intuitions into the geometric character of physical nature which transformed the vague everyday concepts in this domain into clear scientific concepts.[51] Nowadays it is psychology and the other human sciences which are in need of their founding intuitions, which are not the same as those for the physical sciences. For each region has its own characteristic intuition, hence its own evidence and objectivity.

Rather than always relying on "genial pioneers" like Galileo

48. *FTL*, p. 90.
49. *LU*, Vol. I, § 10, p. 25.
50. *LU*, Vol. I, § 6, p. 15. Cf § 48, p. 178.
51. "Philosophy as Rigorous Science," p. 100.

for eidetic intuitions, why not establish sciences whose task it would be to methodically work out the eidetic intuitions of each and every region of human experience? These would serve not only to fix the basic presuppositions for the domains of sciences which still need to be truly launched, but also to maintain in clarity the fundamental concepts of well-established sciences, which have a tendency to forget their foundations in their progress toward new discoveries. And finally it would manifest the articulations between the various sciences at their roots, by placing each of them in the enveloping context of experience in general. At its ideal limit, such a "logic of experience," made explicit through an intertwined network of eidetic intuitions, would be a total rationalization of the empirical.[52] Alongside and beneath the pure formal logic as a theory of theories is to be placed the pure material logic of the objects of experience, particularly as they enter into the various empirical sciences. Each factual science is to have its concomitant eidetic discipline to provide it with the normative guides it requires for the selection of its relevant facts. For contrary to popular opinion, facts do not "speak for themselves" but always appear in a context of meaning in which they find their place. It is this necessary eidetic framework which the material ontologies are to bring out of obscurity, for like the spectacles through which we see, the a priori vision of the *eidos* is usually implicit. And the character of the fact changes when it changes context, e.g., the age or date of a historical parchment established by radiocarbon chemistry. The dynamics of such a change can be assessed properly only in terms of the eidetic relations between history and chemistry.

Since these eidetic sciences are based on intuition, like the empirical sciences, they are also descriptive sciences. Yet unlike the empirical sciences and like the nomological sciences, they operate in a realm of necessity. Yet this necessity is no longer a logical or deductive necessity but a necessity which emerges from the intuition of eidetic evidence itself. Between inductive probability and deductive necessity lies a realm of ontological necessity upon which both depend. Indeed, deductive necessity is only a particular case of eidetic necessity, from which it acquires its own necessity and to which it must eventually be reduced. For Husserl, it is evidence and not conclusions which is to be the paradigm of reason. Rational necessity and intuition

52. *Ideas I*, § 9, p. 59.

are united through the achievement of the absolutely apodictic evidence of an essential structure. For what is to be seen in the intuition are the necessary conditions for the very possibility of its object, that without which the object could not *be*. It is for this reason that the eidetic sciences are ontologies.

Since the eidetic ontologies strive for a necessary rather than a factually contingent existence, the first step in the eidetic reduction is the suspension of the individuality of the objects under study. To be sure, one may begin with a factual object, but only if it is considered purely and simply as a specimen or example of its kind. The starting point may just as well be a possible object conjured by the imagination, which in its freedom from the contingency of fact is the more appropriate base from which to launch eidetic analyses. Hence it can be said that "it is 'fiction' which constitutes the vital element of phenomenology, as of all eidetic sciences." [53] Elevated from the singularity of facticity to the possibility of imagination, the object partakes of the freedom of that faculty and may now be varied at will. Free variation permits the exploration of the endless ramifications to which the object may be submitted, in order to determine the limits of variation beyond which the object would no longer retain its identity. This necessarily invariant structure, which sustains the permissible variations and without which the object would not be what it is, is the essence in question.

In contrast with the passive character of empirical intuition then, eidetic intuition is actively and laboriously achieved. But it is still a matter of "seeing" the invariant identity present in the manifold of possible variations, a process which is neither deduction nor induction. For inductive comparison is based on passive association and is bound to the factual intuition of a certain number of individuals, so that its empirical universal is subject to modification in the event of the discovery of an individual which is unlike the others. While the empirical universal of a range of facts can at best only arrive at a high probability, the eidetic universal, as the invariant of a manifold of pure possibilities, apodictically defines their condition of possibility through a consciousness of the impossibility of their not being, which is precisely the necessity imposed by the presence of the eidetic evidence itself. This necessity emerges after only a limited number of imagined cases, along with the sense that one can go on at

53. *Ideas I,* § 70, p. 184. Translation altered.

will in the open and endless manifold of variants with the same results. And contrary to the empirical field, an eidetic manifold does not consist of a uniform field of similar individuals but may well encompass possibilities which are in direct contradiction with each other, so that the field is a "hybrid unity" [54] held together only by the very intuition of the essence itself.

Even though eidetic variation is hardly deduction, Husserl has explicitly and quite consciously utilized certain features of mathematical idealization in his eidetic method, which is even described with the help of mathematical terms like "variable," "congruence," "manifold," "arbitrarily chosen example." As in geometric imagery, phenomenology selects an example at will, not for the sake of its individual features, but as a guide to a priori universal thought. As a result, both eidetic phenomenology and mathematics are charged with the same paradox. Both insist on emptying themselves of accidental contents in order to be able to roam freely on the pure a priori level of necessary structure, and yet both a priori sciences eventually find that their essential frameworks remain applicable to the factual world. But phenomenological ideation is not mathematical idealization. For one thing, phenomenology remains exclusively in eidetic intuition whereas mathematical idealization is devoted to the preparation of the axioms of a deductive system. For another, ideation is designed to extricate the vague inexact a priori from experience in all of its temporal fluidity, which is an a priori that precedes and underlies that of idealization. This can only be achieved by a purely descriptive science, not a deductive science. Yet the proximity between mathematics and phenomenology is sufficiently close that it prevents Husserl from closing off the possibility of a "mathesis of experience" utilizing some form of idealizing procedure alongside descriptive phenomenology, as a counterpart to it. [55] But phenomenology itself remains a descriptive eidetic through and through.

Through the intuition of essences, phenomenology can provide the most radical foundation for the sciences, their foundation in rational evidence, in which the object purely and simply gives itself to consciousness. The task of the various regional ontologies is precisely that of exploring the different ways in which the object presents itself to consciousness or, to put it

54. *EU*, p. 417.
55. *Ideas I*, § 75, p. 193.

more ontologically, the different modes of Being-object, i.e., the different modes of the objectivity of the object, each of which requires its own categories. There are regional ontologies because there are different types of evidence. And since objectivity is constituted in subjectivity, each ontology has its correlative constitutional theory.

The regional ontology and constitutional theory of material nature hold a preeminent position inasmuch as material reality is the lowest formation and in this sense is the foundation of all other realities.[56] The prototype experience in this region is the perception of a thing. That Husserl centers his investigations on the "doxic positing" which enters most directly into the cognitive and theoretical attitudes is indicative of his central concern to found the sciences. That the affective, practical, and evaluative attitudes which are put out of play here only reenter whenever the issue of the thing as an object of the human sciences is raised, is further indication of the close relation which he envisions between the regional ontologies and the empirical sciences. By way of contrast, it is well known that Heidegger's displacement of the primacy from *Vorhandenes* to *Zuhandenes* moves toward a less scientifically oriented problematic.

Nevertheless, the natural tendency of the positive sciences to assume the thing simply as a given must itself be put out of play in order to arrive at the how of its givenness. Consider this table as an example. In each perception the complete table is given, but only incompletely, from this side or that. As I walk around it, one silhouette blends into another in a constantly changing panorama of views, but it is always the same table which is under view, each time giving itself partially and pointing to further perspectives. Each of its profiles "shades off" into the background of other possible perspectives, and all of them are related according to a definite order or continuum which constitutes the unity and totality which we call this table. Experienced as an ongoing temporal process, this manifold of perspective variations is correlative to the essential spatial dispersion of any material thing. And because the thing gives itself by withholding itself, it claims for itself an independent existence transcending my knowledge of it and so claims title to being real or objective.

56. *Ideas I*, § 152, p. 389.

Since the essential character of a material thing is to give itself by "shading off," it never gives itself adequately or exhaustively, but only relatively. The suggestions of one perspective may be cancelled by another. Under these conditions of partiality, mistakes are always possible, e.g., through hasty interpretation and insufficient exploration. The ambiguity inherent in this objective-relative configuration of a material thing is a source of the motivation of physical science to overcome the relativism of immediate experience in order to reach the object "in itself," which in effect would mean to be able to consider the object from every point of view, therefore to nullify the whole notion of point of view as such. The objectivity of the material thing is like a Kantian idea toward which the scientific community aims its endeavors as toward an ideal.[57]

A much more fanciful and stricter eidetic variation of a perceived thing produces not only "the most unbelievable miscarriages of things, the most insane thinglike specters, showing scorn for all physics and chemistry,"[58] but also uncovers the perceptual strata which underlie the thing perception as such and thereby defines more distinctly what is most proper to it. If the variation does not respect the real context in which things are found, if the thing is taken in isolation, then it manifests itself in a manifold of "phantoms" or sense schemata, where the thing is considered in its "pure bodiness,"[59] as res extensa. There are two possibilities at this level: the empty schema or the spatial form pure and simple (primary quality), and the filled schema, covered with color, pervaded by odor, etc. But a much more elemental level can be imagined, a stratum of pure sensibility which lacks even spatial formation and which is constituted simply on the level of the original time-consciousness.[60] A sound, for example, need not be taken only as a real event emanating from a real object in definite circumstances (the thing stratum), or as a tonal phenomenon appearing in a definite orientation and loca-

57. E. Levinas, La Théorie de l'intuition dans la phénoménologie de Husserl, 2d ed. (Paris: Vrin, 1963), pp. 26–28.
58. H V, p. 30.
59. Ideen zu einer reinen Phänomenologie und phänomenologischen Philosophie, Vol. II: Phänomenologische Untersuchungen zur Konstitution, Husserliana IV, ed. Marly Biemel (The Hague: Nijhoff, 1952), p. 31. (Hereafter cited as H IV.)
60. H IV, p. 24.

tion at a definite position (the schematic stratum), but simply as a pure "sense datum" or *Urimpression* just being born in the "living present" of consciousness. At this level of "syntheses which precede every thesis," [61] there is no question of a thing or an object in the usual sense.

What then is a thing *really*? The decisive factor in the reality or substantiality of a material thing is its relationship to the surrounding circumstances, whereby the schematic phantoms become real properties by becoming "modes of behavior." [62] A real stance is possible only through circumstance. If we consider, for example, the phantoms seen in a stereoscope, it makes no sense to ask whether they are heavy or light, elastic, magnetic, etc. [63] The phantom world is a world of geometry without physics. [64] Extension, while essential to materiality, is only its essential form. [65] The essential content of materiality resides in the relations of causal dependence between the states of the thing and its circumstances. The causality under discussion here is itself perceived and not thought, like the relations between lighting and color, applied force and elasticity, etc. Under these conditions, the thing now emerges as that which remains the same under variable circumstances and which changes in prescribable directions according to the law: "Like consequences under like circumstances." [66] The thing properly appears not as a manifold of schemata but as a manifold of relations of dependence between real properties and surrounding conditions. "A thing is not even a being in general, but the identical in the union of causal dependencies. It is something which can only live in the atmosphere of causal laws." [67]

But the determination of the conditions for the appearance of a material thing is not yet complete. Among the causal circumstances necessary for the perception of a thing is the perceiver himself. The regional essence "material nature" cannot be considered apart from the regional essence "animal nature" or

61. *H* IV, p. 22.
62. *H* IV, p. 44.
63. *H* IV, p. 36.
64. *H* V, p. 30.
65. *H* IV, p. 31.
66. *H* IV, p. 49.
67. *H* V, p. 30.

"aesthesiological body." A *Körper* cannot appear without a *Leib*. For one thing, the confrontation between the two types of body accounts for the perspectival character of the appearance of a material thing. On the schematic stratum, the perceiving body is the zero point, the center of orientation, the absolute here for every there, "a here which has no other outside of itself, in relation to which it would be a there." [68] From this vantage point, the sensed features of a thing find their correlates in kinesthetic sensations localized in the body. Being localized in the subjective body, the kinesthetic sensations are not related to the feature sensations, as other circumstances are, through a real causal relation. Rather, another version of the if-then relation is operative—that of motivation: if I turn my head so, then the thing appears thus, etc., in a motivation series which structures the entire manifold of appearances. The manifold of dependence relations here is of an entirely different order than that which applies to things. Likewise, the body assumes a spatiality different from, even though correlative with, that of things. The orientation of bodily perspectives in terms of right-left, above-below, forward-back is the source of the three dimensions of objective space, and the periodicity of bodily movements like walking is the suggestive source of the objective measurement of space.

How then is the *objective* material thing constituted? The relativism inherent in the experience of a thing can now be traced to a twofold source: the changing objective circumstances in which a thing appears and the changing conditions of the perceiving body. But just as certain circumstances are taken as optimal and favorable conditions for viewing a thing (e.g., normal daylight), so certain bodily conditions are adjudged normal, against which background others are assessed as abnormalities rendering the body anesthetic to one or another possibility of perception. In this way, daily experience spontaneously works out norms which establish an objectivity adequate for its purposes, enabling it to identify an identical substrate of identical properties in the flux of experience. But such an objectivity is still relative to the individual subject. Is it possible to overcome even this relativity and come to a still higher, more "irrelative"

68. *H* IV, p. 158.

objective identity? Following up to the end the rational drive to overcome relativism prompted from the beginning by the perception of the thing, mathematical physics theoretically constructs the *physical* thing, which is accordingly a categorial thought-determination built from the sensory thing. In the process, the perceived thing is so completely reconstructed that all that in fact remains of it is its sheer "passive" givenness as a mere "this," an empty identical "something" which now becomes the bearer of mathematical rather than perceived determinations. For both the so-called primary and secondary qualities are reintroduced into physics in the idealized form of logico-mathematical categories, and the interlacing of causalities which is the real thing is transformed into the functional relations of mathematical formulas. The end-product is a conception of a "thing in itself" which is only "a rule of possible appearances," [69] "a formal-methodic rule of unity." [70] *"The physical thing of natural science only has a formal essence,* it only has a *formula,* and for the rest its essence only consists in the fact that through this formula it is a regulated intentional unity of infinite manifold appearances 'for all men.' "* [71] Nevertheless, this final ideal object is something which initially "announced itself" in the sensory thing, about which the physicist still continues to speak even in his most abstruse formulas. "The thing that he observes, with which he experiments, which he continually sees, handles, places on the scales, puts into the fusing furnace, this and no other thing is the subject of physical predicates, as that which has weight, temperature, electrical resistance, etc. Likewise for the perceived processes and relations which are defined through concepts like force, acceleration, energy, atom, ion, etc." [72]

The process of idealization and objectification is so complete that the thing is now considered as lying not in perceptual space but in an objective and idealized space, e.g., the Euclidean manifold. In fact, this is precisely the decisive step in the constitution of physical objectivity. Here the key role played by intersubjective constitution comes to the fore. For the subjectivity of the space oriented from the absolute here of the body must be

69. *H* IV, p. 86.
70. *H* IV, p. 376.
71. *H* IV, pp. 376–77.
72. *Ideas I,* § 52, p. 146. Translation altered.

neutralized so that every here can be freely identified with every there. This homogenization of space is based on the relations of empathy which exist between subjects and the idealization of the possible change of position between subjects. With space thus homogenized, the objective identity of the this becomes nonrelative with respect to any particular subject or, *ipso facto,* objective to every subject. No bodily subject has a privileged position, each is a here interchangeable with any there. The location of the body becomes indifferent and every subject can represent every other subject. The relativity of the individual subject is overcome through the ideal community of intersubjective reciprocity.

And so the examination of the region of the material thing inexorably uncovers interrelations with the region of the subjectivity as well. "For a complete clarification of the sense and construction of physical nature, the study of subjectivity is indispensable." [73] The region of the material thing is not independent and cannot stand by itself. Rather than being a concrete unity, it is a domain abstracted from a more encompassing concrete context. This interpenetration of the region of the physical thing with that of subjectivity is in one sense obvious to the physicist, e.g., Galileo, "who had to make the subjective thematic and then methodically bracket it." [74] Even so, the elimination of the so-called subjective secondary qualities does not eliminate the scientific subjectivity as impersonal and intersubjective. Both the perceptual and the physical manifestations of the thing retain their ties to the subjective. "Nature accordingly leads to aesthetic corporality, to the psychic, to the spiritually productive subjectivity, to the insight that subjectivity is world-constituting and transcendental—absolute, that all Being is a correlate of the transcendental subjectivity which comprehends everything objective as a correlate of subjective constitutions." [75] The intentional relation permits no sharp cleavage between *Natur* and *Geist* after the fashion of Descartes. Nature and subjectivity are fundamentally inseparable.

The same interpenetration can be disclosed by beginning with any other regional object as a "transcendental guideline."

73. *H* IV, p. 90.
74. *H* VIII, p. 227 n.
75. *H* VIII, p. 225.

Each region per se is abstract. Complete concreteness can be found only in the full universality of the "world-experiencing life" of the transcendental ego.

THE ONTOLOGY OF THE LIFEWORLD

THE EXPANDING NETWORK of relations which develops in the course of the eidetic description and constitutional analysis of a specified object points to another dimension of the problems of eidetic description. For every thing (or animal, man, cultural object, etc.) emerges against a background of totality which is the world in which we live, which itself is subject to eidetic description. Instead of "the way up" from a particular region, there is "the way down" from the world framework within which each region must necessarily find its place. Not that these two approaches are disjunctive. The relative priorities which exist between them are defined by the mutual relations that exist between thing and world. Since we naturally focus on the individual first, the empirical sciences and their concomitant regional eidetics are the most apparent areas that call for investigation. Yet the comprehension of an individual always includes its horizon and background, which in fact enters into the determination of the individual but which itself is usually experienced only implicitly and indeterminately. To overcome the natural gravitation toward individuals in order to explicate their context of appearance requires a special effort of consciousness. And since the world is the condition of possibility for the experience of a thing, a regional eidetic is not complete without its complementary world eidetic. But even when a consciousness of the world is attained, it cannot be overlooked that the world "is only known as a horizon for existing objects and cannot be actual without the knowledge of particular objects." [76] The world eidetic does not absorb and take away the need for the regional eidetics. Despite their inseparable unity, the two types

76. *Die Krisis der europäischen Wissenschaften und die transzendentale Phänomenologie: Eine Einleitung in die phänomenologische Philosophie, Husserliana VI*, ed. Walter Biemel (The Hague: Nijhoff, 1954), p. 146. (Hereafter cited as *H VI*.) English translation by David Carr, *The Crisis of European Sciences and Transcendental Phenomenology* (Evanston, Ill.: Northwestern University Press, 1970).

of consciousness are distinct. The world is not like an individual which can be pluralized "but exists as a uniqueness for which the plural is meaningless." [77]

The world is first of all experienced in a marginal manner, as an empty horizon of untold possible experiences. But the "intuitive method" (!) of imaginary variation is designed precisely to dispel this indeterminacy, to establish the universal forms without which the world would be inconceivable, and to delineate the typicality which divides the world into regions. The procedure for obtaining this total intuition of the world is the same as for the thing, except that we must necessarily begin with the one world given to us through experience. Free variation of this world relative to us exposes the invariant a priori structures of any possible world, free from all conceivable relativities. The horizon structure with its concomitant indeterminacy and infinitely open possibilities is the most immediately manifest of these structures. The historical relativity of worlds points to the pervasive presence of time as a universal form. Another "distribution form" [78] is space, without which any world would be inconceivable. Then there is the universal form of causality, which ties all realities together through action and suffering. These three forms—space, time, and causality—intrinsically intertwined with each other, have already and necessarily appeared in the eidetic analysis of the thing, for all things are intrinsically bound to the forms of the world. Every thing in the world necessarily has temporal duration, spatial form, and a real identity determined through its persistent causal style. Things do not change at random but according to a typical uniformity. It is through this "routine" of things that the world hangs together as a unified whole and that the things find their place in that world.

Out of this identifiable style also emerges the division of the world into its regions. The most fundamental problem here is to comprehend the intuitive articulation of the world into nature and spirit (the latter includes the psychic, personal, social, cultural, i.e., the subjective in general), from which flows the central phenomenological problem of the relations between the natural and the human sciences. [79] The problem manifests itself most intensely in Husserl's attempts to define the character of an

77. *Ibid.*
78. *H* IX, p. 68.
79. *H* IV, pp. 311–12.

eidetic psychology, which is to determine the a priori structures for all the human sciences and, as a result, free them from the tendency to imitate the norms and style of the natural sciences. Rather than assuming that the forms of time, space, and causality for the psychic are the same as those for physical phenomena, eidetic psychology must return to the "things themselves" in their world context. The spatial-temporal localization which is the "principle of individuation" of physical things cannot be applied arbitrarily to my own experience of myself as embodied in the world, since my individuality derives its aseity from itself and not from external conditions.[80] Likewise, motivation, the "causality" intrinsic to the subjective domain, is governed by laws which differ from the deterministic laws of nature. Rather than resorting to physics, psychology must go back to the world of immediate experience for the rationale proper to its unique domain. But in the process of extricating psychology from physics, the incipient relations between the two domains become even more problematic.

In a sense, when compared with the local typicalities of mineralogy, geology, etc., the more comprehensive regional typicalities have a right to the title of general forms of the world, insofar as they in a way extend to all the individuals in the world.[81] Both nature and spirit have a justifiable claim to such a universality. In the strict phenomenological sense already indicated, if anything is to be a reality in the world, it must be material. The so-called "irreal" or ideal objects are "founded" on the *reality* of man and are incorporated in cultural objects like books and works of art. To this extent, physicalism is justified and the psychophysical sciences add a certain comprehensiveness to the physical sciences proper. But all of the natural sciences (physics, biology, psychophysiology) are based on a deliberate abstraction from all that comes into the purview of the personal attitude. The naturalistic attitude "despiritualizes" the world in order to reveal nature as its universal substratum.[82] But this is still accomplished by an attitude and therefore still retains a relationship to the subjective. For nothing is really alien to it; every experienced object is necessarily related to a

80. *H* IV, pp. 297–302.
81. *H* IX, p. 68.
82. *H* IX, p. 383.

subject. The objectivity of physics is still a matter of being true for everyone.

In the specifically spiritual, we are concerned with the life flow of ego-centered acts, most simply described in expressions such as "I hear the noise," "I recall that it happened then," "I don't believe it," etc., already indicative of the intentionality of consciousness. Hence the subjective acts are at once correlated to the objects given in them, so that it is not simply a matter of juxtaposing the internal against the external. Not that the intentional object is real. Such a consideration is not "really" essential in this domain. The intentional object, strictly speaking, is the object as meant. The spiritual is purely and simply the realm of meaning. Even though the real as real is put out of play, it nevertheless enters into conscious life as meant. It is in this way that the spiritual includes in its realm all that is.

Instead of the world-forms of spirit and nature, one usually speaks of the natural world and the human or cultural world. Both are inextricably intertwined in the world of our immediate experience, like a painting and its canvas, as Merleau-Ponty would later put it. The perceived world is natural and human at once and in its entirety. The spatial categories of near-far, for example, apply equally to relations of the lived body and of the community (neighbor-foreigner). Overemphasis of one or the other dimension results in the abstractions of naturalism and historicism, both of which are prevalent in the present situation of European man. On the one hand, there is the claim that science presents the objective world as it is in itself, in opposition to the subjectively relative world of perception. On the other, it is asserted that the scientific world-view is only one among many other possible views assumed by various historical communities. An exploration which returns to the original "lifeworld" is Husserl's antidote to the exaggeration of both tendencies and a partial justification of each. For the lifeworld is the prescientific, pretheoretical world of our immediate experience which is the intuitive ground from which all of our sciences and theories are developed.

The thematic of the lifeworld first emerges as a counterconception to the "scientific world," the world intended and constructed by the theoretical systems of the objective sciences since the time of Galileo. The paradox of the efforts of modern science is that the "merely subjective" lifeworld continues as the source of its evidence and the basis of its verifications for the objective world which is its aim. But with his eyes fixed on nothing but his aim and the means to attain it, the scientist overlooks this background world which still silently and anonymously enters into his formulations. Moreover, the scientist continues to assume the lifeworld as the encompassing horizon within which he carries on his research, for he necessarily works within a community of scientists in scientific institutions within a scientific tradition, among scientists whom he views not as psychophysical organisms and causal functions but as colleagues, hence subjectively. And he is not always professionally engaged but has other interests which presuppose the lifeworld in other ways. Science now takes its place as one cultural world among others, with interests and aims which at once distinguish and relate it with others. The scientific pursuit and its product, the scientific world "in itself," are intrinsically interwoven into the patterns of the lifeworld, which itself is commonly taken for granted, as something that "goes without saying," "a matter of course." Consequently, the view that considers the scientific world to be a replacement rather than a modification of the lifeworld must be rejected. For the mathematically idealized world that science constructs is really a fabric of symbols being made into a garment designed to fit the lifeworld and none other, measuring the size of the lifeworld and none other. In and through its vague typicality, the lifeworld in fact motivates science in the construction of this ideal superstructure, which in the last analysis is still related to its subliminal structural constants. For all of its relativity, the lifeworld is pervaded by an irrelative general structure which precedes the sciences and enters into them as their most basic presuppositions. It is in this invariant eidetic structure that the scientific world-view finds its relative justification and need not be either absolutized or relativized.

From the current scientific point of view, the turn taken here may be somewhat surprising. In order to justify the sciences, we are asked to go back to the everyday world. But the reduction of a strict science to the vague opinions of daily experience hardly seems worthy of being called scientific procedure. Was not science initially motivated precisely by the attempt to overcome the unreliability of such opinions? Is this the "theory of science" which is to replace the traditional logic which, to be sure, has not yet been able to provide the clarity of foundations being sought here? Has not irrational "intuition" always had a lower epistemological value than "rational" logic? Such reactions underscore the revolutionary character of Husserl's phenomenology. The traditional low esteem of *doxa*, vague and relative everyday knowledge, in contrast with *epistēmē*, rational knowledge, is overcome by simply denying the sharp dichotomy between them. There is a latent reason in *doxa* which is to be exposed through a "rational intuition"(!) into the *logos* of the lifeworld. The ontology of the lifeworld is a step toward a "logic of experience" which is to provide the scientific depth dimension to all of the particular sciences. Scientific rationalism is not flaunted but made more radical through a broadened conception of reason.

Perhaps the most extensive specific example of the reduction of the scientific world to the lifeworld provided by Husserl is the celebrated working manuscript cited by Merleau-Ponty as: "Reversal of the Copernican theory: the earth as original *Arche* does not move." [83] Husserl himself views this effort as an initial contribution to a phenomenological doctrine of the origin of nature according to natural science and toward a "transcendental theory of natural scientific knowledge." Its aim is to take us back to the original ground from which the working scientist starts and which he never really leaves behind, even though the advances of science from Copernicus to Einstein may appear to have taken us further from this ground. The widened discrepancy between Einstein's formulations of space and time and the space and time in which our actual life takes place only serve to intensify the need to invest the idealizations of mathematical physics with a sense based on the intuitive environment in which we live.[84] Hence the intention of the "reversal of the Copernican revolution" is not a rejection of Copernican science but an attempt to view it in the milieu from which it draws its most implicit presuppositions and to which it never ceases to belong.

In the fragment under discussion, the lifeworld is seen as the

83. The published title is "Grundlegende Untersuchungen zum phänomenologischen Ursprung der Räumlichkeit der Natur," in Marvin Farber, ed., *Philosophical Essays in Memory of Edmund Husserl* (Cambridge, Mass.: Harvard University Press, 1940), pp. 307–25.

84. *H* VI, p. 343.

aboriginal earth on the basis of which all bodies, and in particular the Copernican earth, are regarded as at rest or in motion. Initially, two notions of the earth are to be distinguished. First, there is the synthetic picture which I form from living in a world whose horizon appears to open onto the infinite in the sense that I can always go beyond the present landscape to Canada, Mexico, etc. Even if I have never done so, I know some people who have and have heard of others who have gone further, etc. From these secondhand accounts, I synthesize a picture of the United States in North America, above South America, etc., finally a picture of the earth as a synthetic unity, analogous to the more direct unity which I develop of my particular field of experience from the continuous and interconnected experiences of its parts. On the other hand, there is the picture I acquire from an available historical world-view, be it primitive, Greek, medieval, or modern. We Copernicans, we modern men say that the earth is not nature in its entirety but simply one of the planets in interstellar space, a body in the form of a globe not at once perceivable in its entirety, but in a synthesis of intertwined individual experiences. If we exclude the stars for the moment, the earth is a total body which carries and supports all of the more readily experienced bodies, and in that sense it is also their ground. And all lesser bodies are obtained from this huge clumsy body of the earth through partition and separation. Now if the earth is a body akin to the visible planets and stars, then the possibility of movement and rest manifest for them must also apply to it. In our prescientific representation, movement takes place on the earth, toward it, and away from it, but the earth itself does not move or rest, for only in relation to it do movement and rest take on any meaning.

Given the modern world-view, how then do movement and rest assume a legitimate sense, one which can be verified through intuition and evidence? The verification of any representation of the world is finally anchored in the verifying I oriented in its perceptual field, around my body as a zero-point to which all other bodies appear as moving or stationary. As *my* body, it is always here, and hence not equivalent to a here which may also be there, which is the here of a body-object. At this transcendental level of the absolute nonobjectifiable here, I experience myself not in motion or at rest but as that relative to which motion and rest make any sense. But there is more. For a motion is experienced as relative to some ground-body experienced as stationary in relation to my body. But this ground-body is itself experienced to be at rest against the background of the earth, which itself is not experienced as an objectifiable body. I can be in a car which in relation to my body is experienced to be at rest. But when I look out, I say that the car is moving, even though what I actually see is the landscape moving past my car. The train next to mine appears to be moving, until I glance at the railroad bed and see that it is really my train that is in motion. These reversals between rest and motion are based on the earth as ground, itself experienced not as a body but as a horizon at absolute "rest," in relation to which motion and that rest which is arrested motion, and therefore still a mode of motion, take on their meaning.

Now if I conceive the earth to be a mobile body, then I must be able to come to an intuition in which this becomes directly evident, hence also to come to a ground against which it is experienced as a body in motion or at rest. It is true that as I move more and more "across" the earth, I in a certain sense experience its "bodily" being more and more completely. I come to know the earth in piecemeal fashion and experience its divisibility into parts, which when separated are in fact bodies capable of rest and motion—relative to the stationary ground of the earth. The earth at rest? The earth as a unified ground cannot be at rest in the same sense as a body which has not only extension and qualities but also its place in space which can change or remain the same. As long as I have no representation of a new ground on the basis of which the earth as a body in motion and at rest can have any meaning, and as long as I gain no representation of an exchange of grounds whereby both grounds become bodies, then the earth itself remains the ground, but not a body. The earth is an all-encompassing whole whose detached parts are bodies, but, as a "whole," it itself is not a body. As a whole, how could it conceivably move?

But is it not possible to fly high enough so that the earth would appear as a globe? From this astronautical view, the earth would then be just one heavenly body among others. Is it possible to so neutralize the ground from which I stem? The new ground could be my space ship. But then I would necessarily transfer to the ship all that I first found to belong to the earth as ground. Is this not similar to the empathetic process by which I understand the body of another only by presupposing my primordial body and all that belongs to it? But through interplanetary commuting, is it not possible to have two earths as ground-bodies, so that one body would be the ground for the other? "But what do two earths mean? Two portions of one earth with one mankind. Both together would be one ground and individually would be bodies for each other." [85]

But what if I were born and reared on a large space ship, so that it would not be characterized for me as a ship in relation to the earth but would itself be my "earth," my primordial home, though my parents are not native to the ship? And since everyone has his own historicity and therefore his own native "land," this would result in a multiplicity of grounds, perhaps as a sky full of missiles. But by means of the intersubjective transfer described from the start, all of these autochthonies can finally be related to *the* earth where each of us is for one another in the open indefinite horizon of world space. For the earth is not simply this facticity of an earth which we moderns have now parlayed into a planet, but the unity of the world-ground as an infinite horizon of possible human experiences determined by its correlation to the totality of a single humanity.[86] The aboriginal earth is the invariant and immutable lifeworld as the horizon of horizons, which is not one of the objects of experience but will always precede all objects, the background against which and by which all objects, Copernican earth included, are located in terms of rest and motion, never exhausted by the work of objectification which proceeds from it. There is only one humanity and one earth as primordial home, and it is the *Ur-Arche* world to which all planets, parts of planets broken off like icebergs from their parent, space ships, missiles, and even the Ptolemaic earth, belong. Since it is the *Arche* and hence the fixed principle by which movement and rest first make sense, can Galileo's *par si muove* apply to it? The time has come to exhume this aboriginal nonobjectifiable earth buried beneath the sedimented deposits of our scientific culture. For though it never enters into the equations of the global earth, it is the starting point from which it is possible to speak of the Copernican earth.

85. Farber, *Philosophical Essays*, p. 318.
86. Edmund Husserl, *L'Origine de la géométrie*, trans. Jacques Derrida (Paris: Presses Universitaires de France, 1962), p. 80.

THE TRANSCENDENTAL TURN

BUT FOR HUSSERL, eidetic rationality alone is not enough. If the plumbing of the foundations should stop with the ontology of the lifeworld, we would have invariant structures which are simply there, as an eidetic facticity. But what of their origin? As soon as we have taken note of the pregiven character of the world, as a presupposition of presuppositions, one more task emerges before the *telos* of a complete rationality is revealed, that of a "science of the universal how of the already given character of the world," [87] which is the transcendental logic of the phenomenon of the lifeworld, its phenomeno-logy in terms of the ultimate giving of meaning which underlies its givenness. The "What?" of the world is to be completed by a consideration of its "How?" It is a matter of investigating the anonymously functioning consciousness in correlation with the "self-evident" horizon of the world and taken for granted along with the world, as is characteristic of an *actus exercitus,* in this case the veritable life of the lifeworld. Instead of living *in* these acts in our natural ways, in which we are overridingly interested in the things of the world given in these acts, we now turn to the field of these acts themselves, *ab ovo,* seizing experience by its umbilical cord, in the very upsurge of the consciousness. The world now appears as the fabric of conscious life, and the problem of the genetic constitution of the world in the incipient consciousness is rendered thematic. We have now reached the heart of the matter of phenomenology, the very origin of experience, the initial emergence of meaning in experience, "the pure and original experience in which things themselves can appear to us immediately in an original way," [88] where "we stand in a sphere of evidence behind which it is nonsense to wish to inquire," [89] "an unquestionable ground which contains all the means necessary for its solution," [90] where nothing need be taken

87. H VI, p. 149.
88. Ludwig Landgrebe, *Philosophie der Gegenwart* (Bonn: Athenaeum, 1952), p. 31.
89. H VI, p. 192.
90. H IX, p. 337.

for granted, as a matter of course, since all is permeated by the transparency of reason. This absolute apodictic ground, self-founding and founding all other experiences, is the true subject matter of the absolute science, transcendental phenomenology.

The task of its elaboration is not easy, indeed it manifests itself as an infinite horizon to the community of philosopher-scientists who enter into its endeavor. The very naming of the problem opens up a vast field of exploration, an intricate network of experiences interwoven into each other and ultimately synthesized to the unique centralizing stream. That the historical Husserl, rooting himself in the Cartesian tradition, attributed this pure centralizing function to the transcendental ego should not distract us from the field characteristics of this subjectivity, as world constituting. The Cartesian way of phenomenology brings us too quickly to the transcendental ego, tending to override its world content. It likewise overexercises the apodictic character of the absolute ground and calls for the counter-reminder that we are standing before "the deepest essential bonds between reason and being in general, the puzzle of all puzzles." [91] As Heidegger puts it in his foreword to Husserl's lectures on time constitution, "the term 'intentionality' is no all-explanatory word but one which designates a central *problem*." [92] Husserl's complaint of the lack of appropriate words by which to overcome the ambiguities pervading the doctrine of the transcendental ego finds a later echo in Heidegger and underscores the tasklike character of the radical problem of the absolute starting point. The *logos* of experience is the *telos* of an absolute science toward which man in his most intimate humanity strives, in solitude and yet as a "servant of humanity." [93] The transcendental life is the life of reason, and the life of reason is the life of humanity. The doctrine of transcendental subjectivity necessarily issues into that of transcendental intersubjectivity and transcendental historicity. The transcendental ego manifests its concrete form in "the philosophizing ego as the bearer of absolute reason coming toward itself" [94] and conscious of its relations to a historical

91. H VI, p. 12.
92. *The Phenomenology of Internal Time-Consciousness*, ed. M. Heidegger, trans. J. S. Churchill, introd. C. O. Schrag (The Hague: Nijhoff, 1964), p. 15.
93. H VI, p. 15.
94. H VI, p. 275.

community of cophilosophers, whose striving for an absolute science is *ipso facto* the achievement of self-understanding and the fulfillment of self-responsibility.

The *telos* of an absolute science is none other than that of Western man, the philosopher turned scientist now fast becoming a technician and in danger of losing his philosophical birthright. The crisis is manifest in the continuing success of science and the continuing lack of success in comprehending its fundamental concepts. Despite their technical prowess of prediction and mastery of nature, the increasingly abstract formulations of science defy basic understanding. Their "theories" are little more than computing machines accompanied by only a bare minimum of the rational insight which the Greeks honored with the name of theory. The technical rationality of the sciences is a relative and one-sided rationality which leaves the other side in complete irrationality.[95]

As Husserl sees it, the illness is objectivism and its cure is the radicalism of phenomenology. To the critical question "What gives science its scientific character?," the Renaissance moderns have fostered their ideal in the rational techniques of a formal mathesis. The result has been the fragmentation of the field of science into countless specialties and branches of *expertise* which still maintain a peculiarly fruitful, though loose, relationship to their parent and sister sciences. Counter to this encyclopedic tendency, Husserl seeks to call Western man back to his original vocation of *theoria* as an infinite task of the totality of the reason whose scientific character is *epistēmē*, knowledge based on fully evident principles and in this way transparently rational.

We have just sketched how Husserl endeavors to bring this about. We have yet to note the all-enveloping way in which he construed this task. For the philosophical-phenomenological sense of science is *eo ipso* the human sense of science, and to be scientific in this sense is the only way to be fully human, to encompass the totality of human experience, theoretical, practical, ethical, aesthetic. A life committed to the "heroism of reason"[96] is a life based on the ideal of a universal science which is to function as the basis for all community life and culture and

95. *FTL*, p. 15.
96. *H VI*, p. 348.

provide all the norms necessary for the cultivation of man through reason. If, then, there is a crisis of the sciences, it is at once a crisis in the very substance of human existence. Whence the urgency of the mission of phenomenology, considered now as a profoundly rational response to the most basic exigencies of an irrational age, in which the sciences have yet to find their fundamental significance in the larger context of human existence. The reductive return is designed to disrupt the hardened irrationality of the dogmatic and even fanatic claims of Science carried to speculative excesses and increasingly removed from its concrete origins, in order to clear the way for the avowal of a more basic naïveté. It begins in the recognition that "the rationality of exact science is on a level with the rationality of the Egyptian pyramids," [97] inasmuch as its surrounding context has been left out of consideration and even the role of the working scientist has been overlooked. Acknowledgment of this more subliminal irrationality will in turn naturally redirect the rational energies of the epoch toward the confrontation of these contextual questions. The archaic return to *doxa* would then become the normal procedure in the telic advance of science, as the indispensable way to achieve a higher rationality, "a rationality incessantly rediscovering its insufficiency and relativity and thereby driven by the effort to conquer its true and total rationality." [98]

97. *H* VI, p. 343.
98. *H* VI, p. 274.

2 / The Mathematization of Nature in Husserl's Last Publication, *Krisis*

Joseph J. Kockelmans

IN ONE OF HIS IMPORTANT ARTICLES on Husserl's phenomenology Eugen Fink has properly drawn attention to the fact that the three major publications which Husserl produced during his Freiburg period (1916–38) deal with the fundamental problems of his phenomenology as it had developed gradually between 1887 and 1916; his purpose was to try to solve these basic problems on a higher level and in a more radical way. In *Formal and Transcendental Logic* (1929) Husserl attempted to show that logic is a correlative unity of formal apophantic logic and formal ontology and, particularly, that all formal logical a priori elements are to be ultimately founded in the meaning-constituting acts performed by transcendental subjectivity. It was his conviction at that time that the problems studied in *Logical Investigations* (1900–1901) were given their final solution in these new considerations.

In *Cartesian Meditations* Husserl returned to the question of how all the convictions arrived at in our "natural attitude" can be ultimately understood in their real meaning and critically justified in the constituting activities of transcendental consciousness. In a very concise, often schematic way Husserl points here to a solution for the basic problems of his philosophy, which despite all of his earlier attempts had not received an adequate answer in either *The Idea of Phenomenology* (1906–7) or in *Ideas* I (1913).

In his last publication, *Crisis*, Husserl finally returned to the problems of his *Logos* article, "Philosophy as Rigorous Science" (1911). After radicalizing logic and epistemology in *Formal and Transcendental Logic* and *Cartesian Meditations* respectively, Husserl in this work attempted to bring to light the ultimate roots of a general theory of science by means of an analogous radicalization of his initial "naïve" view on the issue.

The main goal toward which Husserl aims in his last work is to solve the problems involved in man's theoretical and, particularly, scientific knowledge in a genuinely radical way. In order to do so Husserl takes his starting point in a minute analysis of man's prescientific experience. In his view, the *Lebenswelt*, that is, the world as we immediately experience it in our everyday life, constitutes a very complicated system of relativities, because it is the world as it is immediately "lived" in our culturally and historically determined individual and social life. The "worlds" of the sciences originate from this world and therefore are not only somehow depending upon it but are also somehow opposed to this "subjective," "practical," and eternally "relative" world. For the sciences try to transcend the "subjective," "practical," and "relative" aspects of "the" world and want to understand things in a truly "objective" manner, in the way they "really" are, by using either the methods of the mathematical science of nature or the historical and interpretative methods of the humanistic sciences. In this way the "objective" becomes the ideal of all theoretico-scientific thought which develops from the lifeworld.

Husserl does not question science's pretension to transcend the lifeworld, but he focuses serious attention on the fact that science also, and at the same time, *conceals* the lifeworld without explicitly noticing this. Husserl is convinced that precisely *because* science never becomes aware of this concealment of the world, science everywhere lapses into "objectivism," "naturalism," and skeptic "relativism." Furthermore, science does not quite understand itself either, because it is no longer aware of its own origin, which is to be found in certain fundamental motives characteristic of the lifeworld itself. This is also why science does not see that for a *radical* explanation of its own foundations it needs a subject-oriented interpretation that has its ultimate root in the constitutive analyses of transcendental subjectivity.

From what has been said it can be understood why in *Crisis* Husserl's investigations range over three completely different areas: (1) the naïvely mundane phenomena of the lifeworld; (2) the realm of "objectivism" of the sciences which also remain principally within the realm of the natural attitude; and (3) the constituting subjectivity of transcendental consciousness which precedes and constitutes the lifeworld as well as the "worlds" of the sciences. Husserl wishes to show that, and in what sense, science indeed transcends the immediate subjectivism and relativism of the lifeworld and also that, and in what sense, the mediated objectivity of science is to be transcended by transcendental phenomenology.[1]

Husserl begins his investigation with a question: Can we really speak of a "crisis" of the European sciences? The great successes, particularly those of the natural sciences, and the really amazing technical improvements made possible by science make one believe that such a crisis does not exist. But without in any sense diminishing the value of science, Husserl asserts, nonetheless, that such a crisis really does exist. When he speaks in this context of a "crisis," he merely means that the self-understanding of man in his relation to the world has lost its genuine validity and, therefore, can no longer offer him a clue to guide him in determining his real place in the midst of things and deciding with certainty on his authentic position in the world. The breakdown of man's self-understanding, therefore, means not only the breakdown of man's theoretico-scientific explanation of the world but at the same time the failure of every "practical" orientation in the world. Husserl calls the root of the breakdown of man's self-understanding "objectivism." By this he means what later phenomenologists have called "scientism," namely, the conviction that the truth of the world coincides with what can be expressed in the statements of objectifying science. In this conviction is founded also the belief that on the basis of our scientific knowledge Being is completely and totally at man's disposal, that man's science, therefore, has the capacity for putting everything which is immediately given in experience into a conceptual framework in such a way that, neither for man's knowledge nor for his "praxis" and technology, would there be left over an incomprehensible remnant. It is obviously not the case that in and through science man's reason "projects" the

1. Eugen Fink, "Die Spätphilosophie Husserls in der Freiburger Zeit," in *Edmund Husserl: 1859–1959* (The Hague: Nijhoff, 1959), pp. 98–115, esp. pp. 99–107.

world creatively; and yet his reason is nevertheless able to re-produce the world with its ideas so that every intervention in its course and every change can be calculated with certainty in advance.

But in this way the world gradually loses its character of being that "whole" in which man always already lives, which is simply given to him as never completely available to him. On the contrary, the world disappears increasingly into that which is made possible and in fact constituted by the projects of science. In this way, to an ever-growing degree, "the" world becomes an artificial world projected by the sciences and in which less and less is left over which was *not* of its own making. And most importantly, in such a world man, too, becomes an artificial object which is no more than a product of his own scientific projects. As Husserl formulates it concisely: "Blosse Tatsachen-wissenschaften machen blosse Tatsachenmenschen." [2] Man's reason is no longer the faculty which learns the truth which is "in itself" but is more and more conceived of in terms of its instrumental significance in regard to man's scientific self-pro-duction in a world which is first produced by man. In its main lines this seems to be the core of what Husserl calls the "depriva-tion of meaning" characteristic of modern mathematical science and its technical application and which Husserl in *Crisis* hopes to overcome by means of transcendental phenomenology. [3]

In Husserl's view it has not always been the case that the objectivity which, indeed, is characteristic of science has led to scientism, nor is there any reason to believe that contemporary science necessarily leads to positivism. That this in fact is true becomes clear when one focuses attention on the question of precisely how the positivist conception of science came about in the course of modern history and tries to understand the deeper motives of its genesis. [4] Among the major factors which have influenced this tragic development, Husserl briefly refers to (1) the conception of the meaning and task of philosophy which developed during the Renaissance; (2) the idea that philosophy

2. *H* VI, p. 4.
3. *H* VI, pp. 1–4; Ludwig Landgrebe, "Die Bedeutung der Phä-nomenologie Husserls für die Selbstbesinnung der Gegenwart," in *Husserl et la pensée moderne* (The Hague: Nijhoff, 1959), pp. 216–29.
4. *H* VI, p. 5.

is not a collection of disciplines but an all-encompassing science of the totality of all that is, in such a way that all existing and all possible disciplines can be no more than branches of this unitary philosophy; (3) the Cartesian conception that philosophy is able to encompass all meaningful questions in a rigorously scientific way in the unity of *one* theoretical system which is to be characterized by the apodictical evidence of the methods with the help of which it is brought to light, as well as by its unlimited but rationally ordered progress of inquiry; and finally (4) the fact that philosophy was unable to cope rationally with the highest and ultimate questions of "metaphysics" which fact, in turn, led to dogmatic rationalism, skeptical empiricism, or Kant's criticism.[5]

In other words, the ideal of philosophy which had guided many great thinkers between 1500 and 1800 appeared to be unrealizable in the very domain of metaphysics where it had led to a multiplicity of system-philosophies. On the other hand, in the realm of the empirical sciences the ideal brought such great and unexpected successes that it becomes understandable that gradually a gap developed between philosophy and science which finally seemed to be unbridgeable. Many philosophers have tried to construct a bridge over this gap in order to transcend positivism in the realm of science, which had become its necessary consequence. In Husserl's view none of these attempts was successful, however, because no one clearly understood the root of the problems which are at the basis of this unfortunate historical development.[6]

However, once philosophy itself had become problematic, the sciences had to follow in its wake, because the problems concerning the possibility of philosophy appeared to imply the basic problem concerning the genuine meaning of the sciences and their results and discoveries as well. It is this complex situation which, in turn, led to the "breakdown situation of our time" and ultimately has made man a problem to himself.[7]

In *Crisis* Husserl tries to deal with this complex of historical, as well as philosophical, problems by means of a careful critical analysis of the historical development of science and philosophy since the time of Descartes. This analysis leads to a set of

5. *H* VI, pp. 5–8; *H* VII, pp. 51–199.
6. *H* VI, pp. 6–9.
7. *H* VI, pp. 8–9.

problems for which his transcendental phenomenology in his own view can provide an acceptable answer. In view of this the subtitle of the book becomes understandable: "An Introduction to Phenomenological Philosophy." The book proposes to bring a *new* approach to Husserl's phenomenology as already contained in his earlier works. The novelty of the approach consists in taking modern science, physics and psychology respectively, as points of departure for this endeavor.[8]

Although in what follows I wish to confine my discussion to what Husserl calls "Galileo's Mathematization of Nature," which constitutes a central part of the first major section of the book, I believe it is necessary first to refer briefly to the general context in which this investigation functions.[9]

GALILEO'S MATHEMATIZATION OF NATURE

WE HAVE SEEN ALREADY that since the Renaissance, and especially after Descartes, an essentially new conception of philosophy developed. This new conception of philosophy was somehow connected with a new conception of the meaning of Euclid's geometry, Greek mathematics in general, and Greek science of nature (astronomy) in particular. The starting points of our modern sciences can be seen in two characteristics of sixteenth-century science: (1) the idealization of mathematical entities in the Platonic sense, and (2) the rigorously deductive method which takes its point of departure in basic postulates and axioms and, then, allows us to proceed to an indefinite number of theorems which share in the apodicticity of the axioms. Whereas Greek science, as does classical logic, sees only the possibility of a finite and closed a priori, in the beginning of our modern era it became clear that in this way it is possible "to encompass infinite tasks" which for modern man are immediately connected with the concept of geometrical space. To

8. *H* VI, pp. 8–14.

9. Aron Gurwitsch, "Comments on the Paper by Herbert Marcuse" ["On Science and Phenomenology"], in *Boston Studies in the Philosophy of Science*, ed. Robert S. Cohen and Max W. Wartofsky (New York: Humanities Press, 1965), II, 291–306. See also Aron Gurwitsch, "Galilean Physics in the Light of Husserl's Phenomenology," in *Galileo, Man of Science*, ed. Ernan McMullin (New York: Basic Books, 1967), pp. 388–401.

modern man it is clear that a universal and systematically unitary a priori belongs to ideal space, an infinite but nonetheless determined and unitarily systematical theory, which, starting with axioms and proceeding to theorems, is capable of constructing all imaginable geometrical figures in a deductive and univocal way. What "exists" ideally in geometrical space is already determined in advance in all its determinations. An apodictic thought merely "dis-covers" what was already there in truth.

From this insight gained within the limited realm of geometry, modern man began to conceive the idea of a rational and infinite totality of being with a rational science able to master this totality systematically. He came thus to conceive of an infinite *world*, a world of idealities whose objects are not individually, imperfectly, and incidentally open to man's knowledge but can be brought to light by a rational, systematic, and unitary method. In addition, new mathematical disciplines developed which opened up unexpected possibilities. This fortified modern man in his conception that a rational all-encompassing science in truth is possible. Indeed, the infinite totality of all possible being is in itself already a rational total-unity (*All-Einheit*) which correlatively can be mastered exhaustively by one universal science. Finally, under the influence of this general conception, and identifying the method of this unitary science with mathematics, modern man started to "apply" mathematics to the physical sciences, for which an easy justification could be found in the current Neo-Platonic philosophy. In this way modern man created the completely new idea of mathematical physics.[10]

According to the classical Neo-Platonic view, the real, in greater or less degree, participates in the Ideas, so that it is understandable at once why geometrical insights can be "applied" to the real. In Galileo's mathematization of nature, on the other hand, nature itself becomes idealized under the guidance of the new mathematics. Here one has to ask what is the precise meaning of this mathematization of nature and how can it be *reasonably* justified. Galileo argued as follows in this regard. In our prescientific life the world is given to us through our everyday sense experience in a subjective and relative way. Each one of us has his own appearances of the world which he takes to refer to the real world. Everyone knows that there is often a discrepancy between individual conceptions of the real. This

10. *H* VI. pp. 18–20.

does not alter the fact that we finally believe that there is only one world, *the* world which for all of us contains the same things which only *appear* differently in different circumstances. In the appearances there manifests itself a certain content which is the same for everyone and which we must attribute to the real world. Galileo now accepted as an obvious datum that this "content" certainly includes all that geometry and mathematics teach us about things. In other words, Galileo subscribes to the view that there is a gap between the world as it manifests itself in immediate perceptual experience and the world as it is "in truth," in reality. Because of the subjectivity and relativity of the secondary qualities, science cannot accept the world we perceive at face value and, thus, must try to find the invariable, eternal, mathematical structure which is contained and hidden in the real world as it is immediately given to us in perception. To penetrate through the veil of the appearances and thus to discover the mathematical structure of the world, to disclose it as a mathematical manifold, is precisely the task of science as Galileo conceives of it.[11]

In Husserl's view it is of the greatest importance to make carefully explicit all that Galileo here presupposes as obvious and self-evident. But before following Husserl's investigations in this regard I wish to make two brief, but important, remarks to which Gurwitsch has already drawn attention and which will perhaps be useful in avoiding misunderstanding.

First of all, when Husserl speaks of Galileo in this context, he does not exclusively mean the historical person Galileo, nor when he speaks of Galilean science does he mean the scientific work done by the person Galileo. Rather the expression "Galilean science" refers to the science inaugurated by Galileo and pertains to the historical development of modern science in the whole of the seventeenth century.[12]

It is furthermore important to realize here that the great philosophers between Galileo and Leibniz have tried to justify in their philosophies their firm belief in the mathematical structure of the "real" world. As Gurwitsch has properly pointed out, it is only with Euler that there is any clear awareness of the fact that physics is intrinsically independent of philosophy. From there on it has been generally admitted that science must be accepted and

11. Gurwitsch, "Comments on Marcuse," p. 293.
12. *Ibid.*, p. 292.

respected as a fact. The task of philosophy is merely to account for the very fact of science and to clarify its basic concepts. The same point of view is found in Kant, in most Neo-Kantians, and in all contemporary attempts at a logical analysis of science. The historical significance of Husserl's analyses concerning Galileo's physics lies in Husserl's readiness to challenge and even to abandon the acceptance of science as an ultimate fact and to see it rather as a philosophical problem.[13] It is obviously Husserl's intention to question not the intrinsic value and validity of science but merely our interpretation of it as to its ultimate meaning. Galileo's physics rests on presuppositions. Since these presuppositions were never made explicit and their genuine meaning never clearly delineated, the true meaning of science had been obscured from the very start. Trying to make these presuppositions explicit, to specify their genuine meaning and, thus, to delineate the precise meaning of science and its validity in regard to the phenomenal world obviously does not entail any a priori negative criticism of modern science as such.[14]

In trying adequately to understand Galileo's conception of physics, Husserl continues, it does not suffice to reconstruct what consciously and explicitly has motivated Galileo. We also have to examine all the presuppositions which were implicit in that conception, particularly with regard to mathematics which he used as a model for the development of his conception of physics. This leads us at once to a reflection on the origin of pure geometry. Pure geometry was for Galileo, as it still is for us, a science of "pure ideal entities" which nonetheless always can be applied to the world given in immediate perception. Although in our everyday life we seldom make a clear distinction between the spatial form given in perception and the forms with which geometry deals, we must clearly distinguish between these two realms if we are to understand the genuine meaning of geometry. Once these two realms are carefully distinguished, the question arises concerning the origin of geometrical forms or figures. Upon reflection it becomes clear that they neither immediately originate from perception nor do they find their origin in the working of our imagination, since our phantasy is able only to change sensible forms and figures into other sensible figures. The origin of geometry seems rather to be found in the aware-

13. *Ibid.*, pp. 293–94.
14. *Ibid.*, pp. 294–95.

ness that each geometrical figure in principle at least can always be made more perfect, a straight line more straight, a plain more level, and so on, an awareness that grew with the development of technology, which made an always greater perfection possible. It is clear that by going from the practically realizable perfection to the horizon of imaginable perfection, limit forms begin to delineate themselves—invariant and unreachable poles toward which all further perfection keeps pointing. It is the task of geometry to be interested in those ideal forms, to determine their ideal characterization, and, by starting from those which are already available, continually to construct new forms and figures. Instead of the real "praxis" which is always limited to what is practically possible and deals with real and really possible empirical bodies, we have now an *"idealizing praxis"* which limits itself exclusively to the domain of pure limit forms. In other words, in Husserl's view the "origin" of geometry is to be found in *idealization and construction.* The subject matter of geometry consequently consists in an unlimited and nonetheless finite world of ideal objectivities.[15]

In this "geometrical praxis" we are able to reach something which is always denied to us in the "empirical praxis": namely, exactness. For these ideal geometrical figures can be determined in absolute identity and recognized as substrates of identical characteristics that are methodically and univocally determinable. This means not only that each concrete limit form can be exactly reconstructed, nor does it merely mean that it is always possible to construct ever new limit forms from those which are already "available"; it also means that it is possible univocally to construct all imaginable ideal forms with the help of an aprioric, all-encompassing, and systematic method.[16]

The geometrical method of operationally determining first some, and later all, possible ideal entities from certain primary and elementary forms is somehow connected with the method of measuring and measuring-determination which in our prescientific life is first used primitively and then intentionally and in an orderly way. For measurement and determination by means of measurement are certainly a first attempt to transcend the subjective and relative in the direction of the objective and intersubjectively verifiable. From this, Husserl concludes, it be-

15. *H* VI, pp. 21–24.
16. *H* VI, p. 24.

comes understandable how—once the desire of finding "true and objective" Being had originated—the empirical art of measuring with its empirically and practically objectifying function became idealized and changed into pure geometry the moment the original practical interest switched over into a merely theoretical interest.[17]

It is of importance to note here along with Gurwitsch that when Husserl speaks about the "origin of geometry" he does not use the term "origin" in a historical or psychological sense but means rather a meaning-genesis. In trying to explain the real meaning of the "genesis of geometry," Husserl uses phenomenological investigations which, taking their starting point in historical facts, try to explain the "genuine meaning" of these historical phenomena. As Husserl sees it, the basic geometrical concepts arise on the basis of perceptual experiences by means of *idealization*. Once the origin of the basic concepts of geometry is explained, it is easily understood how, by taking the definitions of these basic concepts as axioms and using certain postulates, an unlimited number of geometrical entities can be *constructed*. By assuming the character of a deductive science, geometry proves to materialize the idea of the Greek *epistēmē* so that it can present itself as the model and standard of all genuine knowledge.[18]

When Galileo in his attempt to found the science "physics" decided to establish a relation between the empirical and the mathematical ideas, he was certainly inspired by what tradition had to offer him: geometry and arithmetic as established in ancient Greece, the application of "classical" mathematics to astronomy, and the art of measuring which aimed at progressively more accurate measurements and a progressively more objective determination of the forms and figures. As far as the latter is concerned, it is understandable that once geometry was born under the influence of the tasks which technical practice had set, it became, in turn, a means for technology; in this way it became applied geometry, offering a method of measuring which enables us in our dealings with the real world to approximate the geometrical ideal limits.

17. *H* VI, pp. 24–25.
18. Gurwitsch, "Comments on Marcuse," pp. 295–97; Edmund Husserl, *L'Origine de la géométrie*, trans. Jacques Derrida (Paris: Presses Universitaires de France, 1962), pp. 14–37.

Accepting these acquisitions of tradition, Galileo failed to investigate the "origin" of geometry and especially the question concerning the origin of the *apodictic evidence* of mathematics. Neither he nor anyone else in his time surmised that one day it would become evident that it is of the utmost importance to make the "origin" of geometrical evidence into a problem.[19]

Taking the attainments of tradition for granted and understanding them within the general perspective of the prevailing Platonic tradition, Galileo argued that wherever such a method is constituted there we have at once conquered the relativity and the subjectivity which are essentially connected with our knowledge of the sensible world. For in this manner we are able to come to a truth which is nonrelative, which is identical for everyone, a truth of which everyone who understands these methods and knows how to apply them can convince himself. Here we have a possibility to know true Being in the way it genuinely is, albeit only via a process of approximation which begins in empirical data and aims at geometrical limits.[20]

However, Husserl says, one must realize that pure mathematics deals with bodies, and the material world in general, merely in abstraction—that is, it is interested only in the abstract forms of spatio-temporal reality which furthermore are to be taken as pure and ideal limit-poles. On the other hand, in our immediate experience we encounter merely real and possibly real empirical figures as "forms" of a "sensible matter"; that is to say, these figures are always given there together with that which manifests itself in and through sensible qualities; these are the real characteristic properties of the material things which can be immediately reached through perception.[21]

Furthermore, if we take the perceptible bodies just as they are given in immediate perception, one sees that they are bound in their characteristic changes: in their spatio-temporal motions as well as in their alterations they appear perceptually to depend upon one another. When such a real, causal connection is not immediately given in perception, we ask immediately *why* things happen the way they do and try to find an explanation in some "cause" or other. We also see that in their mutual causal interdependence things have the "habit" of behaving equally under

19. *H* VI, pp. 26–27.
20. *H* VI, p. 27.
21. *H* VI, p. 27, esp. n. 1.

equal circumstances. And this is true not only for individual things but also for the perceptible world as a whole, which perceptually manifests itself as something which is going to continue its course as it has done in the past. On the basis of what we perceive we are even unable to imagine a world which (manifesting itself as a rational whole) is not bound by this "general style" of causality. If we reflect upon this and apply to it the method of free variation, we will see that all that is found together in our world of perception really belongs together because of an a priori and universal causal interconnection, so that the world is not only an *omnitudo realitatis* but also a genuine whole. This is evident a priori, however little we really experience of concrete causal connections.

This universal causality of our perceptual world makes hypotheses, inductions, and predictions possible. But in our prescientific life all of this never transcends the realm of the approximate and the typical, and it is by no means clear yet how a "philosophy," that is, a scientific knowledge of *the* world is precisely possible, if one sticks to the vague consciousness of totality which is given in immediate perception. It is certainly possible to come to grips with this general causal style of the world through reflection and free variation, but in that way we will only find the evidence of an empty and purely formal generality: each perceptual event is in each point of space and at each moment of time causally determined. But what does this mean in regard to the concrete, real, and determined causality of the real world? It does not make any sense whatsoever to try to genuinely and scientifically understand the world as long as we are unable to find a method which makes it possible to construct, systematically and in advance, the world with its infinity of causal interconnections, by taking our starting point from the few data which are given in immediate experience and which can be ascertained only in a relative way.[22]

Classical mathematics shows us an answer for this problem —at least as far as spatio-temporal entities are concerned. For mathematics, first of all, had already created ideal objects by means of idealization of the material world with respect to its spatio-temporal determination. In other words, mathematics had already been able to show how out of spatio-temporality, as it is given in immediate experience with its manifold of real and

22. *H* VI, pp. 29–30.

possibly real perceptible entities, an objective world can be constituted as an infinite totality of ideal objects which methodically can be determined in such a way that this determination is univocally valid once and forever and for everyone. In this way mathematics had already shown that the infinity of subjective and relative objects which in our prescientific life can be represented only in vague generality can be thought of as objectively determinable and objectively determined in itself by means of an apriorically all-encompassing method.

Classical mathematics had shown, secondly, that by returning from the world of ideal entities to the perceptual world and by using the art of measuring one can reach an objectively real knowledge of a completely new type, namely, a knowledge which is oriented approximately toward the ideal entities of mathematics, in regard to the spatio-temporal aspects of the real world of perception. In other words, by making the ideal and "de-mundanized" geometry into applied geometry one is able to bring to light the possibilities of induction and prediction in regard to the spatio-temporal aspect of the world. Astronomy had shown this in a very concrete and equally convincing way.

As Husserl sees it, Galileo has been the first to ask himself the question whether this objectivation, which for the quantitative aspect of the world had proved to be possible and fruitful, could perhaps be applied to the concrete world as such so as to include all its other aspects as well. It is obvious that in such an attempt the secondary qualities will cause unexpected and quite complicated difficulties because the "mathematization" will here have to take place in an indirect way.[23]

Before entering into the question of how Galileo tried to solve the problem of the indirect mathematization of the sensible qualities which are immediately given to us in perception, we must first explain why in Galileo's view a direct mathematization of these qualities is excluded in principle. It is obvious that these qualities manifest themselves in a gradation of more or less; it is obvious also that these gradations can be measured. But one has to realize here that in the realm of the sensible qualities there is no exact measurement possible, nor is there any possibility of continuously increasing the exactness. The reason for this is that the whole schema which we have used to justify the mathematization of the "quantitative" aspects of the world does not

23. *H* VI, pp. 31–32.

apply in the realm of the sensible qualities because there is no second universal form of the world corresponding to the universal form we spoke about in the foregoing, and correspondingly there is no second "geometry" possible in addition to the one developed by Euclid.[24]

Furthermore an indirect mathematization does not seem to be easy because no one sees how there could be a one-to-one correspondence between the changes occurring in the realm of the sensible qualities and those which occur in the realm of causally determined spatio-temporal events and for which "applied geometry" is able to account.[25] One will evidently say today, Husserl continues, that the "mathematization" of the sensible qualities no longer involves any serious problems in that "colors" are "really" wave phenomena, the frequency of which can easily be determined with the greatest accuracy. However, Husserl rightly remarks, that which through Galileo's first endeavors would eventually become self-evident was certainly not yet evident to him. That is why we must realize that at that time it must have sounded very strange to many people that *all* aspects of the real things which manifest themselves through the sensible qualities must have a mathematical index in the occurrences of causally determined spatio-temporal characteristics and that from these an indirect mathematization of all other aspects of the material things must be possible.[26]

This last remark, however, does not mean that the basic idea of Galileo's physics, as it were, fell out of a blue sky. Examples of an indirect mathematization of some secondary qualities had been known by the Pythagoreans, the possibility of a complete mathematization of nature had been defended by Plato and almost all Neo-Platonists, very interesting investigations concerning the measurability of extensive as well as intensive magnitudes had been available since the fourteenth century, and, finally, Galileo knew about the attempts made to apply the mathematical conception of the infinite to extensive and intensive magnitudes. But all of this does not immediately lead to the indirect mathematization of nature which constitutes the basic conception of Galileo's physics.[27]

24. *H* VI, pp. 32–33.
25. *H* VI, pp. 34–35.
26. *H* VI, pp. 35–36.
27. *H* VI, pp. 36–37.

Up until now we have found only one general idea—better, one general hypothesis—namely, that the world of immediate experience is governed by a universal law of induction which manifests itself everywhere in experience but also hides itself there in its infinity. In Husserl's view, Galileo did not conceive of this idea *as* hypothesis: physics was for him almost as certain and "pure" as applied geometry. Geometry also showed Galileo how this idea could be concretely materialized from a methodical point of view. New methods of measurement were to be developed and pure mathematics was to be further developed. With the help of these new means the universal causality, that is, the universal inductivity of the world of immediate experience, was to be examined systematically. It is to be noted, however, that in this new type of idealization of nature a *universal* exact causality is postulated which from now on includes not only the spatiotemporal but also the other aspects of the real.

In the concrete realization of this great project Galileo was guided not by a preceding systematical reflection on fundamental possibilities or on basic presuppositions of this general mathematization of nature but by the successes and failures of his own attempts. Without ever justifying his conception systematically, he found via a careful application of the newly devised methods that indeed everywhere there are causal interconnections which can be expressed mathematically in formulas. Husserl, however, rightly refers also to the fact that a great deal of Galileo's success must certainly be attributed to Galileo's genius (or "instinct," as Husserl calls it).[28]

At any rate, in the actual measurement of what is given in immediate experience one obviously finds merely inexact, empirical magnitudes and their corresponding numbers. But the art of measuring implies for this new realm, too, that the "exactness" of the measurements can be indefinitely increased. It is an art, not a ready-made method; it is an art which implies the possibility of continuously perfecting its own methods. Since now, according to Galileo's basic conception, the world in *all* its aspects is related to pure mathematics in that the world precisely constitutes the domain of its applicability, the "over-and-over-again" connected with the indefinite perfectibility of the measuring procedures receives the mathematical meaning of the "in infinitum," and thus each concrete measurement receives the charac-

28. *H* VI, pp. 38–39.

ter of an approximation aiming at an ideally identical pole which never can be reached, namely, one specific mathematical ideal entity or at an algebraic formula which corresponds to it.[29]

Since finally, according to Galileo, his method as a whole has a *universal* meaning, one may conceive of the result of the measurement of one individual and factical entity as something which is universally valid for all similar cases under similar circumstances. That is why Galileo can conclude that the indirect mathematization of nature, which materializes itself as methodical objectivation of the world of perception, leads to *general* algebraic formulas which, once they are discovered, may be used to complete the factual objectivation of all concrete cases which can be subsumed under it. The formulas represent universal causal connections, "laws of nature," laws which express real causal dependencies in the form of "functional" dependencies of numbers and which eventually together with other similar laws can lead to "theories." [30]

At this point in his analysis of Galileo's physics, Husserl makes the important remark that Galileo's basic conception is in truth a *hypothesis* of a very peculiar type: notwithstanding its verification during almost four hundred years, this hypothesis is still a hypothesis and will remain a hypothesis forever. It belongs to the very essence of physics forever to remain hypothesis and forever to remain verification. There is evidently progress in physics; physics continually gives us ever better "representations" of what "real nature" genuinely is, but "real nature" *is in infinity*, and, what is more, as a pole which is infinitely far away, "real nature" is an infinity of theories related to an unending historical process of approximation.[31]

Returning to Galileo's physics, Husserl then states that in his view the decisive achievement of Galileo's conception, which according to the total meaning of the physical method makes systematically possible previsions and predictions which transcend the realm of our immediate experiences of the lifeworld, is found in the real coordination of the mathematical ideal entities which in advance are projected in undetermined generality and then are shown in their concrete determinations. Once the mathematical ideal entities are found in their functional interdepend-

29. *H* VI, pp. 39–40.
30. *H* VI, p. 40.
31. *H* VI, pp. 41–42.

ence, it is possible to project the expected empirical regularities of the practical life world.

From this fact it becomes understandable why, seen methodologically, from the very start the main interest of the scientists has been to further develop this mathematical aspect of the method of science, to find new and more adequate formulas and to found them strictly logically. Thus, it is logical that immediately after Galileo the arithmetization of geometry begins by means of analytic geometry and infinitesimal calculus. This process obviously increases the formalization which was already part of the idealization found in the geometrization of nature. All of modern mathematics develops in the direction of increasing formalization, beginning with common algebra and ending in modern set theory and contemporary logic. In these completely formalized disciplines the terms used are deprived of all intuitive content and are defined merely by relations which hold between them and the operations performed upon them. Thus, formalization, which is an essential part of the arithmetization of geometry, necessarily leads to a certain emptying of its meaning. The spatio-temporal ideal entities of applied geometry which still belong to the realm of our intuition are replaced by numbers and algebraic formulas. Instead of intuitively representable constructs we have now systems of symbols and rules for operations to be performed upon these symbols. The system of symbols, in turn, can be "interpreted" in different ways, and thus, in addition to the "syntax" explaining the use of the symbols, there is need for "semantics" the moment a relationship is to be established between the final formulas of the "calculus" and the results of our experiments.[32]

The entities which are brought about by means of idealization, formalization, and functionalization begin gradually to appear as independent and self-sufficient entities. Once established, pure mathematics and formal logic develop autonomously without ever requiring reference to their "origin." That is why the presuppositions which underlie the modern *mathesis universalis*, namely, the experiences of things encountered in the lifeworld, on the one hand, and the processes of idealization, formalization, and functionalization, on the other, gradually fell into oblivion. This, in turn, gave the impression to many scientists and philosophers that contemporary mathemat-

32. *H* VI, pp. 42–45.

ics and logic do not have any presuppositions outside them-selves. All of this obviously does not place any blame on mathe-matics and logic but is merely meant to point to an important task of the philosopher, whose function it is (among others) to clarify the origin and to account for the very meaning of modern science.[33]

Mathematical physics now shares with its instrument (*pure formal mathesis universalis*) its purely formal character; it too developed into a kind of game governed by a well-determined set of game rules. However, the more mathematical physics suc-ceeded in the mathematization of nature, the more manifest were possibilities both of establishing relationships between the deductive conclusions of the formal calculi and newly discovered "facts" concerning nature, quantified by processes of measure-ment, and of making predictions and of looking for verifications. It is in this latter domain that mathematical physics and experi-mental physics closely cooperate. Although at first sight it seems as if the mathematical physicist is interested merely in the "formal calculi" and the experimental physicist in what practi-cally occurs in "real nature," history of science clearly shows that both these branches of physics constitute a harmonious unity and that both, from beginning to end, continuously orient them-selves to the ideal entities constituted by idealization, formaliza-tion, and functionalization.[34]

In Husserl's view it is of the greatest importance to realize that from now on the cooperation between experimental and mathematical physics takes its cause wholly within a changed horizon of meaning: this horizon of meaning refers to a realm of ideal entities, not to the realm of things as immediately given in our experiences of the lifeworld.[35] The mathematically consti-tuted world of ideal entities gradually becomes substituted for the one and only real world which as lifeworld is immediately given to us in experience. This substitution is already found in Galileo in that the geometry which he inherited and applied without further questioning was no longer "original geometry" but a geometry which had already lost contact with the "aborig-inal" sources of our immediate perception and had worked with

33. *H* VI, pp. 45–47; Gurwitsch, "Comments on Marcuse," pp. 298–99.
34. *H* VI, pp. 47–48.
35. *H* VI, p. 48.

ideal entities. The fact that in a geometry of ideal entities these pregeometrical achievements are the basis of geometry's genuine meaning, that is, the ultimate basis of idealization as well as construction, remained unnoticed by Galileo, who in his uncritical acceptance of the Neo-Platonic philosophy of his time thought it obvious that nature possesses a mathematical structure and thus that all that geometry and mathematics reveals *is* the genuine nature of things.[36] "Philosophy is written in that great book which ever lies before our eyes—I mean the universe —but we cannot understand it, if we do not first learn the language and grasp the symbols in which it is written. This book is written in the mathematical language, and the symbols are triangle, circle, and all other geometrical figures, without whose help it is impossible to comprehend a single word of it."[37]

But by overlooking the processes of idealization, formalization, and functionalization, processes which are our own operations in and through which the ideal entities with which physics deals are constituted, Galileo was wrapped up in his own productions to the disregard of both the constituting activities from which these products arose and their ultimate meaning-fundament, the lifeworld, so as to hide it and to become substituted for it. What in truth is merely a method, and the results of that method, is now taken for "real nature"; nature is reduced to a mathematical manifold.[38]

This analysis concerning the "origin" of Galileo's physics leads thus to the discovery and rehabilitation of the lifeworld which no longer can be dismissed as an "objective and absolute" realm of meaning describing the world as it "truly is in itself." On the contrary, the lifeworld underlies, and is also necessarily presupposed by, the elaboration of "objective" nature. What in science is called "objective" reality is truly an objectivation of reality as it is immediately given to us in perception.

Galileo's basic conception of the "real" meaning of the mathematization of nature led to some very influential but unacceptable consequences. This view almost necessarily implies a sharp distinction between "primary and secondary qualities." Galileo, like Kepler, describes this distinction in terms of that which is

36. *H* VI, pp. 54–56.
37. *Le Opere di Galileo Galilei*, ed. Eugenio Albèri, 16 vols. (Florence: Società Editrice Fiorentina, 1842–56), IV, 171.
38. *H* VI, pp. 48–54.

absolute, objective, and mathematical and that which is relative, subjective, and merely sensible. The former constitutes the domain of real knowledge, whereas the latter is the realm of opinion.

Furthermore, if nature in its "true Being" and "in itself" is mathematical and if pure mathematics teaches us the laws which govern all its events with apodictic evidence, then it is very difficult to understand how such a "divine" knowledge could ever be derived from our everyday sense perception. Thus Galileo's basic conception almost necessarily leads to the doctrine of "innate ideas."

On the other hand, if one rejects Plato's conception of recollection and the doctrine of the Forms which it presupposes *as well as* the doctrine of innate ideas and, therefore, subscribes to the empiricist principle that all our knowledge ultimately derives from experience, then one has to face the almost insoluble problem of induction. For how is one going to account for the vital step which leads from knowledge of empirical particularities to general statements which can be accepted as sufficiently founded and which are also powerful enough to serve as "apodictic" premises for subsequent mathematical and logical deductions which, in turn, will guarantee the "truth" of the "laws of nature"? In Husserl's view the sharp opposition between apriorio and apodictic mathematics and the inductive science of nature rests ultimately on a false conception of the genuine meaning of the mathematization of nature. The moment one asks the question concerning the "origin" of Galileo's physics and carefully analyzes all its explicit and implicit presuppositions, it becomes clear that the doctrine of "innate ideas" as well as the classical conception of the meaning of induction are false answers for pseudoproblems.[39]

CONCLUSION

WE HAVE SEEN that in Husserl's view modern physics since Galileo's time has almost always overlooked the fact that "real and objective nature," which physics tries to bring to light (in contradistinction to nature as it manifests itself in our prescientific perceptual experience), is an Idea in the Kantian sense

39. *H* VI, pp. 54–58.

toward which a set of human theoretical achievements converge. Galileo and his successors were not aware of the processes of idealization, mathematization, formalization, and functionalization from which the correlates of the scientist's conception derive their ultimate meaning. By focusing almost exclusively on the "dress of ideas" which science has cast upon the originally given world, they lost sight of the lifeworld upon which the processes of science precisely operate and which, therefore, they necessarily presuppose.

This realization is evidently not the end of Husserl's phenomenological analyses. For it is obvious that although the lifeworld is the necessary meaning fundament (*Sinnesfundament*) of the natural sciences, it itself is for that reason not yet something which can be taken for granted. In other words, the return to the lifeworld does not exhaust itself in "naïve" descriptions. For to such a return to the lifeworld there also belongs a reflection on that which is experienced, taken as it is immediately experienced, a reflection on the subjective achievements in and through which the lifeworld is present to man, and, finally, a reflection on the conditions of the possibility of that experience. Since now reflections on the conditions of the possibility of experience, an expression which is to be taken here in the Kantian sense, constitute the task of transcendental philosophy, Husserl's intentional and constitutive analyses concerning the lifeworld necessarily lead to what he calls "transcendental phenomenology." [40]

However, there is an important difference between the transcendental philosophy of Kant and of Husserl, a difference which immediately pertains to the subject of our investigation here. Kant's transcendental philosophy confined itself to an investigation of the conditions of the possibility of objective Being as it is brought to light by our objective, scientific knowledge. The consequence of this was that in Kant's *Critique of Pure Reason* man appears exclusively as a theoretically knowing subject who is merely interested in entities which are already objectified. Husserl, on the contrary, asks for the conditions of the possibility of that experience which, as the original and "fundamental" mode of man's life in the world, precedes science, and of which science is merely one of the many possible further specifi-

40. *H* VI, pp. 48, 178–93.

cations. This is the reason why Husserl easily escapes the objectivism to which Kant's philosophy almost necessarily leads.

Husserl is of the opinion that once a reduction from the objective world of science to the immediately given lifeworld is performed, an "ontology" of the lifeworld is to be developed whose main function is to reflect upon the conditions of the possibility of our lifeworld experience. The structures in which the condition of the possibility of that experience consist are found not in those structures that are constituted by our theoretical determination of the given data with the help of objectifying categories, but in those structures that, as the temporalization of temporality, as determinations of the original space constitution, and as a certain style of typical causality, refer to a subject which as a bodily and sensitive being finds itself together with other subjects in a world which is always there already before every possible theoretical activity.[41]

But even this "ontology of the lifeworld" is not an ultimate. Also the lifeworld itself refers to, and in that sense presupposes, acts of perceptual consciousness through which it is experienced and presents itself as that which it is and as that for which we take it. It is only when we arrive at consciousness as the universal medium of access to whatever exists and has value, including the lifeworld itself, that our search for foundations reaches its final destination. In other words, our ontology of the lifeworld reaches its ultimate foundation only in the constitutive analyses of transcendental phenomenology.[42]

41. Landgrebe, "Die Bedeutung," pp. 219–20.
42. Gurwitsch, "Comments on Marcuse," p. 303.

3 / Husserl on the History of Science

Theodore J. Kisiel

IN THE WORDS of its American dean, George Sarton, the history of science is a secret history which largely takes place independently of the noisy events that affect the immediate concerns of existence and survival, the business of the market place and the political arena. And yet this secret history is "the essential history of mankind" [1] and is eventually acknowledged as more important for humanity, once the more urgent daily needs are no longer pressing. Prominent businessmen are soon forgotten; great scientists emerge from their obscurity to take their place in the collective memory. Only the history of science is truly progressive—so much so that scientists tend to hastily pass over yesterday's discoveries as "obsolete" in order to confront today's problems. And yet the progress of science eventually hinges on the comprehension, at least on the part of its most able practitioners, of the very sense of science, a sense which Sarton suggests can only be truly found in the study of the origin and evolution of this "most precious patrimony of mankind." [2] The sense of science is intrinsically bound to its profound historical movement, and this history is the history of human civilization considered from its highest point of view, as the manifestation of its intellectual achievement and of "the power of human solidarity, without which there would be no science." [3] As such a distinctive mark of man, its study is indis-

1. *The Life of Science: Essays in the History of Civilization* (Bloomington: Indiana University Press, 1960), p. 64.
2. *Ibid.*, p. 55.
3. *Ibid.*, p. 49.

pensable not only to scientists but to philosophers as well. "The history of science—that is to say, the history of human thought and civilization in its broadest form—is the indispensable basis of any philosophy." [4]

The echoes of Husserl that can be heard in these words, all the more striking because they were voiced by a practitioner eminently noted for his concern with documents and the details of archives, may serve as a contrapuntal introduction to the following study centered around the famous fragment first published posthumously under the title, "The Question of the Origin of Geometry as an Intentional-Historical Problem." [5] The text is a working manuscript rather than a definitive formulation, and contains a series of remarks and suggestions on the conditions and character of the internal history which is the life of science. Husserl begins immediately by setting the problem off from the external circumstances, names, dates, the actual assertions of factual personalities, etc., that constitutes empirical history. For even natural science fundamentally does not proceed empirically but is largely guided by essential insights.[6] Physics made rapid strides only when Galileo and his peers saw that geometry and further mathematical developments supplied an initial clarification of the fundamental concepts of material nature, especially space. Their physical insights not only added to our factual knowledge of nature but also, and more primarily, evolved a formalized eidetic of *res extensa*. Accordingly, the more basic considerations of the birth and becoming of science lie on the a priori level of meaning rather than the empirical level of facts. Hence as Husserl sees it, the "essential history" which transcends the "noisy events" of daily concerns is even more of a "secret history" than Sarton's. But it is a history which can be traced even when the facts are no longer accessible. We

4. *Ibid.*, p. 58.
5. "Die Frage nach dem Ursprung der Geometrie als intentional-historisches Problem," ed. Eugen Fink, *Revue internationale de philosophie*, I (1938–39), 203–25. A more detailed redaction is presented by Walter Biemel in *H* VI, pp. 365–86. A précis of Fink's redaction is presented by Dorion Cairns in *Philosophy and Phenomenological Research*, I (1940–41), 98–109. A translation of Biemel's redaction with an introduction of 171 pages is given by Jacques Derrida in his translation of Husserl's *L'Origine de la géométrie* (Paris: Presses Universitaires de France, 1962).
6. *Ideas I*, § 25, p. 84.

may know little or nothing of the individuals who instituted geometry. But if we begin with what we do know, the body of geometric thought transmitted to us by the tradition, it is possible to backtrack in a regressive inquiry to gain some insight into what the original but now submerged sense *must* have been when it *first* emerged.[7]

Since in its essence it is not a matter of factual men in a factual history, the scientific life bespeaks a new kind of historicity. A scientist necessarily works out of a particular situation, but his attention and activities are directed toward the infinite horizon of *aeterna veritas*, or better, omnitemporal truth, a truth for all time accessible in principle to everyone, which therefore transcends the relativity of the truths of a particular historical situation. Because he cannot achieve this goal alone, each individual scientist is a scientist in the essential sense of this word only as a member of the open community which provides the tradition of knowledge upon which he bases his own research, and where his contributions are verified and take their proper place. The fulfillment of his own work is his particular goal, which in turn serves as a means for further scientific projects on the parts of others. The current "body" of science is a unity of meaning which is the specific raw material for further developments. The life of science is precisely this interdependent progression of research and researchers extending across the generations and moving toward its infinite *telos*. If by contrast the history of art is considered, the same tightly woven network of means and ends is not apparent. Each art work is an end in and for itself. It may be criticized by contemporary artists, but this is not the criticism of co-workers who are co-responsible for the advancement of that particular artistic problem. Each artist works alone according to his own insights, begins for himself and ends for himself, and his work generally does not directly become raw material for the construction of new works. Correlatively, the so-called schools of art are much looser unions than the scientific community. Historicity plays a much more profound role in the life of science.[8]

It is because of this tightly woven network in the progression of scientific meaning that Husserl now insists that it is possible

7. Husserl, "Die Frage nach dem Ursprung der Geometrie," Fink redaction, p. 207. Cf. *H* VI, p. 366.
8. *H* VI, pp. 505–7.

to regress to the most incipient meanings of science solely along essential lines. This backtracking is necessary since to understand a science one must understand it from the ground up and gain an insight into the founding action which originally instituted it, into the process by which its fundamental concepts were created, and into the original spiritual motives of this creation.

Such a reduction becomes doubly necessary in the face of the tendency to overlook and forget the incipient senses as they become buried under the sedimentations of more advanced acquisitions and to concentrate on the more immediate tasks at hand. And yet these hidden senses are still operative in subliminal ways in the current advance of science, so that a full understanding of even the current state of the science calls for their exposition. The high regard that we have for scientific objectivity may even prompt us to accept our most successful sciences without question as self-evident. We may even have to be forced to recall that geometry and mathematical physics are indeed products of a tradition. "So self-evident has this sense [of scientific objectivity] become for us that it already requires an effort to make clear that we have here a product of evolution, whose motives of origin and original evidence must be sought." [9]

THE TRANSMISSION OF A TRADITION

To AFFIRM that science in its essence had a historical beginning is to deny the assumptions of a Platonism which claims that the ideal object preexists the subjective act in which it first emerges.[10] It has its origin then in the creative activities of the inventor, beginning in a project and terminating in the evidence of the successful achievement of the project. The first acquisition prompts further acquisitions not only by the initial subject but by others as well, and across the generations, in such a way that the body of acquisitions of a science form a persistent totality which grows in a continuous synthesis by serving as a "total premise, so to speak," [11] for the acquisitions of further levels. Each scientist is at least implicitly conscious of being involved in this continuous progression of acquisitions moving

9. *H* VI, p. 358.
10. *L'Origine de la géométrie*, p. 29.
11. *H* VI, p. 367.

toward an open horizon of knowledge. Each science in turn is correlated with an open concatenation of generations of researchers working with and for one another, which constitutes as it were "the productive subjectivity for the totality of the living science." [12] Not that there is a collective subject. There are and can only be individual consciousnesses, but their perspectives do not cease to pass into each other. Each is installed within the perspectives of others and at the same time imparts to others his own perspective. It is this generalized system of interactions which constitutes the reality of history.

If we now compare the project in the mind of the initial creator with the total sense of the present stage of a science, it is clear that he possessed a much more primitive sense than the project which developed after centuries of construction upon his initial project, which has since been integrated and reintegrated into ever larger totalizations. Clarification of the relations between initial project and current totality calls for a consideration of the conditions which make the transmission of a science across the ages possible. The problems here are related to the larger problems of the transmission of any literary tradition whatsoever.

The first of these conditions is the repeatability of ideal objects. In opposition to the project and realization of meaning as transient psychic events in the individual geometer's mind, which as such are restricted to a certain time and place, the Pythagorean theorem has a unique existence which makes it accessible to all men at any time as identically the same sense, no matter how often or in whatever language it is expressed. In thus being intersubjectively accessible in identically the same sense in omnitemporal fashion, it is objective in the strictest sense of this term. Such an objectivity can only be "irreal" or ideal, inasmuch as anything real is individuated in time and space and so cannot have the freedom of repetition so essential to the historical persistence of mental products.

The identity of the Pythagorean theorem, the number series, and other mathematical entities in and through their various reproductions find parallels in, e.g., the uniqueness of *the* Eroica [13] or *the* Mona Lisa [14] in and through their reproductions.

12. *Ibid.*
13. *H* IX, p. 398.
14. *EU,* p. 320.

But more important for the historicity of science is the background provided by the uniqueness of language itself in its ideality. We distinguish the sensuous acoustic phenomena from the words themselves. Repeated expression does not multiply a word. When someone has not understood, we graciously repeat the *same* words. We speak of the same book in the countless reproductions of it which physically exist. "Language has the objectivity proper to objects that belong to the so-called spiritual or cultural world, and not the objectivity proper to mere physical nature." [15] Husserl here even speaks of a certain "spiritual corporality" of the word which remains the same in its many reifications or sensuous incorporations. This paradoxical expression underscores a certain limitation to the ideality of language as a cultural product which gives it a certain local character, restricted to the English-speaking world, or the German community, etc. The same applies to the moral ideality of the United States Constitution, which is binding in an obligatory way only for a certain sphere of influence and is truly repeatable as such only within that sphere. From such bound cultural idealities must be distinguished the truly free idealities like the Pythagorean theorem, which is bound to no particular historical community but rather is omnispatial and omnitemporal in its repeatability.[16] Compare, for example, the translatability of the Pythagorean theorem with that of a poem.

Nevertheless, in order to enter into the historical tradition, our scientific theorems must be incorporated in *some* language. For it is through language that the thought in the mind of the individual inventor acquires an existence in the world and thus becomes accessible not only to contemporaries but also and more significantly, through the written word, to later generations. It is language which is the condition of the possibility for the retention and protention of meaning beyond the finite individual and for the tradition. Thus the free ideality of the Pythagorean theorem, intrinsically supratemporal, binds itself to time through the spatial-temporal fixation of the written word, whereby it becomes virtually omnitemporal, i.e., accessible to everyone at all times. Only by becoming temporally bound can it become temporally accessible.

The crucial problem is in comprehending the character of

15. *FTL*, p. 18.
16. *EU*, pp. 320–21.

this general facticity without which a free ideality cannot acquire objectivity historically. If ideal formations are supratemporal in their ideality, they are nevertheless never so without an essential relation to temporality. For they have a historical origin in being formed through the theoretical interests of productive subjectivities and are implicated in historical transmission in such a way that they are necessarily bound to the continued existence of speaking persons. And it is through the medium of language that ideality becomes conjoined to the facticity of life. Husserl describes this juncture in terms of an infinitely open horizon of a universal "language" which is based on the community of men who have a common world in which "everything has its name, or is nameable in a very broad sense, i.e., is expressible in a language," [17] so that each individual can in principle express for himself anything which he finds in this common world. Likewise, through empathy he recognizes that others are in the same situation, so that he can communicate with them and they with him with regard to this common world. All in all, this means that translation from one culturally localized language to another is in principle always possible, no matter how divergent they may be in structure. Parenthetically, it may be noted that this conception of universal language is inseparably intertwined in the correlation between the lifeworld and the historical human community, in contradistinction to Husserl's earlier conception of a universal grammar or eidetic of language in the Fourth Logical Investigation, which sought the forms of signification without which a language would not be language. This earlier conception of an eidetic language, of which actually existing languages are only confused realizations, suggests instead a correlation with a universal consciousness somehow above history and aloof to its movement.

To proceed, in addition to the intersubjective communicability which binds all language together, a linguistic factor of perpetuity is required, one which will overcome the transience of oral communication and the comings and goings of generations of subjects. Objectification through the written word foregoes the need for the continual presence of active subjects by preserving idealities in the form of a virtual communication. Here language as a "spiritual corporality" assumes the fullness of its

17. *H* VI, p. 370.

paradox of giving body to thought, whereby it now defines a spatiality and temporality peculiar to history and tradition, which transcend the alternatives of sensibility and intelligibility, the empirical and metaempirical, real and ideal. This scriptural spatio-temporality creates a sort of transcendental field for the virtual permanence of idealities from which every actual subject can be absent, but which nevertheless must be reanimated by *some* subject if it is not to pass into oblivion. It is through script that we reassume the testimonies of past men and through empathetic memory place ourselves in the position of a Galileo or the Thales of geometry, "as if" we were there.

But the virtual presence of meaning in the body of a word suggests that it is to a certain extent also absent. Like the human body, the linguistic body at once manifests and withholds meaning. And because of a self-evidence that comes from the familiarity of constant usage, words are generally only passively understood, a natural tendency which over the years submerges latent senses even more. Hence virtuality not only preserves meaning but also "seduces" [18] by promoting a passivity toward the meanings preserved; this induces a forgetting that may eventually lead to a crisis in understanding. The loss of original meaning in the current formulations of mathematical physics is a case in point. Rooted in the phenomenon of *Sinnentleerung,* the crisis is indeed a "disease of language." [19] But if this lapse of meaning seems to apply particularly to the abstract symbolism of mathematical language, one should not overlook that this is based on a certain natural lethargy of tradition considered as a passive and pregiven "deposit," which one accepts with the unquestioning attitude generally summed up in the words, "that's the way things are done around here." Such a proceeding forward on the basis of obfuscated presuppositions might even be considered the prerogative of the scientist, who abstains from questions of origin and institution for the sake of progress, an abstention which is even necessary for such progress. But even though the scientist does not return to the remote foundations when he takes up his science and goes forward, he nonetheless may perform a critique of certain aspects of his more recent tradition. It is in this sense that Gaston Bachelard speaks of the history of science as a judged history. And this is essential to the

18. *H* VI, p. 372.
19. *L'Origine de la géométrie,* p. 91 n.

normal transmission of science. The scientist is not completely passive to his tradition, as Husserl's account may lead us to believe. To this extent, he partakes of the self-responsibility of genuine humanity in its struggle against passivity, through the active assumption of positions.

What Husserl asks for in response to the malady of the age is in fact somewhat unnatural, going against the grain of the normal responses to tradition. The extraordinary cure which he prescribes is the reactivation of the most rudimentary meanings which have been "sedimented" in the basic words of a science and then obfuscated through passivity. Confronted with the obscurity of scientific foundations, it is necessary and indeed still possible to unearth these essential beginnings, inasmuch as they are still operative in the present formulations as their supports, though in a submerged form.

THE PROBLEM OF REACTIVATION

A TEMPORALITY that alternates between passivity and activity is the course of human existence and *ipso facto* of scientific life. Interruptions are the rule rather than the exception. Men turn to other occupations, they sleep, the original inventors die, and others take up their work. On both the individual and the community level, consciousness of the evidence for a conclusion passes, the productive activity is followed by a passivity with regard to it, its retention fades. The problem is particularly acute in science, which builds on previous acquisitions to develop new ones. To guarantee the possibility of reactivating prior sense formations, full documentation is indispensable. But if complete reactivation were necessary every time a scientist resumed work, then science itself would not be possible, practically speaking. Each scientist reactivates only what is essential for his particular occupation and assumes the rest. And if these assumptions continue to yield fruitful results, the need for a reactivation which extends to the most primitive levels of his science becomes even less acute. Only when a radical obstacle is encountered, promoting a crisis in the very foundations of the science, is the need for such a backtracking felt. Progressive repetition must now give way to a regressive reactivation reach-

EDMUND HUSSERL / 77

ing to the very sources of the science. But then the documentary resources may not be readily available, centuries of forgetting having obscured even the need for a detailed preservation of the initial halting steps. In fact, the first geometers themselves, being too close to the original evidence, did not feel this need. And the manifest possibility of the practical applications of the laws which they derived quickly led to a habitual praxis which could be readily transmitted without the sense of the original evidence upon which it was based.

Consider, for instance, a "deductive" science like geometry, where in fact more comes into play than simply deductive procedures. An examination of its manuals indicates how it has been transmitted to us. There we learn how to manipulate, by means of rigorous logical procedures, concepts which are ready-made. Instead of showing the derivation of the primitive geometric idealities from their pregeometric raw material, the concepts are illustrated for us through drawn figures. And the practical success of applied geometry does the rest, a success based on technical rationality, rather than on the thoroughgoing rationality which is capable of seeing through its concepts and procedures to their most fundamental evidence. One cannot stop with the axioms of a deductive science, for these are themselves the results of a more radical formation of meaning. Scientific responsibility calls for more than the elucidation of concepts through logical analysis. The reactivation of sedimented senses must be a radical *Be-Sinnung* which fixes the method of production of the original idealities from the prescientific data of the cultural world in well-established propositions which once and for all dispel the vague and illusive comprehension that we now have of the foundations of geometry. Without this capacity of reactivating the institutive activities locked in our fundamental concepts, as well as "the what and how of their prescientific materials," [20] geometry is a tradition devoid of meaning in the true sense, i.e., a sense of its truth, which must comprehend the sense of the entire science and not just its most recent developments.

In the final sections of the "Origin of Geometry" text, which anticipate the objections of modern epistemology and of histori-

20. *H* VI, p. 376.

cism, Husserl proceeds to clarify in what sense reactivation is a historical investigation, and to summarize his conception of history in the central notion of the "historical present."

Objection 1: It seems that reactivation as just described is no different from the search for the epistemological foundations of science in modern philosophy. *Sed contra*, modern epistemology, wary of the "genetic fallacy," assumes an abstract ahistorical attitude which misses precisely the concrete context within which it was possible for geometry or any science to originate. To study the origin of geometry as an intentional-historical problem means to consider it within the total problem of historicity in general. But if this is not a problem of factual history, a search for the "Thales of geometry" [21] or a "history of magic and experimental science" (Thorndike), then what? It is a matter of considering the essential genesis of geometry by recourse to the historical a priori already indicated, the conditions of possibility of history: language, intersubjectivity, tradition (which implies within itself the movement of transmission and the persistence of a heritage) and most important, the entire field of invariants and motivations to which these refer. In brief, it is a matter of placing geometry back within the horizon of the lifeworld.

The entire investigation is to take place on the transcendental level of meaning, where history is "the living movement of the association and mutual implication of original forming of meaning with sedimentation of meaning." [22] Such a *Sinngeschichte* is not the *Nacheinander* of external causality but the *Miteinander und Ineinander* of motivation implicated in an associated synthesis. In three cautionary notes added to Fink's transcription of this text, Husserl on each occasion stresses the need to go beyond the superficially social level of the historical world, in order to ultimately situate the historical movements in the inner historicity of the individuals motivationally implicated with each other. [23] The basis of history is still inner time consciousness, but now with all the complications of the world, the other, and language, involving active as well as passive syntheses.

The unavoidable starting point of the historical investigation

21. *H* VI, p. 378.
22. *H* VI, p. 380.
23. Cf. Robert Welsh Jordan, "Husserl's Phenomenology as an 'Historical' Science," *Social Research*, XXXV (1968), 245–59.

is the historical present in which we find ourselves. When the movement of this historical present is described as a "self-traditionalizing in streaming-standing vitality," [24] one cannot help but be struck by its resemblance to the descriptions of the *lebendige Gegenwart* used to characterize the life of the transcendental ego and representing a basic absolute in Husserl's work. The conception of the "historical present" must be viewed in the same way, this time as a characterization of the inner historicity of the transcendental ego, and with the difference that its self-transmission calls for a historical intersubjectivity of individuals bound together in the continuity of generations, whose concatenated motivations constitute the heart of historicity as Husserl sees it. The centerline is always in the "subjects of historicity, the persons who perform the cultural forming, functioning in the totality describable as the performing personal humanity." [25] But at the same time its self-transmission demands language, particularly the written word, for without language there would be no retention and protention of sense beyond the finite individual. In the historical present, the self-affection of the living present takes the detour of the written word, in which the life of reason runs the risk of voiding itself of the possibility of reactivation, and the word becomes forever mute.

But reactivation is always possible, at least in principle. The original intentional implications of a particular cultural formation like geometry can be traced starting from the historical present precisely because this entire cultural present "understood as a totality, 'implies' the entire cultural past in an indefinite, but structurally definite generality." [26] As a basis for his investigation, Husserl proposes to establish the general and essential structure that is to be found in our own and in every past and future historical present, and which is therefore "the historical present in general" as a total form, the persistent form-system of concrete historical time. The historical present understood in this eidetic sense exposes the historical space for the ideality of meaning, the pure and irreducible place and movement of the totalization of sense and the transmission of history, in the renewed repetition of the constants of the lifeworld and the ideal objects that have been accumulated.

24. *H* VI, p. 380.
25. *H* VI, p. 381.
26. *H* VI, p. 379.

Thus, the reductions of phenomenology are specifically designed to undercut the "genetic fallacy," whether as psychologism or, more pertinent here, its relative, historicism (the second objection that Husserl considers).[27] Certain romantic forms of historicism go so far as to view the history of mathematics and science from the perspective of the time-bound world-views of magic, myth, and alchemy. It is certainly a matter of fact that these temporary world-views to a degree influenced the origin of geometry. But Husserl emphasizes that his intentional-historical explorations are to be based on the invariant content of the perceptual world of pregeometrical experience and are to be complemented by the association of essential motivations which developed geometry into its final form, e.g., the practical arts.

What then are the a priori which were immediately available to the first geometers as matter for their idealizations? Geometry and its kindred sciences are concerned with spatiotemporal shapes, movements, deformations and the like, particularly as measurable magnitudes. No matter what the particularities of the historical ambit of the first geometers may have been, we can be certain that its "transcendental geography" included a world of corporal things related to each other in a nonexact space and time. The forms and properties of some of these things took on a particular importance in the course of practical life, leading to a technical praxis to improve on them and to "perfect" them. Things were accordingly rated as more or less smooth, with more or less straight edges, sharp corners, etc. From such initial estimations, the arts of shaping, polishing, and the like must have gradually developed means for measuring these features through comparisons of equal parts. All this and similar developments must have been accessible to the first man who conceived of the possibility of geometry. The step toward ideal perfection which constitutes geometry must have been prompted by some sense of the relation between the finitude of practical results and the open infinity of the possible horizon on the basis of which they are rated. All these are only a few minimal suggestions of the factors which are to be considered in the reactivation of the historical origin of geometry, in order to see how its meaning *must* have *first* emerged.[28]

27. *H* VI, pp. 381–83, 385–86.
28. *H* VI, pp. 383–84.

HISTORICITY IN A TRANSCENDENTAL LOGIC

REACTIVATION OF ORIGINS ultimately takes place in the larger context of a transcendental logic, whose task is to perform a transcendental critique of the fundamental concepts, methods, and goals of the sciences. As a critique, it holds the validity of the results of a science in abeyance precisely in order to examine this validity, its justification or lack thereof, its correct sense, in short, the scientific character of the science in question. And just like every other cultural product, the sense of a science is established through the determination of its purpose. Sciences are like buildings made according to human purposes, only made from "spiritual material" [29] and with the over-all aim of objective truth, currently "a much disputed, unclear and in the end even an exaggerated goal" [30] as the positive sciences posit it, so that a much more appropriate essence of a genuine science needs to be worked out. And have these structures of a science been built in a "solid" (valid) fashion from the ground up in every step of its construction? Since we are dealing with a spiritual work, we are in a privileged position to assess this by bringing ourselves into direct empathy with the scientific work itself, both as activity and product, but now considered as a pure phenomenon or intention. This we do by placing the finished form of the science back into the "living becoming" in which its sense is generated, and by living through its goal-directed efforts. But now our activity is not exactly the same as that of, e.g., a working natural scientist, who is directly involved with his theme of nature. For through the transcendental turn, we place ourselves in the position of "disinterested spectators" of the workings of science. Yet in a certain sense we do become scientists, speaking, thinking, producing concepts and propositions, conclusions and proofs like a scientist—but with an alteration of attitude. In the transcendental-logical attitude, we find ourselves in a peculiar self-cleavage, living both as scientist and logician, which is the higher ego here. For now we live through the scientist's activity in an original fashion, for the sake of a thoroughgoing exposi-

29. *H* IX, p. 367.
30. *H* IX, p. 368.

tion of it. This includes the exposition of what every scientist implicitly presupposes even before he takes his first scientific step. And so when we turn to the judicative products of this activity, we examine the scientific assertions in terms of both their scientific and prescientific moments, in correlation with the passive and active life of consciousness.[31]

When we thus confront the system of judgments which is the body of a science, each judgment appears in its structural statics as a build-up of sedimented layers and in its genetic dynamics as a sequence of implicated steps. The most primitive level here is the individual judgment emerging from the "nonpredicative"[32] evidence of perceptual experience. Once the judgment S *is* p is made, the sense p will always and persistently cling to S or, if you will, p is "deposited" on the sense S.[33] The resulting Sp can now be the subject of a further predication Sp *is* q, in which q presupposes and depends on the prior predication of p before it can be asserted. This can go on until we arrive at an object with a complex architecture of senses, $Spqr$ . . . , a structure which could not have been reached without the step-by-step progression followed. The metaphor of sedimentation can be misleading here. The final structure is not simply a "heap" of accretions externally superimposed one on the other but an intrinsic implication of "moments" of meaning, where moments are parts that permeate each other.[34] A more fitting physical analogy might be a precipitation induced by a chemical reaction between an exposed surface and an environment followed by a melding diffusion of the precipitate into the main body. But ultimately one must abandon the language of physical causality and describe the process in terms of the motivation more apropos to things spiritual. In this vein, if "association" is used to describe the above constituting process of the genesis of meanings, it must be stripped of its empiricist connotations and considered in terms of the activities and habitualities of the transcendental ego. Passive association enters into the heart of

31. *H* IX, pp. 366–76.
32. *FTL*, p. 186.
33. *FTL*, p. 275.
34. Robert Sokolowski, *The Formation of Husserl's Concept of Constitution, Phaenomenologica* XVIII (The Hague: Nijhoff, 1964), pp. 170–71. For the concept of "moment," see Sokolowski's article on "The Logic of Parts and Wholes in Husserl's Investigations," *Philosophy and Phenomenological Research*, June, 1968, pp. 537–53.

the active genesis of, e.g., the new judgment *Spqr is t* by an apperceptive anticipation of *t* in the renewed experience of *S* already sedimented with the history *pqr*. Both the renewed experience and the implied senses enter into the motivation of the next predication.

When such a judgment is enunciated by the scientific vanguard and enters into the tradition, the most recent sense tends to dominate and the others recede into the background. The familiarity of usage reinforces this process of recession. Nevertheless, these senses are not eliminated but simply lie dormant beneath the surface as implications and presuppositions of the outstanding meaning. Hence each time the judgment is expressed, its implied senses are silently evoked in a passive association which dimly recalls them. Accordingly, it is always possible to reactivate the submerged senses, once again making them evident in their fullest sense. The process of uncovering these hidden intentional implications is in Husserl's terms an "intentional analysis" which, as already indicated, should not be confused with a simple decomposition into parts. Furthermore, it is more than the elucidation of terms through traditional logical analysis, since it must trace its meanings back to the point of reactivating the direct experiences which enter into each and every step of the formation of these complex judgments.[35] For it is precisely at the Archimedean point where the "irrational" fact enters into the structure of reason that the history of meaning is made.[36] Genetic constitution and *ipso facto* the retroactive process of tracing phenomenological origins cannot simply be a deductive elucidation of the content of our concepts, precisely because of the continual presence of this incipient encounter between subjectivity and the world. Each step of the categorial advance of science is made possible only through the incessant return to the presyntactic stratum of experience.

The method of intentional analysis designed to uncover hidden historical presuppositions manifests some affinity with the hermeneutical approach of some of the men who followed Husserl. Even during Husserl's lifetime, his student Hans Lipps was shifting the ground from a transcendental to a hermeneutical logic. Perhaps we can even speak of Husserl's "transcendental

35. *H* VI, pp. 374–75.
36. *Cartesian Meditations,* trans. Dorion Cairns (The Hague: Nijhoff, 1960), § 39, p. 81.

hermeneutics" to contrast it with the "ontological hermeneutics" of Heidegger and Gadamer. For Husserl's center line is not Being but the transcendental ego, for whom history manifests itself in the modifications and habitualities of a "time-consciousness," whose reactivation is more strictly a remembering than Heidegger's conception of retrieve. But in either case, it cannot even be said that the development of a hermeneutics of natural science is "underway." And this, after all, is the paradigm problem posed by Husserl's remarks on the "origin of geometry." Ever since Dilthey, it has been customary to speak of hermeneutics as the general method of the human sciences, especially when one considers history to be central among them. When one then approaches the problem of a "history of science," it is to be expected that the hermeneutical dimension should have some relevance. For natural science is a human work which as such should be decipherable like any other text. But what hidden meanings are we to seek in such an interpretation, especially when we confront a body of meaning expressed in the highly formalized "languages" of mathematical physics? As we have seen, Husserl calls for an ultimate reduction of the formalized languages to the language of the lifeworld as essential to the further development of science itself. But this procedure of peeling away the formal clothing in order to arrive at the naked historical a priori assumes that all meaning is already implicitly present in the beginning language. But what if the algorithms themselves have a life of their own, constantly yielding new and unexpected concepts, as has been suggested by Cavaillès, the Bachelards, and Ladrière? It is to these ramifications and possibilities of the historicity of science, which at times call for a critique and modification of Husserl's transcendental approach, that we now turn.

CRITIQUE AND RAMIFICATIONS

SOME OF THESE RAMIFICATIONS are already suggested by the "Origin of Geometry" text, which in passing alludes to other problems of history in general and the history of science in particular, e.g., progress, historical continuity, and the process of scientific discovery. But Husserl is so concerned with the reduction of the *Sinngeschichte* to its most radical roots that he even identifies his historical investigations to a *Rückfrage* toward the origins. "For a genuine history of philosophy, a genuine history of the particular sciences is nothing but the reduction of the historical sense-formations given in the present with regard to their evidences—along the documented chain of historical references—back to the concealed dimension of the primal evidences that underlie them." [37] Furthermore, in opposition to historicism, Husserl is so insistent on the eidetic invariants and unity of this history that its very historicity is a bit difficult to see. Even a potentially dynamic concept like the "historical present," in analogy with the streaming and living present, comes off a bit static. Yet the central notion of intentionality, as an intuitive intending, bursting forth and passing beyond, invites us to explore not only a certain consciousness of progress but also a progress of consciousness, through discovery. What sustains history is this intentional burgeoning forth under the teleological sway of the quest for *epistēmē*. And it is somewhere in between its overarching archeology and teleology, in a historical present in which the scientist takes up his work in a lifeworld already heavily clothed in the garment of scientific ideas woven by him and his predecessors, that the dynamics of a science must be studied. What is needed here is not a radical retrieve of origins but an examination of what actually happens in the normal transmission of science. "If we want to take into account the very *progress* of science, we cannot restrict ourselves to the reductive examinations of a radical phenomenology." [38]

And this progress, along with the original heuristic power that it implies, may not be as unproblematic as Husserl seems to assume. He portrays the historical movement of science as a process of continuous synthesis and totalization, in which the scientific judgment acquires a complex structure akin to a geological formation of sedimented deposits. But what if science progresses not by accumulation and accretion but by revolution, as T. S. Kuhn suggests, or else by a perpetual revision of contents through deepening and elimination, so that there are losses as well as gains in the internal life of science? The history of

37. *H* VI, p. 381.
38. Suzanne Bachelard, *La Conscience de rationalité: Etude phénoménologique sur la physique mathématique* (Paris: Presses Universitaires de France, 1958), p. 5. Cf. below, p. 417, for a translation of this portion of the book.

physics in the twentieth century suggests that a current sense-formation may not only subsume, but even criticize, indicate the limits, even reject past senses. Kuhn goes so far as to assert that one paradigm (e.g., Newton's) is replaced by another (Einstein's) which is totally incommensurable with it.[39]

Moreover, the exaggeration of the archeological approach to history even suggests the thesis that all the principles of the development of science are somehow determined in advance, that all of its meaning is already implicitly present in the start. But does one know the growth of a tree by knowing its roots? Does one come to the nature of scientific life only by studying its origin? The history of science and philosophy provides ample evidence that the life of reason is full of surprises, with a way of bringing something new which was not even implied in the elementary, e.g., Planck's quantum theory and Gödel's theorem. Without this, there would be no true history, for history (to quote from Ricoeur's critique of Husserl's sense of history) "loses its very historicity if it is not an unforeseeable adventure."[40] Perhaps even at a certain level of scientific thought, its elementary perceptual origins become inoperative or at least minimal, as when non-Euclidean geometry entered physical theory. Even the most basic concepts of a science do not remain fixed but also have a history, as Max Jammer has shown in his tracing of the concepts of space, mass, and force for physics. There is a continual dialectic between these elementary concepts and the latest discoveries, which transform these concepts and shift the foundations of physics itself, so that a reference to the rudimentary experiences of inertia or resistance to force will not do at the present stage of scientific formalization.

There is then a productive dialectic of science which is not visible in its beginnings. To account for this unpredictable development of the rational, Jean Cavaillès[41] concludes that a theory of science must ultimately be a philosophy of the dialectic of the concept rather than a philosophy of the activity of consciousness in the manner of Husserl. Progress would then be accounted for

39. Thomas S. Kuhn, The Structure of Scientific Revolutions (Chicago: University of Chicago Press, 1962), pp. 97–102.

40. Paul Ricoeur, Husserl: An Analysis of His Phenomenology, trans. Edward G. Ballard and Lester E. Embree (Evanston, Ill.: Northwestern University Press, 1967), p. 170.

41. See below, p. 409.

in the fertility of the formal language, which incessantly en-
hances rather than exhausts meaning. The so-called "technical
rationality" which seems to reduce itself to a mechanical production of theorems, in which the creative act of thought is effaced
before the stereotype operation of the calculating machine,
would then also be a manifestation of the unpredictable fertility
in the internal life of the algorithm.

To establish the sense of mathematical physics, we cannot
therefore restrict ourselves to establishing its lifeworld and
subjective foundations. The power of mathematical rationality
that it reveals must be studied in its own right, in terms of the
internal exigency that drives mathematics and mathematical
physics to a progressive deepening and disclosure of new levels
of discourse. Its power to reveal isomorphisms between seemingly unrelated structures leads to the consciousness of a profound coherence among physical laws themselves and provides
the impetus for the search of a more and more comprehensive
theory of the theories, as for example Einstein's generalized field
theory, or the comprehensive cosmic equation that Heisenberg
seeks. Here the abstract consideration of structures is precisely
the source of the purity and fertility of mathematical physics.[42]
An exaggerated emphasis of the power of concrete intuition only
obscures the profound possibilities of establishing the structural
realities that mathematics can uncover. To complain of its *Sinnentleerung*, the deprivation of intuitive content, is to overlook
the peculiar enrichment of sense that formalization is capable of
reaching, a discursive sense and not an intuitive sense, a much
more uprooted and floating sense, capable of enveloping different possible worlds, but nevertheless a *Sinn* in its own right.[43]

Once we restore to mathematical rationality its proper value,
the sense of sciences like geometry and mathematical physics
can be defined no longer simply in view of a reduction to the
lifeworld, but instead in terms of a dialectical movement between the intuitive given and its formalization, in which the
given invites formalization and formalization provides insight
into the structural reality of the given, much like maps provide
formal insight into a land or a landscape. The tension between
the concretizing and the abstractive tendency of thought is not a

42. Bachelard, *La Conscience de rationalité*, p. 186.
43. Jean Ladrière, "Sens et système," *Esprit*, CCCLX (May,
1967), 822–24.

relationship of mutual exclusion but one of mutual fertilization. The lifeworld is like a rough draft inviting schematization, and the apparently autonomous formal structures eventually find their way back to the given. Human thought finds itself suspended between the given and the system as between two horizons toward which it aims but never reaches, let alone resolves.

Husserl rightly signalizes the danger of the seeming autonomy which formalized objects acquire. But on the other hand, with this autonomy, the ideal object assumes a life of its own, as it were, beyond the original context in which it was born. The repeatability of ideal objects, their ideal identity and omnitemporality, does not invest them with a static immobility but in fact frees them for a functional dynamics which simply cannot be explained by any Platonic realism. By being taken up again and again and used in different epistemological functions, as a conclusion or a premise, as a secondary means or a central theme, in one context or another, the very same judgment undergoes an enrichment of its meaning far beyond the narrow confines of its first emergence.[44] To take Husserl's example, consider the many applications of the Pythagorean theorem, as for instance the revolutionary role that it plays in describing the time of special relativity.

All these remarks serve to introduce perhaps the most crucial dimension in understanding the dynamic and ongoing character of science, its very life, namely, that of scientific discovery, of those history-making events which constitute the high points of the history of science. We are concerned here not with the finished results of such events but with the very process of scientific discovery. For science is first of all an enterprise before it is a "body." Husserl himself points out that "these sciences are not a finished heritage in the form of documented propositions, but a living, productive and progressive forming of meaning which continually takes over the documented as a sediment of an earlier production by making logical use of it."[45] Over and over, Husserl iterates the need to reverse the natural tendency of focusing on the products and forgetting the productive activity of the scientist. It is this productive activity of the scientist responding to the sedimented situation of his historical present which is the starting point of the problem of discovery.

44. Bachelard, *La Conscience de rationalité*, pp. 204–5.
45. *H* VI, p. 375.

First, we must describe the situation in which this process takes place. For one thing, the lifeworld of the twentieth century scientist is quite different from that of the primitive man practicing his arts of shaping, which provided the immediate motivation for early geometry. Today's scientist lives in a lifeworld charged through and through with incarnations of the idealizations he develops, in the laboratory equipment that he uses, the computer data which he analyzes, the formalized language in which he thinks. He therefore enters a world heavily clothed in a logical cladding of his own making. Yet this world of Fresnel's mirrors, cathode ray tubes, and punch cards is not so familiar as to be devoid of a horizon of unfamiliarity. It is this "open endless horizon of unfamiliar realities" [46] which points to the problems which beckon to be solved, which operates as a "horizon of motivations" noematically correlated to what might be called our knowledge of the unknown which we wish to know. The specific problems inviting exploration in this field are historically determined by the state of the science, by the level of sedimentation which one takes up. Problems and their solutions must await their opportune time in the progression of a science; they cannot be thought ahead of their time. It is in this sense that tradition, in offering new meaning when the time is ripe, is more than a principle of inertia. *Sinngebung* therefore cannot be restricted only to the productive activity of a subject. And it is language which is the preserve of tradition and thus prepares the field of disclosure of new meaning. It is this concrete historical and linguistic reality in which the productive subject finds himself which can, through his efforts, be transformed into a field of opportunity for discovery. Thus hermeneutical phenomenology situates the process of discovery in a linguistic happening which precedes and underlies any psychic activity and logical control of discovery, a process in which man responsively submits to a hidden reality in the process of giving itself. [47]

How precisely does this process of discovery take place? Let me suggest the following brief schema. It begins with the researcher situated in a constellation of transmitted presuppositions, which are determining in arousing his research interests, selecting his research themes and the winning of new questions.

46. *H* VI, p. 382.
47. Cf. T. Kisiel, "The Happening of Tradition: The Hermeneutics of Gadamer and Heidegger," *Man and World*, II (1969), 358–85.

And the mark of the genuine researcher is his ability to uncover the truly productive questions from the heuristic field of potential discoveries in which he finds himself. The occurrence of anomalies is the immediate indicator of just where the current presuppositions are in need of revision. Reduction of the anomaly to the aporetic background against which it occurs takes one back to the horizon of the original question which the preanomalous theory answered, a question that now must be redirected toward some of its other possible answers. The new sense, suggested through the anomaly from the already-organized context of expectations, is drawn out into the open from the creative potential hidden in the conceptual patterns of the current state of the science. The said/unsaid structure of the question which indeterminately anticipates its answer is possible because of the said/unsaid character of the scientific language itself. For an algorithmic language is still akin to the natural language in its capacity of indefinite yield, returning more than was initially invested in it, always uncovering more of the world of nature.

Such a *Sinngeschichte* is not the history of ideal objects, which always calls for ideal subjects, but a historicity of language itself opening onto the indeterminate horizon of the world. More basic than either a momentary and prelinguistic factual given or an omnitemporal and translinguistic ideal given is the given horizon of the concrete human situation, which is historical and linguistic through and through. Husserl's own conception of the "historical present" of concrete historical time in fact invites such a transposition of the issue from a transcendental to a hermeneutical phenomenology.

Hermann Weyl

HERMANN WEYL was born at Elmshorn, Germany, on November 9, 1885. He studied at Munich and later under David Hilbert at Göttingen, where he received his degree in 1908 and taught as *Privatdozent* from 1910 to 1913. Later he was a professor at the Technische Hochschule in Zurich (1913–30), Göttingen (1930–33), and The Institute for Advanced Study at Princeton (1933–51). He died in Zurich on December 8, 1955.

Hermann Weyl made original contributions to mathematics, quantum mechanics, and the theory of relativity. In his study on quantum mechanics (*Gruppentheorie und Quantenmechanik*) Weyl tried to solve the problem of a unified field theory. Such a theory would ultimately express in one general invariant mathematical equation the basic characteristics of gravitational, electric, and magnetic fields and show that the elementary particles are generated and controlled by the continuous unified field. Many attempts were later made in that direction, but without success. In 1950 Weyl wrote about these attempts: "Quite a number of unified field theories have sprung up in the meantime. They are all based on mathematical speculation, and, as far as I can see, none has had a conspicuous success" (*Space-Time-Matter* [1950], Preface).

Weyl also wrote on the philosophy of mathematics, where he was inclined to Brouwer's intuitionism, and on the philosophy of the natural sciences. It is particularly in this latter area that we find his great interest in Husserl's phenomenology and its influence on his own thought. In order to concretely illustrate this influence from phenomenology we have translated part of the Preface to the first edition of *Raum, Zeit, Materie* and reprinted a section of his well-known *Philosophy of Mathematics and Natural Science.*

4 / On Time, Space, and Matter

Hermann Weyl

WE ARE ACCUSTOMED to conceiving of *time* and *space* as the existential forms of the real world, and of *matter* as its substance. At a determinate moment in time a determinate piece of matter occupies a determinate portion of space; in the conception of *motion* which follows from this, these three basic concepts enter into the most intimate connection. Descartes set forth as the program for the exact science of nature: to construct all becoming (*Geschehen*) from these basic concepts and thus to reduce it to motion. Since the human mind awoke to freedom, it has always experienced *time consciousness,* the temporal course of the world, and becoming as deeply enigmatic; their mysteriousness constitutes one of the ultimate metaphysical problems for whose clarification and solution philosophy has incessantly struggled throughout the whole breadth of its history. The Greeks made *space* the subject matter of a science of the greatest clarity and certainty. In ancient culture the idea of a pure science gradually developed from this science; geometry became one of the most powerful manifestations of the principle of sovereignty which animated that culture. When the authoritative world-view of the Church came to grief in the Middle Ages and waves of skepticism threatened to wash away everything stable, man's belief in the truth clung to geometry as to a rock; at that time it could be set down as the highest ideal of all science

This essay is from the Introduction to Hermann Weyl's *Raum, Zeit, Materie: Vorlesungen über Allgemeine Relativitätstheorie* (1st ed., 1918; 5th rev. ed., Berlin: Springer, 1923). It has been translated expressly for this volume by Joseph J. Kockelmans.

that it can be pursued *more geometrico*. Finally, as far as *matter* is concerned, we have been convinced that at the root of all change there must be a substance, or better, matter, that each portion of matter can be measured as a quantum, and that its substantiality can be expressed in the law of conservation of the quantum of matter which remains the same throughout all changes.

This prevailing knowledge of space and matter, which philosophy has often conceived of and used as aprioric knowledge of unconditioned universality and necessity, has today begun to waver. Once physics, in the hands of Faraday and Maxwell, had contrasted matter with field as a reality of a different category, and, further, in the last century mathematics in all secrecy had undermined our confidence in the evidence of Euclidean geometry through its subtle logical manipulations; it was in our own days that the revolutionary storm broke out which destroyed those conceptions of space, time, and matter which until then had been considered the most solid pillars of natural science— but this only in order to make room for freer and deeper views of things. This revolution was essentially effected by the thinking of one single man, Albert Einstein. As far as basic ideas are concerned, this development today seems to have reached a certain conclusion; but regardless of whether or not we already stand before a new and definitive conception, one has to come to terms with the new conception which has been brought to the fore here. It is also true that there can be no return; the development of scientific thought may very well once again go beyond what has been reached now, but a return to the old, narrow, and rigid scheme is excluded.

Philosophy, mathematics, and physics must participate in the problems which are raised here. I, however, will mainly occupy myself with the mathematico-physical aspect of the questions. I shall enter into the philosophical aspect of the problems merely and wholly incidentally, simply because until now there has not yet been anything in this direction which is even remotely definitive, and neither am I myself able to give the pertinent epistemological problems such answers as I could completely justify to my scientific conscience.

The ideas which are to be described here did not come about through a mere speculative plunging into the foundations of physical knowledge but were formulated in connection with concrete physical problems in the development of science which, full of vigor, pushed itself ahead and for which the old mold had become too narrow—a revision of the fundamental principles was performed each time only subsequently and only insofar as the newly emerging ideas demanded it. As things stand today the different sciences cannot do anything in this sense but proceed dogmatically, that is, in good faith go the way into which they are pushed by rational motives which arise within the framework of their characteristic methods. Philosophical clarification remains a great task of a completely different nature from that which falls within the competence of the different sciences. Here the philosopher must see to it himself; it is not right to burden and hinder the progress of the sciences which are oriented toward concrete realms of things with the weight of the chains of the difficulties connected with such a task.

Nevertheless, I shall begin with some philosophical discussions. As men living our daily life in the natural attitude, we find our acts of perception set over against bodily real, material things. We attribute real existence to them and take them to be fundamentally constituted, shaped, colored, etc., in the same way that they appear to us in perception (fundamentally, that is to say with reservation as to illusions, mirages, dreams, hallucinations, etc., which may perhaps occur). They are surrounded by and interspersed with an indefinitely blurring multiplicity of analogous realities which grow together into one single, always present, spatial world to which I myself belong with my individual body. We are interested here merely in these material things, not in all those objects of another kind which as natural human beings we also find opposite us: living beings, persons, utensils, values, and those entities such as state, law, language, and the like.

For almost every theoretically oriented man, philosophical self-reflection begins with doubts about this world-view of naïve realism to which I just now briefly referred. One comes to understand that a quality such as, for instance, "green" has existence only as a correlate of the "green-experience" in regard to the thing which manifests itself in perception, but that it is meaningless to hang this quality on real things in themselves as a property in itself. This realization of the subjectivity of sense qualities appears in Galileo (just as in Descartes and Hobbes) in closest connection with the fundamental thesis of the mathematico-constructive method of our modern physics-without-qualities, according to which, for example, colors "really" are ether vibrations, and therefore motions. Kant was the first within the realm of philosophy (and he did so with the greatest clarity) to take the next step which led to the insight that not only sensory qualities but also space and spatial characteristics lack objective meaning in an absolute sense, that space, too, is merely a form of our sensibility. Within the realm of physics it was perhaps the theory of relativity which showed for the first time in a completely clear way that, from the essence of space and time as they manifest themselves in our perception, nothing enters the mathematically constructed world. Colors are for that reason "really" not even ether vibrations but mathematical, functional developments whereby in the relevant functions, according to the three spatial and the one temporal dimensions, four independent variables appear.

Speaking generally and limiting ourselves to what is basic, one must say that the real world, all its constituent parts, and all their determinations, are and can be given merely as intentional objects of conscious acts. What is given unconditionally are conscious experiences which I have and must take in the way I have them. It is certainly in no way the case, as positivists often state, that these experiences consist in the mere stuff of sensations; but in an act of perception, for instance, there is indeed an object standing before me in its bodily reality; that experience is related to it in a wholly characteristic way which is known to everyone but cannot be further described; with Brentano one must determine it with the expression "intentional object." While I am perceiving, I see this chair, for instance; I am continuously oriented toward it. I "have" this perception; but only when I make this perception itself into a new intentional object of a new inner perception (which I am able to do in a free act of reflection), do I "know" something about that perception (and not only about the chair) and establish what I have just said. In this second act the intentional object is an immanent one, namely, just as is the act itself, a real component of the stream of my experiences. In the primary act of perception, however, the object is transcendent, that is to say, although it is given in an experience of my consciousness, it itself is not a real component of it. The immanent is absolute, that is, it is exactly as I have it here and now, and its essence can eventually be brought explicitly to attention in my acts of reflection. The transcendent things, on the other hand, possess merely a phenomenal being; they are appearing things which manifest themselves in multiple modes of appearing and multiple "profiles." One and the same leaf looks so and so big, appears colored in such and such a way, depending upon my position and the illumination; none of these modes of appearing can lay claim of itself to the right to present the leaf such as it is "in itself." Furthermore, in each perception the thesis concerning the reality of the appearing thing is undoubtedly implied as part and further specification of the content of the general thesis concerning the real world. However, when we proceed from the natural to the philosophical attitude, and while reflecting on our perception, we no longer subscribe, so to speak, to this thesis; we quietly discover that in it something is "meant" as real. The meaning and the validity claim of this positing now become a problem for us which must receive its solution from what is given in consciousness. In no way do I believe that the conception according to which the becoming of the world is a game of consciousness, produced by the ego, contains a higher truth in regard to naïve realism. On the contrary. The question is merely that one understands that what is given in consciousness is the starting point in which we must place ourselves in order to comprehend the meaning and the validity of our positing of reality in an absolute way. An analogous situation is found in the domain of the logical. A judgment which I pronounce posits a state of affairs; it posits this state of affairs as being true. Here, too, the philosophical question arises as to the meaning and the validity of this truth thesis; here, too, I do not deny the idea of objective truth, but this truth becomes problematic and one which I must try to comprehend from the viewpoint of what is given in an absolute way. "Pure consciousness" is the seat of the philosophical a priori. On the other hand, the philosophical clarification of the reality thesis has to, and also will, show that none of those experiencing acts of perception, memory, etc., in which I grasp reality, gives me an ultimate right to attribute to the perceived object the existence as well as the constitution as I perceive it; this right can be continually considered and weighed by anyone who grounds himself in other perceptions. It belongs to the essence of a real thing to be inexhaustible as far as its content is concerned, and we can approach it only in an unlimited way through always new experiences which partly contradict each other and thus are to be leveled. It is in this sense that the real thing is a limit idea. It is upon this that the empirical character of all our knowledge of reality rests.[1]

The original form of the stream of consciousness is time. This is a fact; however dark and mysterious it may be for our reason, we cannot deny it, and we must accept that the contents of consciousness present themselves not as merely being (as for instance concepts, numbers, and the like) but as *being-now,* filling the form of the enduring now with a continually changing content. Thus it can be said not "this *is,*" but "this is now, but after that no longer." When in reflection we tear ourselves out of the stream and posit its content as an object over against us, then this stream becomes for us a temporal flow whose individual phases are related to one another according to the relation *earlier and later.*

Just as time is the form of the stream of consciousness, so can one rightly argue that space is the form of material reality. All aspects of material things as far as they are given in the acts of outer perception, such as color for instance, possess in themselves the exteriority (*das Auseinander*) characteristic of spatial extension. But it is only when one single coherent real world becomes built up from all our experiences that the spatial extension, given in each perception, becomes a part of one and the same space which comprises all things. This space is a form of the outer world; that is to say, each material thing, without in any way being substantially another thing than it actually is as far as content is concerned, can just as well be at that other point of space as at this one. In this the homogeneity of space is necessarily implied, and it is here that the real root of the concept of congruity is to be found.

If it now were the case that the worlds of consciousness and transcendent reality were completely separated from one another, or rather that the silent glance of perception were to constitute the sole bridge between them, then things would indeed stand as I have just presented them: on the one side, our

1. The exact formulation of these thoughts most closely follows Husserl in *Ideen zu einer reinen Phänomenologie und phänomenologischen Philosophie,* published in *Jahrbuch für Philosophie und Phänomenologische Forschung,* Vol. I (1913). [Later published as *Husserliana* III (The Hague: Nijhoff, 1950).]

spaceless consciousness, which continuously changes in the form of the enduring now, and, on the other side, the spatially extended but timeless reality of which consciousness contains merely a continually changing phenomenon. However, more original than all perception, there is in us the experience of strife and resistance, of action and passion.[2] For a man who in his life is engaged in natural activity, perception serves first and foremost to bring before his consciousness in graphic clarity the determinate starting point for the activity he has planned as well as the seat of its resisting forces. In the experience of action and passion I become for myself a single individual of psychic reality which is connected with a body which among the material things of the outer world has its place in space, and through which I have contact with the individuals of my own kind; it is in that experience that consciousness, without, however, abandoning its immanence, becomes a part of reality, this particular man I am, who was born and who will die. On the other hand, however, consciousness hereby also extends its form, time, to reality: that is why in itself there is change, motion, progress, becoming, and passing away; and just as my will through my body and as moving act grasps across into the real world, so the world is also working (as the German noun *Wirklichkeit* says), its appearances are subordinated to one another in a universal causal connection. Indeed in physics it becomes manifest that cosmic time and causality cannot be separated from one another. The new way in which the theory of relativity solves the problem concerning the connection of space and time in reality coincides with a new insight into the causal connection of the world.

2. [In regard to the German *Tun* and *Leiden* used here, Weyl writes: "Our grammar has only the verbal modes for the active and passive; there are no modes for the expression of a becoming, and much less for a state of affairs."—Trans.]

5 / Subject and Object
(The Scientific Implications
of Epistemology)

Hermann Weyl

THE DOCTRINE of the subjectivity of sense qualities has been intimately connected with the progress of science ever since Democritus laid down the principle, "Sweet and bitter, cold and warm, as well as the colors, all these things exist but in opinion and not in reality (νόμῳ, οὐ φύσει)"; what really exists are unchangeable particles, atoms, which move in empty space. Also Plato (*Theaetetus*, 156e) holds that "properties such as hard, warm, and whatever their names may be, are nothing in themselves," but arise in the encounter of "motions" originating in the subject and in the object. Reality is pure activity; only in the "image," in the consciousness suspended between the motions is suffering. Galileo may be mentioned as another witness, "White or red, bitter or sweet, noisy or silent, fragrant or malodorous, are names for certain effects upon the sense organs." He holds that they can no more be ascribed to the external objects than the titillation or the pain which might be felt when things are touched. A detailed discussion of this is given in the final sections of Descartes' *Principia* and in his *Traité de la Lumière* (the theory of optical perception is indebted to him for important advances), likewise in Locke's *Enquiry Concerning Human Understanding* (Book II, Chap. 8, §§15–22). The subjectivity of

This essay is from *Philosophy of Mathematics and Natural Science* by Hermann Weyl (New York: Atheneum, 1963), pp. 110–25, a revised and augmented edition based on a translation by Olaf Helmer, and originally published by Princeton University Press. The section printed here has been translated by Joachim Weyl and then revised by Hermann Weyl.

sense qualities must be maintained in two regards, one philosophical, the other scientific. In the first place, such a quality by its very nature can only be given in our consciousness through sensation. One sees in it either an inherent attribute of sensation itself or, upon deeper analysis, an entity belonging to the intentional object which the act of consciousness puts before me. But it remains manifestly incomprehensible how quality disjoint from consciousness can be attributed as a property as such to a thing as such. This is the fundamental tenet of epistemological idealism. In the second place, the qualities in which the objects of the outer world garb themselves for me do not depend on the objects alone. They also depend quite essentially upon the concomitant physical circumstances, for instance, in the case of color, on illumination and on the nature of the medium between the object and my eye, and furthermore upon myself, on my own psycho-physical organization. My sense of vision does not grasp the objects where they are; rather, what I see is determined by the condition of the optical field in its zone of contact with my sensuous body (the retina). These are scientific facts which even the realist cannot deny. How differently the world would appear to our vision if the human eye were sensitive to other wave lengths or if the physiological processes on the retina were to transform the infinite-dimensional realm of composite physically different colors not merely into a two-dimensional but into a three- or four-dimensional manifold!

To Locke we are indebted for the classical distinction of "secondary" and "primary" qualities; the primary ones are the spatio-temporal properties of bodies—extension, shape, and motion. Democritus, Descartes, and Locke held them to be objective. Locke expresses himself as follows: "The ideas of primary qualities of bodies are resemblances of them, and their patterns do really exist in the bodies themselves; but the ideas produced in us by the secondary qualities have no resemblance of them at all" (*op. cit.*, Book II, Chap. 8, beginning of §15). Although Descartes teaches that between an actual occurrence and its perception (sound wave and tone, for instance) there is no more resemblance than between a thing and its name, he yet maintains that the ideas concerning space have objective validity because in contrast to the qualities we recognize them clearly and distinctly. And a fundamental principle of his epistemology claims that whatever we comprehend in such a way is true. In support of this principle, however, he has to appeal to the veracity of God, who does not want to deceive us. Obviously one cannot do without the idea of such a God who guarantees truth, once one has grasped the principle of idealism and yet insists on building up the real world out of certain elements of consciousness that for one reason or another seem particularly trustworthy. "He is the bridge . . . between the lonely, wayward and isolated thinking, which is certain only to its own selfawareness, and the external world. The attempt turned out somewhat naïve, but still one sees how keenly Cartesius measured out the grave of philosophy. It is strange, though, how he uses the dear God as the ladder to climb out of it. Yet even his contemporaries did not let him get over the edge" (quotation from Georg Büchner's philosophical notes, G. Büchner, *Werke*, Inselverlag Leipzig, 1922, pp. 268–269). Hobbes in his treatise *De Corpore* starts with a fictitious annihilation of the universe (similar to Husserl's "epochē") in order to let it rise again by a step-by-step construction from reason. But even he uses as building material the general notions which form the residue of experience, in particular those of space and time. This viewpoint has its counterpart in the physics of Galileo, Newton, and Huyghens; for here all occurrences in the world are constructed as intuitively conceived motions of particles in intuitive space. Hence an absolute Euclidean space is needed as a standing medium into which the orbits of motion are traced. Well-known is Galileo's pronouncement in the "Saggiatore" (*Opere*, VI, p. 232), "The true philosophy is written in that great book of nature (*questo grandissimo libro, io dico l'universo*) which lies ever open before our eyes but which no one can read unless he has first learned to understand the language and to know the characters in which it is written. It is written in mathematical language, and the characters are triangles, circles, and other geometric figures."

Leibniz seems to have been the first to push forward to a more radical conception: "Concerning the bodies I am able to prove that not only light, color, heat, and the like, but motion, shape, and extension too are only apparent qualities" (*Philos. Schriften*, VII, p. 322). Also Berkeley and Hume are to be named here. For d'Alembert, the justification for using the "residue of experience" in the construction of the objective world no longer lies in the clarity and distinctness of the ideas involved as it did for Descartes, but exclusively in the practical success of this method. According to Kant, space and time are merely forms of our intuition. Stumpf (*Über den psychologischen Ursprung der Raumvorstellung*, 1873, p. 22) finds it impossible to imagine the atoms as spatial bodies without color, whose play of motion only engenders those oscillations of the ether which are the carriers of color by virtue of their wave lengths; for no more than color without spatial extension could space (according to Berkeley's and Hume's doctrine) be imagined without the raiment of some quality of color. Intuitive space and intuitive time are thus hardly the adequate medium in which physics is to construct the external world. No less than the sense qualities must the intuitions of space and time be relinquished as its building material; they must be replaced by a four-dimensional continuum in the abstract arithmetical sense. Whereas for Huyghens colors were "in reality" oscillations of the ether, they now appear merely as mathematical functions of periodic character depending on four variables that as coordinates represent the medium of space-time. What remains is ultimately a *symbolic construction* of exactly the same kind as that which Hilbert carries through in mathematics.

The distillation of this objective world, capable only of representation by symbols, from what is immediately given to my intuition, takes place in different steps, the progression from level to level being enforced by the fact that what exists on one level will reveal itself as the mere apparition of a higher reality, the reality of the next level. A typical example of this is furnished by a body whose solid shape constitutes itself as the common source of its various perspective views. This would not happen unless the point from which it is viewed could be varied and unless the different viewpoints actually taken present themselves as instances of an infinite continuum of possibilities laid out within us. We shall return to this in the next section. A systematic scientific explanation, however, will reverse the order; it will erect the world of symbols as a realm by itself and then, skipping all intermediate levels, attempt to describe the relation that holds between the symbols representing objective conditions on the one hand and the corresponding data of consciousness on the other.

Thus *perspective* teaches us to derive the optical image from the solid shape of a body and from the observer's location relative to the body. A physical example, taken from among the upper levels, is the constitution of the concepts "electric field" and "electric field strength." We find that in the space between charged conductors a weakly charged "test particle" experiences a certain force $\vec{F} = \vec{F}(P)$ when put at a given place P. Well determined as to size and direction, the force turns out to be the same whenever the test particle is brought back to the same place P. Employing various test particles we find that the force depends on the latter, yet in such a manner that $\vec{F}(P)$ may be split up into two factors:

$$\vec{F}(P) = e \cdot \vec{E}(P),$$

where the vectorial factor $\vec{E}(P)$, the "electric field strength," is a point function independent of the state of the test particle, while the scalar factor e, the "charge" of the test particle, is determined exclusively by the inner state of the particle, depending neither on its position nor on the conductors, and is thus found to be the same no matter into what electric field we may place the particle. Here we start from the force as the given thing; but the facts outlined lead us to conceive of an electric field, mathematically described by the vectorial point function $\vec{E}(P)$, which surrounds the conductors and which *exists, no matter whether the force it exerts on a test particle be ascertained or not.* The test particle serves merely to render the field accessible to observation and measurement. The complete analogy with the case of perspective is obvious. The field $\vec{E}$ here corresponds to the object there, the test particle to the observer, its charge to his position; the force exerted by the field upon the test particle and changing according to the charge of the particle corresponds to the two-dimensional aspect offered by the solid object to the observer and depending on the observer's standpoint. Now the equation $\vec{F} = e \cdot \vec{E}$ is no longer to be looked upon as a definition of $\vec{E}$ but as a *law of nature* (to be corrected if circumstances warrant it) determining the ponderomotoric force which an electric field $\vec{E}$ exerts on a point charge e. Light, according to Maxwell's theory, is nothing but a rapidly alternating electromagnetic field; in our eyes, therefore, we have a sense organ capable of apprehending electric fields in another manner than by their ponderomotoric effects. A systematic presentation will introduce $\vec{E}$, the electric field strength, in a purely "symbolic" way without explanations and then lay down the laws it satisfies (for instance, that the line integral of $\overrightarrow{E}$ extended over a closed curve in space is zero) as well as the laws according to which ponderomotoric forces are connected with it. If forces are considered observable, the link between our symbols and experience will thus have been established.

One may say that only in the general theory of relativity did physics succeed in emancipating itself completely from intuitive space and time as means for the construction of the objective world. In the framework of this theory (which by the way includes all previously adopted standpoints either as particular or as limiting cases), the relation of subject and object may be illustrated by means of a typical example, the observation of two or more stars. By way of simplification we assume the apprehending consciousness to be a *point eye* whose world line may be called B. Let the observation take place at the moment O of its life. The construction is to be carried out in the four-dimensional number space, only for the sake of readier intelligibility we shall use a geometrical diagram instead. Let Σ be the world lines of two stars. The rearward light cone K issuing from O will meet each of the two star lines Σ in a single point, and the world lines

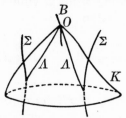

Figure 1. Data on which observation of angular distance of two stars depends.

Λ of the light signals which arrive at O from the stars join these points to O on the cone K. With the help of a construction, describable in purely arithmetical terms, it is possible to determine from these data the numerical measure of the angle ϑ under which the stars will appear to the observer at O. This construction is invariant, that is, of such a kind as to lead to the same numerical measure ϑ if, after an arbitrary deformation of the entire picture, it is carried out anew on the deformed image according to the same prescription. And everything is contained in it—the dependence of the angle on the stars themselves, on the metrical field extending between the stars, on the observer's position in the world (spatial perspective), and on his state of motion (i.e., on the direction with which the line B passes through O; this is the velocity perspective, known under the name of aberration). The angles ϑ between any two stars of a constellation determine the objectively indescribable, only intuitively experienced, visual shape of the constellation, which appears under the equally indescribable assumption that I myself am the point eye at O. If they coincide with those of a second constellation, then both constellations at the moment O appear to be of equal, otherwise of different, shapes.

The objective world simply *is*, it does not *happen*. Only to the gaze of my consciousness, crawling upward along the life line of my body, does a section of this world come to life as a fleeting image in space which continuously changes in time.

An important role in the construction of the angles ϑ is played by the "splitting" of the world into space and time carried out at every moment O of my consciousness. Objectively this is to be described as follows: If e_0, e_1, e_2, e_3 are the components of a vector indicating the direction of B at O, then my immediate spatial vicinity will be spanned by the totality of all line elements (dx_0, dx_1, dx_2, dx_3) issuing from O which are orthogonal to e, i.e., which satisfy the equation

$$\sum_{i,k=0}^{3} g_{ik} \cdot dx_i \cdot e_k = 0, \qquad g_{ik} = g_{ik}(O).$$

Thus the objective state of affairs contains all that is necessary to account for the subjective appearances. There is no difference in our experiences to which there does not correspond a difference in the underlying objective situation (a difference, moreover, which is invariant under arbitrary coordinate transformations). It comprises as a matter of course the body of the ego as a physical object. The immediate experience is *subjective and absolute*. However hazy it may be, it is given in its very haziness thus and not otherwise. The objective world, on the other hand, with which we reckon continually in our daily lives and which the natural sciences attempt to crystallize by methods representing the consistent development of those criteria by which we experience reality in our natural everyday attitude—

this *objective* world is of necessity *relative;* it can be represented by definite things (numbers or other symbols) only after a system of coordinates has been arbitrarily carried into the world. It seems to me that this pair of opposites, subjective-absolute and objective-relative, contains one of the most fundamental epistemological insights which can be gleaned from science. Whoever desires the absolute must take the subjectivity and egocentricity into the bargain; whoever feels drawn toward the objective faces the problem of relativity. This thought is vividly and beautifully developed in the introduction of Born's book on relativity theory.

Within the natural sciences the conflicting philosophies of idealism and realism signify principles of method which do not contradict each other. We construct through science an objective world which, in order to explain the sense data, must satisfy the following fundamental principle. *A difference in the perceptions offering themselves to us is always founded on a difference in the real conditions* (Helmholtz). Lambert, in his *Photometria* (1760), enunciates as an axiom the following special case: "An appearance is the same whenever the same eye is affected in the same way." Here the natural sciences proceed realistically.

For as long as I do not go beyond what is given, or more exactly, what is given at the moment, there is no need for the substructure of an objective world. Even if I include memory and in principle acknowledge it as valid testimony, if I furthermore accept as data the contents of the consciousness of others on equal terms with my own, thus opening myself to the mystery of intersubjective communication, I would still not have to proceed as we actually do, but might ask instead for the "transformations" which mediate between the images of the several consciousnesses. Such a presentation would fit in with Leibniz's monadology. Instead of constructing the perspective view which a given body offers from a given point of observation, or conversely constructing the body from several perspective images, as it is done in photogrammetry, we might eliminate the body and formulate the problem directly as follows: let A, B, C each represent a consciousness bound to a point body, and let K be a solid contained in their field of vision. The task is to describe the lawful geometrical connections between the three images which each one of the three persons A, B, C receives of K and of the locations of the other two persons. This procedure would be more unwieldy; in fact, it would be bound to fail on account of the limitations and gaps in any single consciousness as compared to the complete real world. At any rate, there can be no doubt that in this respect science proceeds in tune with a realistic attitude.

On the other hand science concedes to idealism that its objective reality is not given but to be constructed (*nicht gegeben, sondern aufgegeben*), and that it cannot be constructed absolutely but only in relation to an arbitrarily assumed coordinate system and in mere symbols. Above all the central thought of idealism comes into its own in the converse of the above fundamental principle: *the objective image of the world may not admit of any diversities which cannot manifest themselves in some diversity of perceptions;* an existence which as a matter of principle is entirely inaccessible to perception is not admitted. Leibniz says concerning the fiction of absolute motion (Leibniz's fifth letter to Clarke, §52): "I reply that motion is indeed independent of actual observation, but not of the possibility of observation altogether. Motion exists only where a change accessible to observation takes place. If this change is not ascertainable by any observation then it does not exist." To be sure, many physically different colors will produce the same sensation of red; but if one sends all these various reds through the same prism, then the physical differences will manifest themselves in the perceptible differences between the streaks of colored light emerging from the prism. The prism, so to speak, unfolds the hidden differences to our senses. A difference which can in no way be broken down for our perception is non-existent. This is of great importance as a methodical principle of theoretical construction.

The formula customarily given (Schwarzschild formula) for the metrical field surrounding a mass, such as the sun, can be interpreted as follows, if the coordinates occurring in it are taken to stand for a mapping of the real space into a Euclidean one: "(I) In reality Euclidean geometry holds. But the spherically symmetric field of gravity surrounding the mass center O acts upon rigid bodies in such a fashion that a radially directed rod at P is foreshortened in the ratio $\sqrt{1 - 2\alpha/r} : 1$ (where $r = \overline{OP}$ and α is a constant determined by the mass), while a rod perpendicular to OP remains unchanged." Rods after all are known to change their length with changing temperatures, why should they not react in a similar way to a gravitational field? But in making use of a certain other coordinate system one arrives at the following description: "(II) In reality Euclidean geometry holds. But the rod at P, no matter what its direction, will be changed in the ratio $(1 + \alpha/2r)^2:1$ by the field of gravitation." Both descriptions express the same factual situation. To every possible coordinate system there corresponds a corrective prescription salvaging Euclidean geometry. Yet one is as good as the other. Each introduces into the factual state of affairs an arbitrary element which has no perceptually confirmable consequences and which therefore must be eliminated. And it can be eliminated by employing, with Einstein, none but the physical geometry as it is defined by the direct comparison of measuring rods. (That geometry is, of course, not the Euclidean one.) Each

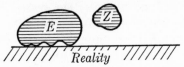

Figure 2.   Schematic representation of a theory with a redundant part Z.

of the two theories can, if properly formulated, be split into two parts: the theory (E) of Einstein, and an addition (Z) which is neither connected with (E) nor touching on reality and which must therefore be shed (compare the schematic diagram in Figure 2).

In Bohr's model of the hydrogen atom the period of the emitted light has nothing to do with the time in which the electron completes a revolution around the nucleus. Though it explains the spectrum as satisfactorily as could be wished, this lack of observable data corresponding to the period of revolution of the electron is felt as a disturbing feature which ought to be removed. In order to clarify the idea of relativity, Poincaré once set up the fiction that overnight, while all consciousness was asleep, the world with all its bodies in it, including my own, had been magnified in a definite ratio; awake again, neither I nor anyone else would notice the change in any way. In the face of such an event science makes common cause with the idealist; for what on earth could be meant under such circumstances by the statement that the world was magnified? A difference may be posited only where the assumption of equality would conflict with the principle that equals under equal conditions (especially equal objective characteristics, location, and motion, of the observer) will be perceived as equal [1] (and with the principle of causality). Between the real world and the given there is a correspondence, a mapping in the mathematical sense. Yet, while on one side there is the one, quantitatively determined, objective world, we have on the other not only what is actually given at the moment but also the *possible* perceptions (perhaps remembered, or expected in response to definite intentions of will) of an ego; and further there enter into this correspondence, besides the unique objective state of the world, the *possible* objective states of this perceiving ego (world line of its body, *etc.*). Helmholtz sets up the principle of the "empiristic view" (*Physiologische Optik*, III, p. 433): "The sensations are signs to our consciousness, and it is the task of our intelligence to learn to understand their meaning." In this one may agree with Helmholtz as he means it and yet be of the opinion with Husserl that the spatial object which I see, notwithstanding all its transcendency, is perceived as such bodily in its concreteness (Husserl, *Ideen zu einer reinen Phänomenologie*, in his *Jahrbuch für Philosophie*, Vol. 1, 1913, pp. 75, 79); for within the concrete unity of perception the data of sensation are animated by "interpretations," and only in union with them do they perform the "function of representation" and help to constitute what we call "the appearance of" color, shape, etc. A dog approaching another dog will see and smell "a fellow dog," an integrated whole that is more than a "bundle of sensations." We merely describe here one of the levels through which the process of constitution of the external world will pass. And there is no denying that the definite manner in which a thing is bodily put before me by means of those animating functions will be directed by a multitude of previous experiences. For how else should we describe this than by saying that "we always imagine such objects to be present in our field of vision as must be present in order to bring about the given impression under ordinary normal conditions for the use of our eyes" (Helmholtz, *Physiologische Optik*, III, p. 4). Helmholtz speaks here of "unconscious inferences." This sounds somewhat questionable; yet he stresses explicitly that only in their result do they resemble inferences, more accurately inferences by

1. This principle cannot be taken as a definition of objective equality but only as an implicit requirement, because the concept of equality occurs in it twice: *equals* under *equal* conditions. . . .

analogy, although the underlying psychic acts probably are quite different from acts of conscious inference and although their effects cannot be annulled by better knowledge. The sense impression of a mirror image, or of a broken rod immersed in water, or of the rainbow, does not deceive; only the bodily object which, as Husserl says, is put before me by this impression is an error. What truly exists can be ascertained only by taking into consideration all sensuous signs, which in the examples adduced above will soon reveal the prevalence of "abnormal" conditions. Only imagine our eyes to be sensitive to light whose wave length is of the order of magnitude of the atomic distances in solids; how difficult it would then become for us to interpret the optical "signs" (the Laue interference patterns)! In the ultimate description of the connection between appearance and reality one therefore does better to ignore all intermediary levels of constitution.

And what significance does this objective world, representable only in symbols, have for the everyday life of man, taking place as it does in the sphere of integrated data of perceptions? Helmholtz answers (*op. cit.*, p. 18), "Once we have learned to read those symbols correctly we shall be able with their help to design our actions so that they yield the desired result, namely, that the expected new sensations will arise. A different comparison between conceptions and things not only does not exist in reality—all schools agree on this point—but a different manner of comparison is inconceivable and would be devoid of meaning. . . . Thus such a presentation (*Vorstellung*) of a single individual body is indeed already a concept (*Begriff*) which comprises an infinite number of intuitions in temporal sequence all of which can be derived from it.[2] The presentation of a single individual table that I carry within me is correct and accurate if I am able to derive from it correctly and accurately the sensations I shall experience when I bring my eyes or my hands into this or that definite position with respect to the table. What other kind of similarity there can subsist between such a presentation and the object represented by it I cannot comprehend" (*op. cit.*, p. 26). In the same sense, Leibniz remarks concerning the Car-

2. [In agreement with a number of philosophers writing in English the term presentation has been chosen here as the equivalent of Kant's and Helmholtz's *Vorstellung* and Locke's *idea.*—Trans.]

tesian principles (*Philosophische Schriften*, IV, p. 356), "Of the sense data we cannot know more, nor do we have to require more, than that they are in agreement with each other as well as with the indisputable dictates of reason and that thus to a certain extent the future may be predicted from the past. To search for a truth or reality other than thus vouched for would be futile— the skeptic may not demand, the dogmatist not promise more." Or Husserl (*Ideen*, p. 311), "To the essence of a thing-noema there belong ideal possibilities of unlimited development of concordant intuitions that follow, moreover, prescribed directions of determinate type." But in the erection of empirical reality discrepancies will occur which will force us to make "corrections." Owing to its empirical character cognition of reality must of necessity pass through errors. "What is given never implies material existence as certain and necessary but merely as presumptive reality. This means that it can always happen that the further course of experience will force one to abandon what with good empirical justification had earlier been posited." (Husserl, *Ideen*, p. 86.) It might well be within the range of possibility that in the moving picture of perceptions every beginning of concordance would irreparably "explode." In that case the attempt to harmonize them according to principles of reason would fail, and no real world would be constituted.

The requirements which emerge from our discussion for a correct theory of the course of the world may be formulated as follows:

1. *Concordance.* The definite value which a quantity occurring in the theory assumes in a certain individual case will be determined from the empirical data on the basis of the theoretically posited connections. *Every such determination has to yield the same result.* Thus all determinations of the electronic charge e, that follow from observations in combination with the laws established by physical theory, lead to the same value of e (within the accuracy of the observations). Not infrequently a (relatively) direct observation of the quantity in question (for instance, of the location of a comet among the stars at a certain moment) is compared with a computation on the basis of other observations (for instance, the location at the desired moment computed according to Newton's theory from the locations on previous days). The demand of concordance implies con-

sistency,[3] yet transcends the latter in that it brings the theory in contact with experience.

2. It must in principle always be possible to determine on the basis of observational data the definite value which a quantity occurring in the theory will have in a given individual case. This expresses the postulate that the theory, in its explanation of the phenomena, must not contain redundant parts.

Hume attempted to uphold with inexorable consistency the viewpoint that the given is the whole of reality. Since it became apparent through him that this viewpoint fails completely in the explanation of those cognitive positions which play a basic role in everyday life and in science, he was indeed the first to reveal the problem of reality in its full difficulty. Reason in its function of constituting reality is described by him as the faculty of imagination. With complete sincerity he confesses the irreconcilable conflict between thought and life, into which he finds himself thrown. To carry his approach through is as impossible as to found arithmetic on nothing but the concretely existing numerals. The positivism of a Mach or Avenarius appears to me merely as a less consistent renewal of Hume's attempt; for in their systems theoretical hypostases, strictly avoided by Hume, play once more a considerable role. But then we are back in the midst of theoretical construction, which supplements the given in the interest of totality, and we are no longer forced to use sense data as our building material. Kant's transcendental idealism reestablished the insights already gained by Leibniz. The content of this Section may be considered as an elucidation of Kant's concept of reality as "that which is connected with perception according to laws." He advances beyond Leibniz in transmuting the old metaphysical ontological concepts of substance and causality into methodical principles for the construction of empirical reality.

In the part on logic we had insisted that existence could not be stated about something exhibited, that the logical symbol Σ_x carries an index x which refers to a blank. This seems to be contradicted by a proposition such as "this chair is real." But the

3. Indeed in an inconsistent theory the formula $e = 2e$ would be deducible, and hence the actual value e as well as $2e$ for the electronic charge could be derived from such a theory in combination with the observational data.

assertion of real existence contains either, idealistically interpreted, the prediction of a multitude of concordant impressions expected in response to certain intentions of will, or, realistically interpreted, the statement that a thing x exists which stands in a certain metaphysical relation to the given chair phenomenon.

Concerning the problem of realism versus idealism we find a striking analogue in geometry, which has a factual connection with it in so far as in the objective world the coordinate system is, as it were, the residue of the annihilation of the ego. As in Section 12, we consider vectors $\vec{x}$ in a plane and represent them in terms of a basis consisting of two linearly independent vectors $\vec{e_1}$, $\vec{e_2}$, thus: $\vec{x} = \xi_1\vec{e_1} + \xi_2\vec{e_2}$. The numbers ξ_1, ξ_2, which are uniquely determined by $\vec{x}$ and $\vec{e_1}$, $\vec{e_2}$, are called the coordinates of $\vec{x}$ with respect to the basis $(\vec{e_1}, \vec{e_2})$. We construe the vectors in our plane as analogues of the objects in the real world, bases as analogues of real observers, the numbers as analogues of subjective phenomena, and thus speak in our analogy of the pair of coordinates (ξ_1, ξ_2) as the "appearance of the object $\vec{x}$ for the observer $(\vec{e_1}, \vec{e_2})$." For the geometric vector plane we can construct an algebraic model, defining a vector $\vec{x}$ as a pair of numbers (x_1, x_2) and the operations of adding two vectors $\vec{x}, \vec{y}$ and of multiplying a vector $\vec{x}$ by a number α as follows:

$$(x_1, x_2) + (y_1, y_2) = (x_1 + y_1, x_2 + y_2), \quad \alpha(x_1, x_2) = (\alpha x_1, \alpha x_2).$$

Calling the numbers x_1, x_2 the absolute coordinates of $\vec{x} = (x_1, x_2)$ and $\vec{i_1} = (1, 0)$, $\vec{i_2} = (0, 1)$ the absolute basis in our model, we realize at once that the absolute coordinates of a vector are its relative coordinates with respect to the absolute basis. Transition from the geometric vector space, in which all bases are equally admissible, to its algebraic model is effected by assigning, as it were, to an arbitrarily chosen basis the role of absolute basis. On the other hand, the individual character of the various bases in the model can be extinguished and all bases put on an equal footing by ascribing objective significance only to such properties and relations as are definable in terms of the two fundamental operations, or, what is the same, as are invariant under arbitrary linear coordinate transformations. The relation of a vector to its absolute coordinates is not objective, but is a special case of the objective relation prevailing between a vector $\vec{x}$, a basis $(\vec{e_1}, \vec{e_2})$, and the coordinates ξ_1, ξ_2 of $\vec{x}$ relative to $(\vec{e_1}, \vec{e_2})$. Our analogy assumes that only the realm of numbers (the appearances) but not the geometrical space (the things themselves) is open to our intuition. Hence the model is the world of my phenomena and the absolute basis is that distinguished observer "I" who claims that all phenomena are as they appear to him: on this level, object, observer and appearance all belong to the same world of phenomena, linked however by relations among which we can distinguish the "objective" or invariant ones. Real observer and real object, I, thou, and the external world arise, so to speak, in unison and correlation with one another by subjecting the sphere of "algebraic appearances" to the viewpoint of invariance. On this issue our theory bears out Leibniz (compare, for instance, *Nouveaux Essais,* Libre IV, Chap 11) as opposed to Descartes, who through his "cogito ergo sum" assigns to the reality of the ego a precedence in principle over the reality of the external world. The analogy renders the fact readily intelligible that the unique "I" of pure consciousness, the source of meaning, appears under the viewpoint of objectivity as but a single subject among many of its kind.

Yet in truth, the absolute subject, I, remains forever unique, notwithstanding the *objective* equivalence of the various subjects. This is in agreement with the facts as I find them. On purely cognitive grounds conscientalism is irrefutable, it can be carried through completely. But for all this the recognition of the "thou" is demanded of me not only in the sense that in my thinking I yield to the abstract norm of "objectivity," but in an absolute sense: Thou art for thyself once more what I am for myself, conscious-existing carrier of the world of phenomena. This step can be taken in our analogy only if we pass from the algebraic model of affine vector geometry to its axiomatic description, where the concepts of a vector and of the two fundamental operations enter as undefined terms. In the axiomatic system it is no longer necessary to enforce the equivalence of all coordinates by abstraction, for in it a definite pair of vectors $(\vec{e_1}, \vec{e_2})$ can be distinguished only by an individual act of exhibition. Pattern and source of any such demonstrative act is the word "I." Thus axiomatics reveals itself once again as the method of a purified realism which posits a transcendental world but is content to recreate it in symbols.

The postulation of the ego, of the "thou," and of the external world is without influence upon the cognitive treatment of reality. It is a matter of metaphysics, not a judgment but an act of acknowledgment or belief (as Fichte emphasizes in his treatise *Über die Bestimmung des Menschen*). Yet this belief is the soul of all knowledge. From the metaphysico-realistic viewpoint, however, egohood remains an enigma. Leibniz (Metaphysische Abhandlung, *Philosophische Schriften*, IV, pp. 454–455) believed that he had resolved the conflict of human freedom and divine predestination by letting God (for sufficient reasons) assign existence to certain of the infinitely many possibilities, for instance to the beings Judas and Peter, whose substantial nature determines their entire fate. This solution may objectively be sufficient, but it is shattered by the desperate outcry of Judas, "Why did *I* have to be Judas?" The impossibility of an objective formulation of this question is apparent. Therefore no answer in the form of an objective insight can ensue. Knowledge is incapable of harmonizing the luminous ego with the dark erring human being that is cast out into an individual fate.

Postulation of the external world does not guarantee that such a world will rise from the phenomena through the cognitive work of reason which attempts to create concordance. For this to take place it is necessary that the world be governed throughout by simple elementary laws. Thus the mere positing of the external world does not really explain what it was meant to explain, the question of the reality of the world mingles inseparably with the question of the reason for its lawful mathematical harmony. The latter clearly points in another direction of transcendency than that of a transcendental world; towards the origin rather than the product. Thus the ultimate answer lies beyond all knowledge, in God alone; emanating from him, the light of consciousness, its own origin hidden from it, grasps itself in self-penetration, divided and suspended between subject and object, between meaning and being.

Oskar Becker

OSKAR BECKER (1889–1964) came to phenomenology from mathematics and continued to pursue original work in this field, making significant contributions toward a modal calculus. As a student of Husserl in the twenties, he enjoyed close contact with the master and had access to Husserl's unpublished manuscripts. Along with Heidegger, he was editor of the *Jahrbuch* in its later years until it was quietly terminated after 1930. From 1931 until his retirement, he was professor ordinarius of the history of mathematics at the University of Bonn. His publications reflect the evolution of his attempts to apply transcendental and then hermeneutical phenomenology to mathematical and scientific problems, culminating in his final decision that "mantic" phenomenology, as he called it on occasion, was the proper approach to such problems and to aesthetics and the unconscious as well. Hermeneutical phenomenology as Heidegger conceived it, which was first taken by Becker to be a concretization of Husserl's phenomenology, ultimately became the counterconcept to the mantic approach. Accordingly, Becker's last book, a collection of his philosophical essays, is entitled *Dasein und Dawesen*. For, according to Becker, the "perduring essence" (*Dawesen*) of nature in its symmetries and structures lies before, under, and outside historical-factic existence (*Dasein*) and therefore cannot be hermeneutically interpreted but only mathematically "divined," i.e., mantically deciphered. Hermeneutical thinking is therefore not all-encompassing but requires the parallel efforts of the divinatory approach into the ahistorical realms of nature, aesthetic existence, and the unconscious—an approach that would be the function of a mantic phenomenology.

The material on the foundations of geometry translated here is Becker's *Habilitationsschrift* under Husserl and, like the work of Hermann Weyl on whom Becker relies heavily, still moves within the milieu of transcendental phenomenology. But Becker more than Weyl tries to go beyond the formal research into the axiomatic foundations of geometry current at that time, in order to penetrate into the phenomenal levels where spatiality is constituted. Operating under the "principle of transcendental idealism," Becker seeks to show that even the intuitive foundations of the domain of the continuum and of Euclidean geometry are rational through and through. Accordingly, two major problems are treated: (1) the rationalization of the intuited continuum by rendering the vague morphology of space into an exact metric through the process of idealization or "going to the limit"; (2) the problem of bracketing not only the empirical contingency of the hypothetical-deductive systems of physics but also the a priori contingency of the axioms of Euclidean geometry, whose laws of essence are still bound to an intuited world of three dimensions, etc. In other words, Becker grapples with the question of how the accidental material content of these axioms can be grounded transcendentally and therefore understood necessarily, thereby eliminating their apparent contingency. In mathematical terms, it is the problem of the relations of Euclidean to non-Euclidean geometry.

The following sections, which are concerned with the "physical applications" of geometry, are selected from Becker's discussion of this latter problem. They represent an early example of the phenomenology of physics under the auspices of Husserl himself and utilize the terminology of what was later published as *Ideen II*. The selections trace the phenomenological significance of the development in physics from causal laws to structural laws.

6 / Contributions toward the Phenomenological Foundation of Geometry and Its Physical Applications

Oskar Becker

THE EUCLIDEAN FORM OF SPACE AS THE FOUNDATION OF CLASSICAL PHYSICS

IN THE PRECEDING INVESTIGATIONS we have studied the "actual" space of intuition solely in terms of its formal constitution. We did not go into the relationship between the form of space and its fullness. Our previous findings had their source in the fact that space is a principle of individuation, and in the constitutive lawfulness through which space as an abstract moment of nature is organized in pure consciousness. We must now turn to nature as a concrete unity of the form of space and its fulfillment. Our knowledge of material nature and of the relation of its laws to those of pure space must now enter into our understanding of the form of space taken by itself. We shall start with the "classical" formulation which Newton gave to the foundations of physics.

The "Subtractive" Process Leading to the Physical Thing

Although the development of physics has progressed continuously and although we can trace this historical continuity from ancient times, it is still valid to view the epoch from Galileo

The following translation of selections from "Beiträge zur phänomenologischen Begründung der Geometrie und ihrer physikalischen Anwendungen," *Jahrbuch für Philosophie und phänomenologische Forschung*, VI (1923), 493–507, 536–37, 547–60, has been done expressly for this volume by Theodore J. Kisiel.

to Newton as the time when "classical" physics was founded. For it was this period which outlined a scientific system in its fundamental lines which lasted for centuries. And even today, after a thoroughgoing transformation which took place for many reasons in the second half of the nineteenth and the beginning of the twentieth century, this system persists as a limit case in the system of "modern" physics. While only Archimedean statics remains from ancient physics, not only the Galilean-Newtonian dynamics but also its over-all conception of the tasks and methods of physical science will always characterize a necessary step in our knowledge of nature. It will never lose its specific value because it is essentially well-founded. This is also the deeper and real reason why Kant's critique of reason could be tied to Newton's *Principia.*

Our task here is briefly to characterize this Newtonian conception of nature from our point of interest, so that it can be contrasted with the current "modern" conception. We must emphasize two points above all: the relationship of spatial properties to immediately perceived qualities, and the relationship of space to causality and physical events in general.

Both questions are already treated in Aristotelian physics. But while "classical" physics is based on Aristotle on the first point, it is opposed to him on the second. The well-known formulation by Locke of an insight which Galileo already possessed, that physics retains only the "primary" qualities of things, i.e., the spatial, temporal, kinematic, and dynamic qualities, and considers the "secondary," color, sound, tactile qualities, etc., to be "appearance" and subjectively conditioned, in the last analysis goes back to Aristotle's psychological doctrine of the common senses.[1] But classical physics stands in direct opposition to the Aristotelian doctrine of the physical significance of place [2] in the cosmos. Aristotle distinguishes (within changes of place [*phorai*]) two types of motion: "natural" [*physei, kata physin*] and "violent" [*bia, para physin*]. To the first belong (excluding animal movements, which do not concern us here) the circular movements of the planets and the movements of light and heavy bodies, which proceed simply under the influence of place. All

1. *De Anima* III. 1–2. 425ᵃ 13 ff. This idea appears even earlier in Democritus (Frag. 55B, l. 11; see Diels, *Fragmente der Vorsokratiker,* I, 389).
2. *Physics* IV. 1. 208ᵇ 8–11.

bodies have the tendency to reach their natural place, the heavy ones to the midpoint of the world, the light ones to the outer cosmic spheres. By contrast, the space of classical physics is the completely uniform homogeneous medium in which physical processes take place, obeying only the forces of physical nature.[3] Kant's conception of the "pure intuition of space" and of space as the form of appearances is based on this representation.

What we must now do is to determine the systematic and essential content of this conception of "classical" physics. The object of physics is the intersubjectively identifiable material thing and its pertinent states, which can thus be comprehended in universally valid judgments. This definition applies to both classical and modern physics. But the objects of classical physics are characterized by the fact that they come into being in a purely "subtractive" manner from the wholly intuited things of perception, which appear to individuals only in this way and in no other way. In other words, certain "qualities" (if we provisionally accept this expression without characterizing its intentional structures), the "primary," persist unchanged even in these "intersubjective" objects, while others, the "secondary," vary from subject to subject according to physiological and psychophysical conditions. We thus obtain the physical object by retaining these invariant "primary" qualities after stripping away the variable "secondary" qualities.

This is roughly the systematic content of the view stemming from Galileo, Descartes, and Locke. We must now bring some highly significant corrections to it from the phenomenological point of view.

It is necessary to distinguish between two constitutive levels of thinghood:[4] the "pure sensory thing" or "phantom" and the

3. Extremely clear formulations of this already occur in Gilbert's *De mundo nostro sublunari philosophia nova* (1651), bk. I, chap. 21, p. 61; bk. II, chap. 8, p. 144; bk. III, chap. 5, p. 241. Cf. Ernst Cassirer, *Das Erkenntnisproblem in der Philosophie und Wissenschaft der neueren Zeit* (Berlin, 1906–7), I, 275–76, 563 n. With its concept of "field" (Faraday), modern physics in a certain sense returns to Aristotelian intuitions.

4. The following distinctions, including the terminology, stem from Husserl (still unpublished, though communicated in lectures). [Since published in *H* IV. Cf. esp. pp. 21–90. Cf. also the first essay in this collection for a discussion of some of this terminology, pp. 27–31 above.—Trans.]

"material thing." The latter is the normal object of our natural perception. Pertaining to it are the specifically "material" and "causal" properties, like weight, inertia, elasticity, viscosity, mobility, etc. There is no sharp distinction between "material" and "causal" properties. We recognize elasticity in the way in which a body reacts to impact, pressure, tension, etc., its weight and inertia in its easy or difficult maneuverability, etc. All these properties of the material-causal level are not in the genuine sense sensibly perceived. To be sure, they are intuitively given through and through and not conceptually or categorially founded upon intuition or even revealed on the basis of an observed lawfulness. But they are still not directly perceived like the genuine sense qualities of color, sound, hardness, roughness, etc. We say that they are "co-perceived," but in a special way. For there are different kinds of "co-perception," first, the kind and way in which the concealed back side of a thing or a thing behind my back is "co-seen" by me without having truly been seen. Here the "concealment" can be overcome, and then I see this thing or that side of it immediately. Second, there is the kind in question here, where certain genuinely invisible properties "are seen in" the sense qualities and structures of the thing, in that they "externalize," so to speak "express," themselves in the sensory.

If we restrict ourselves to the perceived in the genuine sense (including the co-perceived of the first kind), we have the pure sensory thing (phantom) in mind. This phantom is subdivided into the "empty schema" (the empty form of space) and the sensory "fullness" (which consists of the pure sense qualities, optical, acoustic, haptic, thermic, etc.). The visual and tactile data play an important role here. They alone in the strict sense "fill out" the form of space (while sounds, warmth, smells, etc., have a much more indeterminate kind of localization "in" the schema of space). Along with the form of space, they make up the "concrete schema."

The "material" thing stands a step higher than the phantom in the ladder of constitution. It is thus constituted as a unity in a manifold of phantoms, which are connected to each other according to a definite rule in intuitive continuity. A material thing manifests itself as such only in its action and reaction, in its reciprocal interplay with other things like itself, in short, in the causal relations which it as an individual has with all of the individual objects in world space.

In order to obtain a sharper delineation of the ("causal") laws of nature, let us begin with a consideration of the phantom event, the occurrence of the phantom, where these laws become apparent to sense perception. First of all, the pure phantom event, the *kinesis* of the phantoms in the broad Aristotelian sense (their movement, change, coming to be, and passing away, etc.) has its self-contained continuity and essential rule. If a phantom as such is to have stability, its "adumbrations" (its "skia-graphs," its "perspectival aspects," etc.), in which it is given to per-ception, must be subjected to a definite rule: in rotation it must show us its back sides, etc. Even if these "immanent" rules of the phantom event should suffice, there is still a great deal of freedom in the more precise determination of the process. If we now inquire into the laws which govern these free possibilities, we encounter a fundamental distinction between two types of law which arises from a consideration of the relation to intersubjectivity. Every phantom together with its occurrence is first of all given to the individual subject in his consciousness. It is a priori not certain whether it appears in the same way to a second subject. But it is only upon such an eventuality that it can be recognized as an "intersubjective" reality and the law which it obeys be acknowl-edged as universally valid, as a "truth in itself." (A connection of empathy between the subjects in question is thus to be as-sumed.) Those characteristics of the phantoms and their "kine-sis" which vary from subject to subject come to be characterized as "subjective," while those which prove to be identical and constant are characterized as "intersubjective." But with this we have not yet reached the decisive distinction. For there is such a thing as a "normal" subjectivity, so that the characteristics of the phantom which appear the same to all "normal" subjects (whereby "normality" resides primarily in the condition of the body) are to be characterized as "intersubjective" (restricted to the circle of "normal" subjects). If a subject is "abnormal," this manifests itself in an alteration of the total phantom world. Frequently also specific "body feelings" (pain, etc.) accompany the process. By bracketing the peculiarities perceived by an ab-normal subject and its rules, we come to a valid sense of "objec-tivity" (equivalent to "intersubjectivity" between normal subjects) which is useful in daily life. But it is not "exact" and therefore cannot be used as a basis for an "exact natural science" directed toward rationality. Not all of the peculiarities of phantoms can be included in a definite manifold of concepts and laws. But only the constructibility that a rational algorithm provides would permit a judgment valid for all (and not only normal) subjects with regard to properties and states of affairs pertinent to phantoms. Only the propositions and algorithms of formal logic are intersubjectively valid without restriction. This requirement of a universal validity without restriction, of a constructibility through rational algorithms, is sufficient first of all for spatial, temporal, and kinematic properties and relations. Now if the laws of spatial deformation in time (under which movement falls as a special case) were in themselves closed and somehow not connected with the laws of qualitative alterations, we could completely discount the qualitative contents of space and bracket them out of physics as "secondary qualities." But this is not the case. A "geometrical" physics in Descartes' sense proves to be unrealizable. And so we are confronted with the problem of somehow converting the manifold of qualitative variations into a definite manifold. The principle of its solution is as follows: for the sense qualities we substitute physical "material" properties which are measured through their "effect," through the deformation produced by them. They exist only on the basis of this effect. Here we come upon the most fortunate "material" properties, which are "co-perceived" along with the properties of naïve intuition in the "kinesis" of the phantoms. These "morphological" properties, co-perceived in a naïve way, are made into "exact" ("geometrical" in the more generalized sense) properties, which are constructed out of these by virtue of their functional connection with definite "deformations" (geometric-kinematic type) and thus incorporated into the geometric-kinematic definite manifold. This is in its fundamental features the way which leads from intuited causality to the functional coherence of mathematical physics.

In summary, we can thus say that the situation underlying the division of qualities into "primary" and "secondary" is the following: objective, i.e., intersubjectively valid propositions without restriction can acquire their validity only from the rationally constructible properties. These are, first of all, the geometric-kinematic and then the "material" properties constructed out of them by virtue of the deforming and moving effect which they exercise. Subjective states of affairs, at best valid for a certain group of subjects called normal, are based on the genuine sense qualities. But even the morphological spatial structures may in certain "deceptive" circumstances have merely such a "subjective" validity, e.g., in the so-called "optical illusions," as investigated by experimental psychology.

What then follows from this for the relation of space to material nature in classical physics? The geometric-kinematic states of affairs form the foundation of the exact laws of nature. They need not be "in reality" as they appear to be in the individual instance. But in their fundamental structure they still spring from the laws of phantom space. For an "apparent" spatial figure, another "real" one is simply substituted, which itself could just as well be made intuitive.[5] Space is a principle of individuation for the "material" content in the same sense as it is for the sense content of phantoms. Matter is dispersed in it in precisely the same way as the quality of the phantom. Accordingly, all the considerations which we have carried out in this section with regard to intuitive space as a principle of individuation apply to it without alteration. Just like phantom space, the space of material nature according to classical physics is Euclidean.

Geometry and classical physics are thus completely and clearly separated. The geometric (Euclidean) laws form the framework within which the material-causal laws are plotted. Physical occurrences never have any influence whatsoever on geometric relations. Likewise, "place" is completely free of physical significance. This means that the laws of nature are purely causal; the operative forces are bound to matter and exercise an effect on the bodies subject to them. No movement (or alteration in general) proceeds "of its own accord," with the exception of the movement of inertia. The structure of the world, e.g., the distribution of matter in space, is completely "accidental," sub-

5. This cannot be derived strictly from the line of thought which we followed. It is more a matter of a special presupposition surreptitiously made in classical physics, which we will come to later. It is connected with the fact that the geometric-kinematic lawfulness is the starting point and means for the construction of all "exact" laws of nature, which cannot be undermined without having the entire structure collapse.

ject only to the laws of probability.[6] There are no cosmic laws of structure. In spite of this, it is naturally possible to distinguish purely formal mathematical concatenations of function in which time emerges as an (independent) variable from those which are free from time variables. But there is a genuine law of nature only when it can at least be indirectly reduced to concatenations of the first type. Concatenations of the second type which are not reducible to the other type are nothing but "approaches," i.e., arbitrary equations of condition which are grounded no further but only serve to provide precise positioning for the individual mathematical problems of theoretical physics.

There is in this conception of nature as governed exclusively by causal laws an ungrounded presupposition of classical physics which we only want to point out here. It is connected with a conviction already exposed but not further grounded, namely, the belief in the Euclidean lawfulness of the space in which the physical event takes place, which amounts to asserting that this event is to be represented in the mode of a phantom event (even though the phantom event, observed in every case purely by leaving out the "secondary" qualities, does not become a physical event). Both presuppositions mean that the physical event is subject to no new "structural" lawfulness with respect to the phantom event but pertains solely to a purely "causal" lawfulness which does not disturb the world structure.

The sequence of ideas just developed will be of great importance in our later investigations, and its central concepts, "causality," "structure," etc.,[7] will be progressively clarified and will form the chief means for understanding the physical applications of the non-Euclidean geometries.

The Role of Measurement in Classical Physics

We have already characterized the fundamental significance of metric. It serves to bring about a choice among the many

6. This manifestly paradoxical conceptual formulation of the lawfulness of the accident poses a very important problem for transcendental logic which we cannot handle here. To the present day, a truly satisfying grounding of the calculus of probability is still lacking, in spite of the many efforts made in this direction.

7. On these terms, cf. Stumpf, *Zur Einteilung der Wissenschaften* (Berlin: Berliner Akadamie, 1906), pp. 61 ff.

possibilities of topologically equal value and thereby to permit a univocal determination of coordinates. Accordingly, the concept of equality plays a central role: the distances of the topologically designated points are to be divided into equal parts. It is here that the question of the criterion for such an equality emerges. We have, in our phenomenological considerations of Euclidean metric, investigated the constitution of the phenomenon of intuitively congruent transference. This phenomenon clearly provides the basis for the "estimation" of equality. "Measuring," on the contrary, "consists" (to use Riemann's word *besteht*) "in a superimposition of the magnitudes to be compared. Accordingly, measuring requires a means which carries over one magnitude (unaltered) as a standard of measurement for the other." [8] The relation of the two methods for determining magnitudes is this: as long as an "estimate" is possible, a measurement is superfluous. If a measurement is to have a value in its own right, the unalterability of the standard during the measurement does not need to be established on the basis of the estimates but must be grounded somewhere else. If estimation appears as the primary means for the determination of equality, it still possesses the decisive disadvantage of not being exact, and this for essential reasons. Estimation is based either on the sense impression of equality or on the kinesthetic compensability of the intuitive difference of magnitude of the two figures estimated as equal. Now estimation according to sense impression ("measure of the eye," etc.) is essentially only of restricted exactness because of the "approximative" structure of the prespatial continuum and accordingly is not utilizable for the unrestrictedly approximable geometric figures of homogeneous space. The kinesthetic criterion seems to take us further. It clearly extends to all constitutive levels, and it seems that through continual penetration into the inner horizon and repeated application of the criterion of sensible equality, in a way analogous to the case of the "genuine" geometric ideal formations which are defined as "limits of constancy," we can come to an unrestrictedly exact determination of equality. We can, for example, compare very small distances under the microscope by estimation and then compose the length of a larger body out of these small distances in order to

8. *Über die Hypothesen, welche der Geometrie zugrunde liegen* (1854) I, § 1.

achieve a high degree of exactness. But this is only apparently correct. A larger body becomes so immense that it becomes "unsurveyable" when we approach it too closely (as with instruments like the microscope). We thus lose sight of large parts of it when we consider its individual pieces exactly. If the over-all result is to have validity, it must therefore be presupposed that the body to be determined in its magnitude remains unaltered during the entire course of the examination of all of its parts. Indeed, this is a presupposition which is not grounded in the performance of the partial estimates but which nevertheless must necessarily be made if it is to be admitted that the results of the partial estimates are to be joined together into an over-all result. Thus a criterion independent of every estimate [9] is required in order to be sure that a material body remains the same. But this is the same requirement by which we have already characterized the measurement of independent worth. We thus come to the conclusion that an estimate is useless for an arbitrarily exact determination of magnitude, and that accordingly the basic condition for measurement must be fulfilled in order to be able to establish the unalterability of a material body in its magnitude of extension with arbitrary exactness in principle.

Now classical physics in fact makes the most extensive use of the unalterability of a rigid standard. How is the belief in the unalterability of a definite standard founded? Is this perhaps presupposed completely arbitrarily ("conventionally")? No, its conviction in the unalterability of the rigid standards which it employs is guided throughout by rational motives. Inasmuch as it proclaims the autocracy of causality in nature, it can with justification assume the constancy of the standard whenever no altering causation is present. The loci of such causes are the material particles which are distributed in space at random or according to our will. Whether a specific piece of matter exercises effects can be determined by bringing it into proximity with easily altered, "sensitive" bodies ("reagents"). In the selection of a body as a standard of measurement, we begin first of all by making it from the most insensitive material available. This material is discovered by placing it near bodies which strongly affect their environment, by which it is not affected at all or only

9. An estimate of the equality of the entire body "from a distance" for sameness during a certain time would naturally be too inexact.

slightly. Second, we bring the standard thus screened into an environment exercising a minimal effect, in which even highly sensitive bodies do not react. (Example: the meter stick in Paris; insensitive material: platinum-iridium; neutral environment: a cellar with an extremely uniform temperature, etc.). The choice of the standard in classical physics is thus by no means conventional. It depends on certain presuppositions which are based on the presupposition that all laws of nature are causal laws. This includes the presuppositions that all causes are material, distributed without structure in world space, and that the same causes (provided that only all the coefficient causes are taken into account) exercise the same effects. And finally the (most surreptitious) assumption that the intensity of an effect decreases with the distance from its source. And so we see that, on the basis of the starting point that physical reality is material-causal, classical physics with thoroughgoing consistency comes to a grounding of a metric. The starting point itself, with its rejection of a regular world structure independent of matter or even of a structure which itself regulates their distribution in space, is grounded no further than in the requirement of being able to bring the material event to intuition in precisely the same way as it does the phantom event, which functions as its mirror image. It is here that we find a break in the coherence of the system, which serves as the breach used by the moderns to force the bulwark of classical physics. . . .

❖   ❖   ❖

ON THE PROBLEM OF A PHENOMENOLOGICAL INVESTIGATION OF A PHYSICAL THEORY

IF HERE AT THE CONCLUSION of an endeavor to lay the foundations for geometry in a fundamental way, we now turn to the consideration of an apparently special physical theory, such a turn is not obvious and requires some clarification. Accordingly, we shall begin with a brief consideration of the general aims of a phenomenological investigation of a physical theory.

As everyone knows, a physical theory is a collection of a large number of empirical statements into a deductive system. More precisely stated, at the head of the theory stand a few fundamental laws, primarily of a hypothetical character. From these, all the results of observations explainable by the theory can be derived as consequences and with quantitative exactness at that. Such a theory is therefore a hypothetico-deductive system.

But now "deduction" is not to be taken here completely rigorously in the sense of a formal logical deduction. In addition to these hypothetically assumed fundamental laws which are explicitly expressed, a priori-material propositions grounded in the essence of the domain under question enter into the theory, often only implicitly. It is only when we presuppose both the fundamental hypotheses and the unexpressed propositions that we can draw out the individual results in a purely formal logical fashion. The truth content of a physical theory thus comes (1) from the implicit a priori-material propositions, and (2) from the empirical observations brought together in the explicit "hypotheses."

For the phenomenologist, the propositions of an a priori-material nature are the important ones. Since they are for the most part blended in with the empirical parts of the theory or generally appear implicitly in the positive-scientific formulation, the first task of a phenomenological investigation is to expose them in their purity and explicitness. The second task is then to ground these propositions transcendentally.

The following pages do not claim more than a beginning in these two tasks with regard to relativity theory. Their complete solution must be left to the future.

There is no need to say any more about the particular significance of relativity theory. As was stated at the conclusion of the last section, we conceive it as a fundamental part of the methodology of modern physics, in serving to secure temporal and spatial measurement.

[Becker begins his investigation of the a priori-material content of R. T. (relativity theory) with a study of its "mechanical root," largely centered on the problem of the relativity of movement. The approach is more a historical survey of the discussions of this problem from Aristotle's *Physics* to the mechanics of Mach (1883) and Andrade (1898). Because its strictly phenomenological content is minimal, this survey is omitted here. The next study aims at the optical (field-physical) root of R. T., centered on the questions of contemporaneity raised by the pre-supposition of a *finite* velocity for the propagation of light.— Trans.]

❖   ❖   ❖

THE OPTICAL ROOT OF RELATIVITY THEORY (THE PROBLEM OF CONTEMPORANEITY)

Toward a Phenomenology of Contemporaneity

NOTHING IS MORE EVIDENT to the impartial man than the contemporaneity of two events separated from each other by any great distance.[10] But if we go back to the phenomenological constitution of this everyday fact, we soon find ourselves before difficult problems.

Let us first remind ourselves that homogeneous space, which is where we localize these "events separated by any great distance," is constituted from a manifold of aspects or "oriented spaces," and in such a way that no original and instantaneous grasp of all of the homogeneous space is possible. But an original instantaneous "perception" of oriented space is indeed quite possible. For a certain conic section of space is directly seen while what is concealed and behind me is "co-perceived." Larger portions of space than those in my range of vision can be grasped only by successive traversing, hence not instantaneously but over a certain period of time. It is not valid to object that, e.g., the stars that we see in the sky, despite their immense distances, are still given at the same time with our surroundings. For the stars are not given to us in their "true" distance but in the distance of the "horizon" (of the so-called "visually infinite") as definite limit-type horizon-phantoms, which give us no idea of the "actual" stars as defined by astronomy, to say nothing of an original consciousness.

If we now examine more closely to what extent different distant things can be given at the same time in oriented space, we have in visual space the outstanding case of the truly simultaneous perception of distinct and very remote objects. This is due to the fact that vision is a sense of the distant.

10. Here we are thinking first of all of phantom events.

But in tactile space, only objects which are touched simultaneously are perceived, and they can be somewhat nearer or farther only by virtue of the varied distance of the limbs from the trunk. In like manner, the "co-perceived" objects within the "sphere of reachability" can stand somewhat nearer or farther from the center of orientation. For us accordingly, only the visual space, where greater differences of distance are possible, is of significance.

In order now to approach the problem of the metric of time and space in their interrelationship, in which they function as principles of individuation of the world event, we wish first of all to clarify for ourselves the constitution of the phantom event.

If we use the constitution of pure phantom spatiality as our guideline, we have to distinguish three significant levels: the oculomotoric field, oriented space, and homogeneous space.

With regard to the determination of magnitude through estimation, we likewise have three levels: the "oculomotoric distance" (which we wish here to take together with the "sensible"), the "skiagraphic length," and the "phantom length." The first gives itself as the adumbration of the second and this in turn as an appearance of the third. In other words, here we have the phenomenon of perspectival foreshortening of oblique lines and perspectival diminution in the distant view.

Are there analogues for this in the temporal? Do temporal intervals change with distance? In other words, is there a time perspective? Obviously not, as long as we hold fast to the direct perception of the distant through vision. In the pure phantom happening we must perceive two events, which have a definite temporal interval when viewed from a certain location, from all sides and from all distances in the very same temporal interval. If differences arise, no intersubjective phantom happening is constituted, although it may provide a skiagraphic happening which in itself is harmonious throughout from every point of space. But then the "oriented" (skiagraphic) happening viewed from the individual locations does not have the property of being able to serve as an aspect for a phantom happening (tying together all events visible from the various standpoints). And yet there are also (in certain "optical illusions") manifolds of skiagraphs which do not merge in a harmonious way into a phantom.

If we now go to the material happening, first of all, wholly in the sense of classical physics, we have the possibility of coming to a thing event free from contradiction even in cases where no harmonious phantom happening is constituted. When we treat perception by the distance senses (vision, hearing) as a causal effect on our body which is transmitted in space, we can calculate the propagation velocity of this effect and thereby correct the "seen" or "heard" temporal interval of the skiagraphic occurrence.[11] We thus obtain a thing event which can be represented as a phantom event, wholly in analogy with the way in which classical physics elsewhere substructures things to phantoms, which things, even if they diverge from these in spatial properties ("primary" qualities), still can be spatially represented as phantoms. We can thus in classical physics construct an *image* of the "actual" processes which an "ideal observer" who could look through everything would have before his eyes precisely as a phantom event.

And so in the introduction and consideration of the finite propagation velocity of sound and light, it is not really a matter of a "time perspective" but of the transition from the general phantom event which is always restricted to the purely intersubjective material event.

Classical physics here as elsewhere has not really proceeded radically and critically. Here also it is burdened with a presupposition which we have already found in it in a very similar form [cf. above p. 125]. Just as it calls for the thing substructured to the perceived phantom to be presented intuitively so that basically only a phantom (stripped of "secondary qualities") takes the place of the thing, in like fashion it now substructures to the phantom event (or to the skiagraphic event, if even a phantom event is not constituted) a "thing event" which basically is only a second phantom event. This "image character" of the "actual" event, i.e., this perfected intuitive character which would permit the production of a "model" for it, cannot be substantiated. It is not a necessary property of the material event. We can even go further: if we draw all the consequences of the finitude of the propagation velocity of light, we find that it is impossible. Ein-

11. Closer approximations are needed here of the way in which this transmission velocity can be measured as well as of the way in which objective recording instruments can largely free us from the intrusion of psychophysical factors. All this in its fundamental methodology is amenable to a phenomenological investigation.

stein was the first to draw these consequences in a radical way. They form the content of his "special theory of relativity."

On the Phenomenological Significance of the So-called "Special" Theory of Relativity

Freed from all technical details, the fundamental content of Einstein's "special" theory of relativity of 1905 may be briefly characterized in the following way: while it is possible through the introduction of a finite and constant velocity of light for a series of observers at different locations to establish *univocally* the time relations of a definite process occurring at some distance from these observers, *as long as the place of the observation and the place of the process do not move with respect to each other,* this no longer applies when these places approach each other or move away from each other. In other words, for a series of observers remaining stationary with respect to the place of the event to be judged, this event behaves like a phantom event, but this is no longer true for a moving observer.

We must also mention that Einstein thereby presupposes the following: (1) that a transfer of clocks from one place to another is not possible without disturbing their accuracy; that accordingly contemporaneity can be established only through signals with a finite velocity of propagation; (2) that the signals employed have the highest known velocity of propagation (for otherwise we could control the time relations through faster signals transmitted almost instantaneously for the distances in question); (3) that the velocity of propagation is finite and constant.

A more precise axiomatic investigation would be required in order to establish which of these presuppositions are fundamental. Here we can at least state that the first is necessary and the second is required in order to avoid the reversal of a series of events in the use of various signals. The third serves to win specific formulas and is for this purpose the simplest, but to what extent it is necessary is an issue which is in doubt.[12] We can spare ourselves an exact investigation whose difficulty cannot be underestimated, since we shall later interpret the "special"

12. Cf. on this the investigations of P. Frank and H. Rothe, *Annalen der Physik,* XXXIV, 825.

theory of relativity in its positive content on the basis of the "general" theory. Taken by itself, the "special" theory is perhaps not generally susceptible to a fundamental interpretation.[13]

We will accordingly limit ourselves to the following negative assertion: in the movement of the observer, a material event with an "imagelike" character, to which we can substructure a phantom event, no longer exists, and for essential reasons.[14] We thereby take a step which fundamentally goes beyond classical physics. For what is characteristic of classical physics is precisely the "picturability" which a substructuring of the material world through a phantom world purified of secondary qualities makes possible.[15] The same step is taken in the transition from the Euclidean to the non-Euclidean metric. For the possibility of producing a model for the spatial relations of the material world disappeared with the introduction of space curvature. A world whose space is "curved" cannot be structured into a Euclidean space. In spite of this, the phantom world in its inner condition remains undisturbed by this restriction. The only difference is that noncausal "structural laws" result from its occurrence and are regarded as an externalization of spatial curvature. The relations are similar now. Likewise, here the phantom world as such remains undisturbed, at least in its possibility and its inner legitimacy. It of course undergoes a restriction in its scope, namely, to the world of normal everyday distances. But this restriction also exists, strictly speaking, in curved space, since no Euclidean phantom world is identifiable as intersubjectively univocal in the large regions of space. For the disorientation destroys its inner consistency.

13. Hence also all "elementary" derivations of special R. T. in the literature are in a fundamental respect not satisfying (cf. Reichenbach, *Relativitätstheorie und Erkenntnis a priori* [Berlin, 1920]).

14. One may well be puzzled by the absence of any reference to the so-called empirical foundation of special R. T., Michelson's experiment, etc. But our problem does not concern empirical facts but the essential relations which come to light in working with a certain empirical material. On the significance which the "empirical pursuits" of Einstein's theory play in our essential relations, see below, p. 140.

15. Cf. on this J. Cohn, "Relativität und Idealismus," *Kantstudien*, XXI (1916), 222, and the comments above in the section entitled "The 'Subtractive' Process Leading to the Physical Thing," pp. 119–26.

This deficiency of the phantom world, which otherwise binds together the oriented "skiagraphic" worlds, is now replaced by an exactly determined but abstract rule which cannot be represented intuitively, which as a structural law of the world unites all these subjective aspects into an intersubjective "object."

This rule is given mathematically through the law of the transformation of coordinate systems into one another, i.e., through the so-called Lorentz transformation (for uniform rectilinear movements). The symbolic object which persists as identical in the change of coordinate systems (of aspects) is the Minkowskian "world," the "union of space and time." It must be emphasized that this four-dimensional manifold is only symbolic, in spite of the fact that mathematically it shows a closed structure just like Euclidean space.

Of course, we need not overestimate this Minkowskian world in its fundamental significance. Viewed by itself, special R. T. is generally suspended, so to speak, "in mid-air." It is dependent on certain unclarified hypotheses (constancy of the velocity of light, etc.), and moreover is related to uniform rectilinear motion alone.

We shall therefore hold to only the negative facet of special R. T., namely, the impossibility of an intuitive phantom model for the event in the material world. We shall only investigate what kind of possibilities for world structure are opened fundamentally by this negative determination. But with this, we come to the sphere of problems of general R. T.

Search for a Phenomenological Interpretation of Einstein's General Theory of Relativity

As we have indicated above, if we must, in order to do justice to the fundamental significance of a physical theory, single out the components with a priori content and place them within the total context of the constitution of nature, we shall require a fundamental guideline to perform this task. For relativity theory, this is provided for us by the radical conception of the metric problem which we have already reached above. We shall see that the fundamental content of general R. T. lies precisely in its solution of the problem of the *measurement* of spatial and temporal magnitudes. Accordingly, we shall now resume the course of thought followed above.

The infinitesimal geometric solution of the metric problem in freely curved space consisted in the fact that it succeeded, by starting from the principle of the flatness of space in its smallest parts (which can itself be understood group-theoretically), in finding the formal-mathematical approach to the affine and metrical connection which determines the metric of space in its entirety from the infinitely small. But the particular values of this affine-metrical connection at every point of space are, as we saw, defined by the material content or, more exactly, by the character of its structural laws. The question then arose as to how this structural component of the laws of nature is to be distinguished from the causal laws, since both still depend on matter distributed contingently in space. The general R. T. now provides us with the means to solve this problem.

Let us briefly summarize once again all that has thus far been gained in this regard.

1. Andrade, inheritor of the centuries-long evolution of the concept of movement, made a distinction between the "natural" movements of gravitation and inertia (*les cours naturel des choses*) and the "violent" movements under the influence of mechanical forces (tension and pressure; Gauss's principle of "least compulsion"). This suggested that the laws of gravitation and inertia gave us the structural lawfulness of the world which we are seeking. But it was shown that this was not adequate to the formal demands which must be imposed on the laws of the affine-metrical context. We presumed that this was due to the inadequate consideration of the temporal metric and the possibilities of spatial-temporal coupling.

2. The special R. T. provided us with the negative observation that with the assumption of the finite propagation velocity of distant effects (light, etc.), a phantom event can no longer be substructured as a model for the material event. We are thus freed from the objective significance of contemporaneity and confronted with the problem of the fundamental possibilities which now emerge. It is this last observation which provides the key to a truly radical conception of metric.

Now we can still only speak of a time at a definite place. We think we perceive something "now, there" (in the distance), but

138 / Phenomenology and Science in Germany

because of the possible (completely undetermined) time of propagation which the action of the event requires in order to reach
us, we fundamentally do not know the "true time" of its occurrence. We can no longer make a "distant comparison" of time in
different places. A comparison of the clock time of different
places appears as completely conventional.

We can avoid this resignation to conventionalism only by the
same conception of "infinitesimal metric" which we employed in
space. We unite space and time into a four-dimensional manifold and found a "pure infinitesimal geometry" in it. Weyl's
approach to this results in the necessity of the quadratic form of
linear elements *for all dimensions.*[16]

Now we can calculate the laws of the affine and metrical
context in this four-dimensional space-time manifold and see
whether we can find analogous formulas in the known laws of
nature.

Here it becomes clear—and this is the real content of Einstein's general theory of relativity in the expanded form given to
it by Weyl—that the laws of the affine context correspond to the
laws of gravitation and inertia, while the laws of the metrical
context correspond to the laws of the electromagnetic field.[17]
This means that the affine connection defines how a definite
world direction (and any universal vector) is carried over from a
definite point P to the neighboring P_1, while the metrical connection does the same for an infinitesimal magnitude of extension
(in particular cases: a spatial distance or a temporal period).
Accordingly, it is first of all a matter of vectors and extensions in
(four-dimensional) "ether," which still do not coincide with the
vectors and extensions observable in material objects. The relation between the affine-metrical field and the observable vectors
and extensions is complicated and is defined by the kind of
"functions of action" which enter into the "principle of action"
comprising the (structural) laws of nature. These are to a cer-

16. The flatness of the element of space can be founded transcendentally. An analogous transcendental foundation of the element of
space-time does not seem to exist. But it is probably not even possible
to provide an "inhomogeneous" metric in which three dimensions
have a quadratic linear element and the fourth does not.
17. For the following, cf. Weyl, "Die physikalischen Grundlagen
der erweiterten Relativitätstheorie," *Physikalische Zeitschrift,* XXII
(1921), 473 ff.

tain extent arbitrary, i.e., not defined a priori and univocally in every instance. (This will soon be discussed in more detail.) Now the principles of action valid in nature are so constituted that the affine connection is immediately reflected in the "control field" (which regulates the movements that according to the earlier conception proceed under the influence of gravitation and inertia, particularly the planetary movements), so that the transfer of material extensions (e.g., the lattice distances in a crystalline medium) and of time periods (e.g., the frequencies of spectral lines) still ultimately prove to be integrable by virtue of their not readily visible relation to the metrical context of the field, which cannot in itself be integrated. Hence in the "geometry of bodies," there is in fact a curvature of direction (in the "control field") but not a curvature of extension. Physically expressed, this is because of the transfer of "directions" in the "control field" through "persistence," which happens to the "extensions" in the electromagnetic field through an "adjustment" (to the constant radius of curvature of the world). In other words, the affine-metrical context immediately expresses only the transfer through "persistence."

For this, it is evident that the laws of the field of gravitation and inertia and those of the electromagnetic field are a priori until the function of action is chosen. But which field state numerically dominates at a definite field position depends on the matter "producing" the field and its distribution, and this is accidental and can only be defined empirically.

And so we have finally won the structural laws of the world, which at least in their general form are a priori.

With regard to the function of action, which is to a certain extent arbitrary, in choosing it we let ourselves be guided by the principle of simplicity. In other words, we choose the simplest possible function and compare the results gained through it with the experimental results. It is thus a matter of methodic necessity. We operate with a sort of serial development which conforms to the observed course of the world to the extent that observational exactness demands it. Such a development begins with the simplest members (of the lowest order) and then introduces members of a higher order to the extent necessary, in order to attain a suitable degree of approximation.[18]

18. This conception of the connection of a mathematical theory to the results of observations in physics stems from F. Klein (*Vor-*

It is here that the significance which *experience* possesses in relativity theory now manifests itself. It tells us how far we must go in the series of approximations. Perhaps it may also bear on the choice among several equally possible "functions of action." The displacement of the perihelion of Mercury, the deflection of light rays near the sun, etc., thus show that we get by with a definite simple function and an approximation of the second degree in the theory of gravitation (the theory of the affine context) for time. Circumstances permitting, this can be changed in the future, when we refine our means of observation.

The scope of the structural laws of the world now established with compelling necessity is extraordinarily large. It includes all externalizations of the gravitational and electromagnetic field in itself, in other words, all known exact (not statistical) laws of nature. For gravitation and electricity are the only original "powers of nature." And so it seems as if causality is banished from the world. Everything apparently is resolved in structural lawfulness and physics becomes four-dimensional geometry.[19]

But this would lead to untenable consequences for the essence of time. In the formulas which describe the affine-metrical world context (the gravi-electrical field), the space coordinates x, y, z and the time coordinate t are first of all in no way

lesungen über die Anwendung der Differential- und Integralrechnung auf Geometrie [Leipzig, 1902]), and has been further elaborated by H. Dingler (*Die Grundlagen der angewandten Geometrie* [Leipzig, 1911], and *Die Grundlagen der Physik* [Leipzig and Berlin, 1919]). Dingler characterizes this "method of exhaustion" of empirical observations as "synthesis." We agree with his general remarks on the idea of synthesis. He believes that an algorithm can be determined a priori for all of physics on the basis of "simplicity" and this algorithm would provide the basis for all laws of nature. He thus employs the criterion that a series is "simplest" where all of its members are simplest. We cannot accept this. We hold that serial development to be the "most transparent" (the "most rational") which provides a good approximation with the fewest possible members. Its individual members may indeed be fairly complicated. Accordingly, the choice of the series and the kind of "synthesis" is directed by the nature of the individual problem. There is no universal "synthetic primordial structure."

19. This viewpoint is in fact still presented by Weyl in the third edition of *Space-Time-Matter* (1920). In the fourth edition (pp. 237–38, 273–76, 279, 282–84), he modifies it in the mode of thought pursued by the text. On this, cf. the article "Feld und Materie," *Annalen der Physik*, LXV, 541 ff., also by Weyl.

distinguished in the four coordinates x_1, x_2, x_3, x_4, and second, the substitution of $-t$ for $+t$ in every instance yields a valid formula. This means that the peculiarity of time as compared to space and the unidirectionality (nonreversibility) of time is lost. This seems absurd. No matter how the "material" event may diverge from the phantom event, the fundamental character of time must be maintained.

In order to see this, we must once again return to the transition from the infinitesimal geometry of space to that of the four-dimensional space-time manifold. The level of constitution most important for us is the "directional bundle" of oriented space. On the one hand, the Euclidean phantom space is constituted from this bundle. On the other hand, this bundle emerges in the "material world of things" as a spatial element (the flat kind) from which the metric is developed by virtue of the metrical connection. With the introduction of time, this infinitesimal nature of our "basis for construction" in space necessarily entails the giving up of the contemporaneity of distant events, and we arrive at a concept of "local time." But time still does not become an infinitesimal element in the sense of a spatial linear element. It rather contains an unlimited extension into the past and future in its own purely temporal direction.

"I" with my body in space am extended only in a very restricted way, and in relation to the cosmos only infinitesimally. But I endure in time in an unlimited way (in principle). By virtue of the original time stream, "my" orientation in time changes continually and compellingly. A portion of time is never isolated in the same sense as a portion of space. There are always relations between the past and the present in which something identical persists temporally.

My "ego" with my body gives me the idea of a persisting (a "sub-stance") in time which can "act" from one point of space into space. According to this idea, we form the isolated systems of physics, the atoms, electrons, etc. These have their discreteness in space; they are individual in it. In time, they are enduring in a continuous way.

In the four-dimensional manifold, this is expressed in the fact that not "points" (spatial elements) but "world lines" are the genuine elements of reality. These are formations that are infinitely extended in one direction, the "temporal," but are infinitesimal in the other three dimensions, the spatial.

On the constitutional level of the "directional bundle," time loses its distinctive character even less in relation to the dimensions of space. Here also, time and space are the primary and secondary principles of individuation [20] and distinguished as such.

For the four-dimensional continuum, this means that a world line has a tangent at every point, and this specifies the "temporal" direction. The four coordinates can therefore no longer be arbitrarily interchanged. At every point of a world line, a definite "cleavage" of the world into time and space is prescribed.[21] This tangent as well as the world line possesses a definite direction: past to future. "I" live "along" a definite world line, the "now-point" is continually shifted on it: this is the symbol of the "original stream of time."

In a similar way the electron "endures" and now and then sends "actions" into the world, which are then distributed according to the laws of the gravi-electric field. Mie has proposed the theory that electrons, i.e., the ultimate component parts of matter, are a "miscarriage of the field." But he thereby succumbed to the understanding of the causal actions of electrons, e.g., as a light source. Light waves proceed from a (point) "source" and spread out in space, but there are no incoming waves, which might well be possible according to the field laws, which grant the conversion of time variables.

Thus, causality and "matter" once again come into their

20. More exactly, time and direction bundle. The elements of the secondary principle of individuation are the individual directions.

21. Moreover, in order to be able to even describe only the relative movement of parts in relation to each other, because of the general invariance of the equations of movement in the general R. T., it is not enough to put a "universal" coordinate system U which can be chosen arbitrarily into the world, but there must also be a "local" coordinate system K for every part at every moment of time, in which the part instantaneously rests. To put it more precisely, the transformation formula which permits the transition from U to K for every part at every moment of time must be given. (This is of course only possible with the "quasi-stationary acceleration" of the part, i.e., when its world line is determined geodetically through the control field.) This coordinate system K then gives the Euclidean form to the line element in the vicinity of the part, *it permits the "cleavage into time and space"*, and in it the electromagnetic field of the part has a certain "normal form." (Cf. Weyl, *Annalen der Physik*, LXV, 553, 561.)

own. The gravi-electric field is reduced to being the impotent mediator of actions, and its lawfulness is limited to the metrical structure of the world. Physics is once again confronted with the problem of finding the causal laws of nature, and this it has already begun in quantum theory.

And so the real "process of excitation" at the source of excitation (e.g., a light source) is causal and can no longer be described in the formulas of field laws. Since this excitation is always localized "in the electron," Weyl has taken the electron out of the field continuum. In other words, he conceives the world lines of electrons as channels which are bored out in the metrical continuum of the world. The "world" thus has "inner limits" beyond which matter exists and operates causally in the world. The world lines thus become topological structures.[22]

Therefore, to conclude our comments, we now can characterize the fundamental significance of the general R. T. so that it provides a radical solution to the metrical problem in its most universal form in conjunction with the phenomenological laws of essence. It gives us the decisively sharp separation of the structural and causal laws of the world and thus solves the problem posed by the application of a freely variable curved space. It therefore establishes the necessary methodic foundation of physics. Here is where its *fundamental* significance lies, independent of the empirical state of research at any given time.

And so we have phenomenologically investigated all known non-Euclidean forms of space and established their possibilities of application in physics. We have thus thrown light on the relation in which they stand to the Euclidean form in the constitutive build-up of nature. The first part of this work has shown the basic possibility of a rational treatment of space. Now this second part has given a complete overview of the formal organizations which govern the substantial essence of spatiality, arranging them within the great over-all system of nature and freeing them from all the contingency which at first adhered to them. But with that, the problem which we first posed, the overcoming of the contingency of the geometric axioms, is fundamentally solved.

(Conclusion of treatise)

22. Cf. on this "agent theory" of matter, Weyl, *ibid.*, pp. 541 ff.

Martin Heidegger

MARTIN HEIDEGGER, certainly the most influential philosopher in the existential phenomenological movement, was born in Messkirch in the Black Forest on September 26, 1889. After his secondary education he entered the University of Freiburg im Breisgau in 1909, where initially he studied theology and philosophy. Later he applied himself to the study of mathematics, physics, and history. Eventually he decided to devote his life to philosophy. He wrote his doctoral thesis (*Die Lehre vom Urteil im Psychologismus*, 1914) under A. Schneider; his *Habilitationsschrift* (*Die Kategorien- und Bedeutungslehre des Duns Scotus*, 1916) was written under the guidance of H. Rickert. From 1916 Heidegger studied under Husserl, becoming his assistant in 1920. Heidegger taught philosophy in Marburg from 1923 to 1928, and in Freiburg from 1928 until 1957.

Sein und Zeit, one of the most important works written by Heidegger, originated in Marburg between 1923 and 1927. In this work Heidegger carefully explains the sense in which he wishes to employ the phenomenological method. It becomes more than clear that he deviates from Husserl's original conception in many essential aspects.

As Heidegger sees it, phenomenology refers primarily to a maxim which can best be formulated in Husserl's words as "Back to the things themselves." This expression does not mean that one should return to naïve realism. It simply indicates that in philosophy one should renounce all free-floating constructions and accidental findings, all arbitrary ways of thinking and all prejudices, and be guided by the things themselves. Philosophy, however, does not intend to stop with the description of what manifests itself to us immediately. By means of what shows

[145]

itself immediately it seeks to penetrate to that which, though still hidden at first, constitutes the meaning and ground of what is immediately manifest; this is in the final analysis the Being of being (*Sein und Zeit*, p. 31). Later in reflecting on his own development Heidegger wrote as follows about his conception of phenomenology:

> As my familiarity with phenomenology grew, no longer merely through literature but by actual practice, the question about Being, aroused by Brentano's work, . . . remained always in view. So it was that doubt arose whether the "thing itself" was to be characterized as intentional consciousness, or even as the transcendental ego. If, indeed, phenomenology, as the process of letting things manifest themselves, should characterize the standard method of philosophy, and if from ancient times the guide-question of philosophy has perdured in the most diverse forms as the question about the Being of beings, then Being had to remain the first and last thing-itself of thought. Meanwhile "phenomenology" in Husserl's sense was elaborated into a distinctive philosophical position according to a pattern set by Descartes, Kant, and Fichte. The historicity of thought remained completely foreign to such a position. . . . The Being-question, unfolded in *Being and Time,* parted company with this philosophical position, and that on the basis of what to this day I still consider a more faithful adherence to the principle of phenomenology.*

Heidegger has never written a study completely dedicated to the problems usually dealt with in the philosophy of science. However, on many occasions he does bring up questions which modern science poses to man, particularly to that man who wishes to "think" the question concerning the meaning of Being. In Heidegger's view the main issue as far as modern science is concerned is to be found in its function within the totality of meaning which (partly manifesting and partly hiding itself) offers itself today to philosophical reflection. This means, on the one hand, that one understands what science is, how it objectifies being in thematizing it; this means, on the other hand, that one tries to lay bare the metaphysical presuppositions which underlie the current self-conception of modern science. These are the issues on which the essays which follow attempt to focus the reader's attention.

* William J. Richardson, *Heidegger: Through Phenomenology to Thought* (The Hague: Nijhoff, 1963), pp. xii-xiv.

7 / Heidegger on the Essential Difference and Necessary Relationship Between Philosophy and Science

Joseph J. Kockelmans

THE PREVAILING WORLD-VIEW of our contemporary Western civilization is largely controlled by the sciences. A philosophy which wishes to make the fundamental philosophical problems of the time its theme in a manner that appeals to modern man can hardly afford to ignore the phenomenon "science." This is why Heidegger deals repeatedly and extensively with the fundamental problems that the sciences present to philosophy.

The main problems he raises in regard to the sciences are well-known basic questions: what science is; how it is constituted; what is to be thought about its truth, certainty, and exactness; what relationship exists between science and technique; and, especially, what the relationship between philosophy and the nonphilosophical sciences should be. It is to Heidegger's view on these basic questions that this essay limits itself; more specific topics will be dealt with in the essays that follow.

According to Heidegger, science and philosophy are essentially different. One of the differences between these two forms of knowing can be found in the fact that sciences do not "think radically," while philosophy is characterized precisely by the radicalism of its thinking. This fundamental difference, which at the same time implies a profound divergence in method, creates an unbridgeable gap between philosophy and science. Any attempt to pass from the one form of knowing to the other encounters insurmountable difficulties, because no bridge over this abyss exists. Going from philosophy to science or vice versa can be accomplished only by a leap, an abrupt transition by a fundamental change of attitude.[1]

Although scientists generally interpret this view of Heidegger's as a disparaging one, this is in no way his intention. Philosophy does not intend to speak against science; on the contrary, it tries to act in favor of it by attempting to reach a degree of clarity in regard to its true nature that science itself is unable to attain. For science also has another characteristic which becomes immediately evident when one tries to understand what science is—it cannot turn toward the essence of its own field of study. For example, the historian who confines himself to a purely historical approach can never discover what "the historical" in itself is, just as a mathematician is unable to explain the essence of "the mathematical" with purely mathematical means. To science too, the essence of its object of study remains hidden. It is the task of philosophy to ask such questions and to seek for their solution. The fact that science itself is unable to deal with the essence of its own objects forces us to say that science cannot "think radically."

Here again philosophy seems to consider itself superior to science. We must take into account, however, that philosophy is well aware of the fact that it has not yet been successful in trying to discover and express the essence of the mathematical, the physical, and the historical. Strictly speaking, philosophy knows less in this regard than the sciences, which have lived up to their name by making genuine achievements within the limits imposed upon them by the methods they use.

Nevertheless, it remains true that the sciences are one-sided in the sense that, so long as they remain true to their own character, they are unable to reflect upon the essence of their own objects. The impressive results which the sciences have

1. Martin Heidegger, *Was heisst Denken?* (Tübingen: Niemeyer, 1954), pp. 4–5.

accomplished within their own domain have often caused scientists to overlook this one-sidedness. When the scientist begins his scientific investigations he always presupposes a certain realm of meaning which is "already there," whereas philosophy's major concern consists precisely in the radical questions immediately connected with the Total-Meaningfulness to which Heidegger usually refers with the term Being-itself.

A final characteristic of contemporary science can perhaps be seen in the fact that the sciences make things appear only in that kind of "objectivity" which is constituted and maintained by the various scientific objectivations. Philosophy, on the other hand, being primarily concerned with the "Whole," the totality of all possible meaning, or, as Heidegger says, with Being-itself, wishes to show how things come originally to light within the realm of that Total-Meaningfulness.[2]

These vague and as yet ambiguous assertions must be explained in more detail in what follows. There it will become clear from the very start that, as far as science is concerned, Heidegger is not so much interested in epistemological or methodological investigations as in ontological problems. That such a concern does not include any immediate criticism of other approaches to science is obvious, although it is true that this view implicitly claims that a philosophy of science without this basic dimension remains incomplete.

II

HEIDEGGER CLAIMS that traditional philosophy, questioning itself on its fundamental problems, has directed its attention too one-sidedly toward intramundane beings, that is, toward things. The thing itself, in its turn, has been considered too unilaterally in its appearance as the object of theoretical knowledge and of science, so that it becomes perfectly understandable that one may have come to confuse beings with the thing-objects, the "res." For the same reason, Being has received the signification of "reality." It is, furthermore, comprehensible that even the ontological understanding of man has moved into the horizon of this conception of thing and Being. Like all other

2. *Ibid.*, pp. 49, 56–58, 90, 155–56.

beings man is conceived here as present-at-hand and "real." It follows, finally, that in traditional philosophy the concept of "reality" has received priority over all other ontological concepts. Indeed, our view of the mode of being characteristic of man has gotten diverted, and metaphysics, in its problem of Being, has been forced into a direction which lies off the course, because it no longer takes its starting point from originally given data.

Moreover, in classical metaphysics, the question of Being was never formulated in a clear way, since various problems were clustered under the heading "problem of reality": for example, do the beings which supposedly transcend our consciousness really exist? Can we adequately prove the reality of the "external world"? To what extent can this being, insofar as it is real, be known in its being-in-itself? What is the profound meaning of this being called "reality"?

From the ontological point of view the last of these questions is undoubtedly the most important. However, since the ontological problem was never clearly formulated and the right methodology was lacking, this question was always associated and confounded with other questions, especially with the "problem of the external world." For the analysis and description of reality is possible only if man has an appropriate access to the real. But it has long been held that the way to understand reality is by that kind of knowledge which is called "theoretical and contemplative" knowledge and which takes place "in" consciousness. Now, insofar as reality has the character of something "independent" and of something "in itself," the question of the meaning of reality becomes linked, evidently, with the question of whether reality can be independent of consciousness, or whether consciousness is able to "transcend" itself into the sphere of the real. The possibility of an adequate ontological analysis of reality thus depends upon how far that which is supposed to transcend itself (namely, consciousness) has been clarified in its own Being. On closer investigation, however, we will realize that there are actually two problems to be considered before we will be able to pose and solve the question of the ultimate sense of reality, namely: (1) what is knowledge; and (2) is knowledge *the* privileged access to reality? [3]

3. Martin Heidegger, *Sein und Zeit* (Tübingen: Niemeyer, 1927), pp. 201–2.

Now, with regard to the problem of knowledge, traditional philosophy has always separated subject and object. It is not difficult to understand that whoever adopts such a point of view must sooner or later, in some way or other, examine the problem which was formulated clearly and in a critical way for the first time by Descartes. He who envisages a world independent of man necessarily throws man back upon himself. If one then speaks of knowledge of the world, he must interpret such knowledge as a special process taking place "within" consciousness. And the more unequivocally one maintains that knowledge is really "inside consciousness" and has by no means the same kind of Being as the intramundane beings, the more reasonable and urgent the question concerning the clarification of the relationship between subject and object appears to be. For only then can the problems arise as to how this knowing subject is able to come out of its inner sphere and go into another which is "external," and how one must think of the object itself so that the subject is able to know it without having to venture a leap into that other sphere. But in all of the numerous varieties which this approach has taken, the question concerning the Being proper to the knowing subject has been left entirely unasked. Of course we are assured that we are certainly not to think of the subject's inner sphere as a sort of "box." But when one asks for the positive signification of this "inside" of consciousness in which human knowledge is proximally enclosed, then one vainly waits for an answer.[4]

On the other hand, if one interprets knowledge as a manner of Being-in-the-world, then it will be immediately clear that it does not make sense to conceive of knowledge as a process by means of which the "subject" creates for and "in" himself "representations" of something that is "outside," representations which somehow are to be preserved "inside" the knowing subject. For the same reason it is evident that it does not make sense to ask the question of how those "representations" could harmonize with "reality." Thus the questions of whether there is a world at all, and whether its Being can be proved, make no sense if they are raised by man as Being-in-the-world. In his *Refutation of Idealism*, Kant shows clearly the confusion between that which one wants to prove, and that with which one carries out the

4. *Ibid.*, pp. 59–61.

proof, and the means whereby the proof is materialized. Among other things Kant affirms that it is a scandal for philosophy that there is still no conclusive proof for the real existence of things outside of us. According to Heidegger the "scandal of philosophy" is not that this proof has yet to be given but that such proofs are expected and attempted time and again. In all the efforts undertaken up to the present, Heidegger denounces as the principal fault the fact that the starting point is always taken in a subject which is at first worldless or at least unsure of its world and which thus must, at bottom, first assure itself of a world. Being-in-the-world becomes, therefore, something which rests on a preconception, on arguments, on a belief, whereas all knowledge is a mode of man's Being founded in his Being-in-the-world. The problem of reality in the sense of whether an external world really exists and whether such a world can be proved turns out to be an impossible question, not because its consequences lead to inextricable impasses but because the very being which asks the question a priori excludes any such formulation of the problem. Our task, therefore, is not to prove that an "external world" really exists, or to show how it exists, but to point out why man, as Being-in-the-world, has the "innate" tendency to bury the "external world" in nullity epistemologically before going to prove it.[5]

In this perspective it will be understandable why contemporary phenomenology has ceased to conceive of man as pure consciousness. From his very beginning man is essentially oriented towards the world. All the manifestations of his Being are, by that very fact, manners of being actively correlated with the world. At its very origin and in its intimate essence man's subjectivity is intentional and necessarily transcends itself. It is by his familiarity with the world that man is familiar with himself. His Being is Being-towards-the-world. He ek-sists, and as such he is open towards the world. Human subjectivity is not an ego wrapped up in itself. On the contrary, from the beginning it manifests itself as a Being-with, a Being-open-to. For this reason Merleau-Ponty, for instance, calls this primordial fact of existential phenomenology "presence." Others will speak of "encounter" and of "dialogue." All of these expressions, as well as

5. *Ibid.*, pp. 202–7.

Heidegger's term "There-Being," are meant to show that man is not a monad locked up in itself but that he originally is Being-in-the-world and Being-towards-the-world. It is in and through his dialogue with the beings in the world that man lets those beings be what they are, uncovers them, brings their meaning to light. The Being of man is therefore a being-aware of his Being-in-the-world; man becomes present to himself only by his Being-towards-the-world.

Originally man is therefore nothing but a project of the world. There is nothing in man which escapes this Being-towards-the-world. No matter how deeply one penetrates man's subjectivity, one always finds the world there. In every modality of his concrete life man is always an intention who projects himself towards the world, and his ek-sistence as a whole is bound up in his life in and towards the world. We find many modalities in our Being, but all of them are only so many modes of our belonging to the world. Our relation with the world, originally and primordially seen, does not consist in a relation of knowledge, that is to say, a relation which is constituted by and perseverated in theoretical knowledge; on the contrary, this relation totally penetrates our very Being in all its layers and ramifications. Theoretical knowledge and science, therefore, are only modes of man's Being-in-the-world, in which man materializes his Being-towards-the-world.

The first question one must pose then is this: are these modes of Being-in-the-world fundamental, or are they only derivative and founded modes of our Being-in-the-world? Heidegger's opinion is that our Being-in-the-world originally takes the form of a concernful preoccupation with intramundane beings. From the historical and genetic point of view this position is easily substantiated. For man does not rise to speculation or attain to science except by taking his starting point in his concernful preoccupation with intramundane beings, in his "practical" activities, and, thus, in his very life, which completely engages him with those beings. At first the Being of man is a Being-already-alongside-the-world, and this is not just a fixed staring at something that is merely present-at-hand. Originally Being-in-the-world is concern, and as concern it is fascinated by the world with which it is concerned. We come to a contemplative type of knowledge and to "theory" only when we hold ourselves back from any manipulation or utilization, from our work, our "fabrications," our "doing," and in a word from our life in and with the intramundane beings.[6]

But how does this primordial concernful preoccupation change over to a theoretical exploration? In view of the foregoing one might say that "merely looking at beings" is something which emerges from the simple fact that one holds back from any kind of manipulation. What is decisive in the emergence of the theoretical attitude would then consist in the disappearance of the praxis. So if one posits "practical" concern as the primary mode of Being which man factically possesses, the ontological possibility of "theory" would be due to the absence of praxis, and thus to a privation. It is evident that this way of looking at the problem is erroneous. For all praxis and all "practical" dealings have their own ways of tarrying. And just as praxis has its own specific kind of tarrying and circumspection, theoretical research is not without a praxis of its own. We have only to think here of the "praxis" and technique implied in the usage of the complicated instruments of contemporary scientific investigation. Consequently, if we are to explain the existential genesis of science, we must first try to compare the "seeing" proper to our daily concern with the way of "seeing" characteristic for science, and in so doing we must set out by characterizing first the *circumspection* which is the guide for our practical concern.

The circumspection proper to our daily concern as regards intramundane beings first of all implies a certain survey of the totality of the current equipment world and of the "public" environment (*Umwelt*) which belongs to it. What is essential to this survey is that one should have a primary understanding of the totality of involvements within which concern always has its start. Circumspection furthermore implies a certain kind of deliberation. The scheme peculiar to this is the "if-then"; if this or that is to be produced, put to use, or averted, then some ways and means, circumstances, or opportunities will be needed. Circumspection finally presupposes a certain understanding in which that which is considered with an "if" is understood *as* this or that. Thus for every mode of circumspection a certain manner of "seeing" is necessarily characteristic. Now it is precisely this manner of "seeing" which in our theoretical attitude must

6. *Ibid.*, p. 61.

change. Let us try to analyze this change by taking a simple example as a guiding clue.

When we are using a hammer circumspectively, we can say, for instance, that the hammer is too heavy for the work that is to be done. The proposition "this hammer is too heavy" can give expression to our concernful deliberation and signify that this hammer is not an easy one to use in these concrete circumstances. But this proposition could mean also that this being which we already know circumspectively as a hammer has weight, has the property of "heaviness": it exerts a pressure on what lies beneath it, and it falls if this is removed. This way of speaking does not belong to the "language" of our everyday concern, because in it there is seen something which is suitable for the hammer, not just as a tool, but as a corporeal thing subject to the law of gravitation. Why does the hammer show itself differently when our way of talking is thus modified? Not because we are keeping our distance from practical manipulation, not because we are just looking *away from* the equipmental character of this being, but rather because we are looking *at* the thing which is ready-to-hand *in a new way*, as something that is now only present-at-hand. But this is not all. For in the "physical" assertion that "the hammer is heavy," we overlook not only the tool-character of the being we encounter but also something which belongs to any equipment which is ready-to-hand, namely, its place. Its place becomes now a matter of indifference. This does not mean that what is present-at-hand loses its "location" altogether. But its place becomes a spatio-temporal position, a "world-point," which is in no way distinguished from any other. This implies not only that the multiplicity of places of equipment which is ready-to-hand within the confines of the environment becomes modified to a pure multiplicity of positions, but that the beings of the environment are altogether released from such confinement (*entschränkt*). In this way the aggregate of the present-at-hand becomes the theme of theoretical investigation.[7]

The way of "seeing" which is characteristic of the theoretical attitude, therefore, always implies a certain "view" and a new position towards the intramundane beings which now manifest themselves as being no longer ready-to-hand, but only present-

7. *Ibid.*, pp. 357–61.

at-hand. This typical "perception" of the present-at-hand takes place when one addresses oneself to something *as* something and discusses it as such. This amounts to a certain interpretation, and on the basis of such interpretation the theoretical perception becomes an act of determination. What is thus perceived, interpreted, and determined can be expressed in propositions and can be retained and preserved as what has thus been asserted. This perceptive retention of such an assertion about something is itself a way of Being-in-the-world, and it is not to be interpreted as a procedure by which a subject provides itself with representations of something which then remain stored up inside and with regard to which the question of how they agree with reality can occasionally arise.

When man directs himself towards something and grasps it theoretically, he does not somehow first go out of an inner sphere in which he has been encapsulated, but his primary way of Being is already such that he is always "outside" alongside beings which he encounters and which belong to a world which always has already been discovered. Nor is any inner sphere somehow abandoned when man dwells alongside the being to be known and tries to determine its character. And furthermore, the theoretical perceiving of what is known is not a process of returning with one's booty to the "box" of consciousness after one has gone out in order to grasp it; even in perceiving, retaining, and preserving, man, who knows, remains outside.

Be this as it may, it seems to be clear that in theoretical knowledge man achieves a new ontological status towards the world which has already been discovered in his original praxis. This new ontological possibility can develop autonomously. It can become a task to be accomplished, and as scientific knowledge it can even take over the guidance for our Being-in-the-world. But the "commercium" of that subject with the world does not get created for the first time by theoretical knowledge, nor does it arise from some way in which the world acts upon a "subject." Theoretical knowledge is a mode of man's Being founded upon his Being-in-the-world itself.[8]

Theoretical knowledge thus is only a special mode of our Being-in-the-world. The characteristic proper to this mode of Being-in-the-world is that man confines himself to observing the

8. *Ibid.*, pp. 61–62.

world in such a way that he is no longer completely engaged in it. In this "contemplation" there is already a certain stance of man regarding intramundane beings; and correlatively the intramundane beings which are encountered in this way are always considered from a certain point of view. The aspect of the intramundane beings which uncovers itself to man in his theoretical attitude depends upon the original attitude of man towards those beings. As soon as man in his theoretical knowledge takes such an aspect as an object of his critical and methodological investigation, he lays the foundation of a determinate science.

Every scientist, in his theoretical attitude towards the world, begins to delineate a certain region of intramundane beings as his proper object of investigation and research. The delineation of a well-defined domain of investigation is the beginning of all scientific research. This delimitation of a definite region of beings is effected through a thematization which takes, in a primordial way, a certain aspect of those beings as its theme of investigation, and as such constitutes and projects it. It is by such a project (*Entwurf*) that the access to the proper domain of a science acquires its methodological guidelines, that the structure of the conceptual and discursive explanation acquires its first orientation, and that, finally, a proper language is progressively constituted. Thematization, therefore, comprises the original project of the object of investigation as such, the delimitation of the domain of research, the determination of the methods to be used, the first orientation of the conceptual and discursive structure, and the linguistic means of expression.[9] Let us now try to explain this briefly by taking Heidegger's *Being and Time* as our starting point and attempting to elaborate this view with the help of a short commentary.

According to Heidegger, the classical example for the historical development of a science and even, as we shall see, for its ontological genesis is the rise of mathematical physics. What is decisive for its development consists neither in its high esteem for the observation of "facts" nor in its application of mathematics in determining the character of the natural processes and events; it consists in the manner in which nature itself is *mathematically projected*. In this projection something which is constantly present-at-hand, namely, matter, is discovered in ad-

9. *Ibid.*, pp. 363–64.

vance in such a way that a certain horizon is opened in which only what is somehow quantitatively determinable is further relevant (for instance, motion, force, location, time, and so on). Only in the light of a nature which has been projected in this way can anything like a "fact" be found and set up for an experiment which will be regulated in terms of this projection. The foundation of factual science was possible only because the early scientists understood that in principle there are no "bare facts."

In the mathematical projection of nature, moreover, what is decisive is not primarily the mathematical as such but the fact that such projection discloses a certain a priori. Therefore the paradigmatic character of mathematical physics does not consist in its exactness or in the fact that it is intersubjectively valid and binding for everyone; it consists rather in the fact that the beings which it takes as its theme are discovered consistently in harmony with the prior projection of their Being-structure. When the basic concepts of this way of understanding Being have been worked out in detail, the clues of its methods, the structure of its way of conceiving things, the possibility of truth and certainty which belongs to it, the way in which things get founded and proved, the mode in which it is binding for everyone, and the way in which it is communicated—all of these are determined. It is precisely the totality of all these items which constitutes the full existential meaning of science.

The scientific projection of beings which we have already encountered in our circumspective concern lets their mode of Being be explicitly understood in such a manner that it becomes manifest which ways are possible for the pure discovery of intramundane beings. The articulation of our understanding of this mode of Being, the delimitation of a region as subject matter guided by this understanding, and the delineation of the way of conceiving which is appropriate to those beings—all of these belong to the totality of this projecting; it is this totality which we call *thematization*. Its aim is to free the beings we encounter within the world and to free them in such a way that they can throw themselves against (*entgegenwerfen-objicere*) a purely theoretical discovering, that is to say, in such a way that they can become objects. Thematizing objectifies. It does not first "posit" the beings, but it frees them so that we can interrogate them and determine their character. Thus far this is Heidegger's contention.[10] Let us now try to explain this view with the help of a brief commentary.

Whoever applies himself to the natural sciences—to remain within the same example—begins first by adopting a *theoretical attitude.* He disengages himself from his primordial orientation towards the world in which he lived before he had applied himself to science, from the equipmental and surrounding world of everyday concern in which previously he had been totally engaged. But now he wants to "observe" and to "contemplate." Correlative to the assumption of this new attitude toward the world, the world itself in which he has been living changes into an "objective world." Science can, therefore, still be defined as a "theory of the real," but only if one clearly and rightly understands the terms "theory" and "real."

The term "real" in this context signifies everything which makes something to be, which constitutes it; but it means also that which has been constituted and is now present. In both cases the term "real" expresses what that which it indicates has as a proper characteristic, that it accedes to full light, that it abides there, and that it "is." It is essential to all to which man gives birth that it reveal and that it remain in full light. It is characteristic of contemporary science, then, that it brings intramundane beings to light in such a way that "reality" appears as "objectivity": for contemporary science reality is identical with being-object-for. In Greek philosophy the word "theory" put the stress at first on the passive element in the contemplative gaze of man's dealing with intramundane beings in a theoretical way. Nowadays one insists that the active element be involved in this procedure. Whoever considers something in a theoretical way begins by "elaborating" that which he will later contemplate: by that very fact he isolates the object which is to be contemplated from anything else by constituting it in a state of objectivity.[11]

This is why one could affirm with De Waelhens that the natural sciences, as well as every other empirical science, are essentially a theory of the "objective" dimension of reality which, primarily and in the true sense of the term, *is* encounter (in the sense previously indicated). Both science *and* philosophy are a true explanation of reality. The difference resides in the fact that

10. *Ibid.*, pp. 362–63.
11. Martin Heidegger, *Vorträge und Aufsätze* (Pfullingen: Neske, 1954), pp. 46–59. (Hereafter cited as VA.)

each places itself at a different level of explanation and speaks of reality on different levels. Science disregards the intentional movement which directs us toward things; it takes its objects as simply given and does not know that they reveal themselves originally in encounter and coexistence. Philosophy, on the other hand, seeks to describe the innumerable modalities of encounter and coexistence in their noematic and noetic aspects. But if reality is ultimately coexistence of myself with the world, and therefore orientation of the world towards me, and, on the other hand, openness of myself towards the world, within which meaning is constituted in its proper fashion through a great number of modalities, then science, insofar as it is a true explication of reality in the realm of the natural attitude, is nothing else but the theory of the "objective" side of reality.[12]

The following step to be taken consists in what we called the thematization by means of which a certain aspect of intramundane things, or a certain group of them, is taken as the theme of investigation, and as such is constituted and projected. Such a thematization requires first the *demarcation of the region* of intramundane beings which are supposed to be the subject matter of the science in question and then the determination of the *formal aspect* under which they are to be investigated. This thematization must go hand in hand with formalization, functionalization, and quantification.[13]

By *formalization* we mean here the descriptions of beings or events in regard to their formal properties; formalization necessarily implies a certain "abstraction" of some "material" or "contentlike" moments in preference to a group of formal characteristics. By *functionalization* we mean the consideration of formalized phenomena in function of other formalized phenomena according to the general scheme "if p then q," a scheme which is already employed in the realm of our everyday concern in a nonformalized manner.[14] Formalization and functionalization give the scientist the possibility of describing phenomena with the help of rules and laws within the general perspective of the scheme "if . . . then." It is evident that the accuracy of our

12. Alphonse De Waelhens, *Existence et signification* (Louvain: Nauwelaerts, 1958), pp. 107–9.
13. Jan Linschoten, *Idolen van de psycholog* (Utrecht: Bijleveld, 1964), pp. 24–27.
14. Heidegger, *Sein und Zeit*, pp. 359–60.

knowledge of the phenomena in question will depend on the precision with which their conditions are known. The degree of exactness attainable in every empirical science is determined by the subject matter and the thematizing project, that is to say, by the type of formalization which this subject matter allows and permits within the realm of a determinate thematizing project. *Quantification,* the means by which these conditions are described with the help of numbers, is only a special mode of formalizing functionalization. Such quantification permits a very high degree of exactness and, within certain limits imposed by the character of the subject matter and the thematizing project in question, is possible in all empirical science in an *analogous* way. It is evident, too, that in this way the original phenomena will be reduced to a so-called *reductive model,* which is more or less abstract in comparison with the originally given phenomena.

The scientific attitude is thus rooted in a certain thematization. This thematization leaves many possibilities open to the theoretician. Both the region of intramundane things which is supposed to be the subject matter of a certain science and the formal aspect which will be envisaged depend on the proper character of the thematizing project. But however this thematization may be factually, everyone who dedicates himself to an empirical science wants to question a certain region of intramundane things under a determinate *comparable* aspect within the general perspective prescribed by the abstract scheme "if . . . then." By this decision he thematizes these beings in such a way and constitutes them as objects in such a manner that they can no longer be interrogated except in the manner which is already determined in principle by that thematizing project.

Thus, by not wanting to interrogate intramundane beings except under their comparable and even *measurable* aspects, the scientist projects a domain of meaning (*Sinnfeld*) within which only beings of a well-defined kind, that is to say, beings which have either *countable* or *measurable* aspects, can figure. "To be countable" and "to be measurable" are the formal aspects of all intramundane beings insofar as they are the object of the attitude toward the world proper to empirical science. These characteristics of being countable and measurable, however, are not "objective" properties of "objective" things which as such must exist independently of the counting and measuring man in the world "in itself," for there is not such a world. They are but "invitations" which are addressed to man, modalities in which man can encounter those beings. Now, the intramundane beings *insofar as* they are immediately or mediately countable and measurable constitute for empirical science the region of scientific investigation. If the scientist holds himself strictly to the necessary demands of considering these beings and their events only and exclusively in the light of this fundamental conception, his demonstrations will possess a solid form and will attain the exactness so characteristic of empirical science.

The original project in this way determines the orientation which research must take in reference to the question of the concrete methods to be used, that is to say, in reference to the formalization and functionalization to be employed. For, if the entire region has to become objective, then the scientist must try to encounter this domain in all its aspects. But the domain of mundane things is constantly changing. The scientist, therefore, must keep abreast of this change and development and never lose sight of it. For it is only in the perspective of the continuous becoming of the changeable things that the plenitude of their facticity becomes manifest. But this means that facts are intelligible only in the perspective of regularity and law; in other words the scientific description of "facts" necessarily implies the formulation and the verification of *laws*.[15]

But neither the laws, nor the experiences founding them, furnish a scientific explanation of those facts. Scientific explanation requires in addition that the necessary relations between facts and laws be made evident. This is done by means of *theories* in which mathematics plays an important role. For since the facts—because of the quantification necessarily implied in the formalizing functionalization—can speak only by means of measuring instruments, and the laws thus can furnish only relations between numbers yielded by those measuring instruments, it is mathematics alone which in virtue of this original attitude of empirical science towards intramundane beings can give access to the comprehension of the objects thus constituted. The mathematical procedure, in its turn, must take its starting point from experiences and laws in order to return

15. Martin Heidegger, *Holzwege* (Frankfurt a.M.: Klostermann, 1950), pp. 71–76. (Hereafter cited as *HW*.)

ultimately to other experiences or experiments which either confirm or invalidate the ultimate findings. Experiences, experiments, and mathematical procedures are therefore essential to the methods of all empirical sciences.

We may say, therefore, that man in interrogating intramundane beings always assumes a well-determined attitude which is completely different from that of his spontaneous life. But already, in the original contact between man and the different intramundane beings, these beings impose themselves on man as beings which possess "quantitative" aspects of some kind. This fact of being "quantitative" in its different modalities invites man to *compare*. In the horizon of formalizing functionalization the comparison immediately becomes *counting* and *measuring* as soon as man ties this comparison to certain norms by means of counting and measuring procedures. Counting and measuring, which are but special forms of questioning the world, provide us with *numbers* which again invite man to compare. This comparison leads to *laws* which are mathematical relations between numbers yielded by counting and measuring. A great number of laws invite man to order them with the help of mathematics. In this way *theories* are formed which can be controlled by checking their validity with respect to the "facts" in question, by having recourse to representations or *models* of an order other than that of pure mathematics. But in this procedure as a whole, it is man who, interrogating the intramundane beings, looks for relations and establishes them wherever these beings invite him to discover them. For this reason numbers, laws, and theories do not furnish an "objective" description of "objective" qualities of an "objective" world in itself; for numbers, laws, and theories do not arise except in and thanks to the fact that the scientist is intentionally "involved" in the world. This is also the reason why the results of measurements, laws, and theories are valid only within the realm of the domain of meaning constituted by this typical mode of intentionality which fundamentally constitutes the different empirical sciences.

It becomes evident that this method also imposes on the empirical sciences the necessity of an appropriate *language* and symbolism without which the objects which are to be investigated cannot be represented in their proper physiognomy. In the last analysis, however, all of this is already determined by the original thematizing project, as was pointed out previously.

Similarly, the idea of *truth* is already determined in its very roots by the original thematization. Existential phenomenology situates the truth of science neither in an internal relation between a series of concepts and statements, nor in a faithful reflection of a pregiven order of "facts" belonging to a world "in itself"; nor is truth to be described as an agreement between knowledge and reality, with "reality" understood as something which is "in itself." An assertion of empirical science is true as long as the scientist interrogates the intramundane beings in the way in which these beings, within the framework of the typical intentional mode in question, are to be interrogated. As long as the intramundane beings continue to give meaningful answers to the questions which the scientist poses to them, the questions and answers of science remain genuine. An assertion of science is therefore true as long as an experience or an experiment confirms its presumptions which are finally based on a certain theory. All subsequent experiences or experiments may confirm this truth, but they may also demonstrate in a convincing way that intramundane beings are alien to such an interrogation.

In the constraining character of the answers furnished by the intramundane beings existential phenomenology also sees one of the essential arguments in favor of the *certitude* and the *exactness* so typical of the empirical sciences. For the rest this exactitude seems to be the necessary consequence of the schematization and idealizing abstraction proper to the formalizing functionalization as practiced in the empirical sciences, which, in turn, renders possible the employment of mathematics, the exact science par excellence, for a further consideration of the objects of investigations thus constituted. It is evidently presupposed here that in all of these operations the scientist remains within the horizon of the domain of meaning which is constituted by the original thematizing project.

III

At the beginning of this essay we considered the question of whether science is "objective." Let us now in conclusion attempt to answer this question briefly in the light of the preceding explanation taken from existential phenomenology.

Without a doubt it is necessary to state our answer in the

affirmative: science is objective. But in the perspective explained, the term "objective" does not mean that science exactly and precisely attains the real, just as it exists "on and in itself" independent of our knowledge of it, for it is impossible to speak of such a reality unless, in and through science, it appears to us. In science one only speaks of the "real" insofar as it manifests itself to man in function of the original thematization within the domain of meaning proper to the science in question.

And yet science is objective because it keeps to the "facts," because it abstains from all "subjective" prejudices, and because it does not appeal to any uncontrollable a priori. It is objective also insofar as its statements adhere to the demands of the methods determined by the thematization in question.

From this account it follows, too, that the term "objective," taken concretely, has a significance which is proper and characteristic for each individual science. Certainly every science is, in principle at least, "objective," every science is a true theory of the real, but the term "real" has its own particular signification for each science. Each science endeavors to bring to light, faithfully and objectively, an isolated and well-defined aspect of intramundane beings.

It is, therefore, not without importance to remark explicitly that in the foregoing section the existential-phenomenological view on science was illustrated and explained with the help of terms and expressions customarily associated with those sciences which have enjoyed a relatively high degree of perfection for quite some time, namely, the empirical sciences of nature. What was said, however, holds true in an analogous way for all empirical science. For every science the terms "theory" and "objectivity" have their own specific significations. Each science projects its scientific "world," its domain of meaning, in its own way. All of these "worlds" constituted by different thematizations are different, but one is not more true than the others, at least in principle. But although they are different from one another, there is a bond which unites them. This bond is not to be conceived of as the kind which exists, for instance, between the pieces of a puzzle, as if the reassembly of such "worlds" would yield the total and "real" world. The bond among these "worlds" consists in the fact that all of them have been born from the world immediately lived by the community of man.

It becomes evident from this consideration that even though

these "worlds" are relatively independent of one another, it is very difficult and sometimes even impossible to demarcate clearly the frontier between adjacent sciences such as physics and chemistry, biochemistry and biology, physiology and psychology, psychology and sociology, and so on. Although no one wishes to completely identify these adjacent sciences, all scientists know and admit that the domains of investigation overlap; this is attributable to the fact that in each instance the domains of meaning are constituted with the help of an analogously identical method and share in an analogously identical objectivity.

Obviously we have not been able to do justice to Heidegger's views here; but these introductory reflections may serve to set the scene for the ideas which will be developed in the two essays which follow.

8 / Science, Phenomenology, and the Thinking of Being

Theodore J. Kisiel

IN HIS INTRODUCTION to *Formal and Transcendental Logic* (1929), Husserl highlights the phenomenological reflection on the fundamental concepts of the sciences under the leitmotiv of *Besinnung*. Translated by Suzanne Bachelard as *prise de conscience,* this act of deliberately taking thought in order to reflect on one's most anonymous presuppositions is the remedy that Husserl prescribes for the cultural sickness which he diagnoses under the syndrome of the "crisis of the European sciences." It is therefore striking that Heidegger entitles one of his later reflections on science *Wissenschaft und Besinnung,* delivered in Munich in 1953 as part of a series of lectures under the general title "The Arts in the Age of Technology." [1] Its manifest parallels to Husserl permit us to gauge the distance traveled by Heidegger in his journey "through phenomenology to thought," particularly in relation to science. In fact, the explicit theme of *Besinnung* had emerged on occasion in some of Heidegger's lectures several years after *Being and Time* (1927), generally in the context of the relations between philosophy and science. But with the lecture cited above, it moves into the center by being drawn into the arena of *Seinsdenken.* In his 1955 address to a hometown crowd at Messkirch, some of its more idiomatic overtones come to the fore, such as "coming to one's

1. In VA, pp. 45–70. The Munich lecture series included a talk by Werner Heisenberg on "The Picture of Nature in Contemporary Physics," the salient point of which will emerge in our discussion. A translation of this lecture is to be found in Werner Heisenberg, *The Physicist's Conception of Nature* (New York: Harcourt, Brace, 1958).

senses" and "keeping one's wits" in an attitude of soberness and composure (*Gelassenheit*) in order to "make sense of one's situation," and once again the issue is coming to terms with the scientific and technological age in which we find ourselves. Here, making sense of our situation is more a matter of a "homecoming" than the "coming to oneself" which Husserl stressed. But common to both is the movement of return whose purpose is to reactivate the sedimented and forgotten senses which found science and locate it in human existence. Other facets of Heidegger's debt to Husserl will at least be suggested in what follows.

The Husserlian approach to science is strikingly evident in the early pages of *Being and Time*. In terms characteristic of the *Logical Investigations*, science is tentatively described as "the coherent totality of proofs which ground true propositions." [2] The issue of the ontological priority of the question of Being (section 3) refers to the regional ontologies which underlie the empirical or "ontic" sciences. Like Husserl, Heidegger complains of the anemic "philosophies" of science which merely investigate a science as they find it in order to expose its "method" and to establish its logic ex post facto. The current crises of foundations in so many sciences demand not an a posteriori elaboration of concept formation but a research that runs ahead and exposes the structures of the domain of a science, thereby arriving at an interpretation which can suggest possibilities and directions to the factual sciences. That this can be done is shown by the work of Plato, Aristotle, and more recently Kant, whose transcendental logic is really an a priori logic of nature. What physics now needs is a new *Timaeus* which explores the a priori structure of the material world. And biology is beginning to look beyond the vitalism inherited from the *De Anima* and the mechanism inherited from modern physics in order to expose the kind of Being which belongs to the living being as such. Works like Whitehead's *Process and Reality* are a step in the direction of the kind of regional ontology required. But Heidegger's point here is that such speculative cosmologies which interpret the Being of a certain domain are themselves preempted by the need to study the sense of Being as such. Even that phase of the Husserlian program that calls for the "nondeductive genealogy" of the sci-

2. ". . . das Ganze eines Begründungszusammenhanges wahrer Sätze" (*Sein und Zeit* [Tübingen: Niemeyer, 1927], p. 11).

ences and their domains demands the more fundamental eluci- dation of the meaning of Being as Being.

Heidegger had other occasions to refer to the problem of the determination of the domains of science, but now he does so in order to stress the extrascientific character of such considera- tions even more explicitly. Biology, for example, already presup- poses a certain range of appearances, that of the living, which is to constitute its domain of objects. The scope and limits of its field are thus a preconception. This is true of every science. The field in which a science moves is never grounded by that science, but is only taken up and confirmed by it. Every science rests on positions with regard to its domain of beings which are in fact metaphysical positions, which cannot be proven or even suitably thought by scientific concepts and scientific method. What a living thing is cannot be decided by biology as biology. When a biologist does venture to address this matter, he speaks no longer as a biologist but as a metaphysician. Such a metaphysical delib- eration (*Besinnung*) on the essence of its domain is necessary if his science is to be genuine knowledge. The technical domina- tion of his domain, the capacity to control and predict results is a laudable achievement, but technique is not understanding. In spite of these advances, the essences of matter, of life, of ani- mality remain indefinite and obscure within the sciences until the transition is made from scientific considerations to meta- physical deliberation. To avoid confusion, a scientist must recog- nize that an essentially different kind of thinking is needed in the self-reflection on his science, that in fact a leap must be made and not simply a broadening and universalization of the ways of thought which he uses in his research work. This re- quirement signifies not an attempt on the part of philosophy to regulate the sciences but a recognition of a higher form of knowledge hidden *in* every science, upon which the value of that science rests. In fact, scientific research and metaphysical delib- eration are united at a more fundamental level. Historically both are founded on a definite interpretation of Being and move within the aura of a definite conception of the essence of truth. It is on this basis that certain metaphysical decisions have al- ready been made or are being prepared for the fundamental concepts of science. Biological concepts already include meta- physical decisions, manifest in the history of such fundamental words as *physis* and *bios*. Even the idea of a scientifically founded world-view, which confuses the relations between science and metaphysics, emerges from the hidden wellsprings that belong to the metaphysical essence of the modern age.[3]

The extrascientific character of the reflection on the sciences as sciences, and not simply on their domains, should be even more evident. And yet it is commonly believed that someone competent in things biological is *ipso facto* capable of discoursing about his science as a science. But physics itself is not a possible object of a physical experiment, and biology as a science cannot be examined under the microscope as if it were a biological object. It is possible to speak biologically about fish and frogs, bees and beets, but one cannot approach biology in a biological way. Physics as such cannot make any statements about physics. In order to reflect on any science, it is necessary to transcend that science and adopt a transcendental vantage point, to put it in Kantian terms. In fact, sciences are free historical actions of man which evoke such a transcendental deliberation on a continual basis.[4]

Even though it is not possible to think scientifically about science, the scientist as a thinking being can certainly deliberate metaphysically on the fundamental concepts of his science. There are different levels of deliberation, not the least of which is the one in which the scientist himself thinks into the essence of his own science.[5] Einstein, Bohr, and Heisenberg, in the revolutionary changes which they introduced, have been led to certain metaphysical decisions with regard to the fundamental concepts and principles of modern physics. Rather than simply thinking within physics, they have thought into physics, discerning new directions for it, "creating new ways of posing questions and above all holding out into that which is most worthy of questioning." [6] And deliberation at its highest is "composure toward that which is most worthy of questioning." [7]

But the deliberation on the fundamental concepts of a partic-

3. *Nietzsche* (Pfullingen: Neske, 1960), I, 520–25.
4. *Die Frage nach dem Ding* (Tübingen: Niemeyer, 1962), pp. 138–40. (Hereafter cited as *FD*.) English translation by W. B. Barton, Jr., and Vera Deutsch, *What Is a Thing?* (Chicago: Regnery, 1967), pp. 177–79. Cf. also *VA*, p. 65.
5. *VA*, p. 70.
6. *FD*, p. 51. (Eng. trans., p. 67.)
7. *VA*, p. 68.

ular science is not yet this highest possibility, which is on the trail of the questionworthy as such in its presence in the very essence of science. But it is present in the sciences as an "unpretentious state of affairs" which is passed over by them and is in fact inaccessible to them. This latent content which lies at the heart of the matter of science as such is the subject matter of that deliberation which in other contexts Heidegger calls *Seins-denken*. Over and above the foundational crises of the individual sciences is the crisis of science as such, as the present fate of Western man, and it is to this larger issue that deliberation must now respond. Despite all the efforts to demarcate the essence of science which are so fundamentally characteristic of the modern age, the profound state of affairs involved here continues to remain unnoticed. For example, the customary view that considers science as a cultural product of the spiritual and creative activity of men obscures these more profound dimensions that belong to the essence of science. For one thing, science is one of those decisive ways in which we comprehend all that is. For another, the progressively increasing domination which it exercises over modern times manifests how much it operates at a level beyond human control. There is a more profound destiny hidden in science than what can be accounted for by considering science as something man-made, simply a fruit of his curiosity or desire to know.[8]

The essence of science is inextricably intertwined with the essence of modern times, which for Heidegger involves at once the essence of metaphysics and that of technology. However formidable these matters may seem to be, the deliberation on them, far from being an abstract thinking or a high-flown speculation, is actually a "grass-roots" reflection on our own age and its hidden direction. For a thoughtful reflection on the implications of science calls for a return to the very sources of the situation in which we find ourselves. It is in this sense a thinking fully rooted in the earth, an indigenous and autochthonous thinking. It seeks to sense what is incipiently dawning in our atomic-space-automated age, in order to gain a new ground out of which man and his works can flourish within this age, thereby to counter the rootlessness which has been the fruit of technical success.[9]

8. *VA,* pp. 45–46.
9. *Gelassenheit* (Pfullingen: Neske, 1959), pp. 16–26. English

Very much in evidence here are the Husserlian themes of technical *Sinnentleerung*, the resulting crisis of the European sciences, and the need for a return to origins. But the radical *Besinnung* for Husserl still retains the vestiges of a Cartesian meditation in being a self-reflection. One is reminded of the early Heidegger when *Besinnung* in the broad sense is described by Husserl as the case where "man as a person seeks to reflect on the ultimate sense of his *Dasein*," but then the strict, transcendental-phenomenological sense is a matter of "inquiring back to the sense, the teleological essence of the ego." [10] But for Heidegger, more fundamental than the ipseity of either a transcendental ego or a *Dasein* is the "event" which has already happened to us and accordingly pre-cedes us. We have already been begun, and it is here where we must begin in order to make sense of our situation. Accordingly, more originally than becoming conscious, *Besinnung* is a movement of "striking a path which a subject matter has of itself already taken." [11] Heidegger relates *Be-Sinnung* to its Sanskrit root *sent* (way),[12] which proliferates into English most archaically in the root words "send" and "sense." It is a matter of venturing into a sense which is already sending us on its way, in other words, assuming the mission which is given to us. In being given, it is beyond us and therefore not of our own doing, but since it is given *to us,* we are called upon to pursue and overtake it in order to assume it as our own. *Besinnung* assumes the lifelong task of discovering the sense of the historical situation which is at once already ours and not yet ours, thus bringing us explicitly to where we already are implicitly. The peculiar historical structure of this radical reflection is already manifest in Husserl. We are to sense our direction from our origin. The regress to the original sense at once points the way into the horizon of the future. Archeology is *eo ipso* teleology.

Because of the darkness enveloping this most fundamental of our situations, *Besinnung* is "the release toward that which is most worthy of questioning." [13] Because that which is closest to

---

translation by John M. Anderson and E. Hans Freund, *Discourse on Thinking* (New York: Harper & Row, 1966), pp. 47–55.

10. *H* VI, pp. 510–11 n.

11. *VA*, p. 68.

12. *Unterwegs zur Sprache* (Pfullingen: Neske, 1958), p. 53. (Hereafter cited as *US*.)

13. *VA*, p. 68.

us is at once the most difficult to discern and hence farthest from us, the course of such a reflection is a difficult and elusive path, to be pursued with resolute determination (*Entschlossenheit*), "the courage to make the truth of one's own presuppositions and the domain of one's own goals into the most worthy of questions." [14] The rigor and soberness of such a determination is counterbalanced by a certain calm and composure (*Gelassenheit*), resulting in a "relaxed attitude toward things" and an "openness to the mystery." It is in the light of these nuances of a relaxed, persistent, sober, and patient attitude that we have translated Heidegger's version of *Besinnung* as "deliberation," the deliberate way of a life of deliberative thinking.

Now if deliberation is equated with thinking purely and simply, then it must be asserted that "science itself does not think." [15] This intentionally provocative bit of Heideggeriana does *not* mean (1) that scientists do not think, (2) that thinking is superior to science, (3) that thinking should pay no attention to the sciences. As a thinking being, every scientist can move onto various levels of thoughtful deliberation, and in fact does so whenever he moves beyond his method to the problems issuing from the presuppositions of his science. It is in this way that science is always related to thought, though a leap is necessary to move from one to the other. Thinking can hardly be considered superior to science since it always knows less than the sciences, which are fully entitled to be called fields of knowledge. [16] But there is a side which science cannot reach, the essence and origin of its domain and its mode of knowing, to which thinking in the present situation must give its attention, which the sciences are incapable of giving to themselves. [17] The unique and positive essence which science possesses is eminently worthy of thought, especially when we become aware that the essence of modern science belongs to the essence of technology which, as a nontechnological power, dominates the present situation. [18]

14. *HW*, p. 69.
15. *Was heisst Denken?* (Tübingen: Niemeyer, 1954), p. 4. English translation by Fred D. Wieck and J. Glenn Gray, *What Is Called Thinking?* (New York: Harper & Row, 1968), p. 8.
16. *Ibid.*, p. 57. (Eng. trans., p. 33.)
17. *Ibid.*, p. 155. (Eng. trans., p. 135.)
18. *Ibid.*, p. 53. (Eng. trans., p. 22.)

Thinking moves into the unthought of science, to the question of its Being, without the assistance of logic and method, without the intention of formulating theories and ideas about science. It gives us no results, it brings us no knowledge as the sciences do. For thinking is not science, not even the science of science. It is first of all a call from something which needs to be thought and which beckons us on our way, hence a vocation bestowed on us without provocation, a way of life, a certain tonality of existence. It is this tone that we try to accentuate in thinking in order to intensify our resonance with that to which we are already attuned in our present situation. In thinking there is no method nor even a theme, but simply the proximity of the "presuppositions" in which we find ourselves, as our most worthy of questions, which in their very reticence and withdrawal draw us to thought.[19] By letting it draw us into its concealment, into the realm of unthought, we pursue a way which permits access to the inaccessible realm from which scientific method is barred. For that matter, a method is also a way, so that scientific method after all represents a variation of the way of thought, but the sclerosis of uniformity which it tends to provoke makes it a distant relative and even a deviation of the halting but creative way of thought.[20] A method insures results, but the ultimate significance of these results remains obscure until it emerges within the overarching context of the question-worthy situation through which the way of thought wends.

The philosophical tradition itself has tended to obscure this necessity. Even now, and perhaps especially now, philosophy centers its aspirations on being a strict science complete with logic and method. And this has been the case since Plato and Aristotle, whose discussions of theory and logic set the time-honored standards by which thinking is to be measured. In the pursuance of these standards, philosophy has given birth to a plethora of sciences but has exhausted itself in a labor which has taken it away from the element proper to it, the element of thinking. In recent philosophy, the proper character of thought was taken to be the movement of subjectivity, hence a method. In Hegel's *Science of Logic*, the method of speculative dialectic aims at absolute knowledge. In Husserl's *Philosophy as a Strict*

19. *US*, pp. 178–79.
20. *US*, pp. 197–98.

Science, the phenomenological method aims for ultimate evidence. Hegel finds absolute knowledge in the self-knowing subject. Husserl's "principle of all principles" affirms the *de jure* primordiality of whatever gives itself in an "originally giving intuition," thereby absolutizing subjectivity as the original source of evidence. The method of transcendental reduction is designed to bring this subjectivity itself to the state in which it is originally given in its ultimate evidence, where it in effect presents itself of itself. But even this ultimate evidence requires a site within which it can be seen, an open clearing which lets it present itself. It is this situation of openness which all of philosophy has overlooked and which is the proper affair of thought. Condition of possibility of the presence of all that presents itself, the openness as such tends to withdraw and elude all representation, systematic treatment, and methodical regulation. Thinking must let it be so. Its strictness in relation to this state of affairs demands that it not be scientific, i.e., representational, logical, methodical. Theoretical ideas, their degrees of certitude, intuition, and evidence are all to be situated within the domain of the Open. Even the visual metaphors of classical *Lichtmetaphysik* which charge these terms are no longer sufficiently radical for Heidegger, for as he "sees" it, the open domain is more akin to a clearing in the density of a wooded "thicket," hence a thinning or lightening which now makes lighting possible. Accordingly, in thinking we are concerned with a situational aura, an atmospheric modulation (*Wesen*), a climactic clearing of the air which must somehow be "sensed" nonobjectively before it can be made objectively visible in one form or another.[21]

A final contrast between science and thinking which serves to summarize the issue between them: science is "mathematical" and thinking is "hermeneutical." Science is mathematical in a more fundamental sense than its employment of mathematics. The Greek *mathēsis* is a learning process in which we come to know what we already know. Such a project of self-knowledge finds its most fundamental manifestation in the Cartesian *mathēsis* deduced from the unshakable position of *Cogito sum.* It begins in the proposing of propositions which serve as "self-ev-

21. This is a summation of several basic points made by Heidegger in an article available only in French translation by Jean Beaufret and François Fédier, "La Fin de la philosophie et la tâche de la pensée," *Kierkegaard vivant* (Paris: Gallimard, 1966), pp. 166–204.

ident" axioms securing a base for the acquisitions of further knowledge. The security of beginning with what one already knows now provides a solid foundation from which to venture forth with more daring proposals. The boldly active role of human advances on nature manifests itself in the idealizing fictions, hypotheses, and thought experiments of research projects in which mathematics in the ordinary sense, so manifestly a product of the human mind, plays such a large part. A tight circle of methodical precision and control is maintained by the insistence of a return to the familiar through a procedure of certification and confirmation.

Thinking is "hermeneutical" in a more basic way than the methodological connotations which it received in Heidegger's "preliminary conception of phenomenology." [22] Translated from the metaphysical and "mathematical" start which Husserl gave it to the ground which Heidegger seeks to give it, phenomenology is no longer a matter of subjective methodical control but of letting Being, the affair of thinking, show itself, and this means a revelation which is historically situated, and in this sense hermeneutical. It is a matter of reducing the axiomatic positions of science and metaphysics to the aporetic situation from which they emerged, in order to expose the implicit unexamined precedents which they set in the history of Being. Such presuppositions as the opposition of subject and object, its resultant security of clarity, distinctness, and exactness, etc., are then to be understood in the context of the present historical situation, in order to anticipate what this situation calls for. As in hermeneutics in the ordinary sense, it is a matter of reading between the lines to sense the unsaid in the said, with the proviso that one leaps into the movement which takes its course beyond human control, where we venture into the groping insecurity of the ineffable in order to herald the new in our reading of the "signs of the times."

A brief example of such a hermeneutic of science is provided by our guiding essay here, *Wissenschaft und Besinnung*. It is a matter of determining the "essence" of science, or better, in keeping with the historical and hermeneutical connotations of *Wesen*, the "way" of science, its secret "modulation," to which we must now tune in.

22. *Sein und Zeit*, § 7c.

The "Essence" of Science

OUR CONCERN with the essence of science is directed toward science as we now know it, modern science, to be distinguished from ancient *epistēmē* and medieval *scientia* and *doctrina*, each with its distinctive ways of looking at and asking about nature, which in turn are dependent on their interpretation of things in their Being. Because *physis, natura,* and nature take on different meanings, it is not possible to compare these results directly and to judge one in terms of the other. Each must be understood on its own terms. More important than trying to assess which is truer is the attempt to understand the history of the rise of modern science from its hidden sources in Greek science. The external facts of this history are well known, but the issue here is to understand the "innermost driving connections of this happening," [23] the history of the exposition of Being manifesting itself as the history of science and metaphysics.

Science is concerned with what is actual and real. The actual is necessarily related to the active. The activity here is first of all not human activity but the work of nature, as in growth, e.g., blossoming, bearing fruit. What is significant in such processes is that something which was not there before has been brought forth and revealed. Now it is actual, i.e., present and out in the open. Accordingly, the fundamental feature that belongs to the actual is that it is pro-duction, not in the sense that it effects something, but in that it brings something forth. Revelation takes precedence over efficiency. The *ergon* (work) of nature is not yet considered in terms of ergs of energy. Its actuality is a continual "coming to be," its stasis a permanent emergence and appearance.[24]

The stability of the actual can now be considered as something accomplished, finished, and secured. The actual then becomes factual, something done, ready-made. Production becomes kin to manufacturing, the fact is analogous to the artifact. The problem of the artist or technician who effected such a result then comes to the fore. The *Tat-Sache* calls for an *Ur-Sache.* Furthermore, since a fact is finished, it is fixed, se-

23. *FD,* p. 50. (Eng. trans., p. 65.)
24. *VA,* pp. 49–50.

cure, certain, and not "merely" an appearance. The fact stands fast and secure against all doubt and hence is in a position to become an object for the subject in search of certainty in his theory. Actuality, at first possessing the stasis of appearance, now assumes the stasis of a *Gegen-stand*.[25]

Since science is the theory of the actual, the conception of theory undergoes a corresponding shift. Since what emerges and presents itself can be seen, theoretical behavior in the first instance is a pure looking at what comes into view in actuality. Reverence for actuality evokes the care which strives to let something show itself as it appears. In this sense, the simplicity of "just" looking to let something be is hardly passive, but in fact calls for an effort which becomes the highest deed possible for man. The aspect in which something shows itself is an idea in the most original sense of *eidos*. Here are the seeds of what Husserl will call the eidetic intuition which belongs to theory as such.[26]

By contrast, the theoretician of modern science does not play the role of "disinterested spectator" of reality as it appears. For the stasis of appearances is too vacillating for his quest for certainty. The subject matter must therefore first be "treated" to make it more tractable to his investigations. In the distinction of primary from secondary qualities, the vagaries of appearance are sifted out so that reality can be adjusted into a fixed object, which can be handled in controlled experiments and measuring techniques and be made subject to various constants and parameters. Science in fact posits its own object, placing it in a position whereby it can be governed by scientific method. Method has the decisive and absolute priority in such an approach to reality, even to the point of governing which are its possible objects and which are not. They are in effect "way-laid" in advance to prevent any inherent obscurities from entering into the theater of operations and thereby disabling the effective machinery. Galileo readily admitted that such a procedure constituted a "rape of the senses." Though such mental idealizations as the frictionless plane and the freely falling body no longer violate our sensibilities, other more sophisticated concepts, likewise introduced as parameters of control, no longer pretend to an intui-

25. *Zusatz* to *Der Ursprung des Kunstwerkes* (Stuttgart: Reclam, 1960), p. 96. (Hereafter cited as *Zusatz*.) Cf. *VA*, pp. 50–51.
26. *VA*, p. 52; *Zusatz*, p. 97.

tive relationship with reality. Method now reigns supreme over its scientific themes. No longer an instrument in the service of science, it has rather mustered the sciences into its service.[27]

With this development, is it still possible to maintain that scientific theory deals with reality? Is science really the theory of the actual? A current trend tends to consider scientific theories nothing but working hypotheses instrumental in predicting and controlling events. Hence the theory simply amounts to "a supposition of categories which are accorded only a cybernetic function, with all ontological signification being denied to them." [28] And yet in some way, in the very supposition, "it is still the Being of beings about which the sciences continue to speak." [29] When science treats reality to bring certain features into prominence, it in fact reinforces a certain characteristic, which already belongs to actuality, of emphasizing itself in certain ways and standing fixed in that ex-posure as an object. Science simply provokes the actual into an objectivity which it already suggests, perhaps sometimes only fleetingly. But the very emphasis is of necessity a reworking of the actual, so that the resulting theory is literally a re-presentation of reality. The theoretical technique still manifests a mode of revelation, even though it is not the same as that of classical theory. Objectivity is one of the ways in which nature manifests itself, though it is not the fullness of the essence of nature.[30]

THE MODULATION OF TECHNOLOGY

THERE IS A COMPANION LECTURE to "Science and Deliberation" which parallels and completes its course of thought. This lecture, "The Question of Technology," [31] was delivered in the same series, whose over-all theme was "The Arts in the Age of Technology." According to Heidegger, the unique character of modern technology is not in its being applied science, but in its manifesting the initially hidden character of modern science. The way for its emergence was prepared by modern physics,

27. *US*, p. 178.
28. "La Fin de la philosophie," p. 180.
29. *Ibid.*
30. *VA*, pp. 56, 62.
31. *VA*, pp. 13–44.

which represented nature as a system of forces calculated in advance and then certified through experimental apparatus. But ultimately, the essence of modern science resides in the technological modulation which emerges from it.[32]

Technology, in manufacturing the hidden possibilities of both its material and its maker, is a kind of revelation. But instead of the pro-duction of the more receptive *poiesis*, the revelations of modern technology come about by placing nature under duress. Nature is provoked into revealing the hitherto unsuspected sources of electrical and nuclear energy. Coal or oil (or uranium) from the earth is burned (or fissioned) to heat the steam whose pressure turns the generators of power stations, which produce the electricity stored and transmitted across country through grids which supply the appliances which commutate the energy into its various functions. The release, conversion, storage, distribution, and commutation of energy are the modes of revelation here. The complexity of organization calls for a planning in which control and safeguards are the overriding features. Such control and security seek a constancy and consistency of function which demand the uniformity of stock items, reliability of service, supplies of reserves, backup "fail-safe" systems for all possible contingencies, etc. In such an all-inclusive system, the actual is no longer an opposed object (*Gegenstand*) but positioned "stock" (*Bestand*) to be "counted on" for its consistent service. Considered within the transportation system, an airplane is not an object but a readily available component securing the constant possibility of transportation. Each component must necessarily be positioned at its proper "station" within the technological grid which disposes energy, services, and goods. The enveloping character of the System is manifest in the planetary networks of communication, transportation, industrial organization, international monetary transfers, etc. Its provocative character, where nature is sometimes challenged to the point of defiance, appears in the geographical changes imposed by superhighways, the impending realization of weather made to order, heart transplants, "Astroturf," etc. Its "cybernetic" (from the Greek for "steersman") character emerges in the problems of ground and air control of traffic, logistical control of contingencies through insurance plans,

32. VA, pp. 29–31.

polls, weather forecasting and the like, ecological control of pollution, conservation of natural resources, and population control.

For the technological complex includes man himself, who is likewise a natural resource whose energy is to be tapped, converted through training, and distributed into the "manpower" system, which in turn is to be balanced and correlated with the "consumer potential" system, through marketing surveys, controlled distribution, etc. But more fundamentally for Heidegger, man himself is being provoked into pursuing this technological way by an ontological power which exceeds him. Modern technology is fundamentally not of human doing. There is a provocation which poses man with the task of disposing the actual into a system of calculable and reliable components, which eventually draws man himself into this sphere of disposable components. This provocative power which places man in the posture of *agent provocateur* in order to dispose actuality in this way can perhaps be given a name—the com-posite (*Ge-Stell*). "The composite names the gathering of that positioning which posits, i.e., provokes man into revealing the actual by disposing it in the mode of stock." [33] The composite itself is not technological, but the "essence" or modulating source of technology. It is not intended as a generic term for the particular technical constellations which enter into the over-all technological circuit. It rather refers to the mission of the current epoch of the history of Being. As such, Being as the composite is profoundly related to the Greek "syn-thesis" (also *Ge-Stell*) of *physis*, just as the pro-vocation of modern technology still retains resonances with the pro-duction of the Greek *poiesis*. And yet we have here two different styles of ordering beings, two different *logoi*. The modern positing of beings is dominated by the mark of man and his contrivances. With the Greeks, the thetic positing of beings was such as to let them stand in close proximity with their natural revelation. In fact, the highest form of *poiesis* is *physis* itself in its emergence, and the highest *thesis* is to let it thus produce itself in beings. The synthesis is then the gathering of the production of the *logos* of *physis* in beings.[34] Now nature is considered a stockpile of natural resources subject to the provocative hypotheses of modern logistics. The composite thus emerges with a "synthetic" quality

33. VA, p. 28.
34. *Zusatz*, p. 97; VA, pp. 19, 49.

which serves to screen the more fundamental emergence of nature. Nevertheless, in being a mission beyond our control, the composite is also a production of *physis*.[35] Elements and compounds synthesized in the laboratory are no less natural than those found in nature, for they are provoked by a process which is still suggested by nature.

Yet both the synthesis and the composite, in focusing on manifestations in *beings*, belong together in the history of metaphysics, which in its entirety constitutes "the technical interpretation of thinking." [36] This history moves toward its climax in the development of the various sciences within the horizon opened by philosophy since Plato, which in the process sever their ties with philosophy and become autonomous. The sciences nowadays find their organization and direction in the new basic discipline of cybernetics, to which the classical distinction between science and technology, theory and practice no longer applies, and where it becomes clear that the sciences in fact belong to the realm of the "essence" of technology. The basic object of cybernetic "theory" is the social organization and control of human work. Under its auspices, language becomes an informing instrument, and the scientific categories are instrumental working hypotheses whose "truth" is measured in terms of the efficiency with which they perform their task. The more formalized the categories, the more efficient they are, since they are subject to all the controls which the computer complex can offer. The "technical interpretation of thought," whose seeds were planted by Plato, reaches its apogee in the "thinking machine." [37]

Undoubtedly the revelations that ensue from the simulations of "artificial intelligence" will throw light on the character of human intelligence. But the very nature of these revelations of modern technology holds a radical danger to the most basic dimensions of thinking and truth. For example, in the light of current developments of contemporary physics, Heisenberg observes that the physicist, who initially thought he was talking about nature in his equations, now finds that in reality he only encounters himself in relation to nature here. But even this authentic realization can deceive us into a narrow conception of

35. *VA*, p. 32.
36. *Über den Humanismus* (Frankfurt a.M.: Klostermann, 1947), p. 6.
37. "La Fin de la philosophie," pp. 178–79.

man and obscure the dimension in which man is essentially himself. Only a thoughtful deliberation on the power of subjectivity which governs man in this technological epoch can expose how man really exists. But the constricting circle of mathematizing and calculative "thinking" militates against precisely such a breakthrough. For the revelations of the technological composite are such that they tend to exclude every other possibility of revelation. Its demand for control and security serves to filter out all presuppositions which point in directions other than its own. Even its own presuppositions fall into obscurity in the forward-looking progressive pursuit of the obvious benefits of total planetary domination. Even the forgetting is forgotten. It tends to exclude not only the previous mode of revelation as pro-duction, but more significantly, the entire realm of revelation as such, where the oldest and the newest truth may yet come out into the open. For control above all demands the foresight of prediction and can, and in fact does, dispense with the insight of understanding. The most radical danger then is not so much technology, its enormous capacity to destroy mankind, its presumed "demonic" character, or the specter of man's becoming a slave to his own inventions, but rather the technological modality which threatens to turn man away from the possible experience of the most incipient dimension of truth.[38]

In other words, the danger lies in the debilitation of deliberative thinking in a situation that Husserl so aptly described as *Sinnentleerung*, an exhaustion of even the pursuit of meaning as a result of the Western devolution of its norms of thought from the original *logos* to logic to logistics, whereby our subjective position obscures our founded situation. But the re-duction that Heidegger calls for is a return not simply to the origin of meaning as the Greeks glimpsed it but to the origin which is proper to a post-logistic epoch. And this can only be discovered by coming to terms with the scientific-logistic-cybernetic-technological style itself, which after all still retains muted roots in the origin of all origins. And it is deliberative thinking that must practice attuning itself to the advent of the authentic possibilities concealed in the calculative *thinking* which appears to represent its very antithesis but which it nevertheless must learn to com-prehend.

38. VA, pp. 34–36.

9 / The Era of the World-as-Picture

Joseph J. Kockelmans

HEIDEGGER HAS NEVER DEVELOPED a systematic philosophy of science. His interest has always been in another direction, namely, to come to a precise formulation of philosophy's basic problem and to undertake a "radical" exploration of everything that can be seen as an essential and necessary presupposition for this task. This is not to say that his philosophy has never touched upon, or does not have a bearing on, several issues which are of vital importance for a philosophy of science. On the contrary, in most of his publications Heidegger deals explicitly with problems which pertain specifically to the realm of philosophy of science, or are important to its "radical foundation."

In this essay I wish to limit myself to presenting a survey of, and where necessary giving a short commentary on, a public lecture which was held in Freiburg im Breisgau on June 9, 1938, as the conclusion to a series of discussions on the foundation of the "world-picture" of the modern era. The text of the lecture, whose original title was "The Foundation of the Modern World-Picture through Metaphysics," can be found in *Holzwege*;[1] the supplementary notes which are included occupy almost as much space as the lecture itself and were written at the same time as the lecture.[2]

1. *HW*, pp. 66–89.
2. *HW*, pp. 89–104, 344. Cf. William J. Richardson, *Heidegger: Through Phenomenology to Thought* (The Hague: Nijhoff, 1963), pp. 418–22. Heidegger's lecture has been translated into English by Marjorie Grene under the title "The Age of the World View," *Measure*, II (1951), 269–315.

Heidegger begins with a theme which plays a predominant role in almost all of his publications since *Being and Time,* the meaning (*Sinn*) and function of metaphysics. Metaphysics reflects on the essence of being (*Seiendes*), and in each of its forms metaphysics has made a decision in regard to the essence of truth. Each concrete form of metaphysics founds the era in which it comes about, by giving to that era the ground for the course which it has taken essentially through a determinate interpretation of being and a determinate conception of truth. Since this ground dominates all the phenomena characteristic of that era, a thorough reflection upon these phenomena should help one to understand that ground. It is Heidegger's opinion that such a reflection requires great courage because it aims at showing that the truth of its own presuppositions and the domain of its own goals are that which is most worthy of question (*Fragwürdig*).[3]

In a first addendum Heidegger specifies (as one could expect from his other works and notably from his *Letter on Humanism*), that this "ground," this "truth," and this "domain" which constitute what is most worthy of question, consist in Being (*Sein*). In other words, the essence of an era must be understood from the "coming-to-pass of Being's unconcealment" as it dominates that era. For only in this way can that which is most worthy of question be experienced; and it is this *Fragwürdige* which, in the final analysis, precisely founds and determines all achievements which (transcending what is ready-to-hand) aim at what is coming; in addition, it is this *Fragwürdige* which brings it about that a transformation of man becomes necessary of a necessity which springs from Being itself. From all of this it becomes understandable why it is so difficult to gain a thorough knowledge of all that is implied in the very essence of our modern era.[4]

Among the various phenomena which are essential to our modern era, science and "machine technique" certainly occupy an important place. Referring to his essay on technicity [5] Heidegger, in passing, again remarks that all technology requiring the use of machines, as a typical modern phenomenon, is funda-

3. *HW,* p. 69.
4. *HW,* pp. 89–90.
5. Martin Heidegger, "Die Frage nach der Technik," *VA,* pp. 13–44.

mentally different from the "technique" implied in our everyday praxis; it is an independent and self-sufficient transformation of our everyday praxis. Furthermore, Heidegger argues, machine technology must not be misinterpreted as a mere application of modern mathematical physics to our praxis, for, as a self-sufficient transformation of the praxis, machine technology precisely requires the use of mathematical physics. If it is true that all theoretical knowledge is a derivative mode of knowing which necessarily presupposes the "practognosy" which is inherent in our everyday concern, then machine technology can be understood not as something that follows a theoretical science, but rather as what precedes, guides, and "motivates" it. Alluding to the same essay on technicity, Heidegger repeats, finally, that in his view machine technology is the most patent offshoot of the essence of modern technicity, itself identical with the essence of modern metaphysics.[6]

There are other phenomena which are essential to our modern era. In our time *art* has moved onto the horizon of aesthetics; this means that works of art have become objects of experience and that art is conceived of as an expression of man's life. Furthermore, man's doing in general is interpreted and performed as culture, that is, as the realization of the highest values through the cultivation of the highest goods of mankind; when this realization, which according to its essence is such a cultivation, starts to care for itself, it develops into a *politics of culture*.[7] Finally, we have another typical characteristic of our modern era —de-divinization. By this expression Heidegger means not atheism but the bilateral process by which the world-picture first becomes Christianized by making the world-ground into the Infinite, Unconditional, and Absolute, and Christianity then reinterprets its Christianness into a world-picture in order to adapt itself in this way to the demands of our modern era. Taking up some ideas from Nietzsche and repeating some themes from his own book on Nietzsche Heidegger states that in his view Christianity to a very great extent is responsible for the reactivation of this de-divinization as a state of decisionlessness in regard to God. However, he argues, such a process does not exclude religiosity; instead it changes man's personal relation to God to a religious experience. When God has gone, the emptiness so cre-

6. *HW*, p. 69.
7. *HW*, pp. 69–70.

ated is filled with historical and psychological investigations of the *mythos*.[8]

In Heidegger's view the important question here concerns the kind of conception of being and the interpretation of truth which lie at the root of all these phenomena. In this lecture Heidegger confines himself to a consideration of the phenomenon of modern science. The main questions he chooses to deal with include: (1) What is the essence of modern science? (2) What conception of being and truth is founded by this conception? (3) What does the metaphysical ground which gives modern science its foundation tell us about the essence of our modern era? [9]

SCIENCE AS RESEARCH

IN HIS ATTEMPT to answer these questions Heidegger begins by making the general remark that the expression "modern science" refers here to something essentially different from the medieval *doctrina* as well as from the Greek *epistēmē*. This essential difference makes it impossible to compare ancient and modern science and to say, for example, that modern science is more exact than classical science, or that modern science is true whereas ancient science has been false in many instances. In other words, because of this essential difference, which is founded in a different interpretation of being and correspondingly in a different kind of "seeing" and questioning, it is impossible to conceive of ancient and modern science as forms of knowledge which differ merely in degree, and to claim that modern science has made great progress in comparison with ancient science.[10]

As Heidegger sees it, the very essence of modern science is found in research (*Forschung*). True research limits itself in its procedures to a clearly delineated realm of being. The expression "procedure" does not mean merely "method" or mode of proceeding, because such a methodical way of proceeding presupposes that there is already an open realm in which it can move. The opening up of such a realm is precisely the fundamental opera-

8. *HW*, p. 70.
9. *Ibid.*
10. *HW*, pp. 70–71.

tion of research. The delineation of a definite realm of being is brought about by a project (*Entwurf*) by means of which a certain aspect of things is taken as the exclusive theme of investigation. It is by such a project that the realm of being characteristic of a particular science is clearly demarcated, that the access to that domain acquires its methodical direction, and that the structure of the conceptual and discursive explanation acquires its first orientation. In other words, it is this fundamental project which, in the final analysis, determines the rigor of a science.[11]

The classical example for the historical development of a science is, according to Heidegger, the rise of mathematical physics. What is decisive for its development consists in its application of a *special* kind of mathematics for the determination of the character of natural processes and events. It consists in the manner in which nature itself is projected with the help of *modern* mathematics. And modern mathematics can proceed "mathematically" because it is already "mathematical" in a deeper sense. Heidegger refers here to the original meaning of the Greek term *ta mathēmata*. In his view this term refers originally to what man, in his theoretical consideration of being and his practical concern in regard to things, already knows in advance. Since among all the things the Greek man knew beforehand numbers certainly occupied a privileged position, it is understandable that gradually the expression *ta mathēmata* was reserved for the arithmetical. Later when physics developed into mathematical physics this meant first of all that in it (physics) something was to be determined in advance as that which-is-already-known (*ta mathēmata*). And this means concretely the projection of that which (in view of that particular type of knowledge of nature one was looking for) henceforth was going to be called "nature"; in other words, "nature" becomes then the closed totality of motions of spatio-temporally related mass points. Into this outline of what (because of that a priori project) from then on was supposed to be "nature" was furthermore subsumed the idea that motion is change of place, that there is no privileged motion, nor a privileged direction for motion, that space has the property of isotropy and time the character of isochrony, and, finally, that force must be determined by the motion which it is able to produce. Each process and each event

11. HW, p. 71.

becomes visible and must be understood only within the context of this outline of nature. This project of nature receives the guarantee of its certainty from the fact that physical research, in each of its questioning steps, binds itself beforehand to this outline of nature. This "bond," this rigor of research has its own typical character which depends upon that original project. The rigor of mathematical physics is exactness. An event can be considered as an event of nature if, and only if, it is determined beforehand as spatio-temporal kinetic magnitude. Such a determination can be effected by means of measurements and with the help of their resulting numbers and the calculations performed on them. However, Heidegger remarks, the exactness of mathematical physics is not due to the fact that it calculates exactly; it must calculate exactly, precisely because the mode in which it is bound to its own realm of objects by its original project has the character of exactness. That is why the humanistic sciences can be rigorous without for that matter being exact.[12]

REGULARITY, LAW, AND EXPERIMENT

SCIENCE thus becomes research (*Forschung*) through its project; it secures this project by proceeding rigorously. Project and rigor, however, can develop into what they genuinely are only when science proceeds methodically. This, Heidegger says, leads us to a second characteristic of modern science. For, if the projected domain of investigation is to be objectified in its entirety, then it will be necessary to bring this domain to light down through all its layers and ramifications. But, since things are in a constant state of change and development, it is necessary that the scientist focus his attention on this continuous change and never lose sight of it. For it is only in the perspective of the continuous becoming of what is changeable that the fullness of the things' facticity becomes manifest. But we have seen already that it is precisely these "facts" which must be objectified. Science, therefore, must represent in all its procedures changing things as they develop; it must bring this motion to a standstill and nonetheless maintain it as motion. The characteristic of remaining identical to themselves which these

12. *HW*, pp. 71–73.

"facts" possess, notwithstanding the continuity of their change, constitutes what we call their "regularity," Heidegger maintains, while the invariability of the change in the necessity of its course constitutes what we call a "law." It is, therefore, he argues, only in the perspective of regularity and law that "facts" are understandable. Scientific investigation of "facts" in the realm of nature, therefore, always implies the formulation and the verification of laws. The methodical procedures in and through which a domain of objects is brought to light make clear that which is clear already, that is to say, it has the character of clarification. This process is always bilateral. It grounds something which is unknown by means of something which is already known, and, at the same time, verifies what is already known through that which is still unknown. In other words clarification materializes itself in investigation, which in turn, depending on the character of the realm of investigation and the goals of the inquiry, comes about through experimentation. However, Heidegger remarks, physics does not become research *because* of the fact that it performs experiments; rather experiments, on the other hand, become possible where and only where our knowledge of nature has already changed into research. Modern physics can be experimental only because it is essentially mathematical.[13]

We have mentioned previously that in Heidegger's view there is an essential difference between modern science and medieval *doctrina* and Greek *epistēmē*. Here again we can clarify this difference. For neither the Greeks nor the medieval philosophers ever did come to genuine experimentation, nor could they do so in view of the fact that neither *doctrina* nor *epistēmē* was science in the sense of research. To be sure they knew what *empeiria* or *experientia* means: the observation of things, their properties, and changes under varying circumstances and conditions which, provided they are systematically performed, lead to knowledge of the way in which things as a rule behave. In their observations, too, they sometimes made use of measurements and numbers and in certain instances even employed devices and instruments. But all of this was not experiment in the modern sense of the term, because the decisive element was still missing. To perform an experiment means to prescribe a condition according to which a certain totality of motions (*Bewegungs-*

13. *HW*, pp. 73–74.

zusammenhang) can be mastered in the necessity of its course and can be mastered beforehand by our calculations. In other words, an experiment in the modern sense of the term is suggested and governed by laws which, in turn, point to "facts" which will verify or falsify them. Laws which have the character of hypotheses, are not arbitrary but are developed from basic conceptions of nature which the physicist has formed in and through his original project, by means of which he beforehand clearly demarcated the region of things which will constitute the realm of his investigations. Thus, the more he is able to exactly project the basic conception of nature, the more he will be able to perform his experiments in an exact way.[14]

From this, Heidegger continues, it becomes clear why Roger Bacon cannot be said to be the precursor of the modern, experimenting scientist. It is certainly true that Bacon requires *experimenta*, but his *experimenta* are not identical with the experiments of modern science. Bacon merely requires an *argumentum ex re*, instead of the common *argumenta ex verbo*; he demands the observation of things, that is, Aristotle's *empeiria*, instead of an explanation by means of the opinions of "authorities." [15]

A modern research experiment is not just a form of observation which is more accurate with respect to degree and scope. It is, rather, an essentially different procedure which aims at verification of laws within the perspective of an exact project of nature. The function of experiments in physical research is analogous to the function of the "source critique" of the historical sciences of man, provided the expression "source critique" is understood in a very broad sense so as to include the whole of finding, sifting, verifying, evaluating, preserving, and the interpretative explaining of sources. Historical explanation, however, does not lead to rules and laws; nor, on the other hand, does it limit itself to a mere reporting of facts. The historical sciences, just as does physics, try to present something permanent; this can be done only by objectifying history. But history can be objectified only after it has passed by. The permanent in what has passed by, that is to say, that on the basis of which our historical explanation and interpretation evaluate the nonrecur-

14. *HW*, pp. 74–75.
15. *HW*, p. 75.

ring and manifold events of history, is that which has always been there already. By continuously comparing everything with it, it becomes possible to lay bare what is understandable in history and to verify it as its basic outline. The realm of events with which historical research deals extends only as far as historical clarification can reach. That is why the unique, that which occurs seldom, the simple—briefly, what is great in history—is never self-evident and thus must remain inexplicable. Historical research obviously does not deny what was great in history but merely conceives of it as an exception. In Heidegger's view there is no other form of historical clarification possible as long as clarification means the reduction of the unintelligible to the intelligible, that is, as long as history remains research.[16]

SPECIALIZATION, MANAGEMENT, INSTITUTIONALIZATION, AND UNIFICATION

HEIDEGGER TURNS NOW to a third element which is characteristic of modern mathematical physics. He introduces this section of his analysis by pointing out that because each science as research is founded on the projection of a well-delineated realm of objects it is, therefore, necessarily always this particular and individual science. In the further unfolding of this original project through its methodical procedures, each individual science again demarcates determinate fields for special investigations. This specialization is by no means a fatal concomitant phenomenon of the continually increasing incalculability of the results of our modern research. Specialization is necessarily connected with science as research; it is not the consequence but the ground for the progress of all research. Specialization does not proceed arbitrarily; it is oriented and guided by a third characteristic of modern science: modern science is systematic management (*Betrieb*).[17]

In a note Heidegger remarks that the term "management" is not used here in a pejorative sense. However, he argues, in view of the fact that science is essentially management, there is always a real danger that science will become *mere* management and even mere "business." Science becomes mere manage-

16. *HW*, pp. 75–76.
17. *HW*, pp. 76–77.

ment and "business" when, in its methodical procedures, it does not keep itself open and free, when instead of continuously and originally performing its original project, it leaves this project behind itself as a mere datum which does not ask for any further ascertainment, and merely searches for results and their further elaboration and application. Science must continuously fight this danger. Heidegger concludes this note with the remark that in his view the continuous balancing of the essence and un-essence of science as research assures the vitality of modern science as well as of our modern era.[18]

At any rate, to say that science is management does not mean merely that a science is accepted as a genuine science only when it has become fit for institutionalization. For research is systematic management not because its work is done in institutes but rather because institutes become necessary in that science as research intrinsically has the character of systematic management. The methodical procedures through which the individual realm of objects becomes conquered do not just pile up results. Rather, with the help of its own results each individual science prepares itself for an ever new approach. Thus, methodical progress becomes confined by its own results, always more oriented toward the possibilities of progress which it itself has first opened up. The fact that modern science must orient itself toward its own results, as well as toward its own progressing methodical procedures, is the essence of the management which is characteristic of modern research.[19]

In the system brought about by this management, the project which constitutes the realm of objects becomes *built into being*. The arrangements which facilitate an integration of the methodical procedures which can be planned, and which furthermore require mutual checking and communication of the results and regulate the exchange of labor, are by no means merely the extrinsic consequences of the fact that the work of research grows and branches out. They constitute rather a sign which comes from afar and to a great extent is still not yet understood, for they point to the fact that modern science only now begins to enter into the decisive phase of its history and take possession of its own and full essence.[20]

18. *HW*, p. 90.
19. *HW*, p. 77.
20. *HW*, pp. 77–78.

What is at stake in the expansion and consolidation of this institutionalization of science is nothing less than the securing of the priority of the method above that being (namely, nature and history) which is objectified in research. On the basis of their management character the sciences constitute for themselves the solidarity and unity which are appropriate to them. That is why the specialization of contemporary science has created a new type of man. The scholar begins to disappear and the researcher who is part of a research project comes to the fore. The researcher does not need a library at home; indeed, he is continually on his way. He becomes informed on the subject in meetings and congresses. He writes those books which his publisher asks for; the publishers now codetermine what books are to be written.[21]

Furthermore, research is today necessarily oriented toward technology, provided technology is taken to mean what it is according to its very essence. Technology keeps research efficient in its action and work and guarantees its genuineness and reality for its own time. This, in turn, explains why the function of the university has changed in our era. For the effective unitary character and, indeed, the reality of our contemporary university is no longer found in a spiritual power which emanates from it and which should bring about the original unification of the sciences. Its function is now found, rather, in the fact that it makes possible the necessary specialization, justifies it, and makes it understandable. Since the essential and characteristic forces of modern science become immediately and univocally effective in the management of science, it becomes understandable why the different research managements are able to predelineate and to bring about their own characteristic unity with other forms of research.[22]

Heidegger is of the opinion that the real and genuine system of the sciences consists in the fact that they, through continuous planning, keep adhering to one another in their methodical approach and attitude in regard to the objectivation of being. In other words, the systematization of the sciences consists not in a devised and fixed unity that depends on an inner relationship between their contents and subject matters but in the greatest

21. *HW*, p. 78.
22. *HW*, pp. 78–79.

possible, free but regulated, mobility of the commutation and engagement of the different forms of research in the direction of the tasks which at each time appear to be dominant. Each modern science has systematically to follow its own course in further specialization and ramification where necessary or desirable if it wants to remain as, according to its very essence, it genuinely is. This is a necessary condition which the sciences must fulfill if they are to play their true part in modern society. It is obvious, however, that in so doing they must know their place in modern culture and stay with their own tasks and goals.[23]

Modern science is founded on, and at the same time branches out into, the projects of determinate realms of objects. These projects unfold in the methodical procedures which correspond to them and which are secured by the rigor of each science. The respective methodical procedures establish themselves in management. Project, rigor, methodical procedure, and management, which mutually require and determine one another, constitute the essence of modern science and make it research.[24]

Heidegger concludes this part of his essay by briefly dealing with a question which in his view is of the greatest importance if one is to understand the essence of modern science and to recognize its "metaphysical ground." What conceptions of being and truth ultimately underlie and ground the science that becomes research?

As Heidegger sees it, knowledge as research calls being to account for the question of how and how far it can be made available to pro-posing re-presentation (*Vor-stellung*). Research disposes of being either when it is able to pre-calculate it in its future course, or when it is able to post-calculate the past. In this pre- and post-calculation nature and history become, as it were, posited; they become the object of man's clarifying re-presentation which reckons on nature and reckons with history. Only that which in this way becomes object, *is*. Science becomes research only when the Being of beings comes about in a pro-posing re-presentation which aims at bringing each being before itself in such a way that the calculating man can be sure of it.

23. *HW*, p. 79.
24. *HW*, pp. 79–80.

Science becomes research when and only when the truth of being has been changed into the certainty of man's pro-posing re-presentation.[25]

Here Heidegger makes in passing the important remark that this conception of being and truth has dominated modern philosophy from Descartes to Nietzsche. This is one of the main reasons why modern metaphysics is to be transcended.[26]

THE MODERN ERA AND THE WORLD-AS-PICTURE

HEIDEGGER TURNS NEXT to the second part of his essay: What does that which constitutes the metaphysical ground of science as research teach us about the essence of our modern era? This question must be asked, since modern science as research is a phenomenon essentially characteristic of our times. One could say that the essence of the modern era consists in the fact that man frees himself from all medieval conditions and, thus, frees himself unto himself. But although this characterization is true, it is superficial and easily leads to misunderstanding, so that it makes it difficult to understand the essence of the modern era properly. It is undeniably true that man's vindication of his own freedom has led to subjectivism and individualism; but it is true also that in no other era has one seen an objectivism and collectivism that can be compared with that of modern times. Even the thesis that the mutual interaction of subjectivism and objectivism determines the essence of modern times does not yet go to the heart of the matter.[27]

The decisive element in the constitution of the modern era is not the fact that man frees himself from the prevailing conditions unto himself, but the fact that the essence of man himself has changed in that man became subject. This word comes from *subjectum* which as a technical term is the Latin translation of the Greek *hupokeimenon;* it means that which lies before or underneath and, thus, as ground gathers everything toward itself. Taken as such the term does not necessarily refer to man.

However, to say that man is the first and true subject is tantamount to saying that man becomes that being upon which

25. *HW*, p. 80.
26. *HW*, pp. 80, 91–92.
27. *HW*, pp. 80–81.

all other being is founded as far as its mode of Being and its truth are concerned. Man becomes the center of reference of being as such. But this, in turn, is possible only if the conception of being as a whole changes. We must ask now, Heidegger says, wherein this change manifests itself and what is, according to this change, the essence of our modern era.[28]

In his attempt to find an answer for these questions Heidegger takes his starting point in the remark that, when man wants to reflect on our modern era, he usually is concerned about our modern world-picture. The important question, however, is whether or not it is characteristic for every era to have a world-picture and to be concerned about it, or whether it is perhaps typical only for our modern era to seek world-pictures. These questions in turn lead to two others: what is meant here by world-picture? And if one conceives of world-picture as a picture of the world, then one must ask, also, what is meant by "world" and by "picture." Heidegger thinks that "world" stands here for the "beings-in-the-ensemble" and thus comprises nature, history, and the world-ground. In the expression "world-picture" the word "picture" might make us think of a photocopy. However, "world-picture" means more than just a photo of the world. It means the world itself conceived of as a totality of beings pro-posed to man as subject. Opposed to man as subject and pro-posed by him, the world has meaning only in regard to him. In our modern era when we talk of a world-picture, we imply that the beings-in-the-ensemble are to be taken in such a way that they are beings only insofar as they are posited by man's pro-position and fabrication. When a world-picture develops, then, an essential decision is made in regard to what the whole of being is supposed to be. Thus, a thing is insofar as it can be pro-posed by man.

Wherever being is not thought of in this way, there a world-picture is excluded. What characterizes our modern era and distinguishes it from others consists in the fact that being *is* merely as objectified, *is* merely in its pro-posedness. And since our era is the first in which this ever happened, it follows at once that it is not right to speak about an ancient or a medieval world-picture and also that the expression "our modern picture of the world" is a pleonasm.[29]

28. *Ibid.*
29. *HW,* pp. 82–84.

In what follows in the essay itself, as well as in the notes, Heidegger points to very important consequences of this decision about the meaning of being. First, the moment the world appears as something which has meaning only in regard to man, then the fundamental task of man becomes to conquer the world. As Heidegger formulates it: the fundamental movement of modern times consists in conquering the world-as-picture by objectifying projects, calculations, designs, and techniques.[30] Furthermore, anthropology as a philosophical discipline is born —by this Heidegger means that philosophical analysis which explains the totality of beings by taking man both as starting point and as center of reference. For, he argues, if it is true that our modern era must be characterized by the facts that man becomes subject and the world changes into a picture, then it becomes understandable that the more the world is conceived of as that which is to be conquered (that is, the more objective the objects begin to appear), the more subjective (that is, claiming priority) the subject becomes and, thus, the more a doctrine of the world changes into a doctrine of man (anthropo-logy). It is then understandable also why anthropology leads to humanism, which means nothing more than the moral and aesthetic dimensions of anthropology. It is understandable, too, how people can come to "world-views"; for, once the world has become a picture man begins to seek a way of looking at it. It is finally understandable that this basic conception can lead to life philosophies. For, if a being attains status as a being merely to the extent that it is absorbed in some way or other into man's life, then one must account for beings in terms of living experiences.[31]

From all of this it also becomes clear why people in the nineteenth century began to seek values. For, if beings become mere objects of pro-posing re-presentation, then man has to compensate for this by ascribing "values" to beings in such a way that these values become the goal of all interaction with things. This interaction with beings then becomes understood as "culture," values become "cultural values," and, thus, the goal of all human creativity is placed at the service of man himself. Finally, the values become reduced to the level of mere objects

30. *HW*, p. 87.
31. *HW*, pp. 85–86.

which man projects as the goals necessary to sustain his own activity in establishing his place in the world-as-picture.[32]

DESCARTES AND THE ORIGIN OF OUR MODERN ERA: TOWARD A GENUINE CONCEPTION OF BEING AND TRUTH

IN THE REMAINDER OF THIS ESSAY Heidegger tries to explain, first, how the world-picture of our modern era came about, and, secondly, what conception of Being and Truth genuine philosophy has to offer in lieu of that which is implied in the world-picture of our modern era. As far as the first question is concerned, Heidegger sees the origin of the modern era in Descartes' philosophy. He explains this in the following way.

We have seen already that the main characteristic of modern man is found in the vindication of his own freedom, whereby he frees himself from all the ties which medieval Christianity had forced upon him; modern man frees himself unto himself.[33] Medieval man received all his certitudes from his faith.[34] By choosing independence in the name of freedom, modern man was thrown back upon himself so that he had to find certitude in and through himself.[35] The freedom modern man chose was self-determination and, thus, the ground of all his certitudes was to be found in his own self-certitude. This means, among other things, that modern man had to decide for himself what is knowable for him, what is genuine knowledge, and what is certitude. In attempting to find an answer for these questions Descartes realized that the ground of all his certitudes must itself be certain, must be able to justify itself, and must ground all other certitudes. Descartes thought that this *fundamentum inconcussum veritatis* which underlies (*subjectum, hupo-keimenon*) all other certitudes was to be found in his *cogito* [*ergo*] *sum*.[36]

In Descartes' view, Heidegger says, the *cogito* obviously is itself certain because knowing is here known to conform with

32. *HW*, pp. 93–94.
33. *HW*, p. 81.
34. *HW*, pp. 75, 81.
35. *HW*, p. 99.
36. *HW*, pp. 98–99.

what is known, in that both knowing and what-is-known are simultaneously present to one another in one single act of knowledge. The *cogito* justifies itself because it is apodictically evident. And finally, it is the ground of all other certitudes in that it not only is their model but also a necessary and sufficient condition for all of them. For, to use a concise formulation of Sartre's, "the necessary and sufficient condition for a knowing consciousness to be knowledge *of* its object, is that it be consciousness of itself as being that knowledge." [37]

In Heidegger's opinion all of this implies three very important theses. The first thesis is that knowledge is identical with a process of re-presenting (*re-praesentatio*) and pro-posing to itself what is known.[38] From this the second thesis follows immediately: the humanly knowable consists in whatever can be a term of the re-presenting and pro-posing process, that is, whatever can be objectified by such a process and, therefore, any "object." [39] The third thesis is connected with the second and states that certitude becomes understood as truth that is guaranteed by exact calculation, which itself is made possible by the process of objectivation.[40]

For Descartes, Heidegger concludes, being necessarily becomes being-as-object which is present to a subject, and its presence has necessarily to remain within the domain of the subject-object relationship. That in addition to this there must be a much more fundamental form of presence, an emergence into nonconcealment, is for Descartes unacceptable. But by excluding this primordial form of presence Descartes is necessarily driven into the epistemological problem, that is, the problem concerning a possible bridge between "consciousness" and "world."

What authentic thought has to say about this is explained by Heidegger by contrasting the Cartesian conception of re-presentative thought with the pre-Socratic conception of *noein*. Referring to Parmenides' correlation of *noein* and *einai*, Heidegger claims that primordially to know does not mean to re-present and to pro-pose; and, correlatively, that being does not necessar-

37. Jean-Paul Sartre, *Being and Nothingness*, trans. Hazel E. Barnes (New York: Philosophical Library, 1956), p. lii.
38. *HW*, p. 100.
39. *HW*, p. 101.
40. *HW*, p. 100; Richardson, *Heidegger*, pp. 321–23.

ily mean "object." Heidegger interprets Parmenides' saying as meaning that it belongs to Being, that is, that it is demanded and determined by Being, that beings be brought to light. A being is that which emerges and opens itself up; and, insofar as it comes to presence, it comes over a man who likewise is coming-to-presence over himself in that he opens himself up into what is coming to presence, inasmuch as he becomes aware of it (*vernehmen*). Thus a being is not a being insofar as a man has perception of it, that is, has a re-presentation of it in the sense of the Cartesian *perceptio*. Man is rather looked at (*angeschaut*) by beings in their Being; man is seized by beings as they open themselves up in their Being. Man himself is gathered up in the process of coming-to-presence; he is drawn into Being's openness where he is retained and sustained. However, man is not merely passive here; for, in order to bring his own essence to fulfillment he must gather together in its openness that which is opening itself up before him.[41] In other words man, indeed, dwells with beings, but he is not just another being. He is the "mediation" between beings and Being, for he and he alone is *Da-sein*, that is the ek-static domain of the revealing and concealing of Being.[42]

41. *HW*, pp. 83–84.
42. *HW*, pp. 88, 104; Richardson, *Heidegger*, pp. 419–21.

Wilhelm Szilasi

WILHELM SZILASI (1889–1966) was born and educated in Budapest, Hungary, where he was a high school professor until 1919, at which time he emigrated to Germany. During the twenties, he followed some of the lectures of both Husserl and Heidegger. In 1933, he assumed a teaching post in Brissago, Switzerland. In 1947, he filled the chair vacated by Heidegger at the University of Freiburg. In this period of his later life, he was also active in the field of industrial chemistry.

His philosophical work was devoted mainly to the problems of transcendental philosophy and the relations between philosophy and science. The link between these two sets of problems is to be found in the central theme of transcendental experience, upon which the following lecture is based—the experience of experience which constantly opens up new possibilities of experience.

This selection is an example of the application of Heideggerian insights to the philosophy of physics and biology. Two theses are developed: (1) the most proper mode of experience in contemporary natural science is not experiment but theory, an ontological rather than an ontic experience, an a priori experience of structural unities which opens up new conceptual possibilities; accordingly, (2) truth in natural science, the truth founding such an ontological experience, is a kind of intimacy with nature, which is not considered as fixed and eternal but as a happening to which man must be continually responsive.

[203]

10 / Experience and Truth in the Natural Sciences

Wilhelm Szilasi

The Concept of "A Priori"

WHAT I PROPOSE TO DISCUSS can best be approached in a first approximation with a statement from Schelling: "We thus do not *know* nature. Rather, nature *is* a priori, i.e., every individual in it is determined in advance by the whole or by the idea of a nature in general. But if nature is a priori, it must also be possible to recognize it as something which is a priori, and this is really the sense of our assertion."

The word a priori is familiar to you. It calls to mind Kant's doctrine in particular. For Kant, the "a priori" designated the subjective conditions of possibility of experience. Subject in a restricted sense means the "knowing existent." "Subjective conditions" refers to the special capabilities of the existent, prior to any experience, thus prior to any contact with other beings; it means to have available the types of bonds which fashion the impending moments of relation, the impressions, and to think what is fashioned within these available forms of unity. These forms of unity which exist in advance and are already available testify to the fact that the scheme for experience is prescribed prior to any experience. Since what is prescribed reaches beyond

This translation of Wilhelm Szilasi's "Erfahrung und Wahrheit in den Naturwissenschaften," *Philosophie und Naturwissenschaft* (Bern: Francke, 1961), pp. 25–51, was done for this volume by Theodore J. Kisiel. The lecture was delivered in 1949 in the course of the *Dies Universitatis* at the University of Freiburg im Breisgau and published first in *Kosmos, Tier, Mensch* (Freiburg i.B.; Alber, 1949).

the impressions and their bonds, we call the scheme transcendental. The Kantian interpretation of experience and of knowledge is called transcendental idealism.

The Experience of Nature in Its A Priori Transcendental Reality

Idealism in a dogmatic sense is the opposite of realism. It indicates that our knowledge of the universe, with respect to unity and lawfulness, is an achievement of the subjective functions of understanding and reason. It believes that whatever we can say about nature and whatever progress our knowledge makes are ultimately grounded in the self-reflection of spirit and in its history.

It is perhaps not superfluous to point out that Kant did not really consider his thought to be a dogmatic idealism. He states with deliberate and even polemical precision that transcendental-critical philosophy is the "opposite of idealism." He believed that his account of the way in which our knowledge of things is mediated through appearances indeed points to idealism, but the possibility which critical philosophy for the first time in history manifested was—as he says—"to spell out the appearances in order to be able to read them as experience."

With Kant, a new epoch of metaphysics begins. The statement from Schelling is an indication of the turn. Its assertion is twofold: that nature itself is a priori, i.e., it is the transcendent whole which never appears, the hidden unity which defines the irreducible plurality of natural events. Nature itself is accordingly ineffable and unknowable in the totality of its possibilities. If we call it the power behind the appearances, we do so only because we are at a loss for words. The act of naming it does not say what it is. It is no more a "something" than Being itself. In analogy with Being, nature stands in a transcendental relation to natural events, just as Being does to the modes of Being. And ancient philosophy has said the same with regard to Being and *physis*.

Secondly, the statement asserts that the apriority of knowledge is not an isolated phenomenon. Its apriority is established because nature is a priori in relation to natural phenomena. The a priori components of our experience are in immediate relation to the apriority of nature, i.e., all elements ascertainable as a priori are the results of a hitherto unexamined experience which experiences the apriority of nature. If we thus trace the a priori moments of experience to their genesis, we discover a new experience, the experience of nature in its transcendental a priori reality.

This statement would be incomprehensible if the ontological turn and the demand corresponding to the turn were not explicit. The demand insists that we consider with the subject not its empty moment of relation to the object of experience, but that fullness of an existential self-interpretation which the a priori of nature possesses within its constitution. The epochal achievement of Heidegger's *Being and Time* is the fulfillment of this demand, which was first clearly formulated by him.

The Newly Understood A Priori Realism

The turn has two important moments. First, it does not consider the subjectivity in opposition to the total unity of all other beings in the traditional sharp dichotomy of *res cogitans* and *res extensa,* whereby one being, the one who experiences, is specially distinguished and all other beings are made to stand in opposition to it as the objective. It rather experiences subjectivity as a natural process in conjunction with other natural processes. It interprets the meaning of reality in a new way. Reality is the process of the Being of all beings and indeed in such a way that the subjective existent, to put it in an exaggerated way, is also a thing in the interplay of all things.

Second, through the ontological turn, the locus of reality is no longer situated in the interplay of all things, but rather in its structural possibilities, which unceasingly develop anew with each new situation.

I shall in what follows expressly and emphatically advocate this newly understood a priori realism. It is not a frivolous realism. When it asserts that we know the totality in its reality, it means by the real that wherein the knowing existent is also included. And by knowing, it means the a priori objective experience which understandingly inserts every natural experience into the apriority of the whole.

These statements are difficult, and in the beginning they are declarations which are still incomprehensible. Fortunately physics, this kindred sister of philosophy, since it has always been directed to the whole of nature, has the most sensitive organs for the change in our understanding of Being. Its practice in adjusting the subjectivity and in arranging the domains of Being exemplify the change which achieves its articulation and generalization in philosophy. I do not mean by this that physics selects its problems under the influence of philosophy. It is urged on its way by its own problems and by the historical situation.

But it implicitly has the same experience of Being that philosophy expresses. And so, many moments of the ontological turn which accompanies our age are to be read in its work.

With this, I think that I have indicated the connection of the two questions and the two parts of our undertaking. In the first part, I wish to advocate the thesis that *natural scientific experience is theory,* i.e., the objective a priori experience of the apriority of nature. In the second part, I shall try to show that natural scientific truth is a kind of intimacy with the happening of nature and that the happening character of truth is connected with this intimacy.

THEORY AS NATURAL SCIENTIFIC EXPERIENCE

The Twofold Significance of the Term "Experience"

1. FIRST OF ALL, I would like to recall the twofold significance of our word "experience." In every experience, the existent (*Dasein*) has its experiences relative to the first experience. The second experience relates itself not to what is experienced in the first experience, but to what the first experience signifies, or to the way in which the first experience determines in advance what follows with regard to further experiences. In conjunction with this, the existent has also experienced something with regard to its modes of behavior and has learned something for future modes of behavior. We may not understand these two observations as a tautology only because experiencing is a kind of behavior. The new mode of behavior is governed by the known kind and mode of object. Let us listen to what is said in our everyday existence. When we say, "I have had this or that experience with this man, so that I now know how I should behave toward him," we do not think of individual experiences, i.e., we do not give an account of what happened on one

or another occasion. With the statement, "I have had my experiences with him," we do not have the experiences in mind but the man himself, his type and manner. Our interest is not fixed on the content of the experiences, but on the structural unity of possible experiences. We apply this unity to the person of the other; by person we mean this structural unity.

I would like to show that modern physics likewise speaks of experiences of experiences, i.e., not of individual experiences, but of the structural unity of the possibilities of experience.

Where ordinary language speaks of kind and mode, of the mode of experience or of what is experienced, of the kind and mode of that toward which the existent comports itself, philosophy speaks of *modes of Being*. It must thus be shown that modern physics is directed toward the modes of Being of natural phenomena and not toward the phenomena themselves. It manifests its immediate bond with philosophy in its practice, and not in the philosophical reflections which many physicists give after their admirable work is done.

German Idealism and the New Mode of Thought

I must once again point to the epoch-making achievement of Kant. He shattered the naïve belief in the uniqueness of our natural self-evident experience of things. He showed that this experience is tied to definite conditions, among others to the spatiality and temporality of the existent. Accordingly, all that can be experienced comes to the existent in advance in spatio-temporal categorial determinations. The seemingly self-evident experience is not an unconditioned experience.

But when Kant speaks of appearances, he does not mean the same thing as Platonic idealism. He does not insist on a purer reality behind the appearances, a prototype of conditioned experience in its undisturbed harmony, teleology, and immutable eternal truth. It is precisely this possibility of experience that the critique excludes. An unconditioned mode of experience is not to be found in it. But the critique is positive: it distinguishes two different experiences, the natural thing experience and the unconditioned "no-thing" experience. How is this second kind to be made evident? This was the question for the three great Kantian contemporaries—Fichte, Schelling, and Hegel. They brought about a turn in man's mode of thought with the greatest penetration and with a full panoply of individual questions. We are standing in the midst of this epochal turn. It is up to us to pursue this path even further. The one man who, after a long period of latency, has once again made the great decision of these great beginners accessible in a productive way, is Heidegger. The "ontological difference" which pervades his entire effort of thought designates most forcefully the separation, which has always been present historically but was never strictly maintained, between two different modes of experience, under the headings of ontic and ontological experience.

In the second half of the previous century, well-nigh up to the present day and to a certain extent even today, Neo-Kantianism reigned supreme. It assumed from Kant only the knowledge of the a priori forms of experience and not the deeper impulse for which it is the critical starting point. The mode of thought adopted with this assumption is that of the a priori subjectivity. We do not even have the right to speak of experience in the true sense when it means that science is grounded through the achievement of the transcendental subjectivity, "in the self-reflection of the transcendental subjectivity in its achievement of giving and uniting meaning and bringing them into harmony," and that "all conceivable sciences of reality and possibility in essentially predelineated transcendental forms" are to be found in the analysis of the forms of the transcendental subjectivity.[1] But for a long time, physics has itself idealized its modes of experience within this rationally constructive procedure which interprets and exhausts the a priori models of thought.

But its rapid development revealed experiences which neither followed the connections of naïve experience which are conditioned by things and proceed phenomenally, nor could be interpreted as subjective-analytical consequences of thought. These were unexpected experiences which were not to be found in advance in subjectivity. They were equally external, coming from the object side, but in such a way that they placed the dogmatic distinction between subject and object in question. Their "coming from the outside" nullifies the subjective origin, and their nonobjective character refutes the claim to being conditioned by thing categories. This paralleled the change which was already proceeding in philosophy. We have no right to claim

1. Cf. *FTL*, pp. 240–42.

that the philosophy of German idealism, even by way of productive suggestions, might have immediately influenced physical thought. In the last decades, it has itself fallen into oblivion. Still less can we invoke the immediate effect of Heidegger. His clear radicality can come to the aid of the natural sciences only in the future. But in all the changes of the spiritual life of the nineteenth century—in carrying through the dialectics of nature and of history, in developing the ontological experience, which bore its first fruits in early biology, in the investigation of language and the phenomena of art, poetry, and the social structures—a new mode, a new atmosphere of thought was being readied, in which philosophy as science reclaimed its lost role of guide in relation to the sciences. If we can say today that physics, as it did with Aristotle, assumes in its latest development its role as an ontology of nature, we may also invoke the common bond which ties philosophy and the sciences on the one hand, and the sciences and philosophy on the other into a unified coherence of development. This bond is not always evident. Obviously, it must often be renewed, calling for a reciprocal understanding and patience. But it must be done. On it depends the level, productivity, impact, and spiritual stability of an age. This task is being served when I seek to indicate that the mode of thought and of experience of modern physics is based on the enormous revolutionary power of the ontological experience.

The New Kind of Experience in Biology

2. I have already briefly described the beginnings of biology. It was the first of the natural sciences to break through the triple confinement of dogmatic naïveté, dogmatic idealism, and dogmatic transcendental-subjective apriorism. It underwent the experience that its phenomena belong thematically in a domain of Being entirely different from that of physics. It thus had the first scientifically formulated ontological experience, undergone by the great biologists of German idealism, like Johannes Müller, Humboldt, von Baer. Secondly, it found that life cannot be investigated on the basis of transcendental subjective projects of giving meaning, because subjectivity as well belongs to *its* genesis.

Only our own subjectivity is familiar to us. The subjectivity of other living natures, their psychic essence, can only be experienced by us in an objective way. And so the third novel experience of beginning biology was that the subjective unities in their proper, continually productive, and meaning-giving self-containment can be adequately experienced not according to human a priori modes of giving meaning, or as mere thing characters, but only by means of a completely new kind of experience.[2] Schelling's most definitive achievement was precisely in working out this experience as the ontological experience. He distinguished between the productive process of nature, which cannot itself be experienced objectively but as a movement of articulated moments, and the products of the process, which are set off from it and must then be investigated in their objective and phenomenal development according to their categorially defined phenomenal lawfulness. It is not Schelling's fault if his ideas, in passing, have had an apparent impact in the form of obscure vitalism, voluntarism, or entelechism.

The New Kind of Experiences in Modern Physics

Modern physics discovered its new mode of experience when it first established that its progress is determined not simply by new experiences, but by the manifestation of new possibilities of experience (which show the experimenter how far he can come to the best possible knowledge of the real process of nature).

All the great physicists of our time unanimously confirm this. What does this mean? We have often heard that the difficulties and successes of modern physics are connected with the discovery of the domains of the infinitely small (in atomic phys-

2. K. E. von Baer, mostly under the influence of Schelling, indicated for the first time the manifold self-containment, each constructed in its own way, of the subjective spheres of life. In a famous treatise, "What Conception of Living Nature Is the Correct One?" *Reden und Vorträge*, Vol. I (1864), he presented the structural scheme within which the variation of the measurement units of perception and of reaction does not lead to quantitative differences but rather clarifies the formation of spheres of moments of life, even of moments of reaction, as objectively different characters of formation of animal life. The nonspecific, thus nonobjective structural scheme, which can only be experienced ontologically, is thereby made into the foundation for the understanding of the ontic manifold. I have presented the consequences in detail in the lecture. Since they are generally well known as to content, I believe that understanding is better served if I stress only the fundamental points here.

ics) and of the infinitely large (in cosmology). It is not the greatness and smallness which is decisive for the dissimilarity of experience, but the fact that the measurement units of our *natural* experience fail in these domains. They fail in relativistic physics because they cannot be kept fixed and immutable, and in quantum physics because they cannot keep fixed what is to be measured. But do not dwell on this negative face. More positively, modern physics discovers various domains of experience with their own structures. What it experiences is experience *relative to our mode of experience*. This *ontological* experience is what permits new possibilities of experience to be revealed. The discovery of new possibilities of experience, with their own dimensions differing from our specific "natural" dimension, is theory. Modern physics is primarily theoretical in this new sense. It is not a systematic explanation, but an advance thrust. The surpassing of natural experiences brackets these experiences. Our familiar units of measure for time and space are no longer constitutive for experience or what can be experienced, not even in a derivative form, so that smaller and larger units have had to replace the natural ones. No longer are there constant forms of experience which offer units of measurement that are applicable in every domain. Modern physics does not place itself *in* a dimension, it is directed *toward* dimensions, toward their variety and the ineffable ground of their unity.

In classical physics, we marked out a framework for ourselves and introduced constants with their relations of orientation. On the basis of these referential orientations, the experiment marked off the measured magnitudes. These could be arbitrarily large or arbitrarily small. But this did not alter anything in the dimension of experience.

In modern physics, we mark out nothing in advance. We insert ourselves, so to speak, into this world totality; we orient ourselves in it with all of our equipment and seek to understand individual parts, like hydrogen or an electron, out of the cooperation of the unified powers of the totality. Every equation always represents the entire totality of the world (only known a priori, but not sensibly and objectively). As you can see, the theme of modern physics is therefore the *cooperation*, the mode of *interlocking*. The transcendental subjective project is replaced by the temporal experience of a definite scheme of the reality of the cooperation of unknown moments. It is this *interlocking scheme* which is of concern to the physicist. Modern physics does not require (and it even excludes it under certain conditions) the physicist to concern himself with the qualitative observation of interlocking moments. Whichever moment he designates can itself only be experienced as theory, i.e., as the mode of interlocking of operations, a mode characteristic for that which is isolated in the experience of the physicist as a mode of the wholeness of the totality. What the physicist has to deal with are modes of procedure, modes of interlocking, modes of schema. Merely consider by way of comparison the idea of the atom in classical physics. It suffices just to point out that when we now speak of atoms or other elementary particles of matter, we do not mean small and stable bodies, even if without qualities, but a system of mathematical formulas. We are not even in the position of being able to ascribe geometrical determinations (extension, shape) to the atoms. And so we relinquish the classical presupposition which assumed that the elementary particles designate some fundamental moment of nature.

Even the proton does not satisfy the meaning which is pictured in the ontic representation of an elementary particle in thinglike form. It can be resolved into particles for ontic experience, i.e., an experience which corresponds to the experiment within a strictly conditioned ontic domain, without these particles actually being "on hand" (*vorhanden*) there. In spite of this, we speak of the constant mass of protons, i.e., we speak of it as if it were a thing formation.

Evidently then, "proton" can have a double meaning: on the one hand, material in the classical sense, with a definite mass and diameter (i.e., under certain circumstances, it is meaningful to speak of its diameter); on the other, a structural rule which has something to do with the quantum instability of the course of nature. The first experience is the ontic-objective, the second the ontological experience of the nonobjective course of nature within quantum physics, but which includes the initial thing experience.

The historical development of quantum physics itself shows how the new kind of experience was successively discovered only on the basis of the ontic experience. The representation of the atom as a thing experience first made it possible for us to become acquainted with appearances of atoms which were describable as quantum effects. These experiences were incomprehensible as thing effects or as appearances. In a completely new kind of experience, theory experienced the course of nature with regard to the magnitudes, lengths, and order of the steps of its pure motion and the possibilities of Being which vary the structural moments in their structural ties. This system of possibilities of ties and variations is in its essence mathematically describable, for mathematics is the only way to describe structural connections.

We must therefore distinguish clearly. The atoms of classical physics were considered as material objects. But this is true not only of the atoms of classical physics. Atoms actually *are* material objects, and so are protons and electrons. But in which kind of experience? In the ontic natural experience, in which only the thinglike and the objective can really be experienced. Atoms, protons, etc., are objects of the same experience in which tables, furniture, words, passions, social changes, birth and death can also be experienced, together with all changes which lie between such end points or to which the phenomena are subject. Every thing experience is an appearance within the transcendental subjectivity.

But basically, theory experiences atoms, protons, etc., stripped of all sensible or objective qualities, as pure structural formulas, i.e., as the expression of the articulated structure of the course of nature. Nothing subjective, as well as nothing understood in a transcendental-subjective way, is found in this experience. The ontological experience experiences the transcendental objective reality.

Could we equally transform our natural experience, which is not performed with scientific exactness, into a new experience? Could we, for example, strip the table experience of all sense qualities? Certainly. We do it whenever we speak of the experience which we have of every table experience, of the underlying (*hypokeimenon*), of having and of privation (*hexis-sterēsis*), as Aristotle does in his metaphysics. His example, among many others, is the possibility of change which links the pile of bricks with the brick house. In this phase of the example, the brick itself is something perceivable as a thing. But it must be borne in mind that the same considerations of ontological genesis (not that of ontic production) apply equally to the brick, and however far we go back, we can always resolve the material determined as a thing into a union of possibilities of change whose bearer is the *hypokeimenon* (that which persists underneath), without name and predicate. It signifies the Being in need of change in all of the possibilities. Such unions of possibilities of change form the plaiting of the articulated order that bears all beings.

But the classical ontological experience is not radical enough. Its discovery, beginning with the pre-Socratics, was indeed the discovery of philosophy and at once the discovery of science. When I say that it was not radical enough, I refer to the link of this ontological experience with the subjective self-discovery of man among beings as a whole, the transcendental subjectivity of this ontological experience, which oriented itself toward the understanding of Being and not (aside from a few early starts) toward the course of Being itself.

Modern physics is free from subjective restriction, so much so that it includes human self-discovery within the texture of the articulated order. Man himself is resolved into an observer scheme and the scheme is linked with the contexts of possibilities for transformation. The observer scheme is not a subject, but an objective moment of the contextual texture, of the articulated order. Space and time in this new and thoroughly radicalized experience are not forms of subjective apprehension, but real moments of having and privation of a nameless mode that we name "nature."

But why did I say at the beginning that with Kant and the post-Kantians a new turn of philosophy began which is first drawn into a productive transparency through Heidegger's effort? Why was I not content to say that the new level of metaphysics radicalized the classical? Because the decisive factor lies not only in the sharp separation of ontological experience from the ontic, but in the separation within the ontological experience itself. This signifies for philosophy that the classical ontological consideration gets its foundation in the philosophy of philosophy which discovered the condition of possibility of the ontological experience, and indeed not by starting from the subjective ontological experience but from the happening of Being, which itself makes experience possible. In other words, we do not seek the conditions of possibility of experience within the subjectivity; rather, we look for their genesis, as well as that of the subjectivity, in the course of the happening of nature. For the understanding of the enormous spiritual and historical effort which takes place in the natural sciences, this separation signifies that it learns to distinguish between transcendental subjective domains and transcendental objective domains of ontological experience. Physics concentrates on the transcendental objective domains. Since it deals with living beings which are defined as much by their own subjective schemes of possibilities of change as by the transcendental objective articulated structures, biology must advance to a universal domain of transcendental union. As a result of this distinction, quantum theory, when it does not illegitimately overstep its limits and thus destroy its positivity, is never adequate for the mastery of the problem of life.

The Significance of Bohr's Correspondence Principle

3. But the actual philosophical difficulties of physics do not stem from illegitimate claims but from the incomplete distinguishing of the ontological experience with regard to transcendental objective articulated structures and the ontic objects, whose experience is first made possible by the first experience. To put it more correctly, the reason for the difficulty is that physics is just underway toward the experience of the connections between the course of nature and the thinglike phenomenal processes of nature. The only mediating experience achieved to date, not advanced enough to be appreciated, is Bohr's correspondence principle. But a sufficiently radical interpretation of it is still lacking. The principle as Niels Bohr initially formulated it is concerned with the parallelism between classical and quantum physics. It states first that the experiences of classical physics are preconditions for possibilities of experience of a completely different kind, for those which proffer the domain of quanta and atomic connections. Second, the principle states that in all individual problems, there is a link between the object experience of classical physics and the non-objectifiable structural experience of quantum physics. Third, the continuous connections which prevail between the thing elements of classical physics are established by the quantum-physical elementary structures, so that their lawfulness must be brought to experience out of these latter. And fourth: even the most exact experiences of the pattern of possibilities of changes in quantum physics acquire a content or phenomenally describable relevance only when the required return to the correspond-

ing objectively determined domain of macrophysics is performed.

What do these four determinations signify for philosophical understanding? It is first necessary to recall that quantum physics deals with elementary processes. Its theme is the process character of nature, and its most fundamental experience is that this process in general is not objectifiable. Physics motivates the impossibility with the quantum-physical instabilities of the processes of nature, which forbid the representation of two interconnecting parts in an objective process or the determination of a continuous and calculable unity of development between the two portions of the process. These are negative formulations. Another negative observation is that this experience is devoid of the causal relation, which requires the conditions of stability and thingness. Even the observation that an indeterminacy prevails in the process of nature, so that only probability statements are possible, is at first negative when taken by itself.

What is the positive interpretation? What the correspondence principle asserts is not unfamiliar to philosophy. It also realizes ontological experience only in conjunction with ontic experience. For it as well, every single moment of experience is charged with the bond between a thing experience and the experience of Being, which is of course not explicit. Like the correspondence principle, it has at its very beginning discovered that the connections experienced as a thing are founded in an interpretation of Being as "no-thing." But even it has no methodic possibility for fulfilling the experiences of Being concretely, other than by a continual return to the ontic experiences of beings.

The ontological experience of process cannot be separated from the experience of objects. Each is intertwined with the other and indeed in such a way that the ontological experience always accompanies the object experience; everything in process transmutes whatever is definite in the object experience, but still the experience is complete only in unity with the object experience. The ontological experiences of the moment of articulation refer to reality, while the ontic experiences refer to the moment of appearance whose reality is to be interpreted. This is a remarkable bond which poses the most difficult problems for ontology. The continual complementarity of moments (the fundamental supplement which was added to the correspondence principle in physics by Heisenberg) characterizes in a more original manner the unity: course – operation (or, more simply stated, the unity: process – thing appearance) of the reality which is adequate to nature. And so we can establish a new level of adequacy for our presentation. Reality is neither the ontological context of articulation, for it cannot be separated from the phenomena unfolding as things, nor the thing phenomena in their lawful and categorially understood motion, since they would be pure contingencies without their genetic foundation. Conditioned by Being, their unity *is real;* that contingent necessity which is physics permits the composition of calculation schemes, which in turn clarify which objective connections are fundamentally possible. A parallel comment: neither the ontological experience nor the ontic thing apprehension is a cognizance of reality. Not the former because it simply cannot be isolated from the ontic experience. There is no thing in itself behind the appearances. But even the experience of appearances is not real, since the transcendental objective experience is not only of appearances, but also, in complementary unity, of the course of nature which founds them and within which they appear.

The Schrödinger Equation

What we have called the "remarkable bond" is described for physics most clearly by Schrödinger ("The Present Situation in Quantum Mechanics," *Naturwissenschaft* [1935]). The classical physicist understood the ontic process with the help of a model, which was established "by a finite number of suitably selected measurements." We have seen that these numerical measurements were selected in a transcendental subjective manner, i.e., they were determined on the basis of what the physicist understood by "operation of nature." The classical model is the constant in relation to which every alteration of the operation can be ascertained by the (indirect) measurement of the numerical values of the invariant numerical measures (model constants). It is the "bridge of relations and conditions between measurements and measurements." It thus permits the prediction of every alteration of the operation, for the alteration proceeds according to causal conditions. This role also "formally" complies with the ψ function of wave mechanics. It corresponds in this regard with the classical model idea. But this is only a condition of its achievement. The ψ function still records a type of alteration "which does not have the slightest thing to do with the unwinding" (an ontic operation). This alteration does not take place on the basis of the invariance of the systematic unity of the numerical measures. The system itself is altered with every new measurement, and with it also the possible range of expectations. The "catalogue of expectations" is always new. It changes with time. With every new measurement, i.e., with every new demarcation of phenomenal relations proceeding in a thinglike way, the model, which earlier depicted the prescriptions of expectations, is now itself unexpectedly new. "With every measurement, we are compelled to ascribe a unique, somewhat abrupt alteration to the ψ function (the catalogue of predictions), which depends on the *discovered numerical measure* and therefore cannot be foreseen."[3]

Let us bear two things in mind from what has already been said. First, the distinction between the course of nature and individual operations of nature. Second, the discovery that a calculative *scheme,* as the most adequate expression for the experience of the articulated structure of the course of nature, on the one hand presents the step-by-step progression of the change of possibilities (as the physicist says, "it is an instrument for predicting the probabilities of numerical measures"), and on the other frees the complementary for the conditions of experience proper to it, the phenomenal self-demarcation of things, which follows without a break out of the causality corresponding to the new measurement situation. Schrödinger has succeeded in separating the two moments of experience and in linking them, i.e., in presenting their unity so that it becomes clear and evident. For quantum physics, the ontological experience is the decisive one—not the products in their isolated occurrence but

3. It must be emphasized that models and model constants have retained their important methodic significance even in current research, in spite of a change in course which (especially, e.g., in quantum mechanics) only disturbs the external form. The content of the model appears to have become something completely new and different. We can speak on the one hand of a continual change in the idea of a model and on the other of the effort to dispense with models and constants in principle. Important philosophical problems are concealed in these inconsistencies. I have dealt with these somewhere else. Here I only wanted to emphasize the ambiguity of the experience, for which the distinctions cited are symptomatic.

the process, and in such an emphatic way that the ontic phenomena, which cannot be separated from the ontological experience, are likewise ontologized. In other words, what becomes thematic is not their product character, but the process character of their possibilities.

Physics Itself Is Not Yet Philosophically Conscious of Its True Intentions

I do not wish to force any congruence whatsoever between philosophy and the theory of modern physics. For the present, there is unfortunately no discussion of the fact that they mutually interrogate each other. But the metaphysical change in which we stand is so compelling that both still obey the same imperatives even without discussion of their experiences with regard to their modes. All of these experiences have consequences for the natural possibility of experience. Not that the return to the latter objectively supplements the other experience. The return is always richer. Everything whose objective possibility is demanded in the experience of the process structures is also sooner or later brought to light in the experiment of ontic experience. This happened repeatedly in the most recent development of physics; it happens almost every day and surprises us again and again with the richness of our ontic world of experience. This is why I said that the most proper mode of experience in natural science is theory. Experiment has a fundamentally different role in it than it did in classical physics. It marks the change in the domain of experience, a *metabasis*, a transition (return) to another genus, to another context. The experimentally experienced positron (the electron with a positive charge), for example, is not identical with the theoretically "constructed" positron. Its construction marks a moment in which the articulated context is experienced. By contrast, in observation it acquires thing qualities, though it does so, as we must rather say, obviously by way of disclaimer, in order to retain the process character in the experience. In the experiment, emerging as it does in the relevant context and then disappearing, the proton is a matter of fact, a thing. We have experienced it as something entering and leaving our thing world under definite conditions. This experience is enormously important. It completes the theoretical experience, but it does not proceed on the same level. The theoretical experience experiences the positron as a process character, as a moment of process in the articulated structure of the course of nature. Even without artificial organization, the moments of process are converted into thing phenomena. But as to when this takes place, this is fundamentally indeterminable, because it is a matter of two distinct domains and modes of experience. Prediction must deal with the transition. And the probability statements of modern physics relate to it. They are witness to the point that the connection between the ontologically experienced course of Being and the ontically experienced thing processes is itself real. The rule of the demonstration of the particular possibility of transition to the probability statements belongs to the radical interpretation of the correspondence principle. Through it, it is possible to explain for the first time how, in the process of nature, the coming to be and passing away of the ontic phenomena are regulated according to individual type. Here is the true cosmogony, if we understand by cosmos the fullness of beings accessible to us right now, with all of their ontic relations and all of the transmutations to which they are subject.

It should be evident from all this that the argument between causality and probability occurs only because physics has not yet made its true intentions philosophically clear. If I repeatedly stress the necessity that the two modes of experience that are accessible to us must be consistently distinguished from one another, I am only formulating an insight which incessantly compels the great physicists to disengage their mode of experience, the theoretical, from the ontically intuitive mode of experience. Heisenberg quite often emphasizes that in atomic physics every attempt at intuition must be shunned in advance as senseless and aimless, and he demands a quantum mechanics which solely contains relations between atomic physical (to be sure, fundamentally "observable") magnitudes.

It is only when physicists interpret what they do as though modern physics were, because of this distinction, a pure thought construction, that they alienate themselves from the creative power which is operative in their work. The nonintuitive experience directed solely toward relations of magnitude must be recognized as ontological in its validity. Physics thus simply recognizes nature in its true happening.

I hope that I have clarified the significance of the ontological experience in physics and have shown, at least in individual instances, how the ontic experience of appearances is connected with the experience of the real happening of nature.

The Theoretical Experience within Biology

4. I beg your indulgence in making a few more remarks about the theoretical experience within biology. I have already pointed out that the experience of the transcendental objective context alone is not adequate for the ontological experience with regard to life as a specific happening.

This is not the only reason why physics is unable to interpret life phenomena with its own methods; the moment of life cannot be wholly described either physically or chemically. In this respect, especially with regard to the initial emergence of life in the transformation of matter, our refined knowledge and the untold possibilities of experimentation can lead us to definite results. But they would not bridge the fundamental separation, for biology deals with beings which adapt their experiences as real moments to an otherwise experience-free context of Being. Whatever inferior level of consciousness these experiences might have, however limited their mode of understanding Being, they form a unique sphere which, when inserted in its totality into nature's contexts, demands entirely new structures for itself. It was not so long ago that biology ran the risk of understanding the subjective transcendental structural mode of a unique domain in an anthropomorphic way. Modern biology treats the moments of consciousness and experience of animals as "physical magnitudes." The change in direction is most strikingly manifested in Karl von Frisch's investigations into the riddle of the "language of bees" over the past twenty years. The first publications interpreted the dance of the bees purely anthropomorphically. Frisch's further aim was to investigate the grammar and vocabulary which determined the communication of bees. The last publication known to me, on the "Dances on a Horizontal Base" (*Naturwissenschaft* [1948], nos. 1, 2) organizes the subjective impressions and expressions of the bees into a strict scheme in conjunction with the physical conditions. It is clear that the contrast familiar to us, on the one hand systematic arrangement and prestabilized harmony, and on the other causal necessity, is transgressed in the research which provides our example. The idea of systematic arrangement loses its sharpness when what is intended with it finds fulfillment in the scheme of the investigation of the ontological structure of the process of nature. Causal necessity retains its experiential validity in the ontic domain. But it also loses some of its sharpness insofar as it is thought that the causal operations unfold in a network whose structure is continually being altered.

The great difficulties of biology thus stem from the fact that it must differentiate its methods along many lines, (1) according to the ontically describable sequence of the phenomenal operations and phenomenal moments, which a consideration of the quantum-theoretical experiential conditions of its founding course of nature demands, and (2) according to the productivity of the subjectivity, which for its part also has an unstable course between achieved stages and the new possibilities emerging from these. Consider only the problem of mutations or that of the immense multiplicity of animal forms, as A. Portmann does in an important book which has just appeared. Or consider, for example, the theory of evolution or genetics. It has so far not yet clarified how deeply, even if not in a way visible in advance, the true life form codetermines the anatomical form. The anatomical form expresses our kinship with all animals; the life form expresses their insurmountable strangeness. We do not immediately know, when we find purely anatomical-morphological-optical instruments in animals, whether they have the same function, and if so, whether they belong to the same structural dimensions as our own optical organization. And conversely, when these are missing, we do not know which organs are delegated for the operation within the unique dimensional scheme. An expression for dimensional scheme is the life formation. Biology can investigate the life formations isolated in each case only in an infinitely laborious effort. To that end, it must first investigate all the moments which enter into the dimension or have their characters from it, and then as well the kind and the way in which the performance disposition utilizes the entire dimensional unity.

This is not the occasion to go into the ontological experience of biology, e.g., to examine how it is directed toward the unified context of ordination in which the transcendental subjectively determined moments of ordination are coordinated with the transcendental objective branches of ordination of the physical happening. But to avoid misunderstanding, I would like to stress that the subjectivity which is proper in each case for the living being is also a theme of the investigation only in its character as a moment. The regulative principle for observation is the global cohesiveness hidden in the organization of the life process, whereby all cooperating moments maintain a definite characterization according to life performance. This global structure is to be investigated as a scheme of this characterization and inserted within the calculation.

The true theory of biology is still to be developed. Many admirable efforts aim at it. More than a hundred years ago, one of the great founders of this new science, Johannes Müller, instituted the demand to think of life theoretically, i.e., corresponding to its structural unity which shows the interlocking of the specific moments proper to it in schemes suitable to this interlocking, to comprehend all experience and then "to think them into theory."

The Greek designation for the organization of life is *psyche*. A hundred years later, another of the greats, Hans Speeman, articulated the same demand in the work which incorporates the distillation of his life's work, "Experimental Contributions to a Theory of Development." He says:

> Again and again, expressions have been used which do not designate physical but rather psychological analogies. That this should happen must signify more than a poetic image. . . . It must mean that these processes of development, like all vital processes, whether or not they are at one time resolved into chemical and physical processes and can be constructed from them, in the type of their nexus bear a similarity with nothing of all that is as familiar to us as those vital processes of which we possess the most intimate knowledge, the psychic. It must mean that we ourselves, totally apart from all philosophical consequences and solely in the interest of the progress of our concrete and exact basic knowledge, should not forego the advantage of our position between both worlds. This recognition is now dawning in many places. I believe that my experiments have taken a step on the way toward this new and lofty goal.

This last paragraph of the book, from which I have quoted and which resounds as a profound legacy, points to theory and how it is to be understood.

NATURAL SCIENTIFIC TRUTH

Heisenberg's Uncertainty Relation

So FAR, I have spoken of the twofold experience and have attempted to demonstrate that the theoretical experience of modern physics is, according to its own practice, the ontological experience. I shall now speak of the problem of truth. The idea of truth in classical physics was based on the continuum, on the unity and stability of the universe, on the immutability of once established relations between individual phenomena, and on the identity of the selfsame thing, leaving aside its changes of state. As a result of the change of experience, our situation is above all a paradox. None of the determinations of classical physics has forfeited any of its truth content as a result of the new development. And yet our new experiences, which can rely neither on the continuity or unity of the universe, nor on the stability of the thing in itself, nor on immutable relations, are in a definite way *more deeply* true than the experiential statements which are related to the phenomenal world of things. They have no subjective moments. They in fact do not conform to eternal forms or to their pure hierarchy. But they are also not flawed by confusion with the mundane and sensible encumbrances, as Plato and the tradition following him understood human statements of truth. We grope ahead with truths which develop concurrently with the genesis of the contexts of Being.

Thus it is almost like living in opposed truths which still go well with each other. The explanation for this compatibility is given by Heisenberg's uncertainty relation, which expresses the new truth relation of that which was established by Bohr's correspondence principle with regard to the new mode of experience. The remarkable feature of this principle is that it is itself a reality statement. It describes the mode of the course of nature. Over and above this, it designates a completely new way of thought, through which the change of which I spoke is stabilized and acquires its corresponding spiritual atmosphere.

The classical manifestation of complementarity is the double nature of light as a particle and as a wave. The particle properties and the wave determinations are dually coordinated to each other. The truth statements in the different domains are complementary in such a way that, for example, the greater the certainty of the statement concerning the location of the particle, the more uncertain the statement of its magnitudes of motion or of the relations which relate it to the atomic context. The absolute certainty of one mode of statement would correspond to absolute ignorance of the other domain of experience. This alone is already remarkable enough. It suggests the analogous fact that our everyday knowledge has so fallen to the level of the given that any sort of orientation to Being can be veiled to the point of oblivion. But there is something else which is even more remarkable. The degree of certainty or uncertainty in physics can be expressed numerically. According to what has already been said, the product of the two uncertainties is constant. But now Heisenberg made the theoretical assumption that the product of the uncertainties associated with a measurement in the complementary domains must be equal in order of magnitude to the elementary quantum of action. This assumption has proven to be very fruitful in physics. This sounds subjectivistic or contingent. But when we heard the word "assumption" in modern physics, and we hear it quite often, we always regard it as having only a formal kinship with what is meant by "hypothesis." Physical "assumptions" today are not presuppositions but results of a very definite ontological experience, which as such can hardly be immediately founded but which impose themselves in compliance with the guidance provided by the experience and the articulated structures which it manifests. They "succeed" to an entirely new mode from the clarity proper to the situation of a mathematically described context of articulation—neither as deductions nor as subsumptions but as the missing thread which uniquely and by itself can trace the sequence of experiences and thereby unite them.

The Truth Construction of the Physicists

The logic of this truth "construction," which the physicist customarily introduces with the statement "we make the assumption," calls for a thorough investigation. So too does the point that the assumptions are in most cases identifications of two structural magnitudes, e.g., the identification of light intensity with wave amplitude. The most important advances in quantum physics occurred through assumptions of this kind, like those added to classical mechanics by de Broglie and Schrödinger, for example. Thus the impression easily arises even among physicists that what they do, because it is a "construction," is an arbitrary constructing of forms which have no claim to reality. Even though there is not yet enough clarity pervading these questions, I would nonetheless like to emphasize in particular that the truth construction, and with it "constructive empiricism," denotes a completely new kind of construction, a moment of the ontological experience which experiences the apriority of the course of nature by a priori means.

And so it is convincing to an even greater degree that the constant of the product of uncertainties must have precisely the order of magnitude of the quantum of action; that therefore the certainty, perhaps we may even say the "complementary truth level" of a physical statement in one domain and its complementary completion in the other, has a fundamental relation to the quantization of the course of nature.

It would be premature at this time to wish to characterize the truth of the ontological experience systematically. I would like only to accentuate one of its fundamental characters. It says nothing about beings, ontic relations, ontic events. But it says something exhaustive about the possibility of beings, relations, and contexts of events. The mathematically experienced representation of the context of Being retains an a priori introversion with its course, which is not influenced by phenomenal changes, not because it is related to the eternally immutable but because it is associated with the structure which lies at the basis of every change of the processes. With respect to the objective world (in which our history, art, poetry, and social structure are included), our knowledge becomes ever richer, more genuine, more profound. It has a linear continual progress. Our ontological insights do not. They will be altered only because the context of nature is altered. Insofar as they comprehend the scheme of these alterations, they are unshakable. But then they cannot be objectively fixed. They are the inspired readiness to let all changes of possibilities of Being remain as they are and to let them have a hearing. In our facticity, such a character possesses a unique relation of truth: intimacy. I have already repeatedly emphasized another of its characteristics: we do not arrive at new conceptual possibilities on the basis of experiences, but rather we arrive at new possibilities of experiencing on the basis of new modes of experience.

The Concept of "Intimacy"

Intimacy is the highest level of the coexistence of one man with another. It denotes a relation of familiarity which is not erected on individual experiences but already precedes them. It is a priori to such a degree that it already operates in the form of a total readiness in the education of man as such from the first years of childhood. When it has achieved its full effectiveness, its level of mutual acquaintance is such that it can predict how the other will behave in definite circumstances, even if all the circumstances cannot be conceived and still less be predicted. The mutual possibilities of experience can be predicted to the point that even the incalculable situations serve to confirm intimacy. A further moment of intimacy: it regularly permits silent dialogue. This steadfast dialogue which even dominates silence is precisely intimacy. It gets a hearing by virtue of the dialogue, which is not torn asunder into individual attitudes toward one another, or into the words which are exchanged. The words draw their sense and their resonance from the intimacy. I would accordingly like to say that a kind of intimacy characterizes the context of theories. It is the bond of understanding between the human existent and the happening of Being, which does not have to be made explicit and as such cannot be explicated at any given time, but is explicated in every attitude of the existent and in every word which he speaks. The intimacy of a mechanic with his auto manifests itself in his manipulations. We might even say that the auto and the mechanic understand each other well. It is in this way that the existent understands the different domains of Being well. The intimacy goes beyond the individual theories; it is precisely the "understanding-each-other-well" in the theoretical happening. By virtue of its intimacy, theoretical physics has experiences concerning the openness of its new possibilities of thought. It is in this sense that I wish to be understood when I say that intimacy makes possible the dialogue with nature—to put it more adequately, the dialogue between the Being of the existent and the Being of the totality. This intimacy is the transcendental reality which is our common bond.

If we understand the dialogue with nature in this sense, the full scope of Heidegger's thought becomes clear to us, and we grasp what he suggests when he says that Being gets a hearing in the existent.

The dialogue is silent because it is intimacy itself. But it comes to language, as it does in every word expressed in daily coexistence, whoever may say the word. It is in this sense that the Being of beings comes to language and gets a hearing in the existent.

What does this signify in regard to the questions which now concern us? We have indicated that the complementarity principle in its unity with the uncertainty relation institutes a pervasive relation. It allows itself to be generalized even outside of physics in the form of an assignment of a general complementarity or *koinonia,* as Plato has called it in an even deeper ontological understanding. The word denotes a special kind of bond. It clearly excludes the communication explainable in terms of content (like the somatic account of psychic phenomena). But it points to a common prehistory. It imposes its independence over every domain of phenomena. But it demands that the independence be understood out of the common relation, since it precedes every division.

Intimacy is a kind of experience of the prehistory, not in the sense of facts but in the sense of the precedent common relation. The preconceived common relation in our coexistence is language. Its experience in the form of the capacity to speak constitutes the intimacy, i.e., the truth of the capacity to experience not only the uniting but also the separating, and indeed in a continually self-modifying development which only deepens the intimacy, no matter how this development goes or comes to a standstill.

I must forego the further pursuit of this idea here. The same kind of intimacy enters into our new natural scientific experiences. It has its own truth. Since modes of Being are experienced in the experience, the openness corresponding to it is the truth of Being. As such it is never refutable and can never be undone. It is a new possibility of experience and thus a new opening of an irrefutable openness. It shows how far-reaching, in terms of anticipation and the indication of directions, Heidegger's profound distinction between the truth of beings and the truth of Being is, even in this relation. The truth of beings is the truth of the ontic experience. The truth of Being is being able to apprehend in what mode the Being of beings articulates itself in many ways, so that the experiences corresponding to the different domains of beings are united and separated out of a prehistory.

Essence of Historicity

One of the most important results of theoretical physics is the insight that it is fundamentally impossible to constitute a uniformity, in the classical sense of a model, out of the different domains of beings as it experiences them. It thereby itself makes explicit that it sees its deepest experiences in the experience of Being or in its articulations and different modes, and that its highest truth is the openness of the happening of Being, in which it is articulated into different modes of Being. I used the word "happening" and I mean historical happening. In conclusion, I must illustrate in a few remarks what the designation "history of Being" should refer to in this context. It belongs to the historicity of a happening that it never passes away. Even in the ordinary use of the word, the appellation "historical" refers to something which never entirely disappears from our Being, even though it is not always actual. The historical is always "present" at every level and in every mode of our human Being. "Presence" is meant to express that the historical is operative in every present, disappears from no present, even if conscious memory is remiss in bearing it in mind. The essence of historicity is presence and indeed in the mode of continually waiting for actualization. The happening of the always new experience of Being has the greatest affinity with the happening of historicity. It is in this happening that the truths discovered in the different domains of Being are "present," so much so that their factic validity is curtailed with the alteration of the experiential system. The curtailment does not contradict their continually persisting claim to truth. On the contrary, it means their actualization in a newly uncovered, always unexpected truth of experience which renews their legitimacy. But this following upon one another of experience is not, as on a geographical map, a matter of sketching domains next to each other and thus covering a continuum, but rather has a course which can be ontologically experienced, like the course of history. It is not a matter of holding domains together according to a scheme projected in advance, thereby never capable of being experienced in their totality, but the happening of an articulation and of a unity of Being. This unique and authentic happening which governs everything can never be seized in a single glance, since it is always advancing and always underway in unexpected ways.

I would like to mention one more thing. We can never esteem too highly the spectacular achievement of the men who, especially in our century, have brought into play all of their human gifts, fantasy, a sense of harmony and beauty, faith and self-reflection, so that the knowing union with the totality, already sought in the Greek mythologies, and its mysterious happening, exalting us again and again, but also compelling us to humility, has slowly but surely become a scientifically concretized experience. The latest discoveries have taken their starting point in the investigation of light. "The light," says de Broglie, "which illuminates bodies, has also brightened our spirit."

Plato and Aristotle also thought of light in this way, so that for them it was not the visible but the mediating power which gives visibility to all beings and so puts them in the same medium with us, the "seeing things." The age-old question of the unity of Being and the multiplicity of the modes of Being, which determines our vision and action in the new turn, implicitly and unconsciously also guides the deeds of the great scientists of our age, those who continue the destiny of our profession.

I said vision and action. The vision is the theory. According to its essence, theory points to that which is more powerful than man, to the colossal, dangerous, overpowering, as Aristotle points out in the *Nicomachean Ethics*. Our action won supradimensional possibilities by virtue of our intimacy with nature. On the strength of the union with the elementary powers, our bodily possibilities have developed into unsuspected dimensions. Reaching even farther and magnifying itself more and more, our corporality requires—as de Broglie in conjunction with Bergson says—an equally magnified soul. The magnified moral sense, the magnified sense of responsibility for the totality, we can almost say, is that for which we strive in our work, and to which our university, the unified cultivation of all the sciences, the unified preservation of our tradition, also calls you in these meetings.

PART II

Phenomenology and Science in France

Eugène Minkowski

EUGÈNE MINKOWSKI was born in Poland on April 17, 1885. After receiving his secondary education in Warsaw, he went on to study at the medical schools of the Universities of Warsaw and Munich. He received his medical degree in Munich in 1909. After a short period in Kazan, Russia, where he continued his medical education, he returned to Germany to study philosophy. In 1914 he left Germany and became a resident at a university psychiatric hospital (Burghölzli, Switzerland), where he worked under Eugen Bleuler (1914–15). In 1915 he became a volunteer in the French army. After taking French citizenship, he was awarded a French medical diploma and practiced for many years as a psychiatrist at several leading French hospitals. He devoted a great deal of his time to research, publications, and philosophical reflection.

Specializing in neuropsychiatry, Minkowski devoted his first publications to the theory of color perception and psychophysical parallelism. His later publications deal with topics related to clinical psychiatry and psychopathology. In addition to numerous articles in French and foreign journals, as well as other publications, Minkowski wrote three very important books: *La Schizophrénie, Le Temps vécu*, and *Vers une cosmologie*.

Minkowski's philosophy has been deeply influenced by Bergson and the phenomenological movement. Although he only recognizes explicitly the influence of Scheler, in fact, Husserl's work, which is mentioned a few times in passing, and the philosophy of Heidegger certainly belong to the major sources of Minkowski's inspiration.

Although Minkowski's work has been substantially in the realm of the human sciences, we have included in this anthology one chapter of his *Vers une cosmologie* in which he compares natural science with poetry and tries to outline what both contribute to our genuine understanding of the "kosmos." At first sight this essay does not seem to fit into the over-all perspective of this anthology. Upon closer examination, however, it will become clear that, regardless of the many differences in style, approach, and final goal, there is a striking analogy between Minkowski's main concern here and the fundamental concern of all phenomenologists. There is no doubt that Minkowski's study is meant to be a rigorous criticism of all forms of positivism, and, for that matter, of scientism. A similar criticism is found in the works of Husserl, Heidegger, Merleau-Ponty, and many other phenomenologists. Perhaps not all phenomenologists will agree with Minkowski that the realm of the world which science leaves out of consideration is to be designated by the expression "the poetic side of man's life and of the world." In this context some phenomenologists would certainly like to refer to the religious, moral, social, political, technological, and perhaps even other aspects of our lives and of the world, too; but all of them certainly agree with the basic thesis Minkowski has tried to defend here. Furthermore, if one were to take the term "the poetic" in a rather broad sense so as to include everything which presupposes man's "creativity," that is, everything to which Hegel refers with the term "objective spirit," then the relationship between Minkowski and other phenomenologists would become even more striking. His terms "anthropology" and "cosmology" could then perhaps be interpreted as analogues of Heidegger's analytic of man's Being and what he originally called "ontology."

But perhaps we should not stress these parallels too much; suffice it here to point to the fact that Minkowski shares with all other phenomenologists the following views: (1) scientific knowledge is not the only nor privileged way of knowing things and the world; (2) we must challenge the ambition of the sciences to give us a synthetic picture of the totality of the world; (3) it is not possible to reduce philosophy to some kind of systematization of the sciences; and finally (4) philosophy, although essentially different from it, has nonetheless something in common with "poetry." As Heidegger says: "Between these

two [thought and poetry] there exists a secret kinship. . . .
Between both there is, however, at the same time an abyss, for
they dwell on the most widely separated mountains." *

* Martin Heidegger, *What Is Philosophy?* trans. Jean T. Wilde
and William Klubach (New Haven, Conn.: College & University
Press, 1958), p. 95.

11 / Prose and Poetry (Astronomy and Cosmology)

Eugène Minkowski

One night, while quietly nestled down under a fig tree, I looked at a star with that curious passion which captures children and to which my precocious melancholy added a kind of sentimental understanding. . . . She [the governess] pretended to look for me and called me. I answered. She came to the fig tree where she knew I was.

"What are you doing there?" she said.

"I am looking at a star."

"You are not looking at a star," said my mother, who heard us from her balcony. "Can one know astronomy at your age?"

(Balzac, *Le Lys dans la vallée*)

CERTAINLY, at the age of six one does not engage in astronomy, but one can look at a star with "that curious passion which captures children" and to which a "precocious melancholy" can add "a kind of sentimental understanding." Moreover, may it not happen to us at any age that we look at a star and find a particular charm in it because it reflects a whole aspect of our being?

Two ways of looking at a star come face to face in the scene just described: one, the scientific way, wants to see facts in rigorous objectivity and things only in their "materiality"; the "poetic" way does not impose any barriers upon itself and lets its glance wander to infinity to discover in each object an entire world. The mistake of the mother lies in ignoring the second

This article is from *Vers une cosmologie* by Eugène Minkowski (Paris: Aubier, 1936), pp. 163–72, and was translated into English expressly for this edition by Joseph J. Kockelmans.

way. It reveals to us a lack in her soul and makes us take a step backward. The astronomer himself does not go that far. In his spare time he will know how to look at stars as a poet and as one who knows that it is not this poetic thrust toward the infinite which once pushed him in the direction of astronomy.

Science knows only the first attitude. It has as its domain the cold and naked facts stripped of all poetic raiment. Its constant progress is sufficient testimony to the fact that its methods are well founded.

The science of the soul claims to do the same. Like astronomy and physics, it too wants to adhere to "material" facts, nothing but the facts. And without being concerned with the true nature of our mental life, it casts these facts in the mold of the facts of the outer world; it even forges them after that model if it does not happen to find them that way. In this way it adjusts its fundamental notion, namely, that of perception, to the observable fact; it is in this way, too, that under the name of "subjective" it brings together everything which the "sciences" (from the very start and in order to reach their goal) have left behind on their way as a kind of residue. This is the source of those odds and ends, such as sensation, elementary feelings, particular volitions, and even isolated individuals to which one, always in the name of "science," claims to reduce the spiritual life of man and of the universe. This probably also explains that remark of Binswanger which gives us so much to think about, namely, that to this day psychology has never yet succeeded in specifying and delineating the psychic fact in a satisfactory way.[1] And yet what is closer to us, what is it which in its very essence is more accessible to us than a fact of this kind?

But let us return to the scene by Balzac. The generally accepted thesis comes down to this: nature consists merely of observable facts, and anything over and above these facts that we sometimes believe we discover in nature is merely a "song of the poet" who just projects outwardly, without value for science, images which he draws from his own soul.

But why and how then does man generally come to sing the praises of nature? We have already indicated the answer which

1. "To this day no one has yet succeeded in finding a positive, contentlike characterization of the psychical which is essential to all psychic experiences" (L. Binswanger, *Einführung in die Probleme der allgemeinen Psychologie* [Berlin: Springer, 1922], p. 13).

in science one customarily gives to this question. The poet popu-
lates nature with his images in the same way (and to arrive at
such a comparison requires only one step) as the naïve mind
"peoples" it with its deities and the simplistic products of its
imagination. And now one must ask oneself whether man in his
constant progress will not succeed in completely transcending
this unfortunate tendency toward poetry in favor of a strictly
"astronomic" attitude, in the same way as he has been able to
overcome superstitions and the naïve beliefs of former times.
But do we thus not fall back into the error of the mother who
credited only the astronomer with the right to look at stars? And
so the song of the poet would not contain anything which en-
riches our "knowledge" concerning the world! There is something in us which rebels against such a conception.

Besides, even without going that far the scientist will be unable not to maintain his fundamental thesis, namely, that the
poetic thrust extols psychic facts; this thrust at most unveils to
us an aspect of man's nature. Dependent upon imagination it
can teach us nothing about nature itself which, since it is essentially proselike, offers itself exclusively to the purview of science.
But this thesis, no matter how rigorously exact it may appear to
be at first sight, still seems on reflection to be too narrow, too
"dry," too contrary to the data of life. Is it therefore true that the
poetic thrust unveils nothing about the nature of things, about
the nature of the universe itself?

We are thus brought back to the question we asked previously: how does man come to sing the praises of nature? Let
us say immediately that it seems difficult to admit that at a given
moment the poetic thrust appeared within the human community as if by a miracle. Man and nature appear to be too closely
united to one another for "spontaneous generations" of this kind
to come about. How would nature, which is merely prose, give
birth to a being endowed with poetic gifts, and consequently to
poetry? That other thesis which admits that nature itself was
originally full of poetry, and that this is even its real mode of
being, appears much more plausible to us. Science shows us only
one of its aspects. It does so after *"depoetizing"* it, after taking
away all of its fragrance, just as the goal it pursues demands.
But, moreover, man, who is profoundly bound up with nature,
has always made efforts (at his best, and in his own way) to
convey its poetry. More than the scientist who depoetizes, the

poet and the child, in that they truly possess "the naïve" in themselves, are close to the genuine nature of the universe. It is probably useful to meditate here on the meaning that ordinary language gives to the terms "poetry" and "prose" when one speaks of the poetry and prose of life and for the same reason integrates them into it.

But even in that case science would still have nothing to do with poetry. By tearing our being in two parts, it will abandon the poetic side to the poet whom each one of us virtually carries within himself. Yet there we see already that a change is beginning to take place with regard to the problem posed. A "knowledge" creeps into our considerations. Above and beyond the thesis that the world consists of prosaic facts to which man-as-poet *adds his song* as he pleases, we prefer that which in nature embraces all the data which are accessible to us (and which in principle would be unable not to be so) and which affirms that science *depoetizes* the whole in order to free its own domain in that way. Without a doubt, science, or, more exactly, the particular sciences feel themselves to be the masters of that domain, but now perhaps they will claim with less pride to be the sole source of our *knowledge* of the universe; perhaps they will also show less contempt for that "sentimental understanding" which we carry within us. Moreover, in order to defend their position, they can now appeal only to *form*. Science concerns itself only with the prosaic (depoetized) form of the facts and must relinquish to poetry the task of transcribing the poetic side of life.

But even then this thesis still seems to call for caution. Certainly, far be it from us to think of diminishing the importance of the sciences in any sense whatsoever; but we merely believe that we have to challenge their ambition to give us a synthetic picture of the totality of the world, and this because of the fact that from the very start they reject the whole poetic side of it. Would this not give us something essential to *learn* with regard to the general structure of life and of the world? We do indeed insist that the poetic form be the adequate form in order to translate the poetry of nature and of life. But even though all of us potentially are poets in our soul, not all of us are poets in our expressions. But by forever confining ourselves to the sciences, do we not by that very fact abandon our desire to penetrate the poetic aspect of life, or better to penetrate life as a whole? I do not think so. For the regard of the philosopher who in a supreme effort endeavors to encompass in a single glance the whole universe, nature, and man, reaches beyond the formulas, the statements, the language of the scientist, as well as beyond the song of the poet. But this effort could not even come near to what the poetic thrust asks us to *learn* while remaining indifferent. But what form will it assume and what language will it employ in order to tell us what it has glimpsed? Will it celebrate nature in the way poets do? No, because that form is the poet's and not the philosopher's. Philosophy does not try to be just one more poem. But the data which poetry provides for philosophy will be "material for reflection," and philosophy will ask itself whether it can transcribe it into prose. For basically that is the language proper to it; it shares it with the sciences. Only the "material" will be different because now we try to encompass by our effort, in addition to its prose, all the poetry which is inherent in life.

Certainly, its language will feel the effects of this content. It will experience the after-effects; quite often it will knowingly be more poetic than a mathematical formula. It merely prevents the work thus accomplished from ever turning into a poem, for its goal is precisely to transcribe into prose that which constitutes the poetry of life. Perhaps, the mathematical formula even remains its ideal, an ideal, however, from which it will voluntarily deviate more than once. Because of these divergences which he has agreed to, the philosopher will sometimes hear himself called a "poet," but this will not deter him.

Now we see dawning on the horizon the possibility of a cosmology, a cosmology which, contrary to astronomy (considering merely the prosaic aspect of the star in its relations with other stars), tries to encompass the whole which the glance of the child discovers in it by finding there the image of his own soul—and "image" means here something completely different from projection to the outside since image and "object" are here one—and by disclosing a whole *world* in it. This cosmology endeavors to translate into prose, as we have just said, all the poetry emerging from life and from which man-as-poet, in perfect harmony with this life, finds his inspiration.

But is not this prose of poetry, as it appears at first sight, contradictory in itself, and is not cosmology destined in advance to come to a standstill even before it starts, unable to provide us with one single valid assertion other than the pretentious program which it lays down?

Our previous considerations permit us to answer this question. We know that man is closely *allied* [2] with nature not only in the sense that he is a part of it, or as the biological sciences would have it, that he descended from it and is a product of it, but also, and even above all, in the sense that each impulse of his soul finds a profound and wholly natural substructure in the world, and in that way reveals to us a primordial quality of the structure of the universe. This structural alliance is one of the guarantees of the objectivity of life's poetic side. May I refer here to the descriptions given earlier, concerning "reverberating" and "expanding"? May I refer also to this particular characteristic of reality and veracity which reveals itself in each literary work genuinely deserving the name? It is the dynamic qualities, the motions common to man and the universe, which seem to constitute the foundation of all poetic thrust on our part. They, too, constitute the object of "cosmology," which serves as the necessary complement to "anthropology," the scope of which we have previously tried to determine. We believe that we have somewhat prepared the ground for such a cosmology as well as for such an anthropology.

However, it is necessary to specify still further the goal we are pursuing. What is it that the poet ultimately sings the praises of? He sings, one will say to us, the praises of the beauties of nature, love, passions, nostalgia, sadness, and still other emotions which stir the human soul. In this way our cosmology would bring us back to a scientific study of the aesthetic values which are spread out in nature and manifest themselves in human works, or the conflicts—love, hatred, and other passions —which psychology has long since accepted as the objects of its investigations. But all of these are only the "material" for the poet's song. They can furnish the subject of a literary work just as well as they can become the objects of scientific investigations, and that proves to us already that they should not be considered as the very essence of the poetic thrust and thus provide us with the elements of the cosmology toward which our effort is directed.

2. See *La Portée structurale (cosmique) des phénomènes psychiques*, p. 97.

As far as aesthetics in particular is concerned, this cosmology differs from it in that it does not envisage its objects from the viewpoint of the value of the good, but focuses on the fundamental data of a structural order which reveals the beauty of life itself to us, as well as, on the other hand, rising above the common psychological facts in order to discover through these facts the same fundamental structure. In the final analysis this is the same method as that to which we have subscribed in our work on "lived time." In our study on "the investigation of ethical action," our main concern was not to write a moral treatise, and still less to determine the psychological elements which in our subjective life constitute the ethical thrust, but merely to emphasize the essential elements of the structural order which no phenomenon other than the thrust would have contributed to life.

More than once we have already opposed the structure to the content of life, and each time this structure was what in life is the more dynamic and alive. More than once, also, have we insisted on the fact that the psychology of the affections, by placing the notion of *conflict* at the center of its concerns and after grouping all around this notion the various factors which seem to radiate from it, does nothing but indulge itself in one mechanical aspect of man's spiritual life. But in addition to the impulses which *agitate* the human soul there are impulses which constitute its fundamental properties. The poet, just like the psychologist-scientist, remains, as far as the "matter" is concerned that is, dependent upon notions which our common life offers to him, as for example the notion of "conflict." However, this effort is still supported by something completely different from this "matter" from which he himself is molded and which constitutes the content of his work. But beneath all that he feels throbbing in himself notes much more profound; he feels that he communicates with the whole universe in one single movement which, properly speaking, knows neither date, nor content, nor matter. The tale, the characters are nothing; the atmosphere which reverberates around them is for him everything. Man reveals himself as such in that atmosphere in order to merge immediately with the cosmos. And the scientist-philosopher, tired of the splintering and the abstraction of the particular sciences, thirsty for anthropology and cosmology, will follow here the song of the poet and the look of the child and will try to transcribe into prose the impulse which animates them both, the one as well as the other, and propagates without transition throughout the universe.

The principle of structural alliance by its very nature has a universal scope. It carries that universality within itself. It extends to all things. The star, like ourselves, integrates itself into the world in two different ways. It does so by occupying a place in space and by exercising its attraction, or by acting upon the bodies which are there in a completely different way. Together with them it constitutes the (astronomic) *world*. But at the same time it surrounds itself, as it were, with a subtle and imperceptible cloud, full of life and poetry, which, emanating from itself, reflects the universe and which, without appealing to distance or space, integrates it into the whole.

It does this with as much intimacy as possible, since the star now carries this whole within itself and expresses it in its own way. It integrates itself into the *cosmos* whose existence it reveals to us in all of its intimate richness and in all of its primary poetry. And the child, by looking at the star, discovers a whole world in it. It is in the truth. And we have merely to follow him by trying, however, to translate with words that upon which this discovery rests and that in which this particular movement consists, encompassing into one whole the cosmos, the star, and the soul which contemplates it.

Science dissects, opposes, proceeds by means of abstraction, generalizes. At its touch, life comes to a standstill, slips away through its fingers. Science can conceive only of one movement —the displacement of bodies in space—and it resolves this movement into successive positions which it then translates through curves, through what is static. Everything that it touches becomes something immobile, dead nature.

And yet all around us the world reverberates with a thousand melodies, exhales a thousand perfumes, is animated by a thousand movements which make our whole being tremble and palpitate, and we take part in that life so intense, so delicately expressive, albeit impalpable. It is this life from which we derive our forces and the reason of our being, which we would also like to *know*, trying to seize alive, distinguish, differentiate the different movements, the *dynamic qualities* of which they consist, in order to study later their particular affinities, the concatenations to which they give rise. That is the goal which cosmology pursues. Because its object consists in the movements which are common to the human soul as well as to nature, the dynamic qualities as we have just called them, it cannot do anything but animate all it touches. Indeed the whole of "dead nature" comes alive at its touch, revealing to us the meaning of life, man, the cosmos.

But can this cosmology lead us also to a *cosmogony*, or would it not (bound to the contemplation of the present or, to be more exact, bound to a contemplation of phenomena outside of time and space) have to content itself with ever arriving at reconstructing a real becoming with a probable beginning and a constant march toward infinity? This question has something agonizing in it. But does this anguish come from the fact that we, because we are dominated by the notion of genesis, feel completely disabled the very moment the necessity to submit it to a critical analysis imposes itself upon us? Or does it, rather, come from the fact that we really cannot live without it, so that all efforts of our mind which do not allow for it, would be destined to certain failure from the very start and would be merely aberrations of the mind? I cannot answer these questions, but I cannot forego them in silence either. Too important for that, they are called upon to become the source of new meditations.

Maurice Merleau-Ponty

MAURICE MERLEAU-PONTY (1908–61) graduated from L'Ecole Normale in 1930, and after teaching in several *lycées*, returned there as an *agrégé répétiteur* in 1935. After demobilization from the army in 1940, he resumed his *lycée* teaching and was also, during this period, associated with the Resistance. After the war, he became master of conferences, and later professor, at the University of Lyon. Most notable during this period was his association with Jean-Paul Sartre and Simone de Beauvoir as a founder of the periodical *Les Temps modernes*, through which his strong political interests found a ready outlet. From 1949 to 1952, he was professor of child psychology and pedagogy at the Sorbonne, from which he was called to the Collège de France, where he was the youngest man to assume the chair held previously by Bergson, LeRoy, Gilson, and Lavelle, a position which he held until his untimely death on May 3, 1961.

If we should ask ourselves in what sense Merleau-Ponty is to be considered a philosopher of science, it is the fields of psychology and its allied human sciences which would loom uppermost in our considerations. It may seem strange, then, that he should be included in a volume concerned with phenomenology and the natural sciences. The possibility of this puzzlement simply serves to highlight the unique contribution which his phenomenological approach has to offer to the traditional discipline of the philosophy of science. Husserl had already pointed out that even though natural science is the science of nature, the philosophy of natural science is a science of man. Psychology rightly understood can therefore provide a basis for understanding all of the sciences, including natural science. Merleau-Ponty accordingly attempts to trace scientific formulations back to the structures within which they first emerged—the structures of behavior: perception, imagination, expression. These are to be the subject matter of an eidetic psychology which is at once attentive to the findings of empirical psychology. At the same time, the investigation of the genealogy of the objective field of science from the phenomenal field of the perceptual world, whose genesis in turn must also be investigated, ultimately calls for a mundane cosmology correlative to such a psychology. It is this cosmology that Merleau-Ponty was seeking to outline when he died.

The general problem of the applicability of Merleau-Ponty's reflections to a philosophy of the natural sciences is the subject of the first essay, while the second presents a detailed example of his reductive approach to a central notion not only of physics, but also, in the terms in which he treats it, of biology and psychology as well.

12 / Merleau-Ponty on Philosophy and Science

Theodore J. Kisiel

AFTER EDMUND HUSSERL, it is difficult to think of a phenomenologist who has taken science in all of its forms more seriously than Maurice Merleau-Ponty. From the in-depth confrontation of physiology and Gestalt psychology of his first publication to scattered references in the posthumously published fragments, he returns again and again to the problem of the relation of philosophy and science to each other and to the transcendental field of perception which is his unique contribution to the phenomenological search for an experiential absolute. Remarks on this problem constantly crop up in the student notes of the lectures he gave at the Sorbonne from 1949 to 1951,[1] when he held the post of professor of child psychology and pedagogy. The notes include comments not only on psychology but also on the "physics of the soul" and on physics as such. His own work is itself a living testimonial to the essential convergence of philosophy and science that he promulgated and promoted.

It is against this background that his famous and often misconstrued statement, declaring that the first directive of phenomenology is from the start a "disavowal of science,"[2] must be considered. What phenomenology since Husserl has from the start disavowed is not science but scientism in all of its forms,

1. *Bulletin de psychologie,* XVIII, no. 236 (November, 1964), 3–6. The entire issue is devoted to a resumé of Merleau-Ponty's courses as reported by his students and approved by himself.

2. *Phenomenology of Perception,* trans. Colin Smith (New York: Humanities Press, 1962), p. viii. (Hereafter cited as *PP.*)

not psychology but psychologism. According to Husserl, the naïve ontological prejudice of objectivism, so closely bound to classical science, poses the most prominent cultural obstacle not only to the phenomenological drive to return to the "things themselves," but also to the further progress of science itself. Thus the need for bracketing, along with the natural attitude of common sense, the theoretical attitude of positive science and the prejudices which lack of reflection on its bases has fostered. The "disavowal" involved in this procedure is not a move to suppress science and the natural attitude to which science is still related despite efforts to overcome it. The reduction, designed to loosen the soil of the hardened convictions of science and all of the other spontaneous affirmations in which one is immersed, in turn places responsibility on the phenomenology of science to explicate and to thoroughly understand these attitudes and their reasons for being. The critique of science which the reduction carries out leaves nothing implicit, examines everything, in order eventually to assess, according to the "things themselves," what is valid and what is indefensible in the presuppositions of science and its concomitant natural attitude. Such a procedure, though it emphatically resists the identification of the "really real" with the world as studied by natural science, promises to place science on much more secure foundations, truer to the "things themselves," which for Merleau-Ponty is the perceptual world experience upon which a more positive dialectic between philosophy and science would naturally develop.

THE CRISIS OF REASON

FROM A HISTORICAL POINT OF VIEW, phenomenology is so closely linked to science that Merleau-Ponty even asserts that without science, phenomenology could not have come into existence. "Phenomenology could never have come about before all the other philosophical efforts of the rationalist tradition, nor prior to the construction of science. It measures the distance between our experience and this science. How could it ignore it? How could it precede it?"[3] A consideration of Merleau-Ponty's

3. *The Primacy of Perception,* ed. James M. Edie (Evanston, Ill.: Northwestern University Press, 1964), p. 29. (Hereafter cited as *PrP.*)

understanding of the historical situation in which rationalism and science gave birth to phenomenology will thus serve to introduce his views on the relationships between philosophy and science.

For Husserl, according to Merleau-Ponty, the relation between philosophy and science was more than an academic question; it was a problem profoundly interwoven with a cultural decadence that he sought to overcome. The turn of the century was not only a time in which philosophy was struggling to secure its proper existence and its own method against the inroads of scientism but also a period that saw the beginnings of an awareness of a shift in the foundations of the sciences themselves. Husserl's entire philosophy is a response to the simultaneous crises of philosophy, the sciences of man, and the sciences of nature. Coming as he did from the scientific disciplines, Husserl quite naturally brought with him a concern for a new foundation for science, vigorously opposing the spirit of dogmatism of the day concerning the foundations of geometry and physics. "His desire to found the sciences anew is certainly significant in his decision to pursue a radical philosophical investigation." [4] His view was that the crises of philosophy, physical science, and the sciences of man could not be resolved simply by a new account of their methods but also required an investigation of their mutual relations, so that they might effectively join in an advance toward a common truth. The struggle for the existence of philosophy is not independent and opposed to the endeavor to secure the existence of the sciences, but is in fact one and the same. Such a security could be guaranteed only by uncovering the foundation of human reason itself, whose obfuscation is for Husserl the core of the crisis of its various cognitive modes.

Perhaps one of the most striking characteristics of the twentieth-century crisis of reason is the emergence of irrationalism from rationalism itself in some of its forms, ideological, scien-

---

4. The lecture course "Phenomenology and the Sciences of Man" is Merleau-Ponty's simplest and most direct account of his views on the relationship between philosophy and science. It may be found in translation in *The Primacy of Perception*, ed. Edie. The translation given here has been made from the edition of the Centre de Documentation Universitaire. A somewhat different and more extended version of this course is given in the *Bulletin de psychologie*, XVIII, no. 236 (November, 1964), 141–70.

tific, or otherwise. Science has lately developed highly speculative formulas whose ultimate meaning and relation to reality are difficult to fathom. That such formulations, which at times even defy common sense, are yet capable of changing the world has aroused a cult of superstition and idolization beyond reasonable bounds. The public image of Einstein is a case in point. The press flocked to him for his comments on all and sundry subjects as one consults an oracle. He was a superman, thaumaturgist, and perhaps more, "the consecrated place, the tabernacle of some supernatural operation." [5] Even his body must be different from ours, so that a study of the neural energy and subtle circuits of his brain might give us some glimpse of the secret of the sixth sense which evoked the beatific vision of relativity. Evidently an age that can no longer point to a Universal Reason as the source of human insight must still have its miracle workers.

Einstein himself was the last of the classical scientific rationalists. Even in his wildest speculations, he obstinately clung to the belief that these free inventions eventually found their way in some mysterious fashion to a truth set down in the world as it is "in itself." Bergson once suggested to Einstein that scientific time and simultaneity need not contradict the common experience of time and simultaneity, but in fact presuppose this experience as a prescientific evidence out of which physics formulates its more special truth. Einstein admitted that the time we experience is the starting point for our ideas on time, but this holds only for each of us individually and hence is but a limited "psychological" experience without ontological validity and universal value.[6] Science alone gives the truth about time. There is no other reason but the physicist's.[7]

Later physicists have retained the right of free invention but in general have dropped the classical physicist's founding of knowledge in a world in itself, perhaps even dismissing such

5. Maurice Merleau-Ponty, "Einstein and the Crisis of Reason," in Signs, trans. R. C. McCleary (Evanston, Ill.: Northwestern University Press, 1964), p. 143.

6. Maurice Merleau-Ponty, Le Visible et l'invisible (Paris: Gallimard, 1964), pp. 35–36. English translation by Alphonso Lingis, The Visible and the Invisible (Evanston, Ill.: Northwestern University Press, 1968), p. 18. (Hereafter cited as VI.)

7. "Einstein and the Crisis of Reason," pp. 192–97.

questions as "metaphysical." The current attitude of operational-
ism does not concern itself with the problem of the radical
foundation. And yet modern physics abounds in paradoxes
which, if left to stand alone, tend almost unconsciously to au-
thorize unreason. It is precisely Bergson's suggestion that Merleau-Ponty develops as his life task, so that the reason of the
physicist is to become situated not in some divine infrastructure
or in the divine right of a dogmatic science but in the prescientific reason implicated in our existence in a common world of
perception. Not that the paradoxes will be eliminated, but at
least they are to be traced to their genetic instances in the
ambiguities of perceptual faith. For the new notion of reason
that Merleau-Ponty proposes is not some perfectly clear truth in
itself at which we aim asymptotically but the chiaroscuro world
of perception with which we already find ourselves in agreement
even before any explicit affirmation. Paradoxically once again,
the rationalist who dictates perfect clarity as a goal represents
the greatest danger to human reason. The irrational is not to be
forcibly dispelled but to be explored and understood, so that it
can be integrated into a broadened conception of reason which
befits the contingency and historicity of human experience. Such
is Merleau-Ponty's formulation of a life task that he also considers to be the task of our century.[8]

FACT AND ESSENCE

THE WORSHIP OF THE FACT evoked a form of irrationalism in Husserl's day which suggested that even a man's innermost ideas are simply the outcome of external conditioning by
physiological, psychological, sociological, and historical causes.
Thus no philosopher really expresses any intrinsic truth valid for
all time; he simply makes pronouncements determined by his
times and temperament. But the same holds true for those who
enunciate this psychologism, and with this realization we are but
one step short of radical skepticism.

Of course, we could bypass the conflict by relegating the
recording of facts to science and delegating philosophy to an

8. *Sense and Non-Sense*, trans. H. L. and P. A. Dreyfus (Evanston, Ill.: Northwestern University Press, 1964), p. 63.

inner realm of pure thought that transcends fact. The *cordon sanitaire* between fact and idea, time and eternity, positive science and philosophy would then permit a peaceful coexistence if each party would but keep to his side of the iron curtain. But such journalistic stereotypes belie the actual practice of both science and philosophy and obstruct the self-understanding necessary for their mutual advance. The essence of science is in the interpretation of brute fact through schematization and idealization, the construction of intelligible models that attempt to decipher the meaning of the fact. And the philosopher takes his object not from some domain of pure essences but from the same concrete world from which science isolates its facts.[9]

That Husserl's initial reaction to the psychologism of facts seemingly gravitated him toward the logicism of pure essences, as in his search for a universal grammar of language, indicates his own struggle with a dichotomy which in his later years he tends to overcome. In the process, positive science and philosophy would be drawn into interdependence, with both "working in the service of humanity," with each contributing to the participation of all men in a common truth.

That a man is empirically determined by his external social and historical conditions as well as his psychological mechanisms is the truth of psychologism, sociologism, and historicism that Husserl does not wish to deny. But it is precisely the affirmations which arise from these factual determinations of a man's life which are to be suspended in the phenomenological reduction and thus brought clearly in mind and prevented from influencing one's rational endeavors. For a man as philosopher desires not only to factually exist but to exist with an understanding of his situation. And, since understanding is universal, he is called upon to consider his own empirical personality as but one possibility in a larger universe waiting to be explored.

But the movement of reduction is not intended to take us beyond time into a realm of pure logic and thought. Philosophy for Husserl is not a science of eternal truths but a science of the omnitemporal truth, holding for time itself rather than beyond time in a realm of truth purportedly without contact with contingent experience. Phenomenology seeks not to found reason in

9. "The Philosopher and Sociology" is another basic essay on the relations between philosophy and science (*Signs*, pp. 98–113).

some right prior to fact, nor to invest man with some secret power of assuming the role of a universal thinker capable of penetrating to the divine infrastructure of the world of Cartesian rationalism, but rather to affirm a rationality to be discovered in experience itself. As such, philosophy is not a science of definitive conclusions but an infinite task of elaboration of the human situation. This refusal of a priori affirmations and insistence on the primacy of experience justifies the claim of a phenomenological positivism even more radical than traditional positivism, since it also brackets the sense-datum theory and the privilege of primary qualities. And despite his insistence on the primacy of perception, Merleau-Ponty still opposes the a priori reductionism of all other human experiences to perception.[10]

"Reason in our experience"—such is the phenomenological formula that attempts to seize the concrete and the universal at once, thereby removing the barrier erected between the exteriority of facts which is a principle of science and the rational interiority of ideas which is the condition of philosophy. Such a comprehension calls for a way of knowing that is neither purely empirical nor deductive but capable of revealing universal meanings in the particularities of events. What Husserl called *Wesenschau* (intuition of essence) is neither Platonic nor mystical but in fact a concrete and familiar practice not at all restricted to phenomenologists. As I listen to the Ninth Symphony, I can discover, in this contingent experience of a single performance by a particular group of musicians at a certain time and place, something which is independent of these factual conditions, namely, the very *sense of the event*, the Ninth Symphony in its concrete essence. The same holds in the "typing" of persons, of things, and of all the other experiences of daily life. *Wesenschau* is this process, not necessarily instantaneous but usually quite gradual, of the clarification of the meanings to which the consciousness is directed.

As such, its measured employment is operative in all sciences. Both psychology and physics are sciences of facts, each utilizing the inductive method to assemble their facts. But induction merely as the association of facts would be blind if some other element were not operative to provide an insight into what these inductions are treating. Hence these sciences of facts need,

10. *PrP*, p. 25.

and indeed already implicitly include, a reflection on the fundamental notions which supply the ultimate meaning to facts observed and related. Physics made rapid strides only when Galileo perceived that geometry and other mathematics supplied an initial clarification of the fundamental notions of material nature, especially space. His experiments on falling bodies already imply a certain intuition into the meaning of physical body. The development of physics not only adds to our factual knowledge of nature but also evolves what Husserl called an eidetic of physical things. For knowledge of essences is not the exclusive privilege of phenomenologists but is present in all effective knowledge of facts. The sciences, preoccupied as they are with facts, have at the same time been able to uncover something about essences. Galileo in his experimental work had no intention of working out an eidetic of *res extensa*, but the close relation between fact and essence is such that he in effect laid the foundation for such an eidetic.

Just as physics must have its geometry and mathematics, so empirical psychology must have its eidetic psychology in order to explicate the ultimate sense of perception, emotion, imagination, consciousness, meanings which in some way are already operative in empirical psychology. These are, to be sure, not the exact essences of geometry, exhaustively defined through a system of axioms, but morphological essences, inexact by nature, drawn completely from the concrete world of experience. A morphological essence results from an act of ideation, an immediate vision of the essence in the vagaries of experience, while the exact essence is the product of mediate idealization through axioms, which pushes the concrete given to its ultimate ideal limits as it constructs, for example, the "spherical" from the "rounded." Thus the exact eidetic disciplines like axiomatic geometry are to be founded in the concrete eidetic disciplines of descriptive phenomenology, as in eidetic psychology and its descriptions of lived space, which has its own strictness, even though exactness is not possible here because of the fluidity of lived experience. There is no such thing as the "mathematics of phenomena," a "geometry of experience," or a deductive psychology.[11]

Scientific practice viewed in the above manner tends to indicate that induction is not really an abstraction of what is com-

11. *PrP*, p. 67.

mon in a collection of a large number of cases but a reading of the essence in the facts. Through certain impure and imperfect phenomena, the free fall of a body or the properties of gravitating masses are read off, theoretically forged by the imaginative intellect. Even though neither of these pure cases actually exists and even though they are thus idealizing fictions, imaginatively formulated, they are nevertheless founded in the facts, justified not by invoking a large number of samples but by the clarity they shed on the phenomena in question.

Understood in this way, *Wesensschau* resembles induction. An imaginary free variation, of usually a single example which is thrown in and out of focus, delineates the invariable structure of the experience. Thus the essence of melody is that which remains the same through variations of the notes and their relations, and without which there would be no melody. Even induction employs something like free variation when values not actually observed are interpolated. Here again is an indication that at least certain features of the *Wesensschau* are not the exclusive property of phenomenologists.

In asserting the fundamental homogeneity of the inductive and the essential modes of knowledge, differing only in degree, Merleau-Ponty affirms that he is going beyond what Husserl wished to assert. However, he sees it as an inevitable consequence of Husserl's later principle that knowledge of essences is experiential through and through and that essences are not eternal but share in at least some of the contingency of fact (e.g., consider Euclidean space). To this must be added the earlier inverse principle that any knowledge of fact always involves the a priori understanding of essence.[12]

Even though Husserl did not go so far as to declare the fundamental homogeneity of the inductive and eidetic sciences, he did affirm the "parallelism" of phenomenology as eidetic psychology and empirical psychology (and hence more generally a parallelism between philosophy thus understood and positive knowledge), such that a factual discovery and affirmation in the latter has a corresponding eidetic discovery and affirmation in the former.[13] Through his theory of phenomenological experience, he worked to open a dimension and initiate an attitude of

12. *PrP*, p. 72.
13. *Signs*, p. 102; *PrP*, p. 72.

inquiry in which philosophy and science could meet in reciprocal involvement. By contrast, Scheler and Heidegger, who brought philosophy down into the realm of facticity, insist on the pure and simple opposition between philosophy and the sciences of man, between the ontological and the ontic.[14]

DIVISION OF THE SCIENCES

THE INTERRELATION between fact and essence is not the only principle involved in the phenomenological division of the sciences. The doctrine of intentionality, which Merleau-Ponty relates closely to the phenomenological theory of essence through his reinterpretation of the notion of Gestalt, introduces a profound, though not immediately apparent, revision of the relation among the sciences.

Classical physics defined its domain by separating objective from subjective reality. Correlatively, psychology did the same, claiming the subjective domain as its own. Psychology thus not only became the necessary counterpart to physics but also assumed the same ontological presuppositions, approaching the psyche as if it were a natural reality to be viewed objectively by a detached spectator.[15] But difficulties encountered within both physics and psychology have placed these common assumptions in question, thereby orienting each in its own way toward a revision of the subject-object relation, first of all toward recognizing this very *relation* as their subject matter (*Sache*), rather than one substantive reality distinguished from another.[16] Heisenberg, von Weizsäcker, and others have pointed to this trend in physics, and Merleau-Ponty has identified the psychological notion of perceptual Gestalt as a category irreducible to either subject or object, but nevertheless involving both. These tendencies in science reinforce the phenomenological invocation to return to a unified and unifying experience that precedes the distinction between subject and object. According to this revision, the phenomenal field would no longer be divided by parceling

14. *PrP*, p. 94.
15. *VI*, pp. 36–37. (Eng. trans., p. 19.)
16. "The Metaphysical in Man" is another essay significant for our problem. It can be found in *Sense and Non-Sense*, pp. 83–98, esp. p. 86.

out various objective realms to different sciences; each science would establish its domain on the basis of a differing type of behavioral Gestalt, a variant dialectic between subject and object. Division of the sciences is to be based not on substance or thing but on perceptual structure, "forms" that take on global proportions, what Husserl called regional essences.

Some of the old categories might be retained in this scheme, but they would be distributed in a different way. For example, quantity, order, and value or signification, which in the old division were identified as the respective properties of matter, life, and mind, would now become characteristics dominant in their respective level but universally applicable to all of them. For quasi-organic orders are to be found in certain physical processes of distribution (e.g., the ellipsoid conductor, electric current, soap bubbles) which possess an internal unity that is not simply nominal or causal in character but is indicative of an immanent signification. In turn, biology and psychology cannot in principle withdraw completely from mathematical analysis and causal explanation.[17] For like the "soul" and "body" in this new scheme, the universe is no longer divided into neatly separated blocks isomorphic and parallel to each other but rather consists of a series of mutually inclusive "fields" or "worlds," dominions that vary in dominance according to the phenomena under study and the perspectives employed. Consider the crucial example of the human body, where the three orders of matter, life, and mind converge as "three inseparable terms bound together in the living unity of an experience." [18] Objectivistic analysis divides this experience into three orders of "events," events of nature, organic events, and thought events, and relates them in extrinsic fashion by a cause-effect "explanatory mythology." [19] On the other hand, phenomenological description of the essential experiences of the human body finds only a normal human behavior which on occasion becomes disorganized and disintegrates through fracture, fatigue, illness, emotion, or other defects, leading to a less integrated structure of behavior, bringing to the fore one of the subordinate behavioral dialectics, that of organism and milieu, or physical system and topographic condi-

17. *The Structure of Behavior*, trans. Alden L. Fisher (Boston: Beacon Press, 1963), pp. 131–32. (Hereafter cited as *SB*.)
18. *SB*, p. 190.
19. *SB*, p. 191.

tions.[20] In reverse order, infant behavior from fetus to neonate to child manifests an increasingly integrated dialectical structuration in which the final psychological structure includes in restructured modes the infrastructures of physiology and biology. Even in normal adult behavior, a certain perceptual meaning which I actualize is only virtual for an observer viewing my behavior biologically or physically, and in turn his actualized significations are only virtual for me. Nevertheless, the various significations are not contradictory but concordant phenomena reciprocally related in a phenomenal field and not causally related in an objective field. All these perspectives are "rigorously synonymous" [21] inasmuch as they find their common justification in the structures of the perceptual field which is the original horizon of all our perspectives. It is this chiaroscuro world that physics, biology, and psychology share and divide, as observers on the mountains and plain share the various vantage points of a landscape or battle, whereby the differing degrees of integration and structural differentiation which they see establish different but "synonymous" orders of signification, in which each perspective takes its place in the system of profiles which is their common "inner horizon." Physics, biology, and psychology are horizontally related as figure and ground and vertically as "body" and "soul," as infrastructure and its restructuration.

Physics establishes its laws by isolating from a larger physical structure conditions capable of being expressed in simple relations of function to variable. Hence physical laws arrive at an explanation not *of* the structure but *within* the structure which is its condition of possibility.[22] If the encompassing structure should change, the law would no longer be valid. And the law cannot be transposed per se into an order other than the one it partially expresses. The law of falling bodies holds in a field of relatively stable forces in the neighborhood of the earth. The close association of law to its proper structure also means that an experiment does not verify an isolated law but the entire system of complementary laws to which it belongs. For the experiment must take into account and "neutralize" the effects of temperature, atmospheric pressure, and the like in order to focus the effect which is to be subject to "free variation" in the

20. SB, pp. 203, 209.
21. SB, p. 217.
22. SB, p. 193.

experiment.[23] The degree of analytical freedom possible here indicates that physical laws express the least integrated structures, which themselves are approximated only by a constant countermovement of the synthesis of laws into more comprehensive mathematical manifolds. But the summation of partial interactions that the classical systems of laws achieved at best express a poor approximation of the cosmological structures on which they are based. Modern physics finds these poorly integrated wholes inadequate and tends to borrow structural models from perceptual experience that are much more encompassing functional and dynamic unities. The nonlocalizable pervasive properties that recent physics treats might well be related to certain field aspects of perceptual space.[24] For the perceived whole which is the natural world is and always has been the horizon that physical knowledge determines and intends. Without it, science would have no meaning.

Where the unity of an organism is expressed in the same manner as the unity of a physical system, through extrinsic correlation by laws, a certain residue of life is left unexpressed —the organism's capacity for initiating action as manifested in a unique style that calls for a new type of intellection grasping the immanent meaning of this behavior.[25] The physical system establishes equilibrium with existing conditions, while an organism acts with respect to virtual conditions and establishes its own milieu according to a unique style of behavior that follows certain preferred directions. As the behavior is new, so must its science develop a language especially tailored to the original experiences that we have of the living being. The mosaic of animal conduct points to an indecomposable "essence" of the individual, an "a priori of the species" [26] which manifests a vital dialectical equilibrium expressible in qualitative terms and irreducible to a summation of quantitative S-R laws. If life is not simply the sum of the physiological reactions of the organism from birth to death, then the science of life must adopt points of view which grasp the inner signification of the totalities detachable from this process, as already suggested in some of its notions, such as "assimilation," "function of reproduction," and

23. SB, pp. 138–39.
24. SB, p. 144.
25. SB, pp. 155–56.
26. Sense and Non-Sense, p. 84; SB, p. 148.

"adult phase." Such an immediate apprehension of structure in partitive phenomena reads in a single glance an essence or ideal unity which is not directly given in these facts but which nevertheless points to something which the facts suggest.[27] Many such eidetic notions that may eventually serve to express the a priori of biology, such as the rich and confused notion of male and female, are already present in common knowledge as insights ready to be refurbished for scientific purposes.[28]

Human behavior is not structured along the relatively rigid instinctual lines of the animal but manifests an infinite flexibility that expresses itself in a rich variety of unique styles of personality, social institutions, language, art, and science. This wealth of "symbolic forms" of human behavior is a subject of study by a wide range of developing human sciences—except for science itself. The possibility for science to reflect upon itself, not simply extrinsically but in its innermost essence, as a form of human behavior, has been approached cautiously, perhaps because of the tardy development of the human sciences but more commonly because of the abhorrence of "anthropomorphism" imbedded in the scientific tradition since Galileo. Even now, for example, there is a continuing debate on whether the history of science has anything essential to contribute to the philosophy of science.

But the program which established physics as the norm by which the unity of the sciences is to be achieved has not fulfilled its promise. By contrast, Gurwitsch has pointed to psychology as the center line of any future system of sciences. "It is not one science among the others; instead, it is their foundation. Its main task is not to enrich our knowledge of reality as the physical and chemical sciences do but to account for the very knowledge of reality." [29] In the same spirit, Merleau-Ponty frequently utilizes psychology in studying some of the classical problems of the philosophy of science. For example, he establishes the human normality of the experience of objectivity by studying the abnormal variants of Köhler's apes and Goldstein's brain-damaged patient, Schneider, and he examines the genesis of objectivity in the infant's experience of his reflection in a mirror. Such

27. SB, pp. 102, 152.
28. SB, p. 157.
29. Aron Gurwitsch, *Studies in Phenomenology and Psychology* (Evanston, Ill.: Northwestern University Press, 1966), p. 68.

unabashed "anthropomorphism" is a full recognition that science is a properly human endeavor whose genealogy cannot be
investigated apart from man. Even the most abstruse scientific
formulations of the physical world still refer to the human experience of that world and are no less anthropomorphic. To
exclude this experience would exclude not only anthropomorphism but science as well. Such attempts at reductionism are a
defense not of objectivity but of naïve realism and nominalism.
Objectivity necessarily defines itself in the intersubjective experience of the perceived world in which the scientific object is
constituted.[30] This applies to all sciences. We grasp the behavior
of the animal, the infant, the psychotic through our own situation, by analogy and contrast with it. As Husserl says, "The
animal is for us a variant of humanity." [31] The same holds for
the objectivity of the physical object, the structure that physics
studies. For, as Merleau-Ponty demonstrates, the thing as thing
is not a part of the perceptual field of even the higher animals.
For an animal is incapable of retaining an invariant in the
diversity of its aspects, a versatility which is proper to symbolic
behavior and which in fact involves virtually placing oneself in
the position of the thing.[32]

But such symbolic behavior is not yet thought. Then how,
one may ask, does one evolve from the rudimentary objectivity
of human perception to the abstract objectivity of science? Merleau-Ponty's primary interest is actually directed toward the opposite problem—to show that the most abstruse formulations of
thought and science are not rooted in some realm of eternal
truth but derive their origin from the symbolic form of human
behavior operative in the temporality of perceptual experience.

SCIENCE AS SYMBOLIC BEHAVIOR

LIKE ANY SYMBOLIC BEHAVIOR, science expresses the
human capacity to surpass present perception and to operate in
a realm of possibles in which the actual experience is only one
variant among other more virtual experiences. As such, science

30. *SB*, p. 102.
31. *Bulletin de psychologie*, XVIII, no. 236 (November, 1964),
pp. 157, 169, 186.
32. *SB*, pp. 116–20.

is a manifestation of human freedom, as Einstein recognized when he spoke of the "wildly speculative" character of contemporary theorizing, and as Merleau-Ponty emphasizes when he places the "free variation" of the *Wesensschau* at the center of any scientific behavior. Such freedom even extends to the "brute fact," for scientific operations literally "make" the *factum* by selecting and separating those figures subject to mathematical manipulation from the perceptual ground in which they appear. On the other hand, the phenomena invite such treatment and even suggest the schemes into which their figures are to be organized. Merleau-Ponty locates the beginnings of any symbolic behavior in the figure-ground structure of human perception, in which the figure refers to the horizon as to a "vague solicitation," which "arouses the expectation of more," which poses a sort of confused problem inviting exploration.[33] Hence it is the object's own "saliency" (William James's term) which emphasizes a possible direction (*sens*) of research. But the ambiguity of the given is such that it permits a broad range of possibilities to the creative response of human questioning.

Hence science is both motivated and free in its translation of the text of the perceived world. It finds its own way of "letting things speak for themselves." That this way is more closely bound to the typical behavior found in that world than some other symbolic forms is suggested by Merleau-Ponty in a thought experiment in which the Ninth Symphony and Euclidean geometry are presumed lost in cultural transmission, in which case geometry would be more likely to be rediscovered.[34] This does not mean, however, that scientific theory is directly available in the data of perception. "Scientific laws [are discoveries] which are not *given in* the facts but which one finds *expressed* in them." [35] The facts only suggest, man gestures in a scientific way, and both movements belong to a single logic of gestation which lies at the heart of the genesis of any human meaning.

We are here approaching the central phenomenological problem of the transcendental synthesis of receptivity and spontaneity. Merleau-Ponty's first approximation to this problem is in

33. *PP*, p. 4.
34. *PP*, p. 390.
35. *SB*, p. 102.

terms of a synthesis of perception and the expressive movement of the body. He is so insistent that it is symbolic *behavior* that he locates the condition of possibility of all the expressive operations that constitute the cultural world in the self-movement of the body proper which perception motivates. Responding to the directions suggested by the world as perceived, the anticipatory movements of the symbolizing body, set to seek more than is actually given, uncover the inner horizon, the physiognomy, the style of things and thus organize the world along certain typical lines, or in Kantian terms, schemata. It is a *Wesensschau* of the motivated-motivating body that higher symbolizing activities will continue. Even the most abstruse constructions of geometry rely on at least potential gestures of the body sketching its shapes and establishing its relations, evident from the very language describing these constructions, e.g., "by," "on," "through," "extend." "The subject of geometry is a motor subject," [36] rooted in the active body whose intentional motion generates a lived space out of which geometry constructs its own space.

Nevertheless, perceptual structures are necessary but not sufficient conditions for geometry and science, and the passage from perceptual sense to linguistic sense, from behavior to thematization (which is a higher form of behavior) remains obscure for Merleau-Ponty, as he is ready to admit.[37] But it is to be noted that the classical dichotomy of sensation and intellection (and the philosophical dichotomy of psychologism and logicism) has been modified to a synthesis between a perception which is already symbolically organized through bodily gestures and a linguistic understanding which incarnates itself in words and thus situates itself in the perceptual world. As the body anticipates more than is given, so the word is capable of directing attention to hidden variations of things. Here is the one marvel of science and other symbolic forms: the capacity of words to "grow through use, being capable of indefinite labor, of returning more than has been invested in them, and yet relating themselves unceasingly to things." [38] The "patterns of discovery" of human language in some mysterious way resonate with the

36. *PP*, p. 387.
37. *VI*, p. 230. (Eng. trans., p. 176.)
38. *Signs*, p. 194.

"Logos of the aesthetic world," in such a way as to continually disclose its invisible depths, almost as if nature were but the other side of man.[39]

To this mysterious presumptive power of language to divine the sense of the perceptual world must be added its capacity to fix this sense so that others, even those removed in time, can take it up, renew it, and even carry it further. Thus to primordial nature is added a second nature that develops a cultivated perception which makes us see differently, that, for example, sediments a network of meanings which restructures our praxis and language so that the symbolic form of science may eventually evolve. But sedimentation can also arrest progress, and progress may remove us from our sources of knowledge in such a way that we forget them. It is the dialectic of freedom and facticity, of spontaneity and receptivity once again, this time in the historicity of science. What to retain and what to modify in the inherited "body" of scientific formulations is a continuing decision posed before the historical scientific community, which is the real locus of the process of eidetic variation. It is possible that, after several centuries of progress with a notion of physics that perhaps favored its beginnings, science is now on the threshold of a new essence of the material world.[40] Man, situated as he is in his temporal horizons, must return again and again to the task of reading essences in and from their facticity, in an ongoing unfinished task of re-vision. But the essence that emerges from this process is not a positive entity but an invariant temporarily fixed by the presumption of language. Only an effort of total variation can produce an essence free from all factual "contamination," which is possible only to a pure spectator transparent to himself and his experience, free from all latency.[41] Logicism always shipwrecks on the invisible of the perceived world which is the permanent horizon of the scientific endeavor. Its perception is not an incipient science, in the sense of a confused judgment, "a stutter which precedes the clear speech of science," [42] but science is an incipient gesture motivated by the darkness surrounding the figure that beckons in distinctive ways. Its activity is an indwelling, not an overflight of

39. VI, p. 328. (Eng. trans., p. 274.)
40. VI, p. 146. (Eng. trans., p. 108.)
41. VI, p. 149. (Eng. trans., p. 111.)
42. *Signs*, p. 197.

the perceived world. On the other hand, science is not simply transformed sensations, as psychologism would have it,[43] for a measure of decentration institutes itself between science and perception. But it is a temporal detachment, not external, made possible by the imaginative variation of the incarnating word.

"But we have no rigorous theory of symbolism," [44] as Merleau-Ponty admits. Its formulation was the major thrust of his latest works, truncated by an early death. How the eidetic variation of science is sustained by imagination, which in turn is sustained by the word, which itself is rooted in historicity and temporality, and how the imaginary variations of language merge to anticipate the world of silence are questions that take us to the heart of the transcendental problem which is the proper domain of philosophy.[45] "The problem of language is fundamental if one wishes to gain any true clarity on the existence of ideas and cultural objects in the actual world." [46] This attempt to probe the symbolic behavior of the active speaking subject expressing his world promises to add a dimension to the theory of scientific symbolism over and above that of symbolic logic, which regards its language as a passive object.

PHILOSOPHY AS RADICAL REFLECTION

SCIENCE CLAIMS CONCRETENESS through its communion with facts. Yet these facts are abstracted from a much more encompassing context according to the anticipatory guidance of a controlling idea initially suggested though not given in this context. Sometimes highly inventive improvisations are developed to achieve fruitful patterns of discovery. The initial phenomenological reflection on science therefore centers on the dialectic between these "a priori essences" and the facts that follow from them and that in turn suggest new structures. Each factual science is dialectically related to a corresponding regional ei-

43. *PrP*, p. 25. By contrast, Bergson affirms "that perception is a science in the process of being born, science an adult perception . . ." (*The Creative Mind* [New York: Philosophical Library, 1946], p. 126).
44. *Signs*, p. 194.
45. *VI*, p. 290. (Eng. trans. p. 236.)
46. *PP*, p. 83.

detic. Privilege is given to eidetic psychology which reflects on activities operative in all the sciences: the essence of perception, imagination, expression.

But these essences do not constitute a fixed eternal realm but emerge from the temporality of human existence. For essence is the "thickness" *of* the sensible world, its "depth." [47] Furthermore it is *Wesen,* in the active sense that Heidegger has given to essence. Philosophy therefore cannot be confined to a reflection on essences apart from the dynamism of existence. His sense of the historicity of essences led the later Husserl to speak of the essence of philosophy itself in the same way, as a European science and not simply a rigorous science, and to locate the place of philosophy more precisely in the "vivifying present" (*lebendige Gegenwart*) that reanimates past and future, rather than simply in omnitemporality. Even Euclidean geometry was not so omnitemporal that it did not need completion by a later phase of the intentional history of geometry. It is reflection on the origination of geometry (and other sciences) that leads us to philosophy in its most radical mode. The last word, the most profound thought is in the realm of the generation of meaning (*Sinngenesis*). Philosophy, then, is the historical intersubjective endeavor to express the genesis of manifest rationality from the contingency of a more latent reason.

Out of the obscure depths of this dimension of originative experience which is the *telos* of philosophy springs all of our knowledge. In fact, the very obscurity of this region of experience is precisely what motivates all expression, including science and philosophy. If our original experience were completely clear, its expression would be superfluous. But expression, and especially philosophy, is always necessary; even our most advanced scientific experiences are not clear, precisely because they have advanced away from their generative sources. And when a scientist returns to the living sources of his own knowledge, as he may have to in times of crisis, he himself practices philosophy spontaneously. By confronting his formulas with the integral experience from which they were idealized, he corrects for the remotion of the schematizations, the price he must pay for his exactness. On the other hand, the phenomenologist does not pretend to be exact, but he must in some way give strictness to

47. VI, p. 273. (Eng. trans., p. 220.)

that out of which science schematizes, by rigorously describing the domain which even precedes facts and essences. This description which is the ultimate task of phenomenology is not a return to immediate experience as to some nebulous state of prescientific primitivism, but the ongoing attempt to try to understand and to express immediate experience, an attempt which because of the immediacy of this dimension cannot in principle be completely fulfilled. Such regressive thinking does not uncover new knowledge but excavates the layers of meanings already operative in existing knowledge. As such, philosophy is an "archeology." "Philosophy is not a particular body of knowledge; it is the vigilance that does not let us forget the sources of all knowledge." [48]

It is therefore evident that radical phenomenology, which is philosophy for Merleau-Ponty, gains its autonomy after science. Science has the first word concerning knowledge, but philosophy has the last. For the progress of science causes it to depart from its original institutions to the point of forgetting its genesis in favor of the objects it reveals, and perhaps this oblivion was even necessary for the initial development of science. The regress of phenomenology is a response to the unwarranted assumptions that have resulted from this obfuscation. In order to properly evaluate the achievements of science, philosophy finds it necessary to reconquer "a *dimension* in which the objectifications of science preserve a sense for themselves and are to be understood as true." [49] The uncovering of this dimension of the *Lebenswelt* is the first step toward a phenomenology of science. "If we want to subject science itself to rigorous scrutiny and arrive at a precise assessment of its meaning and scope, we must begin by reawakening the basic experience of the world of which science is the second-order expression." [50]

An evident corollary to this regressive movement is the necessity of understanding the progressive movement which brought science to its present position. "We will have to show how physical idealization surpasses and forgets perceptive faith." [51] The regressive reduction to the lifeworld indicated that, prior to the moment of scientific interrogation, I live in a web of

48. *Signs*, p. 110.
49. VI, p. 236. (Eng. trans., p. 182.)
50. PP, p. viii.
51. VI, p. 36. (Eng. trans., p. 18.)

experiences in which the family of material things and other families spin their styles of presentation in a "passive" generation of meaning. In order to arrive at exact essences, it is necessary for me to intervene actively through the imaginative processes of objectification and idealization. The empirical success of the scientific schemes encourages the substitution of its translation in lieu of the original text, and the process of oblivion is complete. But even the most advanced formulations have some reference to the perceived architecture, however remotely and infrequently. It should therefore be possible to reveal the original dimension in the very procedures and results of science itself, provided one reactivates them in such a way that one uncovers what they have concealed from themselves. But this presupposes a knowledge of the original phenomenal field, which remains the first and foremost task.

Once both the forward and backward movements are sufficiently explored, a comparison between the terms of the movements is possible. The structures of perception should in fact be present in the structures of science, but one must be careful in trying to approach the Being revealed in perception through the derivative Being conceived by science.[52] Science does manage to pinpoint certain "traits" of Being, certain joints of the skeleton of the world, i.e., intelligible relations or "essences," not isolated substances. But this physiognomic portrait is in principle not exhaustive of the brute facticity of the world.[53] At most, the world-view of physics may provide some guiding clues to the character of the inaugural experience of *physis*. For example, Merleau-Ponty suggests that considerations of scale in modern microphysics and astronomical physics ought to result in contesting the subject-object cleavage and in leading to a definition of the "real" which would encompass the contact between observer and observed.[54] This in turn could throw some light on the dimensionality of Being which in fact is the original source of such phenomena.[55]

But reduction of the objective field of science to the phenomenal field of perception is only a first step toward the radical reflection that philosophy seeks. The character of the relation-

52. *VI*, p. 208. (Eng. trans., p. 157.)
53. *VI*, p. 279. (Eng. trans., p. 225.)
54. *VI*, p. 33. (Eng. trans., p. 16.)
55. *VI*, p. 280. (Eng. trans., p. 227.)

ships between subjectivity, objectivity, temporality, historicity, intersubjectivity, and language remains unexamined at this level of the description of the *Lebenswelt* and its regional eidetics. A further reduction is necessary to pass from descriptive phenomenology to the "phenomenology of phenomenology" and its confrontation of the "phenomenon of the phenomenon" in a self-scrutiny that decisively transforms the phenomenal field into the transcendental realm constituting it and thus already implied in it. Not that the constituting operation which is the source of all meaning ever achieves a complete grasp of itself. Because of perception, reflection on this level of the advent of Being into consciousness is always a reflection-on-an-unreflective experience in a noncoincidence which was already manifest in the eidetic intuitions that proceed only through the gradual unfolding of free variation. In the essence commingled with contingency, in the encounter of the transcendence of a thing which is nevertheless immanent to my experience, in the visible which is pregnant with the invisible, with a subject which is both *naturans* and *naturata*, infinite and finite, in the synthesis of "wild-flowering mind" and "brute being," the transcendental is and always remains ambiguous.[56] It is on this level fraught with paradox that philosophy truly begins to reflect upon itself, just as science gains a measure of self-awareness on the previous level. Just as it is necessary to probe the subconscious of science, to trace its genealogy, so likewise for philosophy. But the ground here is even more obscure so that Merleau-Ponty wonders at the presumption of such a radical retrogressive ambition: "Is this reason's highest accomplishment: observing the ground as it slips away beneath my feet, pompously calling interrogation what is simply a state of continual stupor, calling research or quest what is merely wandering in a circle, calling Being something that never completely is?" [57] Such is the colossal aporia, the insoluble dilemma of a being whose only access to the immediate is through the mediations of its symbolic forms.

56. *PP*, pp. 63, 365; *VI*, p. 269 (Eng. trans., p. 216); *Signs*, p. xxiv.

57. *PrP*, p. 190.

13 / Merleau-Ponty on Space Perception and Space

Joseph J. Kockelmans

SEVERAL CONTEMPORARY PHILOSOPHERS have defended the thesis that man is to be "defined" as Being-in-the-world.[1] Whoever understands the deeper meaning of this "definition" knows it implies that man's being can no longer be conceived of within the realm of the alternative of the "for-itself" and the "in-itself." For if man were a pure consciousness (for-itself) or a mere thing among other things (in-itself) he could not be "in" or "toward" the world. Man is not a pure consciousness because a pure consciousness is a gaze which can unfold everything and for which everything lies already in the open, whereas man's experience must be characterized fundamentally by the idea of resistance, which, in turn, implies complications, obstacles, and ambiguities. Man is not a thing either. For although it is true that a thing can be said to coexist with other things, it certainly cannot transcend them, since it does not have a horizon, it is not "in" or "toward" the world. It must be noted here that in this conception the world is not found "in" things, but rather at the horizon of things; in other words, the world is not the sum total of all real things, nor is it a mere fiction of the human mind, but that "whole," the "total-meaningfulness," toward which man's transcendence continuously aims.[2]

1. See A. de Waelhens, "A Philosophy of the Ambiguous," in *SB*, pp. xviii–xxvii, esp. p. xviii.
2. Martin Heidegger, *Being and Time*, trans. John Macquarrie and Edward Robinson (London: SCM, 1962), pp. 92–93, 101–2, 114–22, 176–77. Cf. de Waelhens, "Philosophy of the Ambiguous," pp. xviii–xix.

In his main work, *Phenomenology of Perception*,[3] Merleau-Ponty shares this view which was formulated for the first time in this way by Heidegger in *Being and Time* (1927).[4] Merleau-Ponty, however, is of the opinion that Heidegger has neglected to give us an adequate description of what precisely is to be understood by the expression "Being-in-the-world." With Sartre, Merleau-Ponty believes that Heidegger in *Being and Time* situated himself in a sphere of ambiguity, or, perhaps more accurately stated, in a sphere of complexity which at the very outset conceals the fact that not all the pertinent problems are solved by looking upon the very essence of man in that way. According to Merleau-Ponty most of the relevant problems which Heidegger leaves untouched are to be solved at the level of man's perception, because, as he sees it, it is precisely at the level of perception that meaning *originally* comes to the fore. Furthermore, Merleau-Ponty claims, it is evident that in perception the human body plays a predominant role. However, in *Being and Time* Heidegger does not explicitly deal with the problem of perception and the human body is scarcely mentioned. The "projects" which, in Heidegger's view, *originally* constitute the meaning of intramundane things are all taken at the level of our everyday concern. Merleau-Ponty claims that all these projects *presuppose* that man is able to move his body, to act, to perceive. In other words, the projects which Heidegger describes presuppose that in his everyday life man is able to see, to consult his watch, to move his arms and legs, to walk, to orient himself. The fact that a human being is able to accomplish all these different tasks involves no problems only and exclusively on the presupposition that man's capacity of moving his body and his ability to perceive are self-evident. Merleau-Ponty claims that the reader of *Being and Time* realizes too late that the minute acuity with which Heidegger describes the world which we project in our everyday praxis has as its very important drawback a total negligence of the world which is always already there and which in each project we necessarily presuppose. As Merleau-Ponty sees it, it is precisely in this world which is always already there that the paradoxical structure of a conscious being which *must become thing* while hovering over things, rises. In other words, if

3. Hereafter cited as *PP*.
4. Heidegger, *Being and Time*, pp. 78–273 *passim*.

a genuine project of the real is possible for man, then this is so because he takes part in the real in a very radical sense. That is why, according to Merleau-Ponty, a philosophy which "defines" man as Being-in-the-world must take its starting point in a phenomenological study of man's perception in order to show that and how in perception the human body plays a predominant role.[5]

As far as Sartre is concerned, Merleau-Ponty believes there can be no doubt that Sartre has given us a very important and detailed critique of the traditional views of sensation on the one hand, and has developed a systematic investigation of the human body on the other. Taking his point of departure in the earlier investigations of Marcel, Sartre defends the thesis that one must make a clear distinction between the body-for-me and the body-for-others, a distinction without which, in Merleau-Ponty's view, the whole problem concerning the body fades away into confusion and remains defenseless against the fundamental theses of positivism. But although it is true that Sartre's view of the very essence of our bodily being, conceived of essentially as a living dialectic between the body-as-instrument and the body-taken-as-a-bare-fact, is exceptionally fruitful in that it, in the final analysis, allows us to understand how an ek-sisting consciousness can inhere in the world and, at the same time, be a project of that same world, it is true also that this view immediately loses its deeper meaning the moment one conceives of it within the general framework of Sartre's ontology as a whole. For this ontology is essentially built upon the radical and irreconcilable opposition between the "for-itself" and the "in-itself" in which the Cartesian dualism of the *res cogitans* and the *res extensa* is not only restored, but even aggravated. It will not be too difficult, Merleau-Ponty thinks, to see that within such an ontology Sartre's critique of the traditional conceptions of sensation on the one hand and his phenomenological analyses of the human body on the other gradually lose their meaning. For after having separated the for-itself and the in-itself in such a radical way, Sartre has to conceive of the for-itself as a "nothingness" of Being which must unfold itself in the "naughting" of Being.

However, once the for-itself and the in-itself are radically

5. de Waelhens, "Philosophy of the Ambiguous," pp. xviii–xix.

separated, and once consciousness becomes a mere spectator without consistency in its own right, such a consciousness knows or does not know, but it certainly cannot know in different ways; it cannot be related to the in-itself *in an ambiguous way*. As soon as such a consciousness knows, it knows everything; as soon as it speaks, everything is said at once. The qualities which it perceives are perceived absolutely. Such a consciousness is not in the world and, therefore, it cannot be involved in what it perceives. But this involvement is precisely what gives our perception the character of constant and essential incompletion, its necessary perspectivism, the necessity of its being accomplished from a determinate point of view. In his phenomenological analyses Sartre has seen these points very clearly, but in his ontology he is not able to account for them. Notwithstanding his sincere attempts, Sartre is not able to explain that the thing which indeed is immediately present is nonetheless given to us merely in a way which is both evident and ambiguous. For the perceived thing, however indubitable it may be just insofar as it is perceived, always has to wait for the reception of its full meaning from a subsequent exploration. And as Husserl has rightly pointed out, this exploration endlessly delineates new horizons of potentialities.

As far as the human body is concerned, the same situation manifests itself in Sartre's philosophy. He admits an absolute distinction between the for-itself and the in-itself. But as soon as the body-as-instrument comes into the picture, it should become clear that the for-itself, even though ontologically the nothingness of Being, must nonetheless exist in some in-itself; but in that way it carves out a certain facticity *of its own* which as for-itself it is unable to possess. True, this facticity of our body is not easily determined, because it is normally hidden in the projects Heidegger has pointed to, in the general organization which I elaborate by the very fact that I ek-sist. But how is such a facticity conceivable if there is an absolute separation of the for-itself and the in-itself? In other words, if the for-itself is nothing but the "naughting" of Being, then it is difficult to see, once a certain facticity is admitted in connection with it, why not everything is facticity for it and especially why, within my experience itself, there is a facticity which is mine in a very radical sense. As soon as the human body comes into the picture, it becomes clear that our Being-in-the-world takes on a new dimension for which an absolute duality of a for-itself and an in-itself is unable to account.[6]

As Merleau-Ponty sees it, the human body is not a thing, but a means in order to manifest meaning, to make this meaning be, to project and communicate that meaning. The human body is in the world as our heart is in our body: it keeps the visible spectacle continuously alive; it breathes life into the world and nourishes it from the inside; and together with the world it constitutes one single system.[7] The human body is not a thing because—precisely as human body—it is *mine;* it founds the meaning the world has for me, and it founds that meaning in itself and by means of itself. My body is not a thing, because I can have "clear and distinct ideas" of things, whereas it is impossible for me to have such ideas of my own body. If one is to know his own body, he has to "live" it. On the other hand, however, our body has certainly the character of the in-itself; the human body is also a thing. That is to say, one can describe it as a thing in the midst of things. This is done by biology and physiology. But the body as described there is not *my* body, that is to say, it is not the body as I experience it immediately.[8]

If we go on into greater detail, we must say *first* that my body is my way of entering a world to which my body belongs on several and different levels but with which it never completely coincides. As mundane my body is in and toward the world; it occupies a privileged position there, upon which all other places depend and around which they organize themselves. Already on this level my body transcends things in the direction of a world insofar as it gives structure and meaning to them, transcends the relation of causality which is precisely characteristic of the totality of things. *Secondly,* the body also refers immediately to an ego who without the body never could affirm itself, and who, on the other hand, never coincides with the body.

As Merleau-Ponty sees it, our "natural" world manifests itself first to a human body which signifies the world; body and world constitute a unity of mutual implication. It is now of vital importance in this context not to confound this "natural" world with the world as described by the sciences, although it is ob-

6. *Ibid.,* pp. xix–xxiv.
7. *PP,* p. 203.
8. *PP,* pp. 203–4.

viously true that this "natural" world is implied as horizon in the worlds of the sciences. That is why the relationship between the "immediately lived" world and the objective world of the sciences must be brought up in every analysis which focuses attention on the way our human body brings meaning to light.

The place now where the relationship between human body and world materializes itself is generally called "sense perception" or, briefly, "sensation." A careful analysis of sense perception makes it clear that sensation cannot be adequately explained in terms of causal relationships. On the other hand, those analyses show equally clearly that the subject of sensation cannot be described as a constituting thinker either. Sensation is communion. That is why sensation offers us something like a "middle term" between a pure in-itself and a pure for-itself. Formulated from another point of view, one could say that in every act of sense perception the subject is neither purely passive nor purely active. It is not even true that the one (the subject, for instance) gives meaning to the other (the perceived thing). One must say that in the "natural interaction" between subject and thing a meaning becomes constituted, comes into being which is neither in the manner of the in-itself nor in the manner of the for-itself. That in every act of sensation no pure for-itself manifests itself is evident from the fact that the subject as it manifests itself on that level is still a "general" and anonymous subject. The ego which manifests itself on the level of sensation is not yet a personal ego, not yet my personal, responsible ego as I experience it in my thinking and willing. Sensation is more the fruit of a "one perceives," "this is consciously present," than an "I perceive" and "I am conscious of." On the other hand, however, one should not forget that the perceived thing never is a pure in-itself and that the world never is a pure multiplicity.

In other words, the subject of sensation is not my conscious ego but my body. In every act of sense perception, moreover, the perception of the thing and the perception of one's own body vary in mutual conjunction, because in the final analysis they are the two aspects of one and the same "act." Such a view of the human body as subject of perception can obviously not be justified by deductive or dialectic arguments; it can be made acceptable only by careful analysis and description of the concrete modes in which man originally perceives. In these analyses Merleau-Ponty believes he has found time and again that underneath the objective body described by the sciences we find that other body which we are and as such experience immediately. In the same way, he thinks, he has found underneath the objective world of the sciences the world as it appears to us insofar as we are in the world through our body and perceive it with our body. And by studying the immediate contact between body and world, he says finally, we shall find ourselves, because in perceiving with our body the body manifests itself as a "natural ego" and, in that sense, as the genuine subject of perception.[9]

In the following discussion I wish to illustrate these general theses which constitute the core of Merleau-Ponty's major works, using his description of our perception of space as a concrete example.

In Merleau-Ponty's works considerations about space and perception of space receive a substantial amount of attention. In both *Structure of Behavior* and *Phenomenology of Perception* he returns to these questions in various chapters.[10] Nevertheless, I think one should recognize that the problem of space as such cannot be called one of primordial importance for Merleau-Ponty. The chief concern of his works lies in the query about the very Being of man and about the fundamental significance of our body-subject; he explains and justifies his views on these issues by means of reflections utilizing human behavior and perception as primary themes. In these reflections the space problem is recurrent, but only as a touchstone for the general theses he wants to defend.

Although Merleau-Ponty's prime objective is to shed more light on the essence of man and the fundamental significance of the body-subject,[11] in the considerations which follow I shall focus my attention primarily on his view of space. In so doing I hope to find an answer to these specific questions: Exactly what is space according to Merleau-Ponty? Which spatial forms must we distinguish? What mode of Being must we attribute to space? What are its main characteristics?

9. *PP*, pp. 204–6.
10. *SB*, pp. 201–20; *PP*, pp. 98–147, 148–53, 217–37 *passim*, 243–98.
11. Remy C. Kwant, *The Phenomenological Philosophy of Merleau-Ponty* (Pittsburgh, Pa.: Duquesne University Press, 1963), pp. 11–30, and *passim*.

SPACE PERCEPTION AND SPACE

ACCORDING TO MERLEAU-PONTY consciousness is not an absolute transparent reality; neither does an absolutely opaque reality exist. On the level of perception the knowing subject manifests itself as a reality that lies between a true in-itself (*en-soi*) and a pure for-itself (*pour-soi*). Time and again we find the intermediary mode of Being in every mode of perception, as, for example, in the perception of space.[12]

Kant drew a sharp distinction between space as a form of our intuition and the things which are given in this experience. This conception of space is obviously not concerned with the relation between something containing and something contained, since such a relation is only possible between two things. Neither is it concerned with a relationship of logical inclusion such as exists between a class and an individual member of it, since space, in contradistinction to logical classes, precedes the "parts" one can distinguish and isolate. According to Kant, therefore, space is neither the logical nor the real "setting" in which things are arranged but only the means whereby the positing of things is made possible. In this conception, therefore, space is not ether in which things could float, nor is it an abstract quality common to all things. We must think of it rather as that on the ground of which it is universally possible to bring things into connection with one another.

One can approach the space problem from at least two sides: either we do not reflect but just live among things, in which case we see space vaguely as the environment in which things are, or perhaps as a quality common to all things; or else we do reflect and grasp space by its roots to discover then that spatial relations only exist and "live" through a subject who describes them; in that case, Merleau-Ponty says, we go from a "spatialized space" to a "spatializing space." In the former case, my body appears together with the things and their mutual concrete spatial relations as an irreducible multiplicity. In the latter case, however, I discover one single indivisible capacity which consti-

12. PP, pp. 374–77; A. de Waelhens, *Une Philosophie de l'am-biguïté: L'Existentialisme de Maurice Merleau-Ponty* (Louvain: Publications Universitaires, 1967), pp. 1–8, 185.

tutes space. In the first case, we are concerned with physical space and its differently qualified regions; in the second, it is a question of the abstract homogeneous and isotropic geometrical space.[13]

It is well known how this difference has become confused in modern space conceptions, even at the level of scientific thought. Consequently, it is necessary to confront it with our experience of space, which (even according to Kant) has the last word in all knowledge of space. Are we really placed in a dilemma of either *perceiving* things in space or *conceiving* of space as the indivisible system governing the acts of synthesis performed by a constituting consciousness? [14]

Orientation in Space

Merleau-Ponty is of the opinion that it is difficult to see and express what space as given in immediate experience precisely is, because the originally given space is hidden under layers of meaning which have their origin in our theoretical, and especially scientific, elaborations of what is immediately given. This is why he prefers to resort to exceptional cases to show how space dissolves before our eyes and then takes shape again. As a first example he chooses Stratton's experiment,[15] by which the images, through special glasses, appear unreversed on the retina.[16] According to this experiment a subject who is made to wear such glasses first experiences the environment as upside down. On the second day of the experiment, the environment no longer appears as inverted, but the subject now has the feeling that his own body is upside down. Between the third and the seventh day the body gradually begins again to occupy a "normal" position; this is particularly the case if the subject is very active; it does not occur, however, when the subject continues to lie motionless on a bed. During the experiment as a whole

13. PP, pp. 243–44.
14. PP, p. 244.
15. G. Stratton, "Some Preliminary Experiments on Vision Without Inversion of the Retinal Image," *Psychological Review*, III (1896), 611–17; "Vision Without Inversion of the Retinal Image," *Psychological Review*, IV (1897), 341–60; "The Spatial Harmony of Touch and Sight," *Mind*, XXIV (1899), 492–505.
16. PP, pp. 244–45.

external objects gradually begin to look "real" again, and actions which were at first liable to be misled by the artificial situation finally reach their goals infallibly once more. At first it is almost impossible to place a sound, but by the seventh day the subject is able to locate a sound if the source of the sound is seen as well as heard. At the end of the experiment, when the glasses are removed, objects are no longer inverted but for some time appear "strange," whereas motor reactions remain reversed for a time.

A psychologist is generally inclined to give the following explanation of this experiment. When the subject of the experiment has put on the glasses, his field of vision at first appears unreal and everything seems to be upside down. With the glasses on the subject experiences the visual world given to him as if it had been rotated 180°, and *consequently* as upside down. At the same time, however, his tactile world has remained "normal." Thus both worlds no longer coincide and, particularly as far as his body is concerned, the subject has two irreconcilable representations: one made up by earlier tactile observations and the visible "images" which he still retains within himself; the other made up by the new visual experiences which show him his body as being head downwards. It appears, however, that such a reconciliation is not impossible; it takes some time and is the more easily accomplished depending upon whether or not the subject is active. The experience of a visually guided movement teaches the subject how to bring the visual and tactile data in harmony with one another. At first the subject seems here to "translate" the new visual experiences into the old well-known space, by explicitly reflecting upon the situation; later it becomes a habit, and the old conception fades away. When the subject has learned to feel *and* to see his legs as "down below" once more, so that here, also, the visual and tactile experiences correspond again and the visual and tactile worlds completely coincide, then the confusion of "top" and "bottom" comes to an end.[17]

Merleau-Ponty considers such an explanation of Stratton's experiment incomprehensible. For in this experiment one presupposes that the "top" and "bottom" in the field of vision are connected with the direction of head and feet, *insofar as* this direction is given *in the image*. On the contrary, he maintains that the orientation of the field cannot possibly be given by the

17. *PP*, pp. 245–46.

content of what appears in the field. Were this so, then these contents themselves would have to have an orientation of their own; "top" and "bottom," "right" and "left," however, are not absolute. Of course, one can say that the new field of vision is "upside down" in relation to the old one, or in relation to the tactile field. But these fields, too, have no absolute orientation in themselves,[18] because their orientation obviously changes during the experiment, without anything whatsoever having to happen to the constellation of the stimuli. In other words one cannot consider the world and orientated space as given along with the contents of sense experience, or along with our body taken by itself, because the experiment rightly proves that *identical* contents can be successively taken in different ways. Apparently the question here is: how is it possible that a thing is able to appear to us as "the right way up" or "inverted," *and* what do these expressions precisely mean?

The empiricist considers the perception of space as the reception within ourselves of a real and given space and the phenomenal orientation of things as a reflection of the orientation of these things in the world. For the intellectualist the orientation depends solely on the points of view which the subject successively takes. But it is obvious that just as a coordinate axis has no orientation in space unless there is a reference system outside it, *and so on,* in the same way must the spatial organization of the world be indefinitely postponed. "Up" and "down" do not have absolute meanings. According to the intellectualist, thus, it is simple to prove that only for a subject constituting it can there be any question of direction and that a constituting mind can trace out all possible directions, even though it itself has (through lack of a real and absolute starting point) neither direction nor space.

Empiricism and intellectualism are unable clearly to formulate and a fortiori unable to solve the problem which Stratton's experiment poses. Empiricism is willing to take the actual orientation of my bodily experience as the fixed point one needs if he is to understand that there are directions for me; but both experience and reflection show that no content is in itself orientated. Intellectualism starts from the relativity of the directions but

18. PP, pp. 217–30; de Waelhens, *Une Philosophie de l'ambiguïté,* pp. 174–79.

cannot stand outside this relativity in order to account for an actual perception of space. Space experience is, therefore, not to be understood by the consideration of contents, nor by a pure synthetic activity. The space of our perception is not the space of things; neither is it a spatializing space. We shall have to look for a solution in another direction.[19]

Merleau-Ponty now appeals to another experiment which, in referring to Wertheimer,[20] he describes in the following way. Let us suppose that a subject is able to see a room in which he himself is, only through a mirror which reflects the room at an angle of $45°$. The subject will at first see the room slantwise. If someone else begins to walk around in the same room, he appears to the subject as leaning to one side as he goes. A picture falling down along the door frame seems to be falling obliquely. The whole situation is strange. But after a few minutes a sudden change takes place: the walls, the second person, and the line along which the picture falls, again become vertical. This experiment, which is analogous to Stratton's, has according to Merleau-Ponty the advantage of showing that an instantaneous redistribution of high and low takes place without there being any motor exploration on the part of the subject. We have already learned that it is not right to say that the inverted image brings about a repositioning of the new spectacle. Now we see that such an exploration is not even necessary and, consequently, that the orientation is constituted by a global act of the perceiving subject. One is inclined to say here that the observer had already accepted a certain spatial level before the experiment, in respect to which the initial scene perceived in the mirror appeared to be oblique. Now it is possible that, without further objective happenings whatsoever, a new spatial level suddenly becomes accepted in which the scene, during the experiment itself, becomes normal and straight again. It is then as though some of the objects in the scene, which in regard to the original spatial level appeared to be oblique, suddenly and "autonomously" begin to act as fixed reference points around which the initially accepted level begins to revolve. In this explanation of the experiment one does not make the mistake of realism which uses the visual spectacle as a source of directions in space; for in our explana-

19. PP, pp. 247–48.
20. G. Wertheimer, "Experimentelle Studien ueber das Sehen von Bewegung," *Zeitschrift für Psychogie,* LXI (1912), 161–265.

tion the originally provided spectacle does not give by itself the new up-and-down axis. Our explanation, however, does assume that the new scene is orientated with respect to a certain earlier environment. The question now is: in what does this already accepted spatial environment consist that (as it were) constantly precedes itself because the constitution of every new environment already presupposes another? Furthermore, another important question is: how is it possible for certain objective points of a determinate environment which is already accepted as such to appear as fixed reference points that cause us to constitute a new environment? And what do "top" and "bottom" mean ultimately? [21]

In the first place, we hold that the "spatial level" cannot be identical to the orientation of our body. The consciousness of our own body undoubtedly contributes, according to Nagel, to the constitution of this spatial level, but it is, regardless of certain exceptions, certainly not the only factor. From Wertheimer's experiment it is clear that sometimes one can accept an orientation which is different from that of our own body, at least so long as the body remains passive. If, however, the body is active and moving, then it is an essential factor in the constitution of a new spatial level. One might be inclined to suppose that the vertical of a spatial level is the direction fixed by the axis of symmetry of our body taken as a synergic system. But even this conception is exaggerated. It is better to formulate this as follows: that which is of importance for the orientation of a scene is not my body as it actually is now as a thing in objective space but my virtual body as a system of possible activities the "phenomenal place" of which is fixed by its situations and its tasks. My body is there where there is something to be done.[22] It is further evident from Wertheimer's experiment that a reorientation appears only when the scene observed in the mirror demands a subject who has to live in it. Then the virtual body moves the real one so that the subject no longer feels himself bound to the world in which he first lived. And instead of his real arms and legs the subject suddenly feels the arms and legs which would be necessary for his being able to walk and work in the scene. It is then that he suddenly inhabits this scene, and it is then that the original

21. *PP*, pp. 248–49.
22. *PP*, p. 250.

spatial level revolves into its new position. The spatial level is, therefore, a certain form of possession of the world by my body, "une certaine prise de mon corps sur le monde." [23]

From a close comparison of several normal as well as abnormal cases it appears that such a level can form itself in different ways. It can be the case that it is constituted and projected, for lack of fixed reference points, solely by the bearing of my body, as is shown in Nagel's experiment, according to which a subject who tilts his head on one side holds a stick obliquely, when he is asked to hold it vertically. It can also be that it is mainly fixed by the requirements of the scene, namely, if the subject accommodates himself more or less passively to the demands of the scene, as is shown by Wertheimer's experiment. Normally, however, it comes into being through a harmonious connection of my motor intentions with the requirements of the perceptual field. In this last case my effective body coincides with the virtual body that is demanded by the scene, while the effective spectacle in its turn coincides with the setting that my body projects around itself. [24]

In the normal way, therefore, a spatial level is created when a pact is made between my body as the potentiality for certain movements, or as that which demands certain privileged planes, and the observed scene as an invitation to those movements and actions, or eventually as a stage for these actions. This pact constitutes space for me and gives to things a direct power over my body. The constitution of a new spatial level is therefore only one of the ways in which we can project and constitute a full world. My body has a hold on the world only when my perception presents me with a scene as clear and as varied as possible, while my motor intentions as they develop receive from the world the answers they expect. This maximum of clarity in perception and this maximum of certainty in my actions together define a perceptual ground, a basis for my life, a general setting for the coexistence of my body with the world. It seems that we can understand Stratton's experiment exactly only when we make use of the notions "spatial level," and "my body as the subject of space." [25]

23. PP, pp. 98–147, 250. See also de Waelhens, *Une Philosophie de l'ambiguïté*, pp. 118–42.

24. PP, pp. 250, 383–88; de Waelhens, *Une Philosophie de l'ambiguïté*, pp. 277–81.

25. PP, pp. 250–51.

Nevertheless, we must try to pursue our analysis further. One could ask oneself the question: why are clear and sharp perception and sure action not possible unless in an *orientated* phenomenal space? We could suppose that this is to be explained only by the fact that absolute orientation is already given in the world to which the subject has to adjust himself. In our inquiry about perception and its conditions in which we want to place ourselves inside perception, we are not permitted to presuppose such an orientation. According to Merleau-Ponty, in a phenomenology of perception the difficulty comes down to this: the constitution of a new spatial level always presupposes another already given level; and so space appears continually to precede itself.[26] This contention is in no way a proof of the failure of our reflections; on the contrary, this contention puts us on the track of the nature of space, and this in a way which will bring us really to an insight into its essence. It is essential to space that it continually is *already* constituted. One can therefore never understand it if one withdraws to a perception without a world.

Therefore, we must not ask why being is orientated, why all being is spatial, and why the existence of our body with the world constantly polarizes our perception and, thus, causes a direction to come into being. These questions can only be posed when we start from the idea that these facts are accidental to the subject and the object, thus when both should in themselves be indifferent with regard to space. Perception, however, shows that they are presupposed in our primordial encounter with things: being is identical with being-situated. If we want to understand this, we must first bear in mind that the being-object of a thing consists not in its being-for-a-thinking-subject but in its being-for-a-gaze which meets this thing under a certain orientation and otherwise fails to recognize it. Perhaps we may express the same idea in the following manner: our perception would contain no outlines, no figures, no backgrounds, no objects either, and it would, consequently, be a perception of nothing, or rather no perception at all, if the subject of perception were not this gaze

26. PP, pp. 251–52. See also 100–102; and Oskar Becker, "Beiträge zur phänomenologischen Begründung der Geometrie und ihrer physikalischen Anwendungen," *Jahrbuch für Philosophie und phänomenologische Forschung*, VI (1923), 385–560, esp. pp. 454–57. (Selections from this work appear above, pp. 119–43.)

which has a grasp on those things only insofar as they have a certain orientation, and if the orientation in space were a contingent characteristic of the thing. This orientation is the means by which I recognize a thing for what it is and by which I am conscious of it as an object. Just as, therefore, each perceived thing immediately or mediately is involved in the perceived world, and just as a perceived world without orientation cannot be grasped, in the same way can being not be dissociated from orientated being. It is thus also without any meaning to try to find a "basis" for space and to ask for the level of all levels. The very first level is on the horizon of all our observations and perceptions, but this horizon can in principle never be reached and never be thematized in an explicit perception. Every spatial level in which we live can appear only when we can cast anchor in some setting which is already given to us. Even our very first experience can be spatial only on the ground of an orientation given beforehand. Our very first experience therefore must have found us already at work in a world, which, however (because we are speaking here of our very first experience) can in no way be defined.

I myself, therefore, cannot orientate the world, and neither is the world orientated in itself. It necessarily follows, then, that my first perception of and my first grasp on the world are the execution of a pact formed earlier between a certain x and the world in general. Underneath my concrete ego I therefore discover another subject for which a world already exists before I am there myself, and which defines my original place in it. This subject is nothing else but my body, not my actual body as instrument of my personal choice and as directed toward an already defined world, but my body as a system of certain anonymous functions. This still blind adherence to the world appears not only at the very beginning of my conscious life but continues to give meaning to every further experience of space, since it is to be reassumed at every moment. Space and perception, therefore, refer me constantly to my existence, to the part which my body exercises in all my activities, to a contact with the world which is older than my thinking. This especially is the reason why both are so difficult to thematize.[27]

27. de Waelhens, *Une Philosophie de l'ambiguïté*, pp. 190–91, 318–20.

Space, therefore, is not an object, nor is it a synthesizing act of a pure subject; neither can it be perceived because it is presupposed in every act of perception; [28] nor can we see it emerge from our constituting activity, because it is essential for it that it already be constituted.[29]

Depth

One comes to a similar conclusion when one subjects the perception of depth to a minute analysis. The classical conceptions deny very positively that it is possible to see depth. Both the reflexive analyses of intellectualism and the considerations of empiricists such as Berkeley tacitly presuppose that depth is nothing other than breadth which one sees from the side. It is exactly this supposition which makes depth invisible. For if one takes depth to be a juxtaposition of simultaneous points in one single dimension, then it is clear that I cannot see this juxtaposition if this series of points lies exactly in my direction. Both conceptions furthermore presuppose that space must be isotropic.

Merleau-Ponty does not agree with either conception. One can consider depth as breadth seen in profile and thus maintain an isotropic space only when the subject can leave his definite place and abandon his point of view on the world in order to *think* of himself as having a sort of ubiquity. Only for God who is everywhere is breadth immediately equivalent to depth. No explanation is therefore given by either system for the *human* experience of the world. Each only tells you what God might *think* about it.

The world itself certainly invites us to think of it as isotropic, and everyone accepts without theoretic consideration the equivalence of depth and breadth, which is an integral part of the *self-evidence* of our intersubjective world. But it seems here as though both the philosopher and the man in the street forget the actual originality of depth. In view of the standpoint we have taken as phenomenologists, however, we know nothing of the world and of objective space as yet; we wish to describe the

28. *PP*, p. 254.
29. *PP*, pp. 252–54.

phenomenon of the world as faithfully as possible, and this on the level in which we live and in which knowledge and science have in no way yet deformed or leveled the individual perspectives. More than the other dimensions of space it is depth which especially compels us to relinquish our bias about the world in order to lay bare the primordial experience from which that world springs. One could therefore call depth the most "existential" dimension, because it belongs most clearly to our perspective and not to things. Therefore it cannot either be extracted from or put into that perspective. It shows us a certain indissoluble tie between things and ego, whereas breadth and length could be conceived of as relations between things. Merleau-Ponty is of the opinion that by rediscovering the vision of a depth which is not yet objectified and which does not consist of mutually external points, we shall once more be able to transcend empiricism and intellectualism.[30]

According to the objective way of thinking, one says, for example, that the piano is farther away from me than the table, because there is an interval between both which one does not *see* oneself, but which reveals itself by the apparent size of the piano. This is even more evident when I see a car driving off. The comparison between the apparent size and the actual size of a thing gives things their definite place in space. One can explain depth also by the convergence of the eyes. According to Malebranche, the distance of a thing is equal to the height of a triangle of which the base and both base angles are given to me. In short, in classic theories depth experience rests on the deciphering of certain given facts, such as apparent size, convergence of the eyes, etc. All of this holds up only on the basis of knowledge concerning a world of unchangeable things in themselves and of a previously given space, since the signs mentioned which would be able to initiate us into the experience of depth can mean spatial relations only if they are included a priori in one and the same objective space, that is, if space is known to us a priori. However, should perception be the primordial contact with the world, then one may accept no objective relation whatsoever which is not yet constituted on that level. The mistake made in the classic conceptions therefore is that one describes

30. PP, pp. 254–56.

two facts (apparent size and convergence) from the viewpoint of a spatial world which is already constituted, and not from that which one grasps from the inside.[31]

According to Gestalt psychologists it is certain that neither the convergence of the eyes nor the apparent size of things is explicitly known and that they nevertheless play a role in the perception of distance. They conclude from this that both elements are not signs but necessary conditions for the perception of distance and depth. In this way one combines the vision of phenomenology with that of objectifying knowledge in a way which does injustice to both. There is no compromise possible in this instance; one has to choose here between phenomenology and behaviorism.

In Merleau-Ponty's view convergence and apparent size are neither causes nor conditions nor signs of distance and depth; they are profoundly present in the perception of depth, analogous to the way in which a motive is present in a decision. A motive is a certain antecedent which influences only by its meaning; the decision confirms the meaning as being valid and gives it strength and effectiveness. Motive and decision are, therefore, two elements of one situation: the former is the situation as a fact, the second is the same situation as taken up. In this way the death of my friend can be a motive for a journey which I am going to take now, because his death is a situation that requires my presence there. By deciding to make the trip I confirm the motive as valid and I take up the situation. The relation between the motive and the motivated act is therefore a reciprocal relation. In approximately the same way there exists a relationship between convergence, apparent size, and depth: the former do not cause depth to exist in some miraculous way; they tacitly account for it, insofar as they both already contain depth in their meaning; they motivate it. They themselves are two ways of looking at a distance.[32]

Perspectives can also be explained in the same way. When I see a road before me that finally disappears into the horizon, I cannot say that the edges of the road are given to me as being parallel or convergent; they are given to me as "parallel in depth." One could think also that a man at a distance is smaller than he is when standing beside me. But this is not always right;

31. *PP*, pp. 256–57.
32. *PP*, pp. 257–59.

it is only so when I detach the distant man from the perceived context. In all other cases he is neither bigger nor smaller, nor even of the same size; it is the same man, but now seen from a distance. One can say only that the man at a distance is a less articulated figure and that my gaze has less hold on him. One can say also that he does not completely occupy my field of vision and that his form is too little structured to exhaust my power of clear vision. This field contains more or fewer things, according to whether I see them close by or far off. Thus it appears that apparent size is not to be defined independently of distance: both implicate each other.

We can therefore conclude that convergence, apparent size, and distance are inseparably tied together. They are mutually synonymous not because the subject constitutes objective relations between them, but just because it does not detach them from one another, because they are in themselves only abstract elements of one and the same situation. We still possess the object which moves away from us; we continue to have a hold on it. The growing distance is not a growing externality, but it only expresses that the thing is beginning to slip from the hold of our eyes. Distance itself could therefore best be described by saying that it is that which distinguishes a superficial and sketchy hold on a thing from the exhausting hold which is characteristic for nearness.[33]

It is especially illusions in relation to the perception of depth which make us accustomed to considering depth as a construction of our mind. These illusions can be evoked artificially with a stereoscope; the same effect can be obtained also by certain perspective drawings, such as those of cubes. The interesting point of such drawings is that one can generally see them in more than one way. I see these "ambiguous" figures first in one way and then in another, according to a certain plane or a certain line or figure that I fix, from which I then can follow the course of the others. If one considers similar cases it is apparent that my gaze is not primary and constituting but that my gaze is called for, suggested, motivated by the given figures. Every fixation always is a fixation of something which offers itself to me to be fixated on.[34] Not my thinking but my perceptive grasp is the genius which gives to things the precise answer which they are

33. *PP*, pp. 259–61.
34. *PP*, p. 264.

awaiting in order to exist for me. Seen in this way depth is that dimension in which things or elements of things implicate each other, while breadth and height are the dimensions according to which they are juxtaposed.[35]

It is possible to consider depth, with Straus, as a spatio-temporal dimension.[36] When I say that an object is seen at a distance, I mean that I already hold it or that I still hold it. It is therefore equally in the past or in the future as it is in space. Of course one can argue that this is only so for me and that in itself the perceived thing exists at the same time as I now perceive it, because distance is a relation between simultaneous things and this simultaneity is contained in the very meaning of perception. This is right, but the coexistence defining space is not alien to time; this coexistence is the "appertaining" of two phenomena to the same temporal wave.[37] The relation between the perceptive act and the perceived thing does not join both *in* space and *outside of* time; they are contemporary. In other words, the *ordo coexistentium* (Leibniz) is not to be separated from the *ordo succedentium*. Perception gives me a "field of presence" in a wider sense of this word.[38] This field stretches out in two dimensions: in the dimension of here and there, and in the dimension of past, present, and future. It is the second dimension which makes the first completely understandable. I have here-now the object at a distance without explicit positing of the spatial perspective, just as I have also in hand here-now the immediate past [39] without any distortion and without any "recollection" pushed in between them.[40]

As we have already noted above, one has to rediscover in depth as a relation between things (which is objectified depth), a primordial depth which gives meaning to the first and which consists in the density of a medium in which as yet no things

35. *PP*, pp. 261–65.
36. Cf. Erwin Straus, *Vom Sinn der Sinne* (Berlin: Springer, 1935), pp. 302–6.
37. *PP*, p. 265.
38. *Ibid.*
39. Edmund Husserl, "Vorlesungen zur Phänomenologie des inneren Zeitbewusstseins" (ed. Martin Heidegger), *Jahrbuch für Philosophie und phänomenologische Forschung*, IX (1928), 367–496, esp. 397–401.
40. *PP*, pp. 264–65.

are. In ordinary perception and particularly in special cases, depth manifests itself as something which does not yet operate between objects, and thus, a fortiori, does not yet fix any distance between them, and which, strictly speaking, is merely the opening of perception upon some "phantom" which as yet is still scarcely qualified. Just as "high" and "low," "right" and "left" are not given to the subject together with the perceived contents but are constituted at each moment together with a spatial level in regard to which things arrange themselves, so also is depth only proper to things through the fact that they situate themselves in respect to a level of distances and sizes which defines "far-off," "close by," "big," and "small" even before an object is chosen as a standard. Often we call a thing "huge" or "tiny," "nearby" or "far-off" without there being any comparison of this thing with any other object, or even with the size or the objective position of our own body. These expressions, therefore, have only a reference to a certain hold of our phenomenal body on its surroundings. Thus depth cannot be understood as something which belongs to the thought of an acosmic subject; it is a possibility of a subject engaged in the world.[41]

Just as height and breadth cannot be immediately defined from the side of observed objects but are full of meaning with respect to a spatial level in regard to which things are situated, so also depth and size are only proper to things in view of the fact that these things are situated with respect to a level of distances and sizes that defines "far-off," "nearby," "big" and "small" before any measuring rod.[42]

Here we originally set depth over against height and breadth, because the latter appeared at first sight to be relations between things, while the former immediately revealed the tie of the subject with space. In the foregoing it was apparent, however, that in the final analysis height and breadth, too, are defined as the best hold of our body on the world. Height and breadth as relations between things are, therefore, really derivative and secondary phenomena: height, breadth, and depth are by nature all three "existential" relations.[43]

41. *PP*, pp. 265–67.
42. *PP*, p. 267.
43. *Ibid.*

Movement

One could say that perhaps movement consists in a change of position, although it is not possible to define it in that way. Objective thought described this position in terms of relations in objective space. The description of motion given above is then understood in an analogous way in terms of intramundane relations, in which view the experience of the world is simply taken for granted. From what has been said it is clear, however, that the origin of the positing of space is to be sought in a preobjective situation of the subject who fixes himself to his environment. It must now be possible to discover beneath the objective idea of movement a preobjective experience in which motion for him who perceives it will appear as a change of the subject's hold on the world. If we think of movement and wish to give a philosophical description of it, we immediately put ourselves in an epistemological position. We then ask: what, strictly speaking, is given to us in movement? One then wants to avoid the "appearance" in order to discover "the truth" concerning movement; one wants to say what movement is "in itself." One often does not notice that in this way he already reduces the phenomenon of movement and that, together with the idea of truth in itself, there creep in already certain prejudices and presuppositions which will hide the genesis of movement for us.[44]

If you throw a stone from your window into the garden and want to think "clearly" about this phenomenon, you have to analyze the data. Then you will say that the stone itself is not changed. Movement is no more than an accidental attribute of the moving thing. The resulting change can only be in the relation between the stone and its environment. Once this difference between the moving thing and the movement itself is made clear, it follows that a movement without a moving thing is impossible, that it is impossible, also, for a movement to exist without an objective reference point, and, thus, that there can be no absolute movement.

Nevertheless, this idea is in fact a negation of movement itself; if we are too rigorous in affirming the difference between movement and the moving thing, we actually say that the mov-

44. PP, pp. 267–68.

ing thing does not move at all. The moving stone must be different from the stone at rest; without that, no movement is possible and all the difficulties of Zeno immediately return in such a way that escape is impossible. We must conclude, therefore, that during the movement the moving thing does not remain completely identical to itself, and that movement is not a pure *denominatio ab extrinseco* in regard to the moving thing; movement does not merely consist in the change of objective spatial relations between the moving thing and its environment.[45]

Psychology, in opposition to the explanation given by objective thought, posits that in a psychological description the identity of the moving thing does not manifest itself. But such a conception is also untenable, since a movement without a moving thing that circumscribes it from beginning to end and constitutes the movement's unity, is nothing.[46]

We are consequently compelled to conclude that both the logician and the psychologist are wrong in their conceptions of movement. We can perhaps say, also, that both are right, since both see the case correctly but put the accent too one-sidedly and too heavily on one of the essential aspects involved. If we want to account for the phenomenon of movement adequately, we shall at least have to endorse the two following theses: (1) in every movement there must be present a certain *mobile,* or perhaps even better, a certain *movens* that can explain the unity of movement; (2) this one *movens* is, however, not absolutely identical under all phases of movement, but it is that which remains identical to itself *in* these phases. It is not necessary that the moving thing be already accurately defined by a certain group of qualities; it is sufficient that there is something that moves. The mistake made by the intellectualistic logician is, therefore, that he wants to posit in the phenomena that which he would like to see in them, while he really ought to let the phenomena themselves speak. The psychologist does do so, but he forgets that the phenomena can be the appearances of a movement only if they are appearances of one and the same *movens,* of the same appearing thing, of one single something which makes itself known through these appearances.[47]

45. *PP,* pp. 268–70.
46. *PP,* pp. 270–72.
47. *PP,* pp. 272–74.

If one, therefore, wants to come to a correct solution of the problem, one must maintain that movement is there before there is an *objective* world, that there are phenomena before the being itself which one gets to know in the phenomena is known in its different aspects, and that these phenomena already have their meaning before they are thematized. This phenomenal sphere is not antilogical, but it remains continuously prelogical.[48] Only the thematization of movement refers to a mobile which in itself remains perfectly identical, and therefore to the relativity of movement. If one takes the phenomenon of movement seriously as it manifests itself, then one takes the world that appears in it not only as a world of things but also as a world of pure transitions. That which is "in transit" and which we have recognized as being necessary for the constitution of every movement is to be defined in terms of the typical way of "passing." [49] A thing is determined in the first instance as this thing not by reason of its static properties but by its behavior. Accordingly, the preobjective being "in transit," this not yet thematized *movens*, posits no other problem than that of implied space and time, about which we have already spoken. For we have said that the "parts" of space must not be thought of as juxtaposed according to height and breadth but coexist because they are all drawn into the one and only hold of our body on the world. And, as we have pointed out, this relation is temporal even before it is spatial. Things coexist in space because they are present to the same perceiving subject and because they are enclosed by one and the same wave of time. But the unity and individuality of each time wave are possible only if each is enclosed by the preceding and following waves, and if the same pulsation of time which caused *it* to well up keeps back the preceding in retention in order to anticipate the next one in protention. It is only an objectified time which consists of successive movements; the lived present on the contrary encloses in its density a past and a future. The phenomenon of movement manifests this spatial and temporal implication in the most tangible way. We know of movement and a moving thing without any explicit awareness of the different objective positions which the moving thing will have to take. Movement is a modulation in an already familiar environment.

48. *PP*, p. 275.
49. *Ibid.*

But in this we are again faced with our central problem, namely, how this setting which forms the background for every conscious act, constitutes itself for us.[50]

In objective reflection it has always been accepted that no absolute movements are possible and, therefore, that all movement is relative.[51] Now that we have localized movement once more *in* the moving thing itself, we must face this problem again. Strictly speaking, a real relativity, as it should be if movement were merely a change in the spatial relationships, is inadmissible. I cannot force myself to *see* the stone as at rest and the garden and myself as in motion. I *see* that the stone moves; the garden and I myself are at rest. The movement, therefore, is *in* the stone.

Furthermore, every moving thing has its own background, its field in which it moves. We have come to the conclusion already that in each movement there must be a moving thing; we see now that each movement has to have its own background. One could say that the edges of the visual field are the fixed reference points with respect to which the movement in the field takes place. The edges of the field, however, are not formed by one or several lines or points: our field of vision is not a definite piece which is cut out of the objective world. We see as far as the hold of our gaze extends, far beyond the zone of clear vision, and even behind us. When one reaches the limits of the field of vision, one does not suddenly pass from seeing to not seeing. Besides, that which we really see is always up to a certain point not seen. Therefore, the limits of the field of vision are only a necessary element of our organization of the world; they are not objective contours.

But it is nevertheless true that an object that moves crosses our field of vision and changes its place in it and that movement outside this relationship to the field can have no meaning at all.

50. *PP*, pp. 98–101, 275–76; de Waelhens, *Une Philosophie de l'ambiguïté*, pp. 120–22.

51. Merleau-Ponty obviously deals here not with the theory of relativity, but merely with the philosophical problems connected with the relativity of movement, problems that have been discussed very often by philosophers since Descartes. See, for example, H. Bergson, *Matière et mémoire* (Paris: Presses Universitaires de France, 1946), pp. 215–20; N. Hartmann, *Philosophie der Natur: Abriss der speziellen Kategorienlehre* (Berlin: de Gruyter, 1950), pp. 231–34.

According as we give to a certain portion of the field the value of figure or background, it manifests itself to us as in motion or in rest. With this statement we make movement not a relative something but only a structural phenomenon. For the very special relation which constitutes the movement is not a relation between *things*. What makes part of our field count as an object in motion and stamps the remainder as stationary background is merely the manner in which we define our relations with them by our gaze. Thus the relation of the visible and moving thing to its background passes through our body.[52] If the hold of my body has once anchored itself to a certain thing, differentiation is immediately made between the moving thing and the stationary background, and only then is the moving thing defined as moving. It seems to us that only this is meant when one speaks of the relativity of movement.

But how is the separation between the stationary background and the moving thing precisely constituted? Certainly not by explicit perception, because the reference points to which we anchor our gaze are not objects. These reference points continually have the peculiarity that they are always *already* there. They do not present themselves directly to our perception. They are therefore the result of a preconscious process the results of which continually appear to us as *already* there. In cases in which we can freely choose our anchorage, such as in a moving train, our perception is cut off from its context, from its past. Then we do not perceive with our whole being; we play a game with our body. If, however, the life of our body is integrated in the demands of our concrete being, then this choice is not given to us. The relativity of movement consists in the possibility which we have, to change our ground within the world. Once engaged in a certain setting, we see movements appear before us as something absolute.[53]

Lived Space

Until now we have spoken only of the *perception* of space, thus of the knowledge which a "disinterested subject" might have of spatial relations between objects and their geometric

52. *PP*, pp. 101–2, 278.
53. *PP*, pp. 276–80.

qualities. And yet, even in our analysis of these abstract functions which do not in the least exhaust our spatial experience, we have been led to admit as a necessary condition of spatiality the establishment of the subject in a setting and his close attachment to a world. In other words, it has become clear by now that spatial perception is a structural phenomenon which can be thought of only in connection with a field of vision which motivates our perception of space by suggesting to the subject a possible reference point. The classical problem of space perception must be reintegrated in a more comprehensive problem. In asking oneself the question of how, in an explicit intentional act, spatial relations and spatial objects with their spatial "qualities" are actually determined, one admits that he has not yet consciously taken cognizance of our experience of the world. This question, in other words, is a secondary one because it is a question about activities which appear only in the background of a world already familiar to us. In the natural attitude I have no isolated perceptions; there I do not posit this object as beside that one along with their objective relations; there is a stream of experiences there which (implying each other) elucidate each other both in their simultaneity and in their succession. Only those perceptions to which we ourselves give meaning by the attitude we take up, or which answer the questions we have put ourselves, appear to us as individual activities. They cannot help us in our analysis of the field of perception, because they all presuppose this field. A first perception independent of a background which is already constituted is inconceivable, as we have shown. Every real perception presupposes a certain past of the subject in which somewhere a secret activity must be found by which, for the first time, we have worked out our original environment.[54]

More suitable for our investigations are the space experiences of abnormal subjects, such as the space experiences of schizophrenics, of people who have used certain narcotics, and the space experiences of our dreams. The mythological space experiences of "primitive" people are also of the greatest importance here.[55] In these cases it appears that, if one has once connected space experience with our implantation in the world, there is always a primary spatiality for every modality which this

54. *PP*, pp. 280–81.
55. *PP*, pp. 281–87.

implantation can assume.[56] In none of these cases do we experience a physical or geometrical space, but it continually appears that an existential, lived space precedes that objective space; this lived space is defined in each case by the typical grasp of man's body on the world.

After analyzing and discussing several of these examples, Merleau-Ponty wonders what, strictly speaking, could be the philosophical value of these and other similar speculations about the, so-called, anthropological spaces. Are these anthropological spaces genuine spaces? Can they exist and be thought of "by themselves"? Do all these forms of space not presuppose after all, as a necessary condition of their possibility, the existence of an objective, geometrical space and a pure consciousness which constitutes it? Does mythical space not necessarily rest on the consciousness of one single objective space? Is space not obviously objective and unique? Is it not essential to space that it is the "absolute outside," correlative to, but at the same time the negation of, subjectivity? Does this space not necessarily embrace everything which one can imagine? Strictly speaking, is it not nonsense to want to found geometrical space on the primary spatiality of human existence, since, after all, reflection knows only itself and things, with the result that a spatiality of the subject is inconceivable? After these questions of objective thought Merleau-Ponty begins by admitting that these considerations about anthropological space in point of fact contain *no thematic or explicit* meaning. Objective thought can therefore get no hold of them. These considerations, however, do have a nonthematic, implicit meaning and one which is not of less significance, because objective thought must precisely draw on the nonreflective; for objective thought is really no more than the elucidation of the life of our nonreflective consciousness. Objective thought denies the value of dream phenomena, of myth, and, generally speaking, of our existence, because it cannot thematize them. In this way it rejects the facts and really itself in the name of the possible and the evident, forgetting that the self-evident must be founded on facts and that the signification of each objectifying reflection goes back to an original perception. That is why it rejects the anthropological spaces as being confused appearances of the true, unique, and objective

56. PP, p. 283.

geometrical space. In fact, however, this relationship is different: geometrical space is founded on our original human spaces.[57]

But do we in this way not return to the errors of psychologism? We can rightfully pose the question if in this view every type of subjectivity, and even every form of consciousness, is not enclosed in its own private life, since it may be asserted that there are as many spaces as there are distinct experiences of space and that the space experiences of the child, the madman, and the primitive cannot be converted to those of a normal, "civilized" adult. Have we here not substituted a purely psychological cogito which remains within the domain of its own incommunicable life for a rationalist cogito which encloses in its individual ego a *universal* constituting consciousness? Does phenomenology in this way not terminate in the negation of all being and all meaning? Are we thus not confusing here phenomena with *mere* appearances?

According to Merleau-Ponty, it is certain that mythical consciousness, consciousness of our dream world, consciousness of the mental patient, and the perception of a normal man, notwithstanding all the differences, are not enclosed in themselves as "islands of experience" cut off from each other; this does not mean, however, that every experience must be regulated by an absolute consciousness. In phenomenology the most important reason why one refuses to see an absolute geometrical space in the various anthropological spaces and why one (generally speaking) refuses to relegate every experience to an absolute consciousness of these experiences is especially this, that a unity of perception so conceived makes impossible the diversity which we actually find in the world.

Mythical consciousness is open to a horizon of possible objectifications. In this, one must see not, as Comte did, an explanation of the world and an anticipation of science, but merely a project of someone's existence and an expression of the human condition in regard to the world. Matters are not different in a dream. This link between subjectivity and objectivity which already exists in mythical and in childlike consciousness and which always is present in dreams and even in madness is a fortiori to be found in every normal experience. I never live

57. *PP*, pp. 287–91.

completely in anthropological spaces; I am always attached by my very roots to a natural world.[58] Anthropological spaces, therefore, continually present themselves to us as being constituted on a *natural space*. But this statement requires a very precise explanation.[59]

In trying to explain his view Merleau-Ponty emphasizes the anthropological character of space and demonstrates that different forms of space experience are given. There is a mythical, primitive space, a proper spatiality of hallucination, a space of our dreams, etc. If space is really co-constituted by our intentionality (and this is essential for every meaning), then it will have to vary with our intentions. He admits, therefore, the existential value of these different space experiences but gives the philosopher-phenomenologist the task of elucidating them.

In this elucidation he absolutely refuses to admit an objective, geometrical space within these anthropological spaces which could unmask these forms of space from the very start as subjective, as *mere* human appearances. Although he accepts the value of the anthropological spaces and defends the thesis that man actually is able to exist in them, he wishes on the other hand to rediscover a natural space in perception itself. Thus he refuses on the one hand to accept an objective, geometrical space which from the very beginning could lay bare the *merely* human character of the anthropological spaces, but on the other hand he admits that one must accept a natural space after all and that only on this basis can the human spaces be genuinely understood as human spaces. That is why he writes that man never *completely* lives in anthropological spaces but always remains rooted in a natural, nonhuman space.[60]

Then he continues that he has sometimes said that space is existential but that one could say as well that our existence is spatial, since it opens itself on to an "outside" by means of an inner necessity. In the original contact between this *necessary* spatial existence and the world there is a moment that escapes our freedom and arbitrariness; it is exactly this moment which makes philosophical reflection of space possible, and only on this

58. *PP*, p. 293.
59. *PP*, pp. 291–93.
60. *PP*, p. 293.

basis is there any sense in making a distinction between a "myth-ical meaning" and a "meaning for the philosopher." [61] There is, therefore, a natural and original space, but this is certainly not the geometrical space, since the former is not clearly and explic-itly known. If one wishes to know something more of it, one must try to understand how our existence in one simple move-ment projects worlds around itself which hide objectivity for me; but we must also show the same objectivity as a goal for the teleology of my consciousness which places these worlds against a background of a unique natural world. [62]

In the constitution of this natural world my body plays an important part. For it is my body which places me in a human world by projecting me first into a natural world which can always be discerned as underlying other forms of world, just as the canvas underlies the picture. [63] There is, therefore, already a substrate of meaning in me which is not subject to my freedom. This stratum of meaning in the world is not a pure in-itself. It too must come into being by a dialectical relation between the intending subject and the world, but this intending subject is not yet a free subject. It is merely a body-subject, an impersonal, or even better, a prepersonal subject. It is only due to this body-sub-ject, to this prepersonal totality of intentions, that there is a natural world, a natural thing, a natural space, that there is an absolute stratum of meaning to which each act which gives meaning must point. [64]

We have seen already that one could characterize man by saying that he is an intentionality directed toward the world. It appears here again, that a double stratum is to be distinguished in this intentionality: (1) on the one hand we find here the stratum of intentionality which belongs to an anonymous sub-jectivity whose necessary intentions constitute a necessary stra-tum of meaning so that no freedom is found here yet; (2) on the other hand, we find a stratum of intentions which breathe the spirit of free personal life. Here we can speak of an ego in the literal sense of the term; here we are in the domain of free-dom and creativity; the intentions which we find in this sphere

61. *PP*, pp. 293–94.
62. *PP*, p. 294.
63. *PP*, p. 293.
64. *PP*, pp. 253–54, 325–26.

constitute a stratum of meaning which is really subordinate to our freedom and creativity.[65]

SUMMARY AND CONCLUSION

IN THESE REFLECTIONS ON SPACE Merleau-Ponty constantly reacts against the conceptions of intellectualism and empiricism, or (as he sometimes says) the conceptions of intellectualism and realism.[66] In his opinion the original and primordial space which the philosopher has to bring to light cannot be identified with the "physical space" of empiricism, nor with the space as form about which Kant speaks, nor with a realistically conceived "objective" space of the sciences which one could perhaps call a homogeneous, isotropic, and geometrical space.[67] Nevertheless it is clear that this remark does not imply a definitive rejection of these conceptions of space.[68] He seems to adopt the point of view that *for the time being* it is absolutely irrelevant what the intrinsic value of these conceptions about space may be; all that matters to him is that one learns to understand that these conceptions of space do not describe space in the way in which it originally announces itself to us in our *primordial* experiences, because these conceptions are in his view obviously based on certain presuppositions about man, the world, the things, and their mutual relations. Classical philosophy, be it rationalist or empiricist, immediately adopts an epistemological point of view; it asks what actually and really is; from the very start it wants to avoid "mere appearances" in order to find the "genuine truth." One does not seem to notice, Merleau-Ponty says, that in this way he approaches the phenomena in the wrong way, because one reduces the original phenomena and introduces presuppositions which eventually will hide for us the genesis of space.[69] In this manner one posits in the phenomena what one would like to find in them, whereas actually the phe-

65. PP, pp. 439–40.
66. When Merleau-Ponty speaks of "realism," he always has a special kind of realism in mind which certainly is of the empiricist variety.
67. PP, pp. 243–44.
68. SB, pp. 215–20. Cf. H VI, pp. 179–82, 192–93, 227, 356, 375–78.
69. PP, pp. 267–68.

nomena themselves should speak.[70] One furthermore adopts the
point of view that being-object for a thing primordially means to
be an object for a reflecting, thinking subject instead of being
object for a perceptual gaze.[71] In the final analysis, however,
these basically unacceptable views go back to wrong conceptions
about man, world, and consciousness. Once one has learned to
understand that man is a "transcendental Being-in-the-world," [72]
that his consciousness must be described as a "being directed to
things by means of a body," [73] then one will understand also that
our consciousness cannot be characterized first and foremost as
an "I think," but must be described far more as an "I can," [74] in
other words that consciousness above all is a mode of being
engaged in the world.[75] From this it becomes clear *why* for a
thing to-be-object cannot be identified with to-be-for-a-thinking-
subject, *why* for a thing being-object must consist first and
foremost in being-for-a-gaze which constitutes the meaning of
this being on the basis of the world immediately given to this
gaze.[76] It finally becomes clear, then, *why* it does not make sense
to try to found a philosophical conception on an "objectively"
pregiven world of "objective" things mutually connected by
"objective" relations.[77]

As far as space is concerned, Merleau-Ponty wants first to
describe space as it manifests itself to us originally in perception, and his major concern here is to keep his description free
from all prejudices and every unjustified presupposition.[78] What
one is to think of the space conceptions of objective thought is a
question which is to be considered later, because the answer to
this question depends in any case on the results of our phenomenological description of our space perceptions.

What space as it manifests itself immediately in our original
space experiences actually is, is difficult to say because the
originally given data are hidden under layers of meaning which
have their origin not in perception itself, but in our theoretical

70. *PP*, pp. 273–74.
71. *PP*, pp. 251–52.
72. de Waelhens, *Une Philosophie de l'ambiguïté*, p. 1.
73. *PP*, pp. 138–39.
74. *PP*, pp. 136–42.
75. de Waelhens, *Une Philosophie de l'ambiguïté*, p. 139.
76. *PP*, pp. 251–52.
77. *PP*, pp. 52–63.
78. *PP*, pp. 251–52, 256–58, 267.

and especially scientific elaboration of what is immediately given. Few philosophers and scientists will deny the thesis that all knowledge takes its starting point in perceptual experience. But the perceptions from which most philosophers and scientists take their point of departure are not pure and original perceptions but experiences blurred by spontaneous, scientific, and philosophical presuppositions or even prejudices. Even the perceptions of a man in the street are already distorted by a projection of layers of meaning which do not belong to the actual perceived phenomenon but have their origin in theoretical reflection which, whatever its nature may be, is always objectifying. This is the reason why in Merleau-Ponty's view neither the perceptions of the philosopher and the scientist, nor the perceptions of the man in the street offer a safe starting point for a phenomenological description of space, because, as we have said, none of these perceptions appears to be genuinely original. To come to original space one will have to remove all the layers of meaning which common sense, science, and philosophy have added to the originally given data, and this must be done by means of a special reduction which leads us back from the objective world of objectifying thought to the original lifeworld. Such a reduction shows us that somewhere underneath objective thought a preobjective experience can be found [79] which takes us to a "natural" space and a lived world.[80]

On the level to which such a reduction leads us, we know nothing of an objective world as objectifying thought describes it, nothing of objective space either. There we just wish to describe carefully the phenomena as they manifest themselves immediately in perception. We wish to bring to the fore there the primordial experiences from which world and space arise.[81] Merleau-Ponty believes that such a primordial experience can best be approached from a detailed description of abnormal cases, because there prejudices can best be recognized and thus more easily eliminated.[82] Such a description will make it clear that there are original phenomena which are anterior to every form of objective being, phenomena which have meaning even before they are thematized. Such a realm of phenomena is obviously

79. *PP*, pp. 267–68.
80. *PP*, pp. 293–94.
81. *PP*, pp. 254–56.
82. *PP*, pp. 244–45.

prelogical, and that is the main reason why objective thought has never been able to get a hold on them. The prelogical, nonthematic, implicit meaning of original phenomena is of greater importance than the meaning which objective thought tries to bring to light because "objective thought itself draws on the nonreflective and presents itself as an explicit expression of nonreflective consciousness, so that radical reflection cannot consist in thematizing as parallel entities the world, or space, and a nontemporal subject which thinks of them, but must go further back and seize this thematizing act itself with the horizons of implication which give it its meaning." [83]

If we now further limit ourselves to this realm of original phenomena and ask ourselves what we can learn here about space, then, according to Merleau-Ponty, we can still direct our attention in two different directions so that our phenomenological description of "original" space must contain two different parts. Let us once more see how Merleau-Ponty introduces these two parts. After speaking about the problem of orientation, the problem of depth, and the questions connected with our perception of movement, he goes on as follows. Until now we have spoken merely of the *perception* of space, that is to say, of the knowledge which a disinterested observer might have of spatial relations between objects and their geometric qualities. And yet, even in our analysis of these *abstract* functions we have been led to admit as a necessary condition of spatiality the inherence of the subject to the world; in other words, even there we had already to come to the conclusion that space perception is a structural phenomenon. This classical problem of space perception must now be reintegrated into *a more comprehensive* problem. The reason for this is, Merleau-Ponty says, that the descriptions of the first three sections (orientation, depth, movement) were limited to a description of *individual* intentional acts in which spatial relations and spatial objects become "constituted" for a *disinterested* subject and, thus, had to leave out of consideration the question of how the field or *world* to which these acts necessarily refer, and which they equally necessarily presuppose as a condition of their possibility, establishes itself and how this world is originally related to an obviously interested subject in and through a whole stream of experiences. This more compre-

83. *PP*, p. 289.

hensive problem is the subject matter of the last section devoted to "lived space." [84]

After describing different forms of lived space Merleau-Ponty asks himself what the precise philosophical meaning of these and similar descriptions of anthropological spaces could be. Do not all these forms of space necessarily presuppose the existence of an objective space? How could one ever found objective space on the primary spatiality of human existence as this manifests itself in these various anthropological spaces? Merleau-Ponty answers these questions by claiming that the various anthropological spaces do not presuppose an *objective,* geometrical space but, indeed, refer to a more primordial space, which he then calls the *natural* space.

It seems to me that such a position is clear only if one can find an answer for the two following questions: (1) What is the precise relationship between the *natural* space referred to in the fourth section and the original spatial level which was mentioned in the first three sections? (2) What is the precise relationship between natural and objective space?

As far as the first question is concerned, the answer is simple in my opinion. The original spatial level to which a description of our perception of space *points* is the same as the natural space which, in all forms of lived space, is pre-understood. Both expressions, *original spatial level* and *natural space,* refer from a different point of view to that original spatiality which is constituted by the not yet conscious hold of our body (taken as a system of anonymous functions) on the world. That is why original or natural space is not a thing, nor the totality of things, nor a quality or property of things, why it is not the result of a synthesizing act of consciousness, why it cannot be perceived, and finally why one cannot even see it emerge from the original "acts" in and through which it became conscious. For natural space it is essential that it always is already constituted in anonymous functions of our body-subject.

As far as the second question is concerned Merleau-Ponty is of the opinion that objective, geometrical space appears before us only when we thematize perceptual or lived space, without questioning its origin.[85] Objective, geometrical space cannot be divorced from orientated or lived space, because it is merely an

84. PP, pp. 280–81.
85. PP, pp. 383–88.

explicitation of them from a certain point of view. The question now is how we can comprehend space as pure exteriority by thematizing our perceptual and lived spaces, for a phenomenological description of this original spatiality reveals it as essentially an implication space. Merleau-Ponty sees the solution for this question in the fact that perceptual or lived space contains the figure background structure which is essential to every concrete hold of my body on the world. One can conceive of this figure background structure as a skeleton or general scheme which can be isolated and idealized. Abstraction and idealization of this basic structure gives us the homogeneous, isotropic sum total of all possible "points" in which lies the very essence of geometrical space.[86]

According to Conrad-Martius the space problem is one of the most difficult problems that exists.[87] As yet there is no satisfactory answer to this problem that few philosophers have left untouched. Heidegger holds that the still existing embarrassment with regard to the very Being of space is not so much rooted in the inadequacy of our knowledge of space itself as in the lack of a fundamental transparency of the possibilities of Being itself and their ontological interpretation. A solution for the ontological problem of space, according to him, presupposes that the question of Being be liberated from the narrowness of the incidentally available and mostly rough conceptions of Being. Heidegger furthermore believes that the problematic concerning the Being of space, in regard to this phenomenon itself as such and in regard to various phenomenal spaces, must be turned in such a direction as to clarify the basic possibilities of Being in general.[88]

It seems to me that we must see in Merleau-Ponty's considerations concerning space the most valuable contribution to a solution of this age-old and undeniably difficult problem, and this not only because of his penetrating phenomenological descriptions but also because of the ontological interpretation of them.

86. *PP*, pp. 101–3, 383–88. Cf. de Waelhens, *Une Philosophie de l'ambiguïté*, pp. 122–23, 277–81.
87. H. Conrad-Martius, "Realontologie," *Jahrbuch für Philosophie und phänomenologische Forschung*, VI (1923), pp. 159–333, esp. p. 214.
88. Heidegger, *Being and Time*, pp. 147–48.

Gaston Bachelard

GASTON (LOUIS PIERRE) BACHELARD was born in Bar-sur-Aube on June 27, 1884. While he was a postal employee he studied mathematics and physics, earning his *licence* in 1913, then teaching science for some time thereafter. He received his Ph.D. at the Ecole Normale Supérieure in Paris in 1919. Following this he taught successively at the Collège of Bar-sur-Aube (physics and chemistry, from 1919 to 1930), the University of Dijon (philosophy, from 1930 to 1940), and finally at the Sorbonne (history and philosophy of science, from 1940 to 1954). After his retirement he lived in Paris and devoted the greater part of his time to his publications. For several years Bachelard was the Director of the Institute for the History of Science. He died in October, 1962.

To characterize Bachelard's philosophy is both easy and difficult. It is easy in that one can truly say that he tried to further develop the basic ideas of the general movement in philosophy of science in France known as "la critique de la science," that in his philosophy the influence of Boutroux, Bergson, and Brunschvicg can be found, and finally that he came to a view rather close to that defended by his friend Ferdinand Gonseth. However, these characterizations, although true, in no way specify the uniqueness of Bachelard's basic ideas. Perhaps his philosophy can best be characterized by the term "dialectic," but then it must be immediately added that his philosophy does not "have any relationship whatever to an aprioric dialectic" and that "above all it cannot be really mobilized around Hegelian dialectic." * According to Bachelard, both philosophy and science must be understood as processes, as movements which continuously "go on." The decisive element in both is the actual situation taken not as a final stage but as a phase in which the past is still present and the future is already predelineated. In the actual situation in which philosophy and science find themselves one discovers various views represented. Bachelard wants to transcend these views in the direction of a kind of "superrationalism made up of rational systems which are simply juxtaposed." For him dialectic "merely adds a margin of very exact surrational organization to an existent rational organization," which simply helps him "to veer from one system to another." In other words, Bachelard's dialectic is built not on the principle of contradiction but on the principle of complementarity.**

Bachelard is of the opinion that in philosophy of science one finds oneself mostly before an insoluble dilemma. The philosophers limit themselves to considering general principles whereas the scientists confine themselves to describing highly specialized results. Many philosophers involved in philosophy of science find themselves faced with the dilemma of an aprioric knowledge of the general and an aposterioric knowledge of the immediately given and do not pay enough attention to the most important trait of contemporary science, namely, the continuous interchange of rational and experimental results—between the a priori and the a posteriori, between rationalism and empiricism within the actual scientific praxis itself. What is genuinely characteristic of contemporary science is that it tries to understand the empiricism of the facts while applying the rationalism of the principles. This is why philosophy of science develops dialectically in the continuous interchange of these rational and empirical elements, without ever reaching an absolute and final point. Man's knowledge is in principle incomplete.

Gaston Bachelard did not limit himself to a "dialectic" philosophy of science. His philosophy develops in two different directions, in the direction of science and in the direction of art. At first sight these two "aspects" of his work seem to be completely different and often even to conflict with one another. Nonethe-

---

* Gaston Bachelard, *The Philosophy of No* (New York: Orion Press, 1968), p. 116.

** *Ibid.,* pp. 116–17.

less, they find their origin in a common center and, in their mutual dialectic relationship, need one another in that they must purify one another. Hyppolite has rightly pointed out that the very core of Bachelard's philosophy is to be found in the fact that he wants to elucidate man's creativity in science and in art, a creativity that finds itself time and again opposite an insurmountable obstacle (the contingent world) which it transcends but never completely leaves behind.

Explicit references to phenomenology are very rare in Bachelard's works and most of them are ambiguous. Bachelard's interest in phenomenology shows itself mainly in his later works. As far as this aspect of his philosophy is concerned, we find elements of Hegel's, as well as Husserl's, conceptions of phenomenology. Hegel's conception is more related to the content of Bachelard's thought, whereas Husserl's influence manifests itself particularly in the descriptive method he uses. One thing is certain, however—Gaston Bachelard did not believe in a "pure phenomenology," that is, in an original and exhaustive description of phenomena, but he tried as carefully as possible to describe two basic intentional phenomena, which presented themselves to him "in person," as it were, namely, the phenomenon of contemporary science and the phenomenon of modern art.

In order to preclude misunderstanding one more remark is in order. In the essay which follows Gaston Bachelard uses the term "phenomenology" several times. As is clear from the context, this term as he uses it here refers *not* to Husserl's phenomenological philosophy but to that conception of phenomenology found in the works of many modern physicists such as Mach, Boltzmann, Einstein, and many others, who explain fundamental concepts of physical theories merely descriptively on the basis of immediate *physical* experiences.

14 / Epistemology and History of the Sciences

Gaston Bachelard

The knowledge which is the most ancient from a historical point of view need not necessarily remain the basis for the comprehension of facts discovered later.

—Mach, *La Mécanique*

HISTORICAL RECURRENCES

SINCE OUR GOAL IN THIS WORK is mainly to study the efforts of rationalism to reorganize itself on the level of wholly new experiments of modern physics, we can center all our philosophical observations around the new mechanical theories. One will note quite soon that in this realm the specific problems become general problems. Nowadays the philosophically important issues reveal themselves in a second approximation just when the generalities of a first point of view have shown their insufficiency. Our syntheses require vivid attention to the details of reality, to the most subtle contradictions of experience. We therefore certainly remain within the realm of active rationalism when we follow science in its attempts at experimental precision and theoretical synthesis.

For example, wave mechanics appears to us as one of the most comprehensive scientific syntheses of all times. It truly is a

This essay from *L'Activité rationaliste de la physique contemporaine* by Gaston Bachelard (Paris: Presses Universitaires de France, 1951), pp. 21–49, has been translated into English expressly for this edition by Joseph J. Kockelmans.

historical synthesis. In fact, it is a cultural synthesis which implies the bringing together of several centuries of culture. As Louis de Broglie has pointed out: "Quite a number of contemporary scientific ideas would have been different from what they are now, had the roads which the human mind took to reach them, been different." [1] This one remark poses the whole problem concerning the objectivity of science, in that it places this objectivity at the junction of human history and man's attempt at the actuality which is essential to all scientific investigation.

Thus a question which the philosopher certainly must ask himself is: at what level of scientific thought is the history of thought integrated into our scientific activity? Is it exact to say that scientific activity which searches for objectivity can assume as a constant rule that it starts from a *tabula rasa?* In any case, to limit ourselves to wave mechanics, one can scarcely imagine a *direct* pedagogy, a pedagogy which is founded upon *immediate* experiences. All such pedagogy is necessarily an exercise in knowledge *transformation.* Here the mind can educate itself only by transforming itself. In order to understand the meaning of wave mechanics, in order to pose the problem in its complete fullness and to appreciate the vital issues of the rational reorganization of experience implied in this new doctrine, it is advisable to go through a long historical preamble.

But here a paradox emerges: it would be a grave mistake to believe that this historical synthesis was historically prepared, and to say, according to the customary expression of historians who want to "embody" history, that this discovery "was in the air." In fact, Fresnel's physical optics had completely replaced Newton's physical optics when Louis de Broglie proposed a new science which associates certain hypotheses of Newton with hypotheses of Fresnel, in order to study the behavior of particles which did not belong to the science of either Fresnel or Newton. Nothing could show better that scientific synthesis is a *transforming synthesis.* Even before this association, before this synthesis, Einstein had without a doubt seen the necessity of defining a quantum of radiation (which soon was called "a photon") in order to explain photoelectric phenomena. . . . But the synthesis of corpuscular and undulatory hypotheses was not yet

1. *Physique et microphysique*, p. 9.

envisaged in its generality. No historical reason propelled science in the direction of such a synthesis. Only a kind of aspiration toward the aesthetics of hypotheses could open the double perspective of ideas which characterizes the mechanics founded by Louis de Broglie. It is the fact of applying undulatory themes not only to light but also to matter which has shifted the problem and expanded the discussion.

This broadening of perspective is such that one cannot rightly appreciate it without a softening of the traditional philosophies. When one studies the numerous synthetic processes which are brought into play in the mathematical development of wave mechanics and the way experimental phenomena which at first sight are quite different are interconnected here, one becomes progressively convinced of the insufficiency of the viewpoints of classical philosophy. Such methods and such vast syntheses cannot be examined philosophically without a polyphilosophy which provides the framework for a classification of the realist, formal, rationalist, and even aesthetic values of the new science.

If, therefore, one wishes to determine the epistemological functions of the scientific revolutions of our era, one must accept an outspoken *modernism;* one must educate oneself in the inspiration underlying a new scientific spirit by making a fresh start even in the case of the experiments of classical physics. For example, from the moment one understands that there is a diffraction of electrons just as there is a diffraction of light, one must realize that the theme of light diffraction is to be revised. In fact, the purely undulatory science of photons, that is, the new-style wave mechanics of photons, has discovered paradoxically that it is behind in regard to the wave mechanics of electrons. The recent investigations of Louis de Broglie concerning the theory of light have precisely the tendency to erase this historical paradox. Thus the theory of light which was undulatory in the old style and which has become corpuscular in the photon style must make a special effort to become undulatory in the new style.

One sees therefore that contemporary science is of the order of a "re-thought" thought and of a re-framed experience. Mach himself said, agreeing here with Volkelt: "I also readily agree that the concepts, barely determined at the beginning, must first

undergo a 'retroactive consolidation' by means of a circular return of knowledge." [2]

But the *difficulties* of the new sciences point in themselves to
the psychological novelty of these sciences. The philosophy of
these sciences will change as soon as one admits this concept of
psychological difficulty as a concept of positive epistemological
determination. In summary, the contemporary mechanics (relativistic mechanics, quantum mechanics, wave mechanics) are
all sciences without ancestors. Our grandnephews will, without
a doubt, have no interest in the science of our great-grandfa-
thers. They will conceive of it as merely a museum of thoughts
which have become inactive, or at least of thoughts which no
longer have value except as a pretext for educational reform. If
we may put it this way, the atomic bomb has already pulverized
a large sector of the history of science; for in the spirit of nuclear
physics there is no longer a trace of the fundamental notions of
traditional atomism. One must conceive of the nucleus of the
atom in terms of a dynamics of nuclear energy, and no longer in
terms of a geometry which merely deals with the arrangement of
its constituents. Such a science does not have a counterpart in
the past. It provides a particularly clear example of the historical
break in the evolution of modern science.

And nevertheless, notwithstanding its revolutionary character, notwithstanding its character as a break with the regular
historical evolution, a doctrine such as wave mechanics is a
historical synthesis, because history (stopped twice in some of
its well-established ideas, namely, those of Newton and Fresnel)
makes a fresh start and leads to a new aesthetics of scientific
thought.

Thus, the new viewpoint defines a new perspective in regard
to the history of science, a perspective which poses the problem
of the *actual* efficacy of this history in our scientific culture. In
fact, it is a question of showing the work of a history which is
already "judged," a history which must take care to distinguish
between error and truth, the inert and the active, the destructive
and the fruitful. In general, is it not true that a history which is
understood is no longer a *pure* history? In the history of science
one must necessarily understand, but one must also judge. Here
more than anywhere else Nietzsche's opinion is correct: "The

2. Ernst Mach, *La Mécanique,* trans. Emile Bertrand (Paris:
Hermann, 1904).

past is to be interpreted only through the greatest force of the present." [3] The history of empires and peoples rightly has as its ideal the objective story of the facts; it demands of the historian *not to judge*. And if the historian imposes the values of his times on the determination of the values of bygone times, one will accuse him rightly of following the "myth of progress."

But here there is an evident difference: for scientific thought, a progress is demonstrated, can be demonstrated, and its demonstration is even a pedagogical element necessary for the development of our scientific culture. In other words, progress is the very dynamism of scientific culture, and it is this dynamism which the history of science must describe. It must describe it by judging, evaluating, and removing all possibility of returning to erroneous notions. History of science may stress the mistakes of the past only in order to push them aside. In this way one encounters the dialectic of *epistemological obstacles* and *epistemological acts*. We have made a long study of the concept of "epistemological obstacle" in an earlier work.[4] The notion of "epistemological act" which we now oppose to the notion of "epistemological obstacle" corresponds to the jolts of the scientific genius who introduces unexpected stimuli into the course of scientific development. Thus, there is a *negative* and a *positive* element in the history of scientific thought. And here these positive and negative elements are so clearly distinguished that the scientist who sides with the *negative* element puts himself outside the scientific community. Anyone who limits himself to living within the coherence of Ptolemy's system is no more than a historian. And from the viewpoint of modern science that which is negative belongs to a psychoanalysis of knowledge; it must be checked if it tends to reappear. On the contrary, whatever remains *positive* from the past will become operative again in modern thought. This positive heritage of the past constitutes a kind of *actual past* whose working is manifest in the scientific thought of the present.

One must therefore understand the importance of the historical dialectic which is *characteristic of scientific thought*. In

3. Friedrich Nietzsche, *Considérations inactuelles: De l'utilité et des inconvénients des études historiques*, trans. Henry Albert (Paris: Mercure de France, 1907).

4. *La Formation de l'esprit scientifique: Contribution à une psychanalyse de la connaissance objective* (Paris: Vrin, 1947).

summary, one must constantly form and reform the dialectic between past history and the history sanctioned by the presently active science. The history of the theory of phlogiston is outdated because it rests on a fundamental error, on a contradiction of a chemistry which concerns itself with weights. A *rationalist* cannot be interested in it without entertaining a certain bad conscience. An *epistemologist* cannot be interested in it except insofar as he finds in it motives for a psychoanalysis of objective knowledge. A *historian of science* who takes pleasure in that theory must know that he is working in the paleontology of a scientific spirit which has disappeared from the scene. He cannot hope to have influence on the pedagogy of the sciences of our times.

Contrary to the phlogiston hypothesis, works like those of Black on *heat* (even if they contain parts which must be done over again) crop out in positive experiments determining the *specific heat* of substances. It is safe to say that the notion of *specific heat* is a notion which *forever* is a scientific notion. The works of Black can therefore be described as elements of a *sanctioned history*. There is a constant interest in knowing them theoretically, elucidating them epistemologically, and following their incorporation in a whole of rationalist concepts. Historical philosophy, epistemological philosophy, and rationalist philosophy can find a motive here for a spectral analysis in which the nuances of a polyphilosophy branch out.

One will perhaps smile over the dogmatism of a rationalist philosophy which inscribes a "forever" upon a truth held by a certain school. But there are concepts which are so indispensable to a scientific culture that one cannot conceive of the possibility of being led to abandon them. They cease to be contingent, occasional, and conventional. To be sure, they are formed in a historical atmosphere which is obscure. But they have become so precise, so clearly functional, that we need not fear the possibility of an *educated doubt* in their regard. At most they are exposed to that general skepticism which affects all science, to that skepticism which is always ready to speak ironically about the *abstract* character of our scientific notions. But this easy irony cannot encroach upon the rationalist oath which attaches a culture to indestructible concepts, an oath which affirms "forever" an exact epistemological value. Reason has themes to which it is faithful. It recognizes quite well the notions which

imply a future for thought, notions which are signs which guarantee that a culture has a future. The philosophy of the continuity of notions whose value is established is therefore certainly
faced with a problem of historical relationships, relationships
through which the rational progressively dominates the contingent.

One sees then, the educative necessity of developing a *recurrent history,* a history which can be clarified by means of the
finality of the present, a history which starts from the certainties
of the present and then discovers in the past the progressive
formations of the truth. Thus scientific thought confirms itself
in the story of its own progress. This recurrent history appears in
the works of actual science in the form of historical preambles.
But it is too often cut short. It forgets about too many intermediary phases. It does not sufficiently prepare the pedagogical formation of the various differential thresholds of our culture.

Of course, this recurrent history, this judged history, this
evaluated history neither can nor will put our prescientific men-
tality on a sound footing. Rather, it is destined to help us become
aware of the force of certain barriers which scientific thought in
the past has formed against irrationalism. It is in this sense that
Jean-Baptiste Biot wrote in 1803 in an *Essay on the History of
Science During the French Revolution:* "The encyclopedia was a
barrier which forever hindered the human mind from going
backward." One finds here a kind of "Declaration of Rights" of
the rationalist man which one will be able to illustrate the
moment he considers the history of the sciences as a realization
of the progress of their rationality. The history of science will
then appear as the most irreversible of all histories. By discovering what is true the man of science bars the irrational. Irrationalism can, without a doubt, arise from other sources. But from
then on there are roads which are blocked. The history of science
is the history of the failure of irrationalism.

But the struggle is never over, and it seems necessary for
each generation of men of science to reaffirm the stand of
rationalism and assess time and again the balance of the history
of science. Sometimes the dialectic enters into the abandoned
history; and the history which forms an integral part of science
is very delicate. It is therefore, philosophically seen, very instructive. For example, one can say that the excellent book of F. K.

Richtmyer changes its historical perspective at the point where, after retracing a short history of science, he declares that the works of Maxwell are to be studied "as an integral part of the fascinating story of modern physics rather than as a part of the history of physics." [5]

The doublet, *story* and *history,* is presented here in a particularly vigorous opposition. What "fascinates" the scientist is the *story* of science, that is to say, history provided with a finality of reason, a finality of the truth, a finality of technical realization. The *story* is of much greater interest than the *history.* The *story* has a remarkable pedagogical value which surpasses the simple values of erudition.

The historians of the sciences are often hostile to these determinations of values; but without confessing it, they themselves deal with the *human evaluation* which is characteristic of scientific work. In fact they do not fail to describe the *struggle of the genius.* These struggles of the genius are often analyzed in the simple dialectic between social misfortunes and personal success. In these great legends told with predilection by the historians, the man of genius fails socially and succeeds intellectually—and the future justifies him. Posterity belongs to him. The *value* of a man of genius becomes a kind of appanage to the "city of science." The story of these evaluations is found time and again on each page of the history of the sciences.

Summarizing, we believe that we are justified in attributing this essential characteristic of evaluation and valorization to the very history of the sciences. Scientific truth is by definition a truth which has a future.

Moreover, as soon as one follows the astonishing progress of the mathematization of the physical sciences, there appears a new motive of valorization which must be emphasized, for it is one of the dominating philosophical aspects of wave mechanics upon which we slowly but surely shall concentrate our commentary.

Indeed, with mathematics incorporating itself into the physical sciences, *apodicticity* makes its appearance in the organization and explanation of our experiences. The value of the mathematical concatenation which connects the principle with its

5. Floyd Karker Richtmyer, *Introduction to Modern Physics* (London: McGraw-Hill, 1934), p. 79.

consequence is added to the value of the concatenation which connects the cause with its effect. Physical cause and mathematical consequence interchange their concatenative value. It is not necessary to see in the convergence of these antiquated themes of philosophy a simple verbal declaration of unity. We will have to return to the fact that quantum chemistry uses semiempirical formulas (we might as well say semirational). One does not hesitate to substitute experimental results for solutions of integrals which are too difficult to calculate. And so integrals are solved experimentally. One will find a proof of this if one reads in Glasstone the section entitled: "Experimental Determination of Resonance Energies." [6] But the proofs show abundantly that these are instances which fall between an elaborated rationalism and a perfected technique. Here one could even mention the amazing technicality of the new computers. But without insisting on this machine example and remaining within the region of transaction between rational theories and technical experiments connected with them, one sees clearly enough that science constitutes itself by means of the increasingly powerful connections of applied rationalism. One passes from the verified truth to the established proof. In its dominating dynamic of progressive mathematization, the history of science is thus a confirmed, double-checked, and coordinated truth. It describes the most comprehensive philosophical synthesis. Little by little—wave mechanics is a striking example of it—mathematical and theoretical physics together constitute a homogeneous theory; the hypotheses of physics are mathematically formulated. The scientific hypotheses are henceforth inseparable from their mathematical form: they are truly mathematical thoughts.

In this attempt to grasp the essence of the *value* in which the effective history of science consists, one must also point to the fact that pure mathematics finds *unexpected* applications in contemporary physics. The fact that the polynomials of Legendre, Laplace, and Laguerre arise in century or half-century intervals, in the study of the energy levels of the hydrogen atom (and of atoms which are a bit more complicated and therefore can be compared with it)—this fact shows the activity of a rationalist valorization with sufficient clarity. The empiricist will not be struck by these *unexpected* applications. He believes that

6. Samuel Glasstone, *Theoretical Chemistry*, 2d ed. (New York: D. Van Nostrand, 1945), p. 137.

mathematics is merely a simple means of expression. We will have to show that the synthesis between physical and mathematical laws is much closer. One must break with this commonplace so dear to skeptical philosophers who consider mathematics merely as a *language*. Rather, mathematics is a *thought*, a thought which is certain of its language. The physicist thinks experiments with this mathematical thought. We do not think much of a physicist who speaks of the different energy states of an atom without referring to the "Hamiltonian," to the mathematical expression of the energy. This is the reason why all philosophical exposition of the new mechanics requires a constant reference to a mathematical rationalism. To comment on the experimental results of this mechanics without giving the theoretical and mathematical preparation for it would be to bypass the great lessons of synthetic philosophy.

On the other hand, a philosophy which in this case were to take its inspiration from mathematical realism would still be as inadequate as empiricist philosophy. In relation to physics the polynomials of Laplace, Legendre, and Laguerre are merely schemes for the organization of our knowledge. One must understand the epistemological function thereof by locating oneself in the very center of abstract-concrete thought, in the very center where *algebra* becomes united with the *organization* of an experiment, where algebra thinks the experiment. If one were to think the phenomena concretely by means of forms and structures, he could imagine a world of pure geometrical essences, a world of Platonic ideas which are educed through reflection on the always imperfect and confused structures which sense experience yields. But the core of the experimental determinations of contemporary science does not follow the direction postulated by a Platonic realism. To speak the language of existentialism, the *algebraic project* does not pursue a goal inscribed in reality. One must maintain a consciousness of the abstraction at the same time as one uses abstract plans in order to give form to experience. In other words, abstract thought could be eliminated in favor of the description of a concrete being, whatever the tonality of this concrete being may be. Contemporary physical science is thus an indissoluble union of the abstract and the concrete. It does not aim at an ontology. Rather, it materializes ontogeneses. In my opinion one must therefore certainly characterize it in its complex philosophy as an ontogenetic epistemology, as an active rationalism, as an applied rationalism.

In order to find the genuine centers from which the history of the physical sciences radiates, one must thus constantly go back to those points where the first mathematizations take place, as well as to those points where the mathematization transforms itself. If we could revive these great historical moments in which the mathematical graft is implanted in the seedling of the experiment, they would yield a kind of *dialectic of curiosity*. Indeed, in addition to this empirical curiosity which calls us toward the carefully examined phenomena, a rationalist curiosity takes place, a curiosity which is interested in the mathematical relations which connect the aspects of the phenomena. In this sense Delambre writes: "As far as light, weight, motion, and the impact of bodies are concerned, all of this nowadays falls almost entirely within the competence of geometry." [7] And vividly aware of the astonishment which Coulomb's science provoked, he adds: ". . . one has even tried to submit the phenomena of magnetism and electricity to calculus." Only an assiduous reader of the enormous prescientific literature on electricity and magnetism will be able to account for the power of *evaluation* accomplished by the mathematical information of the natural phenomena of electricity and magnetism. He will then appreciate the strangeness of the clarity, the oddness of the reduction of the phenomena to what is essential to them, the curiousness of the fact that the phenomena of electricity are put in relation to the phenomena of magnetism by technical experiments as well as through the formulation of mathematical laws. Coulomb's "balance" and Coulomb's law announce a new era for the science of electricity. This sudden algebraic rigor which imposes itself on an ever-expanding phenomenology still baffles the mind unsuited for scientific culture. It is of importance for him who likes science. In its mathematical development electromagnetism would give us innumerable examples, which are more complicated and consequently more interesting, of a geometrization of physical experience, geometrizations of the same type as the first geometrical information which struck Delambre.

7. Jean Baptiste Delambre, *Rapport historique sur les progrès des sciences mathématiques depuis 1789* (Paris: Imprimerie impériale, 1810), p. 284.

But since we must limit ourselves in this work to a particular category of phenomena and thus to a regional rationalism, we are going to follow in its main lines the development of the mathematization of the modern theories of light.

[THE DIALECTIC "WAVE PARTICLE" IN ITS HISTORICAL DEVELOPMENT]

WHEN IN THE ENLIGHTENED CENTURIES one follows the efforts to constitute a science of light, one is quickly struck by the existence of an obstacle to a precise determination of the problems. This epistemological obstacle stems from naïve realism which holds that light is a *material substance*. Thus some begin the study of the phenomena with an over-elaborated phenomenology. They want to start, and they believe it prudent to begin with a sum of effects which is as complete as possible in order to determine the cause. For instance, the effect of light on vegetation is put at the top of the list of effects to be explained. One thinks that the color of plants, that the color of flowers, is a *direct* production of light. Through the action of light the plants acquire taste, odor, and even "combustibility." Are the fruits of sun-kissed countries generally speaking not "more fragrant, more savory, more resinous"? Resin is light matter which in burning emits absorbed light. According to Macquer, it is light which produces "the oil of the plants." [8] De la Métherie supposes that among the principles of fire, light, and air there are "transformations without end." A century earlier Newton himself had written: "The changing of bodies into light, and light into bodies, is very conformable to the course of Nature, which seems delighted with transformations." [9]

Even when the assimilation of the nature of light and corporeal nature is realized through the use of mechanical reasons, one is not necessarily relieved of substantialist confusions. Fourcroy, too, remarks that light is deflected when it passes close to solid bodies (phenomenon of diffraction); he sees in this an argument for asserting the material character of light, which

8. Macquer, *Dictionnaire de Chimie*, III, 142–43. See also our article, "Lumière et substance," *Revue de métaphysique et de morale*, XXXIX (1934), pp. 343–66.
9. *Opera* (London: Nichols, 1782), IV, 241.

thus is subject to gravitation just as everything else which exists in the heavens as well as on earth. Given the fact that at the end of the eighteenth century the forces of gravitation and the forces of chemical affinity were considered to be of the same nature, Fourcroy could conclude that the changes which light causes in chemical substances prove that light is a body and that it produces these phenomena of diffraction by means of "a chemical attraction." [10]

Whether one takes the notion of substance as defined by an abundant set of qualities or makes it into the root of a fundamental quality such as attraction which affects all bodies, one does not in this way succeed in delineating the domains of chemistry and optics. Consequently, a new science was born: photochemistry, which studies the working of light (or more generally, of radiation) on chemical reactions. But this science was soon to become a science of energy rather than a science of substance. And it is precisely the positive history of photochemistry—a history which itself is also fascinating—which relegates to the rank of outdated history all the stories which have been told about the substantial qualities of light.

In this simple instance we thus encounter a *real philosophical impurity*. Substantialism, realism, materialism—these are the many nuances which one ought at least to have determined in order to define philosophically the evolution of thought in the brief period of time separating Macquer and Fourcroy. Obviously substantialism, realism, and materialism do not exhaust the philosophical possibilities of approaching the phenomena of light. One has not yet come upon the core of an objective study of light phenomena by saying that light is material or that it consists of light particles. Objectivity is not satisfied with a philosophical declaration made so hastily. From now on we must convince ourselves that scientific objectivity is *terminal*. It is established in the most developed part of scientific investigation. The realism attributed to the material phenomena of light hides the multiple nuances of thought implied in a discursive study of these phenomena. When Emile Meyerson ascribes Newton's theory of light particles to substantialist intuitions, he exaggerates their *qualitative* aspect: "As far as the luminous bodies of Newton are concerned their kinship with the qualitative atoms of

10. Antoine-François Fourcroy, *Eléments d'histoire naturelle et de chimie*, 4 vols. (Paris: Cuchet, 1786), I, 112.

Bérigard is equally manifest." [11] This comparison is not completely correct, for the characteristics of the particles in Newton's optics remain in a way "exterioristic," notwithstanding some accidental aspects such as the one we have noted above. One studies the *behavior* of the particles rather than the particles themselves. One characterizes this behavior by means of the phenomena of reflection and refraction, all of which are phenomena specifying the relationships between particle and *exterior* milieu. When Newton, in order to explain the phenomenon of "rings," suggests the hypothesis of fits (alternatively fits of easy transmission and fits of easy reflection), it is wrong to emphasize the word "fit" in the sense of a fit of bad humor. [12] The succession of two fits would lead us to envisage rather a comparison with the succession of phases of an undulatory movement. Newton's rings are, as we know, interference phenomena. We shall refer to them later. They can be explained perfectly by the wave theory. For the moment here we must emphasize this tendency of Newton's corpuscular theory toward undulatory explanations and object to too close an adherence to the usual and too realistic an interpretation of a word as special as "fit."

Permit us again to take this opportunity to make a remark on the use of a picturesque language in physics. For example, similar observations could be made with respect to philosophical commentaries often brought up in connection with the "free will" of electrons. As we shall see later, the problem here is to attribute a certain probabilism to the behavior of a particle. Then the physicist turns to a *psychological image*. Some metaphysicians let themselves be taken in by this. They force this psychologism beyond all limits, so far that they make it into an intimate psychology of the electron. Obviously, the physicist did not intend that. He merely wanted to give substance to the "without cause" which allows him to use freely the theses of the probability calculus.

At any rate, Newton's theory of fits and the theory of the "free will of particles" of Bohr and Dirac develop in the same chiaroscuro of a rationalism which otherwise is very distinct and very clear. Within this chiaroscuro one finds the problems which are not yet scientific, the problems which are still inexact. If philosophy wants to learn something in this region of scientific

11. Emile Meyerson, *Identité et réalité* (Paris: Alcan, 1908).
12. *Opticks*, pp. 120–39, 179, 184–201.

thought, it must avoid solidifying the arguments dogmatically. It must not assimilate too fast, in favor of its own systems, that which bears the mark of subtly formulated differentiations. In this manner science constantly offers to philosophy occasions to acquire the spirit of philosophical subtlety.

But we must still show in a more explicit way that the various types of particles which contemporary science considers are, strictly speaking, not *substances*. One must not force realist nuances upon the story of the historical dialectic of corpuscular and undulatory conceptions. We shall see that in the organization of themes discussed by science, light, whether wave or particle, is scarcely more than the subject of the verb *"to propagate with the velocity of light."* In fact, all energy which propagates with the velocity of light corresponds to the energy of a "generalized light" or, according to the standard term, to the energy of radiation. The fundamental characteristics which we now shall have to add to this *mobile* found in the movement of propagation are few in number. We shall discuss them as we go along by calling to mind some historical remarks, in this way making a start on what could eventually become a complete recurrent history of the science of optics.

Without concerning ourselves further with naïve realism with respect to luminous matter, let us simply recall the dialectical phases of the theory of the *propagation* of light as found in modern times.

Descartes' thesis is particularly relevant. It postulates, as you know, an instantaneous propagation. Light phenomena have the character of a shock. They are transmitted through space as if space were a *perfect solid*. As is well known, Descartes, here as everywhere else, is able to avoid the introduction of occult qualities, of specific substantial qualities. For Descartes light is not a substance. By founding his view on the simple laws of reflection and refraction, Descartes establishes catoptrics and dioptrics as pure geometries of light.

Descartes' theory, however, contributes no valuable themes to what today is called *physical optics*. Moreover, observing an astronomic irregularity in the recurrence of the eclipses of Jupiter's satellites, the Danish astronomist Roemer showed in 1676 that light takes a noticeable time to travel the distance from Jupiter to Earth. The transmission, however rapid it may be, is not instantaneous. Much of Descartes' cosmological views are refuted by this simple fact. Since the time of Roemer, the velocity of light has become a kind of universal constant. This number allows us to *think* the immensity of the stellar world. This is, on the cosmic level, a clear example of abstract-concrete determination. We are not able to concretely *imagine* a distance which amounts to light years, that is to say, the distance which light travels during one year. But we can discuss it *abstractly* from the simple fact that we attach the notion of number to the dimensions which defy our imagination. Descartes was forced to fill his heavens with vortexes close to the solar vortex without in any way being able to determine the magnitude of vortexes other than those of our solar system. He did not have any basis for posing the problem concerning the size of the universe. Here we touch in passing upon a remarkable paradox: Descartes' world of extension is in no way a world of measurement. Descartes' physics is a physics of unmeasured objects, a physics without equations, a geometrical representation without a specified scale, without mathematics. Descartes' physics belongs in no way to what in the modern conception of the term is called mathematical physics.

Let us therefore leave Descartes' physics in its historical solitude. It will not return by recurrence when, as in the case in these hurried pages, one wishes to revive the preparation of the dialectic "wave particle."

This dialectic begins with Huygens (1629–98), although, as a matter of fact, the notion of wave in Huygens does not exactly imply the notion of undulation in the actual sense of the term, with its precise reference to a rigorous periodicity of the oscillating movement. Taught by the simple spectacle of a wave which runs on the surface of water, Huygens paid little attention to the duration of one oscillation of the liquid as it went up and down. He mainly emphasized the movement of propagation and explained the geometry of the enveloped waves by starting from the smallest, posing and then solving the interesting problem of the neutralization of the movements behind the wave.

But the really new philosophical aspect of this idea must be sharply distinguished here: the waves must explain the rays, the theory of waves must construct "the reality" which is the ray, or also—and this is an unexpected softening of the naïve realist view—the theory of waves must impose, to the detriment of the realism of the ray, the realism of the wave. We will have to insist later upon the fact that the notions of wave and ray are geometrically complementary. But *realistically*, the ray is visible and the wave is not. Huygens thus proposes a displacement of realism, an overthrow of realism, or at least a change of the dominating form of realism. In those instances one may grasp all that is philosophically positive in the work done by scientific thought. To say that the light wave is a hypothesis does not explain the binding character of the wave notion. The light wave in Huygens appears clearly in the perspective of an abstract-concrete thought, in the sphere of an abstraction which has to prove the concrete characteristics associated with it.

Moreover, in Huygens' theory the wave notion has immediately a remarkable epistemological value, for this notion leads to the *construction* of the refracted ray. The construction of the refracted ray appears as a clear coordination of concepts. It links two empirical facts which correspond to two velocities of the propagation of light in two different milieus. *Huygens' construction is a definitive acquisition* for science. It is "forever" in science. It is an epistemological value which detaches itself without difficulty from the historical course of scientific thought. And when it becomes clear that the same construction principle explains the *double refraction* equally as well as it does the simple refraction, the usual refraction, one can then assess the inductive value of well-constructed theories. The phenomenon of double refraction in fact escapes our common-sense interpretations. That an incident ray divides into two refracted rays was something destined to be even more troublesome to the psychologists, who already claimed to be acutely aware of the false problem concerning the errors of our senses when meditating upon the bent stick. Philosophy gained here by renewing its stock of images. The use of simple images blocks the investigation of complex phenomena. It is precisely the complex phenomena which give us the complete phenomenology. Future science will show that one can produce the double refraction in media which at first only yield the phenomenon of simple refraction. In Huygens' construction one sees therefore the importance of having a synthetic view on the totality of the phenomena of refraction. The value of a phenomenal synthesis unites here with the value of a coherent theory.

Even more than the images which Descartes took from the realm of extension, the themes of Huygens' geometrical wave bar all reference to occult qualities of luminous matter. Of course, one has to come to the nineteenth century in order to find a complete equation for the wave surface of a medium in which the elasticity is different for the three dimensions.[13] We point to this later development only to show that a scientific notion such as the wave notion is rich in problems as soon as it reaches its mathematical expression; one has said everything when one takes a mathematical expression to be a translation of a phenomenal being. The mathematical notion is suggestive also in many other ways. It opens the way to various rationalist inquiries, to experimental investigations which a simple examination of the phenomena does not suggest.

It is obviously impossible to condense in a few pages all the dialectical functions of a work such as Newton's even if one were to arbitrarily limit oneself to investigations in the field of optics. Even if one were to take the space necessary to develop the whole problem, difficulties which derive from the extreme subtlety of Newton's thoughts would still remain. For instance, Newton often simultaneously directs his polemic against the theses of Descartes and Huygens. Sometimes both of these doctrines are evoked in the same sentence: "If light consisted in pression (Descartes) or in motion propagated through a fluid medium (Huygens), or in an instant of time (Descartes) or in a certain interval of time (Huygens), it would bend into the shadow." [14]

In the second place one would simplify things to an extreme if one were to point to Newton as to someone who rigorously adheres to a corpuscular theory. In fact, undulatory intuitions

13. See the report read by Ampère to the Académie des Sciences on August 26, 1828. Fresnel had found this equation by supposing that it would be of the fourth degree.

14. "If light consisted only in pression propagated without actual motion, it would not be able to agitate and heat the bodies, which refract and reflect it. If it consisted in motion propagated to all distances in an instant, it would require an infinite force every moment, in every shining particle, to generate that motion. And if it consisted in pression or motion, propagated either in an instant or in time, it would bend into the shadow" (*Opticks*, bk. III, query xxviii, p. 232).

are in no way foreign to Newton. He has defined in a very modern way the physical conditions which luminiferous ether must fulfill in order to be able to transmit what he calls a *continuous* motion. He has faced up to the paradox which shows the necessity of an ether which is very rarefied and nevertheless very elastic—of an ether thousands of times more rare than air and thousands of times more elastic than a usual solid body.

But it is especially the theory of "successions" produced by the alternate "fits of easy reflection and easy transmission" which marks Newton's optics with a value having the character of a compromise between the corpuscular and the undulatory theories. According to Newton: ". . . light is in fits of easy reflection and easy transmission, before its incidence on transparent bodies. And probably it is put into such fits at its first emission from luminous bodies, and continues in them during all its progress." [15]

It should be well understood that the particles do not leave the luminous bodies, which would give some the sign of easy reflection and others the mark of easy transmission. That would mean conceiving of the particles as having a quality which they do not possess. All the particles during their course maintain the faculty of being successively in the one and then in the other kind of "fits." A particle which has just been reflected can then be transmitted in another piece of glass. Each particle thus has the double temporality of successive abilities.

In short, Newton already found himself faced with the problem of accounting for interference in his experiments of the "rings." We shall see with what constancy all interference phenomena which manifest themselves as a kind of periodicity in space involve the necessity of imposing a periodicity upon time. A phenomenon of structural repetition calls for a phenomenon of rhythmical repetition. Newton already knew that the strictly corpuscular character is unable to explain interference phenomena. Newton's optics is therefore in the final analysis corpuscular in its simple model and pre-undulatory in its scientific theory. The corpuscular model suffices to explain the common phenomenon of reflection and the diffusion which one can present as the rebounding of particles on a rough surface. In order

15. *Ibid.*, bk. II, prop. xiii, p. 179.

to explain Newton's rings, to account for the first phenomena of interference, one needs less simple principles—deliberately artificial principles. This gives us proof of the philosophical multiplicity of scientific thought in action.

In short, although Newton manifests a preference for corpuscular theses, his theories of light possess a genuine dialectical sensibility. That accounts for why they have long been able to provide the basis for positive and solid instruction. We shall give an example of this solidity when we later bring up the teaching of Jean-Baptiste Biot. One must also note on the other hand the excessive simplification with which some minds, judging the problems of Newton's optics superficially, have adhered to the corpuscular conception in the narrowest sense of the term. Fourcroy, as we have seen, gives us a clear example of this abusive simplification. La Métherie, who even exaggerates the simplistic deductions, states that the luminous bodies are perfect spheres which, if they were otherwise, would be unable to obey the exact geometrical law of reflection. Simplifications of our intuition thus provoke a decline of epistemological values. This decline shows clearly enough that the history of science carries more than just the values of progress in its main stream.

Let us draw attention also to the unexpected importance of an unusual phenomenon, of an artificial phenomenon, such as that of Newton's rings may seem to be. Certain philosophers will claim that a lack of proportion manifests itself in taking one's instruction exclusively from particular phenomena. It is in this way that a philosopher of nature such as Franz von Baader (without a doubt moved by the real mysticity of light and heat) does not hesitate to declare the corpuscular theory of Newton to be *absurd* because, he says, one cannot represent a light phenomenon without a perfect continuity.[16] For a philosopher such as Franz von Baader, the physicist who pretends to study light on the basis of the unusual and accidental phenomena of diffraction turns his back on what is of fundamental and prime value in the world of phenomena.

The example of von Baader suffices, it seems to us, to judge the lack of efficacy of a previous philosophy with respect to the values of science. Philosophy of science must follow the actual

16. Eugène Susini, *Franz von Baader et le romanticisme mystique*, 2 vols. (Paris: Vrin, 1942), I, 223.

work of scientific thought. It must disregard the too general themes of former philosophies.

In the evolution of contemporary science it is always possible to find themes of continuity. And regarding the history of the science of optics, which interests us at present, it suffices to limit ourselves to the themes of geometrical optics of light rays in order to have a remarkable example of this continuity. It is not without reason that in the elementary books of geometry a straight line is defined as the path of a light ray. The phenomena furnished by mirrors present themselves in a quasi-natural geometrization. The shadows, the dark room, the magic lantern give rise to problems of elementary geometry. Geometrical optics is a kind of geometry. As such it has the privilege of regular progress, the privilege of making progress without regressing, which is the exclusive historical characteristic of mathematics. Thus Newton carries on the work of Descartes, and Euler in turn carries on the work of Newton.

But this continuity of geometrical optics makes a new oscillation in the theories of physical optics only more remarkable. In fact, Euler (1707–83) criticizes Newton's corpuscular theory and defends the wave theory. In his *Letters to a German Princess* (which is necessarily elementary) Euler piles up the usual criticisms against the corpuscular theory: "If the sun were to emit continuously and in all directions such streams of luminous bodies with such an enormous velocity, it would seem that the sun's matter would soon be exhausted." [17] "However small one supposes the particles to be, one would not gain anything; the system would always remain equally objectionable." [18] And since all the rays which come from the stars cross in all directions "hunted by a terrible force," the firmament would be nothing but a muddle of light "in terrible agitation." [19] In the hypothesis of particles the transparent bodies would have to be pierced with *straight pores* in all directions: "Thus we have here bodies which are completely sieved and which nevertheless appear to us quite solid." Then there is the argument of our burst eyes. In fact, how could the eye remain uninjured when it becomes

17. *Lettres d'Euler à une princesse d'Allemagne*, ed. A. A. Cournot, 2 vols. (Paris: Hachette, 1842), I, 69 (Letter of June 7, 1760).
18. *Ibid.*, p. 70.
19. *Ibid.*, pp. 72, 74.

pierced by a dizzying flood of particles? Euler could conclude his letter by saying: "Your Highness will undoubtedly be astonished that this system (of particles) has been devised by such a great man and embraced by so many enlightened philosophers." And in his next letter, using an imprecatory style which may well astonish us, he deplores the fact that man is subject "to such sorrowful relapses" and that he could ever fall "into such absurdities."

We are calling attention to all these repercussions caused by a discussion exclusively based on common-sense models because it is against these repercussions that we believe that the establishment of a psychoanalysis of objective knowledge would be useful. Would a philosopher who claims to defend the continuity of common sense and scientific knowledge still admit such arguments? To maintain them at the threshold of culture is tantamount to accepting the laziness of a mind which is satisfied with hastily framed models. Contemporary science has rightly freed itself from the objections of the uninformed. The objection of the "burst eyes" has never been raised again in objection to the existence of photons.

After the letters dedicated to the critique of Newton's corpuscular theses, Euler writes positive letters to explain to the princess the notion of ether, that thin and elastic medium which fills the interstellar spaces as well as all the pores of transparent bodies. And Euler undertakes to develop the great analogy of sound and light. This analogy, which persists as a leitmotiv of the elementary culture, is (all things considered) specious. It provides an overly facile unity to our general phenomenology. Let us look carefully at the hurried character of this analogy: "Light rays are nothing but vibrations transmitted through the ether, just as sound consists in vibrations transmitted through air. There is therefore actually nothing coming toward us from the sun, just as little as what comes from a bell when its sound reaches our ears." Without a doubt, as Cournot says: "One would have to go into numerous details in order to show the consequences of these various hypotheses and to compare them with the observed phenomena." As a matter of fact, the analogy neither can nor ought to remain on the level of phenomenology. The analogy is meaningful only when one is dealing with a comparison of the two rational organizations of the science of optics and the science of acoustics. We are thus always referred to the mathematical information of the phenomena. It is there, let us repeat, that the continuity of science resides, notwithstanding the variations of the norms established by realism for the interpretation of physical phenomena.

Moving from Euler to Biot we find that the intuitive bases have changed again and that there is a new change in the realism of light. Jean-Baptiste Biot gives life again, full and abundant life, to Newton's theory. But a new aspect must be noticed: Euler was a great mathematician; Biot is a great professor, and one can depict him as the significant witness to a new era of teaching. His *Treatise on Physics* in four volumes, which appeared in 1816, was to put its stamp on education in physics in France for twenty years. The great schools founded during the Revolution and the Institute which assumed a growing authority during the Consulate and the Empire are among the many cohesive forces for science the moment it becomes a social reality. The notion of the "city of science" and more particularly the notion of the "city of physics" which we have proposed in order to measure the efficacy of a teaching rationalism find an exact application here. It suffices to refer to the *Lectures on Experimental Physics* of Father Nollet (1769) in order to convince oneself that in one generation teaching changed in *niveau*, changed in direction, and changed in function. Father Nollet had readers, whereas Biot needs students. The "city of physics," founded in the beginning of the nineteenth century, is no longer supported by the interest of amateurs. It calls for "workers."

One will perhaps be amazed that we give such great importance to this highly social character of taught science. But the new necessities of a rational and technical organization of science must be understood at their roots. Physical science becomes deliberately technical. Constructive rationalism cannot satisfy itself with primitive, clear ideas and "natural" convictions. But in our recent work we have already sufficiently insisted on the dialectic between teaching and taught rationalism so that we can limit ourselves here to point to a characteristic which is too often forgotten by the historian of the sciences: the influence of the school is henceforth a strong one. One must learn from the masters before doing personal work; one must learn from the human books *before* reading in the book of nature, as was said in the eighteenth century. Anyone who *studies* the *Treatise on*

Physics of Jean-Baptiste Biot does not waste his time. Such a book contains all the solid past of the preceding physics and prepares the mind to take part in the science as it was in action in the first quarter of the nineteenth century. Such a book still instructs. It teaches more than just history.

The manner in which Biot supports the corpuscular intuitions is, moreover, full of philosophical teachings. He puts himself resolutely before the essential difficulty of the corpuscular hypothesis: if the light ray is a set of specific particles, how then does it happen that certain particles are attracted toward the interior of a transparent substance, whereas others are repelled by the same substance? Are there two kinds of luminous particles? This hypothesis is unacceptable because the reflected ray which falls for a second time upon the same transparent substance is again divided into two rays: one of these rays is reflected and thus repelled by matter; the other is refracted and thus attracted by matter. Since the substance of all luminous particles can sometimes be repelled and sometimes attracted, one must in the explanation pass from *attribute* to *mode*. In other words, one must suppose that each light particle, whatever its color may be, is subject to a *modal alternative*. One must suppose that the particle constantly undergoes physical modifications which make it change insofar as *its physical state* is concerned; these modifications alternately bring it to a state of easy reflection and to a state of easy transmission, as Newton formulated it.

Let us see further in what terms Biot refers to these modalities: "One must note that the [luminous] molecules which are reflected are *perhaps* not in the same physical state, or in the same circumstances in regard to their motion, as those which are refracted; now it suffices that this difference be *possible* in order that there not be a necessary contradiction in the two opposed consequences drawn from the phenomena with respect to the two states of the particles." We have italicized two words of the text in order to show how little Biot requires of his hypotheses. It suffices that they be *possible* in order that one may build upon them. This epistemological nuance must be retained because certain philosophers think that they can make it into a mark of all epistemological theory concerned with hypotheses in physics. But this is only one nuance among many others, and, in a moment, in Fresnel, we shall see a type of scientific hypothesis which implies more and is more precisely mathematized. Biot insists less on the coherence of our information; he rushes to experimental proofs for the plausibility of his hypothesis. He evokes "a host of proofs" which confirm the *modification* of the *substantial* character of luminous particles.

In fact, we return constantly to the same conclusion: this *modification* amounts to imposing a rhythm on the motion of the particles. In a transactional theory such as Biot's, the luminous particles thus receive an undulatory character, or at least a temporal character which in the classical wave theory is simply reinforced by a fundamental undulatory intuition.

But this wave character which Biot accepts remains in his physics a characteristic which is merely tacked on; it is not an active element in his explanation. The strong rational adhesion of the oscillatory theme to the mathematical functions of trigonometry has not yet really founded the mathematical and experimental theory of interference. It is necessary that mathematics take the lead in order that the experiments may find their full coherence.

Finally, there is Fresnel who founds physical optics on an indestructible basis. At this moment in history one can even affirm that a point of juncture between rational conceptions and technical experiments about light phenomena has been established *forever*. Fresnel's work will always maintain a cultural value which one will have to take up. Certainly later one will be able to remove some of its elements, modify the content of certain concepts, but the interconceptual organization of the rationalized techniques will scarcely suffer from this. From Fresnel on it makes sense to speak of a rationalism of interferences. In a certain sense this rationalism of interferences may be isolated as a regional rationalism. One does not need to know the whole of physics, nor even the whole of optics, in order to take possession of this domain, in order to acquire in this realm great certainty in regard to the rational information about our experiments.

And this rationalism of interferences is clearly going in the direction of applied rationalism. In fact, it is precisely the rational organization which provokes and varies the experiments, because the luminous interferences scarcely attract the attention of *common experience*. In his *Notes on the Letters of Euler to a*

German Princess, Cournot was still able to write in 1842 with respect to interferences: "These curious phenomena." These must be understood as *exceptional* phenomena able to arouse the curiosity of the uninformed. This is tantamount to saying that there is no *everyday experience* of interference phenomena. Courses and textbooks describe experiments in which the phenomenon is materialized through provoking two centers of disturbance on the surface of a liquid. But these are experiments performed after Fresnel's time. They are performed by the professor in order to illustrate his lecture on light interference. Such isolated phenomena, which are really constructed by the technicians, give evident arguments for the thesis which shows the break between common experience and scientific experimentation.[20]

Fresnel's theory was barely accepted before *technical* experiments were conducted in great number. The number of instruments as well as their variety clearly prove the importance of interferometry. We stand here before a scientific past which is alive and will be forever actual. A whole section of the "city of science" comes to instruct itself here. Young students will come to receive here the great lessons concerning the precision of measurements.

Let us not forget also to note the *indirect* character of the measurements of interferences. By measuring the space of Fresnel's fringes, one is brought to *think*. The measurement here is a moment of thought. The fact which these fringes constitute is without interest if one considers it outside its theoretical framework. We believe that one would blur all philosophical values by speaking here of an *empiricism of interferences*. The rational mark is truly a trademark in this instance.

Moreover, the *fact* of interference is so delicate that one sees immediately the necessity of conducting the experiments properly. And one demands of the young student that he know how to perform them, how to bring them about time and again. One day Bouasse was indignant at a poster he found in a teaching laboratory: it recommended to the students who came to work at the optical bench not to *disturb* the Fresnel mirrors. Bouasse began immediately to disturb the dihedron of the mirrors, convinced as he was that technical culture consists in restoring the setting

20. Cf. *Le Rationalisme appliqué*, (Paris: Presses Universitaires de France, 1949), chap. VI.

and making the phenomenon of the fringes stand out in its maximal regularity by going through all the phases of a well-geometrized thought. Only exercises such as these give the mind the precision of modern scientific techniques.

But we do not have to go further into the history which, henceforth completely positive, is the result of Fresnel's investigations. In this chapter our goal was simply to mark the dialectical evolution of the wave theory and the corpuscular theory. We were able to limit ourselves to determining certain "historical centers" by evoking the great names of Descartes, Huygens, Newton, Euler, Biot, and Fresnel, in order to summarize the "internal contradictions" of the history of optics. Obviously we have not been able to go into details of the polemics; that would have entailed writing a book rather than a chapter. But concerning these polemics, even though only hastily raised here, the epistemologist must point to general philosophical observations. These polemics have two clearly different poles: some consist in the objections of common sense; others are suggestions originating in the mathematical organization. And it is not difficult to realize that the first group, those originating in common sense, are scientifically inactive. To an objection by common sense taking into account common experiences, common sense answers with common-sense experience. In these polemics one ends up explaining light by sound, only to lose consequently the specificity of the phenomena. Another cause of thought's immobilization is found in the too general cosmological views which can hardly be relevant for a study of physical phenomena. How many pages have been written on the *exhaustion of the sun!* If this huge body loses billions of small bodies each second, what then is going to remain of it? This suffices for Euler to convince a princess to abandon Newton's theory.

It is at the other pole of the polemics, where geometry and measurement are the arguments, that science is active. We have noted this activity in connection with the geometrical constructions of Huygens, in connection with the calculus concerning Newton's rings. We have been able to make the same remarks, in a more complete survey, in connection with the experiments of Malus and Biot on polarization. But in this respect Fresnel's works are models of science in action. Not cosmology but instruments, not objections but proofs, not analogies but measurements and equations. And so a *body of concepts* appropriate for the coherence of technical experimentation constitutes itself. Even if these concepts have their counterparts in common experience, they must be redefined with precision and become integrated into a system. There is no scientific knowledge on the level of an *isolated concept*. Epistemological values, therefore, must be judged according to their contribution toward theory construction. Science does not correspond to a world to be described. It corresponds to a world to be constructed.

If one has followed the history of the corpuscular and undulatory theories in all of its fluctuations, one may be tempted to profess a certain relativism and even an explicit skepticism concerning the value of physical theories. One has even come to see the theoretical activity as something which is always uncommitted, the mathematical information as something which is always flexible enough to adapt itself to any experiment, whatever it may be. The philosophical theses of Pierre Duhem are symptomatic of this "educated" skepticism. For him there is no longer a crucial experiment capable of deciding between two theories which are as dissimilar as the corpuscular and the wave theories of light. Fizeau's experiment, which *was* historically crucial in that it stopped the further development of corpuscular hypotheses, *could have been* not crucial. The protagonists of the corpuscular theories *could have assimilated* the experimental conclusions of Fizeau by means of appropriate mathematical transformations. By allowing reason a "delayed repartee" one would give posthumous success to it.

In short, to say that thanks to supplying manipulations all theories have validity is tantamount to saying that they have validity only as proofs of the assimilative power of mathematics, or as a particularly mobile loquacity of the "mathematical language." Our theses of epistemological recurrence, of the reorganization of history's values, do not go so far as the theses of Duhem. We believe that the assimilation of Fizeau's experiment by a corpuscular theory could not have taken place without a collision with acquired rationality, and without the blurring of the rational values of that time.

Generally speaking, it seems to us that each theory defending the equivalence of hypotheses does not sufficiently take into account the epistemological value. Moreover, can the classical philosophical theories appreciate the notion of epistemological value in contemporary science? In an address on the occasion of Max Planck's sixtieth birthday in 1918, Einstein described the real epistemological situation as follows, Hermann Weyl tells us: "The historical development has shown that among the imaginable theoretical constructions there is invariably one that proves to be unquestionably superior to all others." [21] This *superiority* is not merely a question of fact. It is not simply characteristic of a historical moment. This superiority of the explanatory values of a hypothesis shows itself clearly in rational convictions. It is precisely the sign of a rational value, a cultural value, an epistemological value. It is science's destiny that rational values *impose* themselves. They impose themselves historically. The history of science is led by a kind of autonomous necessity. Philosophy of science should systematically take as its task the determination and classification of the hierarchy of epistemological values. General discussions on *the value of science* are quite futile if one does not see that all scientific thought makes one sensitive to a psychic value of the highest rank.

But the influence of skeptical theses in regard to scientific thought remains visible in our times. Contemporary physicists, while working with an unconditioned belief that the enigmas can be solved, accept at the same time a floating philosophy. One physicist has been able to say, for instance, that on Monday, Wednesday, and Friday he believed that light is an undulatory motion, on Tuesday, Thursday, and Saturday he believed it to be a stream of particles, and on Sunday he rested from believing.[22] This one-week genesis, even if it summarizes the history of three centuries, ignores the progressive emergence of epistemological values.

And it is precisely when one comes to the great syntheses of wave mechanics that the mastery of the mathematical information is such that one cannot satisfy himself with a vague relativism and thus realizes that an "educated" skepticism is out of style. Guided by the theory of wave mechanics, one has brought to their proper places the corpuscular intuitions as well as the undulatory intuitions. There is no longer a question of attribut-

21. Hermann Weyl, *Philosophy of Mathematics and Natural Science* (New York: Atheneum, 1963), p. 153.
22. Cf. John Adams Eldridge, *The Physical Basis of Things* (London: McGraw-Hill, 1934), p. 248.

ing an *absolute ontological value* to either one of these intuitions. The intuitions come *after* the mathematical determination. The intuitions are clarified by their mathematical signification or, to be more exact, the intuitions come to illustrate certain more or less abstract mathematical theses.

All the predications which lean too much toward *realism* are soon worn-out, erased, removed. Thus the material wave to which one first had attributed the very realistic function of "piloting" the particle has been transposed into a probability determination. There is no longer anything left of the "waves" but the probable. And we shall have to show that the *mobile* of wave mechanics is a body which has less reality than other bodies.

Of course, it is quite possible that an evolution of theories will force certain aspects of the phenomena back in the direction of corpuscular intuitions.

It is precisely this game in which realism in turn becomes reinforced and weakened, that constitutes the philosophical sensibility of new theories. Philosophically one would not be able to characterize these theories as a whole. One must scatter the philosophical spectrum of traditional philosophies if one wishes to specify philosophically all the characteristics of contemporary physics and chemistry.

Jean Cavaillès

JEAN CAVAILLÈS (1903–44), in the course of the brief span of his professional career, wrote a number of short but rich tracts on the epistemological issues of mathematics, logic, and science in general, some of which, like this last work of his, were published posthumously. *On Logic and the Theory of Science* may be considered his most important philosophical work. The prefaces to the French editions included here supply the necessary clarifications on the circumstances and background of the book and its author, as well as a suggestion of its impact on the phenomenological movement.

It is hoped that the difficulties involved in reading the necessarily condensed style of this prison book will be somewhat alleviated by a study of some of the allied contributions in this collection. Especially related are the essays on Husserl and the selections by Suzanne Bachelard and Jean Ladrière, who have continued the work of a "phenomenology of rationality" along the lines suggested by Cavaillès. To complement the following overview of the more salient points of this rich text, which scarcely begins to exhaust its suggestive possibilities, the bibliography includes several studies on the work of Cavaillès. But the text itself stands in its own right as a remarkable document, whose pages, "stripped of all secondary thought, have that abstract beauty which has become a rarity in our times." *

* Gabrielle Ferrières, *Jean Cavaillès, philosophe et combattant* (Paris: Presses Universitaires de France, 1950), p. 232. This book is a complete biography of Cavaillès. The remark is quoted from a

The book is divided into three untitled sections, dealing respectively with Kantian philosophies of consciousness, logical positivism, and Husserl's phenomenology. The issue is the essence and destiny of the theory of science in view of recent developments in logic and new insights into the riddle of mathematical reality, where the problem of the relationship of mathematics to physics is a recurring theme. What a theory of science must do is to establish an equilibrium among the various aspects of science: its subjective and objective aspects, as both an ordered system and a perpetual progression of knowledge. The former antinomy is found in Kant's vacillation between psychology and logic and in Husserl's notion of intentionality. As Cavaillès sees it, neither of these philosophers of consciousness manages to achieve the necessary balance. The logicists have emphasized science as a system of demonstration to the neglect of everything else. That progress is constitutive of science is a thesis dear to Leon Brunschvicg, who had a profound influence on Cavaillès' early intellectual development. But Brunschvicg exalts the autonomous initiatives of the human mind to the point of derogating the determining norms and the established order within which it necessarily moves, and these are viewed as an inertia to be overcome by the creative mind. Science is thereby limited to the absolute interiority of a spirit which wars with the external forces of conservative pedagogies and consecrated authorities. It is against the background of these positions that Cavaillès attempts to shift the center of gravity of the theory of science from a focus on its conscious activity to a concern for its conceptual dialectic. This emphasis on the dynamics of science itself is also why *enchainement* has generally been translated here as "sequence," to suggest not only the usual "concatenation" or "connection" but also the step-by-step movement that enters into such a dialectic.

The first part begins with an account of the difficulties in Kant's theory of science. The basic difficulty is that Kant turns from a consideration of science in its own right and reduces it to consciousness. Science is only a product of the faculties of consciousness, which is absolute, irreducible, a priori. Logic, which reputedly directs consciousness, is ultimately defined in terms of

---

brief study of Cavaillès' work by Gaston Bachelard, which is appended to this biography.

the a priori forms of consciousness. Such a transcendental logic is an empty and abstract logic, indifferent to the bearing of the object on its structures, having no reference to an ontology. It is a logic which exists even when every object is set aside, and therefore it hardly warrants being called a body of knowledge. The issue is compounded by Kant's uncritical adoption of traditional syllogistic logic, which resists integration into the transcendental logic envisaged by him, his indecision on the role of the mathematical organon in science, and his lack of a sense of the progression intrinsic to the life of science.

It was Bolzano, pursuing a philosophy of science along Kantian lines, who perhaps for the first time considered science as such and in its autonomous movement, without subordinating it to the absolute of consciousness. In regarding science exclusively as a demonstrative system, he paved the way for the logicists of the twentieth century, whose theory of science is the topic of the second part of Cavaillès' book. Cavaillès begins by establishing, in his own terms, the two aspects of demonstration that have been distinguished in the course of this formalistic approach to science: on the one hand, the paradigm, the posited meaning that results from the operation of demonstration, the primary formality of the formal system itself, whose structures are to be classified by the theory of science; on the other, the dynamics of the thematic, the positing meaning of the operation as operative, the more reflective formality which is the syntax of the formal system, whose rules of construction are to be developed. This distinction is not a separation, for the thematic can in turn be the occasion for paradigmatic considerations. The most recent logicists, in equating their theory of science with the general syntax of the syntaxes of all formal systems, in effect seek the comprehensive paradigm of thematization in general.

Cavaillès was one of the first Frenchmen to master the technicalities and intricacies of the logical positivism which was then radiating out of Vienna. In the second section, he concludes that its formalizing approach contributes immensely toward clarifying and specifying a theory of science but certainly does not constitute and found it, as the positivists claim. Despite its "principle of tolerance," it is the old dream of panlogism, and thus a totalitarian conception of science. The theory of science is not equivalent to logic. Other facets of science must be invoked to complete it.

Carnap's ideal of a general syntax is expressly the quest for a "logic without ontology." Its aim is to *prescribe* the use of scientific language and not to *describe* the world. His antimetaphysical predilection impels Carnap to forego even the correspondence theory of truth that the early Wittgenstein still maintained and to adopt a simple coherence theory. Even the so-called protocol sentences are ultimately not the result of direct observation but are based on the pragmatic choice of one's syntactical commitments. But Carnap's initially simplistic view of syntax was immediately countered by Tarski, who pointed out that formalization is not complete without a definition of the elemental objects which enter into the constructions. In analogy with the results of Gödel's theorem, syntactical formalization cannot complete itself but must ever remain open to another level, that of a reference to objects. For Cavaillès, this reference to an exteriority means that logic must ultimately be completed by an ontology. Even now, Carnap refuses to admit this, for when he speaks of an "ontology" it is still a matter of a question internal to the linguistic system, where the real is simply anything which can find its place within this system.** All external questions are "metaphysical" and therefore nonsensical. If one wishes to speak of a material beginning that precedes formalization, there is the system of signs which, if one wishes to go that far, are reducible to the marks on paper. However, the sign is not an object of the world, for it implies a reference to previous acts and sequences, whose very nature involves a reference to an actuality without which science would not be science. The difficulty is especially evident in the deficiencies of the logicist account of the relationship of mathematics and physics, whose coordination is necessarily preceded by a mathematical translation of the experimental object, a process that eludes all formalization and demands an ontological basis. A doctrine of science, which must come to terms with the complex site and sense that constitute the notion of a "physical theory," cannot pretend that natural science is not at once the science of nature.

Husserl's phenomenology (the subject of Part III), through its notion of intentionality, promises to restore the balance between the claims of logicism and a Kantian theory of consciousness and at the same time correct their deficiencies. The import

** "Empiricism, Semantics, and Ontology," *Revue internationale de philosophie*, IV (1950), 20–40.

of intentionality is already manifest in his conception of formal logic, which is centered on the equivalence of content and difference in direction of an apophantic and a formal ontology. Apophantic, the theory of judgment in view of its forms of meaning, implies a reference to the acts and operations of a judging consciousness. Formal ontology, which studies the forms of the meant object, is ultimately destined to refer to the individual in the real world. The mathesis is not a closed system of forms but necessarily involves an application to the world. Otherwise, it is merely an empty mental game. A formal logic thus finds its roots in a material logic, and both are based on a transcendental logic which justifies them in the constituting activity of an intentional subjectivity.

But Kant's dilemma is not thereby bypassed, for this subjectivity is itself subject to norms that call for a governing logic that is not a transcendental logic, which means that transcendental logic itself is not absolute. Moreover, the theses of logical empiricism still lurk beneath Husserl's formulations of the relationship between mathematics and physics. If a physical theory is simply an empty mathematical form applied to the invariant intuitive content of the lifeworld, if mathematization is thereby only a technique for idealizing and organizing predictive activity in this world, if it does not augment our knowledge of the world but only represents an abstract interlude and complication of our more direct concerns, if mathematics finds its justification only through its ultimate reference to this world, if an exaggeration of its role only promotes an obfuscation of intuitive meaning (*Sinnentleerung*)—then mathematics does not have its own content of knowledge and is merely a tautology. This positivistic thesis stemming from Wittgenstein is again evoked by Husserl's view of axiomatics as a nomology, whereby all the posterior deductions are reducible to the prior axioms. But Gödel has shown that such a tautological nomology holds only for manifolds that envelop relatively small domains. The truly mathematical theory, which reaches for the infinite, cannot be dominated in advance by consciousness in the act of positing axioms. What in fact is first posited is an operation or system of operations whose directive possibilities are unpredictable, whose results evoke further developments which in turn cannot be dominated. And as one of its deductive fields develops, its ramifications reverberate through the entire body of mathematics, which develops accordingly. All this amounts to a new notion of deduction which a philosophy of consciousness cannot account for. For the consciousness now is not a fixed absolute; it also progresses along with the progression which is intrinsic to the definition of science. It is this secret life of science, whose intelligibility is dispersed in concatenated moments that preclude comprehension in one fell swoop, whose progression is at once creative and necessary, whose rhythm of expansion involves discontinuous steps that bring suppression as well as resumption, which makes Cavaillès conclude that the fulcrum of a theory of science is to be found in a dialectic of the concept rather than in the activity of consciousness. One can only guess how he might have developed the particulars of this dialectic. Whether such a dialectic is alien to Husserl, whose last manuscripts also probe into the essential historicity of science, is open to question.†

† Cf. Jacques Derrida's remarks on Cavaillès in the introduction to his translation of Husserl's *L'Origine de la géométrie* (Paris: Presses Universitaires de France, 1962), pp. 157–59.

15 / On Logic and the Theory of Science

Jean Cavaillès

PREFACE TO THE 1960 EDITION

IN SPITE OF ITS DIFFICULTY, this book has come a long way. With the first edition long out of print, a second edition has become necessary. This second edition is the textual reproduction of the first, which was polished to perfection through the faithful efforts to Georges Canguilhem and Charles Ehresmann.

The contemporary logician deliberately considers as "prehistory" all the logical literature preceding the publication in 1910 of the *Principia Mathematica* by Whitehead and Russell. And since this publication, logical studies have developed at a rate so rapid in directions so diverse that it can be said, without yielding to skepticism, that any attempt at synthesis is doomed to "grow old fast." It might even be said that logic and current events are practically inseparable nowadays. Yet the book which Jean Cavaillès wrote nearly twenty years ago, in 1942, is still timely, for the logician of 1960 as well as for the philosopher. Thoroughly saturated in the new logical culture, the author of this book has in fact found his way back to the fundamental inquiries which a philosophical awareness necessarily forces on the logician. In a sense, modern logic shares the fate of all the sciences in being a discipline which can be constructed and perfected without endeavoring to inquire radically into its original meaning. Husserl

The following translation of the prefaces to Jean Cavaillès, *Sur la logique et la théorie de la science*, 2d ed. (Paris: Presses Universitaires de France, 1960), and pp. 1-78, has been made expressly for this book by Theodore J. Kisiel.

recognized that what makes science possible is fortunately not the reflection which penetrates to the essence of things but the scientific instinct. The scientist, in order to build, need not involve himself in the preliminaries of philosophical critique. But logic, insofar as it is a theory of science and not only a particular science, cannot be content with that "hidden reason" which acts implicitly in every science. What basically happens here, at the heart of a single discipline, more so than anywhere else, is the rivalry of the science which claims to rid itself of all philosophical tutelage and of a philosophy which sometimes disdains to inform itself. Can this problem of modern logic be formulated more directly and, if we may say so, more definitively than Cavaillès did when he wrote, "The reference to technique is a subterfuge," and, several lines later, in recalling Gödel's results on the theory of demonstration, "Here technique takes its revenge by subverting the constructions realized in an abstract realm that surpasses it"?

This book, in which an entire mathematical and logical culture is continually taken for granted, is nevertheless a book dear to the philosopher. To be sure, the reader will have to inform himself if he wishes Cavaillès' formulas, often rendered enigmatic by their conciseness, to yield their meaning. But once he has overcome his insensitivity to the problems of deductive science, the philosopher will find himself in familiar territory. He will never have to confront a history of naked facts or a garrulous interpretation. Nothing extrinsic or accidental will detain this inquiry into the essence and end of the theory of science. When he drafted this text, Cavaillès wrote to Albert Lautman: "I have tried to define myself in relation to Husserl, somewhat in opposition to him." Since the publication of the first edition, the studies in phenomenology and the French translations of Husserl's writings have become more numerous, perhaps inspired by Cavaillès' reflection. Hence the knowledge of Husserl's work will make the context of Cavaillès' reflection more evident. And in return this reflection will reveal the problems of Husserlian philosophy in an incomparable way.

Far from books, in the heroic solitude of a prison, Jean Cavaillès wrote this book. It is a book of meditation for the philosopher.

GASTON BACHELARD

Editors' Preface

SOME WORDS OF EXPLANATION appear necessary at the beginning of this work by Jean Cavaillès, his last. After completing his philosophical theses in 1938, Cavaillès began preparations for a new step in the work of expressing his own thought. But one year later, the war designated him for other duties. Taken prisoner in May after a courageous campaign in the winter of 1939–40, Cavaillès escaped to Belgium while being transferred to Germany and in October of 1940 resumed his courses at the University of Strasbourg, then relocated at Clermont-Ferrand. It is also known that he was not satisfied simply to resume his professorial work, that he did not consider himself demobilized by the armistice, and that he was one of the four or five founders of the first Resistance movements in France. Cavaillès' work in this domain, until his second and final arrest in August of 1943, was staggering.

This task nevertheless did not detract him from his philosophical work. The two were not really separate for him. The return to reflection in the heat of action seemed to him indispensable in order to preserve his sanity. It was his intention, as he confided to us on several occasions, to write a *Treatise on Logic,* but he added laughingly: "I shall find time to write it only in prison." This is just what happened. Sailing for England one night in August of 1942, Cavaillès was arrested on a beach near Narbonne and taken to the military prison at Montpellier. In order to overcome the despair of captivity, it was then that he undertook to write the work whose project he had now brought to maturity.

One may well wonder how Cavaillès could draft in prison a text in which numerous references are made to less common works. At that time, General de Lattre de Tassigny was in command of the military region of Montpellier. He knew and had a high regard for Cavaillès. Through his authorization, friends could visit Cavaillès in prison and bring him books. Albert Lautman came from Toulouse to Montpellier to bring some highly specialized texts which he possessed. When in the month of November the Germans retaliated for the landings in Algeria by occupying the southern zone, there was some vacillation and lack of decision in the military command. General de Lattre de Tassigny was arrested, under well-known circumstances. The military tribunal of Montpellier closed the Cavaillès case because of insufficient evidence. But the prefect of Hérault issued a warrant for the arrest of Cavaillès. He was sent to the camp at Saint-Paul-d'Eyjaux near Limoges. There he remained, if we may put it thus, just long enough to finish his work, and then escaped with his manuscript in his pocket in the last days of the year 1942. It was only a matter, he said, of putting the references at the bottom of the pages before turning the manuscript over to the publisher.

It was this final work of touching up that circumstances prevented him from accomplishing. In March of 1943, Cavaillès managed to get to England. He returned in May. In June, he barely escaped arrest by the German police. In August, he was arrested by German counterintelligence forces. In the interim, he had as a precaution entrusted a typewritten copy of his work, corrected by him, to his sister, Mme. Ferrières. A second copy, of which some pages were found in his room on the rue Chardon-Lagache after the German search, was kept by him after the final revision.

Cavaillès on several occasions stated to his sister and to us that he had no illusions about the difficulty of his text and that it would need a long introduction. He intended to write it but never realized this project. This preface, of course, does not in the least pretend to supply that introduction. We have limited ourselves to the purely material work of definitively establishing the text and investigating the references, without which the manuscript could not be published. Cavaillès, in short, has left us a work which is complete but not completely polished. When the clarity of the text or of the citations seemed to us to require the addition here and there of some expletive, we have always placed it in brackets. All the notes at the bottom of the pages are ours, with the exception of three indicated as being by the author. With regard to the citations between quotation marks, it will often be observed that they are rather free though always faithful in spirit. This should not surprise us, given the conditions under which Cavaillès worked and his working method as revealed by his other works. The title of the work, *On Logic and the Theory of Science*, is ours. For it is clearly not a treatise on logic. And since this text represents a part of the complete work but lacks the introduction projected by Cavaillès, there was no ground for considering a title standing for the whole. The title we have proposed is more a formality than a program and withholds all reference to the spirit of the doctrine it covers. It is simply the resumé of the reading, without premeditation or rethinking.

The decision to publish this text as it stands, without an introduction, was made by the family and a group of Cavaillès' friends. It seemed that an explanatory introduction made by anyone but himself could after all only be a commentary, bringing to light that level of philosophical and mathematical culture which Cavaillès precisely wished to be taken for granted, no doubt judging that those who did not make the effort to understand did not deserve to be enlightened.

We now present this text to the public with the assurance that it will raise, through its own importance and through comparison with the other works of our friend, all sorts of problems related to the profound intention and to the genuine significance of a work so tragically interrupted. That these problems cannot honestly receive their necessary solution will only render more striking the void left in philosophy by the death of him who rests in the cemetery at Arras, under the cross which identifies him as "Unknown No. 5." ‡

Strasbourg   GEORGES CANGUILHEM
May, 1946   CHARLES EHRESMANN

CAVAILLES' TEXT

IT IS SAID in the *Course on Logic* [of Kant] that to have recourse to psychology would be "as absurd as to draw morality from life. It is not a matter of contingent rules (how we think) but of necessary rules, which must be drawn from the necessary usage of the understanding, which we find in ourselves without psychology." [1] Yet the beginning of the *Course* unfortunately

‡ On November 11, 1946, the body of Jean Cavaillès was placed in the crypt of the chapel at the Sorbonne.

1. *Immanuel Kants Werke,* ed. Ernst Cassirer, 11 vols. (Berlin, 1912–18), Vol. VIII: *Logik,* p. 134. (References to the Cassirer edition are hereafter cited as "Cassirer.")

recalls that of Arnauld. "Everything in nature happens according to rules, including the exercise of our faculties. Likewise the understanding . . . Understanding is to be considered as the source of rules in general. But according to what rules does understanding itself proceed? We cannot think and use our understanding except in conformity to certain rules." [2] In other words, science is the product of certain faculties, understanding and reason. Logic can only be defined afterwards in relation to these faculties, even though it claims to direct them. An abstract definition of these faculties will no doubt be given. Understanding, the source of rules, is "the power of judgment," and all of the judgments are functions of the unity of our representations, while a function must be understood as "the unity of the action of ordering different representations under a common representation." [3] But it remains that the notions of action and of power, which make sense only by referring to a concrete consciousness, intervene here in a fundamental way, not to mention the notions of order and of unity which, far from defining logic, are posterior to it.

The necessity of rules, i.e., their unconditioned normative character, thus remains subordinate to the absolute of a consciousness whose presence and essential structure—which is consciousness in itself—are an irreducible which no rational content defines. There is nothing prior to consciousness. But what is important is what is being thought here, not directly attained or intuitively posited in an original act. What is important, for the definition of logic as well as for any discipline, is the initial term to which a development will be connected in an intelligible way. The test of the theory of consciousness as far as logic is concerned is the determination which it provides of the content of these apodictic rules.

Here again we discover the kinship to Port-Royal. Logic is no longer a matter of a reflection of the mind upon its acts. Instead, it is "knowledge through themselves of the understanding and of reason according to form." [4] Understanding and reason, no matter how abstractly they may be described, remain powers of the

2. *Ibid.,* p. 332.
3. *Ibid.,* p. 408. In fact, the definitions cited by Cavaillès are found exactly in this form not in the *Logic* but in the *Critique of Pure Reason,* Transcendental Analytic, bk. 1, chap. 1, sec. 1.
4. *Ibid.,* p. 333.

irreducible consciousness and as such are characterized by the property of an internal self-illumination. The act is present to itself and can thus determine itself. But what is an immediate determination which would not be realization, and how to separate it from its singularity? The problem of method (or of rule) is resolved here by recourse to the notion of form.

It is because the self-knowledge of understanding and of reason take place "according to form" that they are possible—inasmuch as they bear on an absolute whose form yields their results—and that they produce a necessity. By recourse to form, the philosophy of consciousness strengthens itself and likewise illuminates itself, at least the way Kant presents it. In fact, the ambiguity of the formulas in which the nature of the invocation of our thought intervenes then becomes inoffensive. The starting point is indeed the actual, the immediate experience of an actual consciousness with its empirical accidents, but the absolute finds itself isolated as a result of a double process of elimination.

In the first place, the contingent is expressly rejected from it insofar as it finds itself implicated in a concrete experience. This is the passage from the empirical to the pure or to the a priori. There are two movements here: a positive one in which the a priori reveals itself independent of all experiences and conditioning them, as in mathematics; a negative one insofar as the empirical manifests its essential fragility in the unpredictability of its characters, in its inclusion of that which to some degree is unlawful. One of the fundamental difficulties of Kantianism appears here, in the positing of something totally empirical which, radically heterogeneous to the concept, does not permit itself to be unified by it. If experience is the singularity of an instant, no imaginative synthesis can integrate it into the unity of consciousness. The application of the synthesis as an act upon a datum presupposes a preliminary definition of the datum, as any sort of possibility that can be considered independent of the act. It is thus already in consciousness, as an element which is positively perceived and in a certain relationship with the act—unless the act alone is considered. In other words, a negative positing of the empirical, even if it were only to eliminate it, is inadmissible. Since what is at stake through its rejection is the securing of pure consciousness, there must be a way of relating it to something else. But in essence this "something else" is not consciousness. It accordingly eludes all attempts to grasp it, and the suspicion arises that this pseudo-empirical is only the consciousness once again, denying itself in a game in which it is the first to be deceived, leaving no way of distinguishing in itself degrees of absoluteness or of necessity except through the intelligible sequence of the contents themselves. But then it is these contents which must be attained; they are really what is essential in their movement, and the primordial pseudo-experience of the consciousness dissipates before the autonomous dynamism which they manifest and which no longer leaves room for anything but them. A purification takes place only in a setting where all the levels can be situated and be given meaning. If it were merely a nothing of intelligibility, the impure could not be deleted. But the doubt rebounds upon the positive movement. If the a priori is an a priori of condition, like the representation of space in relation to perception or mathematical thought in relation to physical thought, both condition and conditioned must be located within a system, or at least may be considered as such. Accordingly, either the kind of connection between them is already given—which presupposes a known logic to posit this absolute consciousness which is to reveal it and upon which it depends—or it is uniquely realized each time; but then it is the sequence itself which of necessity will take its course, and it will no longer be a question of purification.

The second elimination isolates the formal from the material. But the notion of matter is a limit notion, in itself devoid of meaning. This is what Hegel was obliged to affirm. "A matter (or content) without its concept is something extraconceptual, therefore without essence." [5] Here therefore we can no longer proceed positively. But a process of radical abstraction seems to provide the solution. "General logic abstracts from every content of knowledge, i.e., from every relation of knowledge to its objects." [6] Not only are the objective contents neglected but also the way in which they present themselves to knowledge. The formal coincides with the act of thinking in general, i.e., with the act of unifying diverse representations under a single one. It

5. *Greater Logic:* Introduction to the third book, *On the Concept in General,* ed. Lasson, vol. II (IV of the *Complete Works*), p. 232. We owe the communication of this reference to the kindness of André Kaan.
6. *Critique of Pure Reason,* Transcendental Logic, Introduction (Cassirer, III, 82.)

s not a question of thinking this empty thought or of carrying
out the abstraction itself, but of having the assurance that logic
exists even when every object is set aside, characterized as an
internal armature not directly attainable by consciousness but
which posits it as an original essence in the presence of the
object. "Similarly universal grammar comprises the simple form
of language in general," [7] without the words which belong to the
language, where language in general equally eludes every concrete grasp. It remains to be seen whether the comparison is not
lame, whether logic thus defined can actually be realized. First,
the notion of a universal language raises serious difficulties. In
particular, the words—or semantic system—certainly do not
represent a matter in relation to the corresponding syntactic
system, but both admit of elements of variation and permanent
elements. Then, the process of abstraction is here applied to
something actually concrete for which, on the one hand, the
process of positive elimination can be realized (by the finite and
actual comparison of different languages), and [for which] on
the other hand there is a possibility of dissociating individually
verifiable concrete totalities from the intelligible connections
heterogeneous to them, inasmuch as these concatenations unify
them. The abstraction which gives logic its radical character
falls to the ground. This abstraction does not acquire a positive
qualification either from the aspect of matter, since it bears on
the indefinite "every object," or from that of form. How is a
science possible if it has only the notions of unity, plurality, and
representation at its disposal? What can be drawn from the
requirement of the agreement of thought with itself except eternal repetition? In order for agreement to assume its full meaning, there must at least be a differentiation within thought, and
the occasion for disagreement must already possess a content.
But then logic would be transcendental or dialectical logic. Now
general dialectic or a cathartic of the understanding is unlaw-
fully grafted onto logic. The notion of negation is no more a part
of the preceding definition of logic than the notions of concept,
judgment, reasoning, and method. To be sure, we can repeat the
radical operation for each of them, eliminating all objective
content and regaining that pure form of unity. But the disturbing thing is that we always regain a selfsame unity and that

7. *Logik,* Cassirer, VIII, 332.

there is no way—which may not forfeit the abstract—to tie these four unities together. It is because the actual consciousness establishes definite relations between them that the four abstractions realized separately permit the supposition of the persistence of abstract relations. But can we indicate them by referring to nothing but the emptiness of logical identity? What is the subject and the predicate, what are the categories defining the judgment, the rational sequences or science in general, if we do not refer to an ontology, as Aristotle's two *Analytics* do or as another analytic after Leibniz outlined. There must be a substrate or substance in order to distinguish subject and predicate. The act of judgment must be acknowledged as an act that can be reached as such and linked with the act of reasoning. But a direct characterization presupposes knowledge, i.e., construction of the object of the concept (here judgment and reasoning) in intuition. Now Kant refuses to make logic into "an algebra by which hidden truths can be discovered." [8] He likewise refuses to identify general logic with transcendental logic.

Yet these were the only two ways to make logic into a body of knowledge, since in the second case "it has before it a manifold of the sensibility which the transcendental aesthetic offers to it in order to give a matter to the pure concept of the understanding." [9] For the rest, the Transcendental Aesthetic does not play a necessary role here, as the abstract part of the transcendental deduction shows by considering only the unifying activity of thought in the presence of a receptivity supplying the matter of its objects—without the intervention of the proper forms of this receptivity. What is important is the synthesis performed by the understanding upon a sense manifold, i.e., the primordial logical operation. "The same function which gives unity to different representations in a judgment also gives unity to the simple synthesis of different representations in an intuition, a unity which in general terms is called the pure concept of the understanding." [10] But what is this concept outside of the synthetic act? We clearly see that Kant wants to respect the possibility of an understanding which would not receive the manifold to be unified from any other faculty, but would produce

8. *Ibid.*, p. 339.
9. *Critique of Pure Reason*, Transcendental Analytic, bk. 1, chap. 1, sec. 3, § 10 (2d ed., 1787). (Cassirer, III, 96).
10. *Ibid.* (Cassirer, III, 97–98.)

it itself. "We do not have the slightest conception of such a power."[11] So we ask ourselves if such an understanding would have something in common with the one which the formalizing analysis isolates and whose legislation defines logic. "The same understanding . . . , through the same acts [by which] it established the logical form of a judgment in the concept [in availing itself] of the analytic unity also brings a transcendental content into its representations by means of the synthetic unity of the manifold in intuition in general, by reason of which they are called pure concepts of the understanding, applying themselves a priori to objects which general logic cannot realize."[12]

The formal priority of analytic unity over synthetic unity consequently becomes at least dubious. Where can this analysis truly be realized? Here we have reference not only to *consciousness* but to *a world* which it would think and whose plural structure would be preserved by the process of abstraction. This is actually what the *Course in Logic* makes explicit when the traditional definitions are considered: "A concept is a representation according to common or discursive notes."[13] It originates from three classical operations: *comparison* of three representations among themselves, in relation to the unity of consciousness, *reflection* on the possibility of understanding different representations in one consciousness, finally *abstraction* which suppresses everything in which the representations differ. In other words, the unity of the empirical concept must be borrowed from experience; it is the analysis of a datum. But if the abstraction which isolates the understanding retains this analytical character, it must maintain the notion of a determining datum. We then no longer see how to come back to the synthetic stage. If our interpretation of the reference to consciousness is correct, when the elimination of what is extrinsic makes the absolute nucleus appear, this cannot be the same understanding which was synthetic at a step of lesser abstraction and becomes analytic at its extremity—no more, for that matter, than the possibility of analysis being a foundation for synthesis. If the philosophy of consciousness can provide a logic, it must arrive at an irreducible act, the act of unification. From the transcendental deduction, we sense almost fully the malaise which comes

11. *Ibid.,* bk. 1, chap. 2, sec. 2, § 17 (*in fine*). (Cassirer, III, 119.)
12. *Ibid.,* bk. 1, chap. 1, sec. 3, § 10. (Cassirer, III, 98.)
13. *Logik,* Cassirer, VIII, 399.

from the utilization of general logic as a guiding clue and a preliminary ground, received ready-made without critique or justification. But the notions which it uses—quality, quantity, relation—either are of alien origin (and to be justified if they are retained afterwards) or are posterior to the act of synthesis. Besides, how can logic be called transcendental analysis if it does not replace the ancient theory of *logos* in an authenticity without division? The collaboration with traditional logic is impossible. In a philosophy of consciousness logic is transcendental or it is not.

But then it is an ontology at the same time. This is acknowledged clearly enough in the *Report on the Progress of Metaphysics since Leibniz and Wolff,* in order to subordinate it to metaphysics "for which it is only the vestibule." [14] It is a curious thing and a consequence of this dual inspiration that science is not directly subordinated to logic, in spite of the *Analytic of Principles.* In the first place, general logic, reduced to the role of *canon* in relation to science, juxtaposes, following the Port-Royal tradition, a chapter on method to chapters on the concept, the judgment and reasoning. "Just as the elementary doctrine of science has the elements and conditions for the achievement of a knowledge, so the general theory of method, as the other part of logic, deals with the form of a science in general or of the way to tie the manifold of knowledge into a science." [15] This definition represents a change in relation to the Cartesian definition by putting the accent on the formal notion of science, but it could not succeed because of the inadequacy of its theories of judgment and reasoning. Upon the distributive unity of understanding, reason superimposes the collective unity required by the ideas and which has no other instrument than the syllogism. Since its only procedure is subsumption, science would then fatally assume the Aristotelian uniform of a hierarchizing classification.

Now in the second place, on the contrary, for science the *Organon,* i.e., the discipline "which indicates how a particular knowledge must be put on its feet," is "mathematics . . . which contains the foundation of the extension of our knowledge in view of a certain usage of reason." [16] In the *Analytic,* the differ-

14. *Ibid.,* p. 238.
15. *Ibid.,* p. 443.
16. *Ibid.,* pp. 333–34.

ent principles direct or found the extension of our knowledge with the same right as the axioms of intuition. The principle of causality, essential source of questions, is extramathematical. Yet Kant previously declared that there is science only insofar as it is mathematical. Is it simply a matter of expressing relations which are actualized in intuition? But we cannot dissociate a meaning and an expression of a relation: to what extent does causality, tied to the hypothetical judgment, express itself mathematically?

The same difficulty is found in a magnified form in the *Metaphysical Foundations of Natural Science,* where the requirement of a scientific ideal based on the notion of demonstration leads, as a result of its indecision between the syllogism and mathematical construction, to the creation of that pure and necessary part of a science from which its development is deduced through the addition of empirical principles. It is well known how, in the execution of the program, pseudo a priori elements and empirical elements are joined in an inextricable fashion for phoronomy, dynamics, and mechanics. The notions of effective velocity (in a movement distinct from mathematical displacement), of inert force, of active force already presuppose a recourse to experience. But in what do they consist? Is it a matter of a process of incomplete abstraction? We do not see the limit which obliges him to stop, unless it is the extrascientific consideration of a physical universe. Neither do we see, as a consequence, the authority which can come from it. These are hardly simply unelaborated notions from the vernacular which serve as guides here. Now if the subsequent development of science is deductive, therefore analytic, all the empirical elements to come must already be found concentrated in the synthesis which produces these notions. A particular experience either offers no interest or overturns the edifice—unless the demonstration is of a mathematical order, through a construction of concepts. But then the physical concepts must be represented completely within mathematics, which Kant does not admit and which moreover raises the difficulty of the specific character of physical construction in relation to mathematical construction.

Finally, mathematical demonstration is hardly defined with clarity. The validity of the construction which permits one to start from the concept is based on the unity of the formal intuition of space. But the extraintellectual character of this intuition renders illusory every effort to transform any science whatsoever into a deductive system, beginning with geometry. The Euclidean model itself—perhaps unknown to Kant—is impossible to maintain. In fact, geometry would consist of nothing more than findings connected to each other, with the connecting bond having no other authority than the autonomous affirmation of an act. Here again it is the recourse to consciousness which is indispensable. [But] can we speak of an irreducible element when it is no longer a matter of pure thought but of a sensible thought whose form seems as arbitrary as the spatial form? As for the unity of the latter form, it is a simple postulate which the uniformity of development of geometry could guarantee, if this unity existed and if it were legitimate to consider it within the Kantian system that destroys it.

The authority of method, as logical canon as well as mathematical organon, is thus reduced to the preeminence of a formality which does not even have an irreducible simplicity to guarantee it. Transcendental Analytic can indeed procure for science its framework, since "all of the empirical laws are only particular determinations of the pure laws of the understanding,"[17] so that "understanding is not only a power of making rules for itself through the comparison of phenomena, but is itself the legislation for nature."[18] The type of science, its striving toward a classical mathematical type as well as its mathematical extension, completely neglects the bearing of the object on the structure of the theory. The theory is given in advance once and for all. The indifference to the object, the third characteristic of the Port-Royal Logic, is thus represented here by the subordination of matter to a form which tends to absorb it, even in the case of mathematization. There is no science as an autonomous reality and characterizable as such, but a rational unification, according to a fixed type, of a manifold already organized by the understanding, or a survey of a mass of evidence without plan or discovery.

Two possibilities are still open for the theory of science along Kantian lines, depending on whether the accent is put on the notion of demonstrative system or on that of mathematical orga-

17. *Critique of Pure Reason*, Transcendental Analytic, bk. 1, chap. 2, sec. 3 (*in fine*) (1st ed. 1781). (Cassirer, III, 627.)
18. *Ibid.*

non. To the first belongs the logical conception inaugurated by Bolzano and continued simultaneously and in different ways by the formalists and by Husserl. To the second belong the epistemological philosophies of immanence, as the philosophies of Leon Brunschvicg and Brouwer may be labeled.

It is perhaps preferable to forego the examination of the latter until our scientific epistemology has been systematically developed. The notions which they invoke are too closely tied to the development of science for it to be possible to specify them in the course of a simple classification of points of view. Besides, Brouwer's mathematical philosophy, arising from a technical problem, has been interpreted in different ways. Thus H. Weyl, in admitting that he is faithful to the orthodoxy of the school, wishes to relate himself to Husserl.[19] Yet it seems that the true thought of the master, expressed for example in *Mathematik, Wissenschaft und Sprache*,[20] or in the works of Heyting, is oriented in a different direction. In the first place, mathematics is an autonomous becoming, "more an act than a becoming," for which a definition at the origin is impossible but whose moments in their necessary interdependence betray an original essence. From the dyad to the elaborated theories, there is continuity and unpredictability. The only kinship with Husserl is the reference to an act. But this generative act and criterion of true mathematics must situate itself concretely, submit itself to conditions of actual accomplishment. If there is accordingly no method in the traditional sense, there is in fact a domination of the course of science by rules. They can in truth be modified at any time, according to the theory to which they are applied. Nevertheless, they have a common principle, the requirement of a positive constructibility, the refusal of an existential affirmation which refers to a collectivity merely posited in the abstract by virtue of an indefinite state [translating itself], when all is said and done, through a negation (or an indetermination): refusal of the excluded middle and above all of nonpredicative definitions. What relation this rule has to traditional logic, and to what extent it can replace or transform it, is what in part is specified by the formal developments of Heyting and above all by the role

19. On the same subject, see Cavaillès' note in *Méthode axiomatique et formalisme* (Paris: Hermann, 1938), p. 33.

20. *Monatsheft für Mathematik und Physik*, XXXVI (1929), 153–64.

played by the intuitionist doctrine in the problem of the foundations of mathematics. Formal ontology as well as a more detailed realization of mathematical epistemology must then intervene. We can only discuss two difficulties here. First of all, the reflection on the essence of mathematics—which founds the intuitionist norm—must be situated in relation to the spontaneous movement of its becoming, since it demands an amputation or rather a redress of classical mathematics. It is a question of knowing whether there is a reference to an absolute consciousness characterizable in other respects, to the content of concepts submitted to a dialectic which itself can also be apprehended, or finally to the irreducible specificity of the mathematical movement. But then the second question poses itself: how to distinguish the mathematical movement within the general advance of science or even of culture? "Mathematics," says Brouwer, "is the ordering of the world, rational thought of the world"—without submitting the terms "world" and "rationality" to any further critique. The relation to physics in particular remains vague. If every science is defined as a type according to Brouwer's rule, it is because here again mathematics serves as an organon, but to such an extent that it absorbs the rest. It has been observed that intuitionist mathematics is particularly useful in modern physics. Is it not because the intuitionist attitude is first of all the attitude of the physicist, because the representation of a world, in which the mathematical act is performed and which determines it by furnishing it with at least a point of departure and a point of application, remains a primordial and perhaps a dominating element? The independence of a direct theory of science thus finds itself rather gravely handicapped. However seductive it may be at first, and however supple its utilization in being thus linked with the advance of science, such an attitude leaves too many initial questions open, perhaps also too many vague ones at the end of the road, to be able to eliminate without further ado the other logical points of view.

The same remark applies to Brunschvicg's epistemology. In reaction against the logicism of Frege and Russell in which it saw a renewal of the Aristotelian tradition, it places thought, as a creation escaping every norm, in juxtaposition with its linguistic expression, which as a social phenomenon falls within the ambit of both the illusions of the city and the laws of nature. The requirement of communication on the one hand pushes to the absolute that which was only a movement within a progression and which took on its true sense in the transition which it realizes and on the other hand transposes it into a system whose structure (e.g., the deductive syllogistic form) finds its justification within an organization or a social history which are themselves only parts of nature. The *idola tribus* is the revolution of the past, asleep and petrified; the presumed canon of science is a rule of pedagogy. Thus the disputes over the Cantorian infinite simply mark the resistance to a new creative thrust; likewise the periodic reappearances of the same paradoxes, like that of Epimenides, proof of the incapacity of language to express the indeterminate power of thought. But this indetermination itself remains a problem. The progress of consciousness is undoubtedly detected not externally through an increase in the volume of its results, but through an intensity by means of the spiritual enrichment that refined concepts attain or through a unification of disciplines previously separated. It remains that progress by its very essence appears [only] after it is realized, that as a consequence the science which as such detects it on the one hand locates itself with difficulty, and on the other cannot claim to dominate science. This is moreover not Leon Brunschvicg's wish: rational immanence eludes every grasp outside of the idea. But is there still room for a philosophy which is not a simple explicitation of the scientist's intentions? Can it even be asserted that the history of progress still does not remain external, a useful cathartic for the scientist to protect him from social temptations, but that only the actual sequence of intelligible contents is on the level of the spirit? Even that cannot be satisfying. The terms of spirituality and immanence presuppose the possibility of an asceticism or of a deepening of consciousness other than simply scientific comprehension. What is needed is either the absolute of intelligibility which legitimizes the Spinozist superposition of the idea of an idea, or the reference to a generative consciousness which has the property of grasping itself immediately in its authentic acts. In both cases an ontological analysis seems necessary. On the other hand, no answer is given to the questions of epistemology. Here again all the sciences are intertwined in the same movement. In particular, it is impossible to distinguish mathematics and the science of nature. The being of the world, of a world posited externally and which it is the vocation of consciousness to reduce to terms of interiority, subsists as a determining condition of science. To know the world, to comprehend the world—here is a program which already represents an abandonment of creative autonomy, a surrender to a necessity which is related to nothing other than itself.

Emphasis on the necessary character of science is precisely Bolzano's overriding concern. Science is above all demonstrated theory. Bolzano in the *Rein Analytischer Beweis* [21] took issue with the overly facile recourse to evidence, an evidence that Descartes invoked only for the simple natures and which for Kant regulated all geometric reasoning. The crisis of growth of algebra then required a change in the type of evidence, as is shown in the *Stages of Mathematical Philosophy*.[22] For Bolzano, it was a matter of the radical transformation of verification into demonstration. On the mathematical level the inspiration is Cartesian, an achievement of intellectualization through analytical geometry, an achievement made necessary by infinitesimal calculus. The paradox of the actually infinite obliges one to reject the geometric continuum as a simple nature. Now, already the syncategorematic infinite of differential calculus claims a reference to a truly unique infinite as an absolute term. Thus in Leibniz, however much he rejects the infinite number—and does not see the possibility of a plurality of infinites—the actual division of matter at the infinite makes the arbitrarily small increment of a variable possible. Wherever we stop we hit upon an existing element that can serve as an extreme to the increment. The well-founded phenomenon of space has its intelligible base in the infinite extranumerical multiplicity of monads. Aside from other motives—philosophical or historical—Leibniz has a reason for relating mathematics to logic. Not only spatial intuition but number as well is relegated to the level of the imagination, inasmuch as it is by nature repugnant to the infinite, according to the classical antinomies reviewed by Leibniz' contemporaries. Through a revolutionary reversal, it is number which is driven out of the realm of perfect rationality and the infinite which comes into it. But it is no longer a question of the human intellect embracing a complete sequence in a single glance, even if this is only the system of the terms of a series.

21. (Prague, 1817). New ed. by B. Jourdain (Leipzig: Engelmann, 1905).
22. By Leon Brunschvicg (Paris: Alcan, 1912).

The necessary bond seen between two terms guarantees the whole. The power of extension by iteration or combination is both a source of novelty and a caution of intelligibility. In the divine understanding, the rational homogeneity of the finite and the infinite is thus expressed in the universality of logic. What is necessary is what can be demonstrated. This is the source of Leibniz' idea of the *ars combinatoria* and of the universal outlines of science and of the *ars characteristica*. The poverty of the means employed should not obscure the sense and direction of the enterprise. Total science thus defined posits the absolute and represents the only way of attaining a part of it.

Bolzano considers—and fails to resolve—the same problems of mathematical legitimacy. After the difficulties with the principles of infinitesimal calculus with which the eighteenth century was embroiled, it was he who first correctly defined the limit and introduced the notion of set, from which a twofold philosophical enrichment of the Leibnizian vein emerged. First of all, the very being of science is submitted to critique, in order to determine both what constitutes a science as such and the motive for its development. If we put aside the imperfections due to the times, the idea is decisive for our problem. Perhaps for the first time, science is no longer considered as a simple intermediary between the human mind and being in itself, depending as much on one as on the other and not having its own reality. Now science is regarded as an object *sui generis,* original in its essence, autonomous in its movement. It is no more an absolute than an element in the system of existing things. If we can speak of a science of a country or of an epoch, we do not mean something which may be included among the natural realities, but affirmations localized in space and time within the sociological phenomenon and belonging to science. Hence science is not even situated within the universe of cultural objects, characterized by the participation in a value which such objects manifest. On the one hand, contrary to these, its mode of actualization is extrinsic to it and not so closely tied to value that this may, as with a work of art, essentially implicate it in the accidental exteriority of a sensory system. On the other hand, it requires unity, i.e., it cannot be reconciled with an actual multiplicity of singular realizations. There are not different sciences or different moments of one science, not even the immanence of a single science in various disciplines. But these disciplines are conditioned among themselves in such a way that the results as well as the meaning of one science require, insofar as it is a science, the utilization of others or the common inclusion within a system.[23] A theory of science can only be a theory of the unity of science.

This unity is a movement. Since it is a question here not of a scientific ideal but of realized science, incompleteness and the requirement of progress are part of its definition. Simply an autonomous progress, a self-enclosed dynamism, without absolute beginning or end, science moves outside of time—if time signifies a reference to the lived experience of a consciousness. In it, change is growth in volume through the spontaneous generation of intelligible elements. On the one hand, every concept or system of concepts, through that which it poses to itself, is at once exclusion and need of the Other. In this sense, the representation of an absolutely simple infinitude of all knowledge is an image without any relation to the reality of militant science other than pushing to the limit a property of movement, namely, the absorption of the prior by the posterior which justifies it and to a certain extent suppresses it. But the road should not be abolished, if we want it to be followed. The true sense of a theory is not in an aspect understood by the scientist himself as essentially provisional, but in a conceptual becoming which cannot be stopped. On the other hand, even for the sciences of nature growth occurs without external borrowing. There is a break between sensation or right opinion and science. Experience, far from being insertion into nature, is on the contrary the incorporation of the world into the scientific universe. Even if its sense is not elucidated, even if it appears as an opaque body, an obstacle to theories actually thought, its value as experience lies at once in its detachment from a world of singularity and exteriority, where that which is does not have significance beyond its actual (and determined) existence, and in the virtual unification over which it must necessarily preside some day. Thus scientific autonomy is simultaneously expansion and closure, negative closure in its refusal to borrow from or terminate in what is external to it. If total knowledge does not make sense—there is a hiatus with an absolute consciousness as real as the one with opinion, so that there can be no question of either preparing for

23. Whence the idea of a hierarchy according to relations of dependence, with a subordinated science utilizing the results of the preceding ones as regulative principles. [Cavaillès' note.]

it or starting toward it—neither does radical extrascientific knowledge. In order for it to be posited as outside, it would have to be placed on the same plane and would therefore already be an experience. Science is a Riemannian volume which can at once be closed and without anything external to it. No method issuing from this theory of science can recover the Cartesian decision: *sub scientia non cadit*.

The difficulty soon appears not only in justifying and specifying these characters but in situating the discipline which posits them. The theory of science is also a claim to validity and to intelligibility. It wishes to be the science of science and therefore a part of itself. Accordingly, its assertions must not be constitutive of a particular development but must appear immediately in a self-illumination of the scientific movement, yet distinguishing themselves from this by their permanent emergence. Such is the role of structure. In defining a structure of science which is only a manifestation to itself of what it is, we specify and justify the preceding characteristics, not by an explication which would have its proper place and would in its turn be an object of reflection, but by a revelation which is not distinct from the revealed, present in its movement, a principle of its necessity. The structure speaks about itself. But it is only a way of imposing itself with an authority which borrows nothing from the outside; it is only a mode of unconditional affirmation, the demonstration. The structure of science not only is demonstration but is identified with demonstration. In it the essential traits are again encountered: unity, necessary and indefinite progression, finally closure upon itself. The internal rule which directs it posits each of its steps; it is entirely in them and impossible to grasp *ne varietur* in any of them. We are reminded of Descartes' difficulty with the connecting evidences—or simple natures. The toe holds can be multiplied, and if the demonstrating link consisted in these, others would have to be superimposed upon them indefinitely. There is in reality no essential distinction between the hardened rings which seem to mark the terms and the movement that traverses them. But the movement does not stop. Demonstration, simply by the fact that it posits the goal, extends and ramifies the domain created by means of combinations which it establishes as soon as they are possible. Finally it cannot be allied with the undemonstrated. We again meet the Platonic reserve against the *dianoia* which lends its hypothesis to the visible world, an arrangement without justification from which nothing necessary can follow. True science does not depart from the demonstrated. The modern conception of hypothetico-deductive systems is subject to the same critique. How can a principle or a union of principles, which in their content and in their totality are not themselves intelligible, be the starting point for an intelligible development? The heterogeneous alliance of a verified pure concrete and a mode of rational sequence is a simple image without thought. If there is science, it is entirely demonstration, i.e., logic.

The problem which then arises is the apprehension of this principle in its generating movement, to find this structure again, not by description but apodictically, insofar as it elaborates itself and demonstrates itself. In other words, the theory of science is an a priori, not prior to science but the soul of science, not having external requisites but requiring science in its turn. There is a twofold difficulty with Bolzano's solution. If it avoids subordination to a historical existent or to the absolute of consciousness, it must itself posit the totality of what it attains, to discern afterwards, if it can, the permanent essential element of what is mobile through it. It is, on the one hand, a construction of a pure theory of rational sequences, and on the other a relationship to science as it has developed. Without the resolution of these problems, scientific epistemology cannot constitute itself directly as primary, which is its ambition. But it is posterior to the analytic which gives content to its object, and to ontology which brings the object into being.

II

THE TENDENCY of a faithful theory of science is such that the demonstrable is not given its proper due. But unity does not mean uniformity: within the identity of its essence, the demonstrative can assume many aspects. Two dimensions in particular can be distinguished: a realm of singularities where the demonstrated adheres to the demonstration to the point of being indiscernible from it and characterizing a single moment of science; and the set of sequences in the strict sense which, although they are indispensable only to the extent that they actually demonstrate something and as a result cannot be renewed in their integrity, present a kinship of type according to groups, a mark of the unity of movements which can be manifested in the abstract. Thus emerges the notion of logical form indispensable to a theory of demonstration. The process of separation is two-fold: longitudinal, coextensive with the demonstrative sequence; vertical, establishing a new system of conjunction that uses the old as a base from which to start, no longer as a stage traversed by a movement but as an object of reflection in its true bearing. In each case, a property constitutive of the essence of thought (or of intelligible sequences) manifests itself: the *paradigm* and the *thematic*.

The *paradigm* is characteristic of the actualization, not of an actualization *hic et nunc* in the lived experience from which the extrinsic is eliminated, in the simple seizure of thought by itself, but of an actualization required by the sense of what is posited, i.e., a relationship which as such is affirmed only in the singularity of realization of the sequence, but which calls for this singularity only in an indefinite way; it therefore suppresses it in positing it and thereby reveals an internal principle of variation. From arithmetical reasoning on the finite integer to the most abstract sequences, the same liberating dissociation of meaning occurs. "If *it is* is said of the one which is and of the *one* of being one, and if being and one are not the same thing but equally belong to this thing . . . does it not necessarily follow that the one which is is a whole and that one and being are its parts?" [24] The being of the relation consists in what it adds to its origin and is therefore different from the necessity which makes it one. In spite of this necessity, it affirms an independence which is translated into relative indifference which in turn is the source of plurality. "And so the one which is will be an infinite plurality." [25] And so already for the identical judgment of identity where the repetition neglects what is repeated; so for each of those mathematical moves where the connecting act, as soon as it is realized, becomes the connecting type; so for that indefinite flight toward meaning which, liberated as a result of the intelligible setting and fabricated from it, immediately escapes "as in a dream" and thereby posits its originality as well. This alone is what makes polymorphy in the single rational sequence possible, those suc-

24. Parmenides 142d. [Cavaillès' note.]
25. Parmenides 143a. [Cavaillès' note.]

cessive fractures of independence which on each occasion un-leash upon what comes before the imperious profile of what necessarily comes after, in order to surpass it. The synthesis that Kant discloses within thought requires no furnished or different manifold, but simply itself, which is a multiplicity through its moments and its progress. What is unified is not given in advance as diverse, for how could it be given if not already within a synthesis? And to presuppose it for an analysis is to transform it in spatial imagination. What is unified is really the elaboration of the acts insofar as each of them, forgetting and realizing itself at once within a meaning, posits its own being only as an element of a set recognized as a plurality and at once as a basis from which to initiate new acts.

And so the synthesis is coextensive with the production of what is synthesized. The later developments will furnish examples of this. What is important here is the disengagement brought about with each suppression of singularity. This is what is represented in logical calculus by the rule of substitution, i.e., the possibility of replacing in the new element that from which it actually proceeds with something else equivalent to it from the new point of view.

This is the source of the distinction at each step between matter, the singularity as origin, and form, the actual meaning. This is likewise the source of a distinction which, when projected into the absolute, would extend from one end of the general sequence to the other, like a continuous flaw through the nodes of the particular distinctions. It is an image favored by language, sometimes the consequence of an ontology as well. The illegitimacy of it is evident, since it misunderstands what it generalizes, namely, the motive of the necessarily progressive passage from the act to its meaning. There is no meaning without an act, and no new act without the meaning which produces it. It remains that we can, for a certain length of the rational chain, by placing ourselves immediately at the last term, consider its meaning as the unique form all along the successions of acts. We proceed in this way in the systematic exposition of a mathematical theory, where the initial inventory of the proceedings springs both from the analysis of the final meaning of the sequences and from the artifice which consists in considering these chains as preparations for this meaning without intermediate or ultimate renewal. This is the *moment of the variable:* in replacing the determinations of acts by the place vacated for a substitution, we progressively raise ourselves to a degree of abstraction which gives the illusion of an irreducible formality. This is what Leibniz tried in passing to the absolute through the mirage of an infinite whose simplicity makes conditions and conditioned simultaneous. Such are the attempts toward the algebraic or geometric art of characteristic, the theory of determinants, the symbolism of infinitesimal calculus, where in each instance the desire to preserve only what is essential manifests itself. Such finally is the reduction of all judgments to the predicative judgment, of all reasoning to repetition or to the distribution of a single and identical formula. Here the spatial image of juxtaposition, the utilization of an elementary combinatory, which preserves the simple characters of the finite as it reveals itself to itself (resigned to justifying every hiatus in an opaque way) within the infinite, are at once tied to the origin of the enterprise and a cause of its failure.

But formalization is realized only when the rules which regulate the structures are systematically superimposed on their outline. *Thematization* [26] takes its start in the sequence seized en route, a trajectory which moves toward meaning. Thought no longer goes toward the created term but starts from the modes of creating in order to provide its principle through an abstraction of the same nature as the other one, but directed transversely. The theory of the syllogism provides some rudimentary examples—*nota notae est nota rei ipsius* and other rules—where we see that it is a matter not of grinding out a general model under which all the species of syllogisms can be ordered but of a new intelligible development taking its start in the *vis probandi* of the argument. The works of Kant and Lachelier are in this direction, in contrast with the classifying tradition of forms.

But the most numerous examples appear in mathematics: theory of groups, theory of linear operations, of matrices, topology of topological transformations. If Leibniz was here again a precursor, the rules which he gives scarcely surpass the trivial, and we must wait for Hankel and especially Grassman for a systematic development. These efforts toward an effective theory of operations are the historical origin of the calculi of Boole,

26. Here begins the examination of the second of the processes of separation distinguished on p. 375.

Schröder, and Frege and the general formal systems. The process is in itself not conditioned solely by the structured character of the sequences whose principle is the morphological law but by the very dissociation between meaning and act which longitudinally gives the general principle. The preceding analysis was incomplete. In the moment which liberates the meaning, there appears a duality between *positing meaning* and *posited meaning,* between the signification of an operation as "operated" or *performed*—apart from the problem whose exigency created its active singularity and stripped of the accidental character of its starting point through the possible substitution—and its signification as *operating,* i.e., no longer the sense of the passage but of its *quomodo,* where the result is no longer considered in its essence, however pure it may have become, but in its simple position of a result which results, consequently an indication of the modes which have produced it and to which our interest returns. Thus addition, which the longitudinal process renders indifferent to numbers, with letters being added, becomes multiplication or abstract addition, for which the transversal process gives the laws of associativity and of commutativity. In the first case, the notion is purified following in some way the same lines, by the positing of increasingly abstract forms. In the second, the new form which is constituted by the principles of the first appears on another level.

The dual interplay of the two processes is evident. On the one hand, not only are both born from the same emergence of meaning, but also the abstraction of the first favors the second. This manifests itself in the descriptive definitions of certain very elementary notions (powers of irrational exponents, Lebesgue's integral) where it is important not to misunderstand that it is a question of the position of the new act, prolonging the previous acts in spite of the rupture, since it includes them as a particular case. The transversal process is indeed reinforced by their retroactive influence, as the theory of operations indicates. On the other hand, like all meaning the positing meaning as an act for longitudinal development, i.e., every positing meaning is at the same time a posited meaning of another act (which may recall the traditional principle that every idea has a formal reality). Thus, as soon as it is initiated, the movement of deepening makes way for a new sequence of the first species. The idea of the idea manifests its generative power on the level which it defines without prejudice to an unlimited superposition. Henceforth the problem is posited equally for relations between longitudinal developments tied to two positing senses of acts situated at distinct points of the same inferior longitudinal development. Here we have an unlimited intelligible complication which at once shows how the image of the separation between matter and form in the rational sequence was simplistic and how a systematic study of forms is indispensable. There is no formalism without syntax, no syntax without another formalism which develops it.

The theory of rational sequences (judgments, reasoning, systems of reasoning) is thereby not only justified in its claims but situated and initiated in its development. If the accidental is excluded, if both necessary form and principles are brought to light, formalizing is a process of founding. The theory of science takes over the heritage of logic, surpassing even its ambitions. Insofar as it identifies itself with the system of all possible formalisms, it absorbs rather than canonizes the totality of formalizable demonstrations, and so the totality of science. This was the solution at the time of Frege and Dedekind. Mathematics is a part of logic, which here means that there is nothing more in mathematics than certain formal systems. And it neglects the problem of a demonstrative knowledge external to formalisms, so that their relation to formalisms, e.g., in physics, remained undetermined. The progress made from Frege to contemporary logicists like Carnap and Tarski coincides with the distinction of the two meanings: logical theory does not have its justification in their revelation but is the second meaning, inasmuch as this meaning is developed longitudinally in acts; logical theory is not the totality of formal systems but the totality of syntaxes of all the formal systems. Here is the source of the principle of tolerance, which Carnap placed at the head of his treatise: "In logic there is no canon but the unlimited possibility of choice among the canons." [27] Here is likewise the source of the

27. *Logische Syntax der Sprache* (Vienna: Springer, 1934), § 17. Cavaillès' quotation is not found exactly in this text of Carnap, no more than in *Abriss der Logistik* or in *Der Logische Aufbau der Welt*. On another occasion, in his article on the Vienna Circle at the Prague Congress (*Revue de métaphysique et de morale* [1935]), Cavaillès, in referring to this same principle of tolerance of syntax, quotes a text from page 45: "In logic there is no morality. Each person can construct his form of language as he understands it."

solution to the problem of the relation between mathematics and physics: mathematics is all of the formal systems, and physics is a certain privileged system resulting from the principle of choice that experience constitutes. There is a coordination between formal relation and sense phenomena, by means of an evidence *sui generis* which belongs to the other type of demonstration distinguished, where the demonstration adheres to the demonstrated. It is through this that physical theory is formally determined.

A precise examination of the logicist position requires the actual definition of syntaxes [and] therefore cannot be done here. But from the start two essential difficulties appear. In the first place syntactic formalization: Tarski is one of the first to have clearly dissociated the plane of primary formality and the plane of its syntax, which belongs to another formality. While, prior to this, syntax was defined in ordinary language without appealing to any definite type of demonstration for its deduced laws, its more profound study demands its formalization. But to define the formal system S_1 of the syntax S, we must define the syntax of S_1 which is realized within a system S_2, etc.—an apparently inoffensive regression, since it does not enlarge the base set of all the syntaxes. Although it is a matter of superposition, we find ourselves led to choose, in favor of the syntax of a system S_i on the same level as it, e.g., among the systems S_{i-1} previously defined. This initial system must undoubtedly still be posited. It is a result obtained in the actual act of formalism that every system containing arithmetic can formalize its own syntax. The secondary act for which the positing meaning of the primary act is a posited meaning then coincides with it. There is here a sort of return of thought upon itself which was impossible to predict before its realization and which assumes its true scope only in it.

The difficulty is elsewhere, in the question of knowing how to construct the system which is the basis of all syntaxes. What Carnap calls the general syntax is only a set of abstract rules whose entire précis is still borrowed from actually realized mathematics and from its syntax. The syntactic imagination seems to lose itself in the void of a radical abstraction. With the precisions that have been given, it could even be shown that the paths predicted in advance, where later science was to have busied itself, have remained barren. There is a more serious flaw here than an error in prediction, a misunderstanding of the essentials of formal sequence, namely, that its progress is necessary and in every instance conditioned by the real. A position simultaneous with all those that are possible, even though nonrepresentable and as such simply admitted in order to serve as a basis, is in contradiction with the notion of a formal system whose signification demands a generation through successive thrusts and transcendences. That all may not take place in a single stroke has nothing to do with history but is the characteristic of the intelligible. To misunderstand it is to leave the security of its immediate presence for a projection whose internal emptiness as well as the lapse into the historical appears in connection with the actualizations of a time and their accidental veneer. There is no attainment of an absolute, but a hypostasis of systems and procedures which exist only as transitory. To abstract from the type is not to fix but to arrest the essence.

On the other hand, the formal definition of a system is not complete with the enunciation of the syntax. It is again to the credit of Tarski for having constituted in its originality semantics alongside syntactics as such. It is in fact a question of not only giving the form of statements invested with meaning (rules of *structure*) and the modes of passing from one group of propositions to another (rules of *consecutiveness*) but of defining the objects themselves, the elements and intervening components with their properties in the sequences: variables, functions, individuals, demonstrations, definitions—in short, introducing the concepts of the system. This role of semantics raises a problem which Carnap had already attacked elsewhere, in distinguishing descriptive syntaxes and strictly logical syntaxes. What does describing signify for an intelligible system? The very notion of a complete formal system is at stake here. For an incomplete formalization (i.e., the simple precision of a process of sequence) the separation between positing meaning and posited meaning is immediately manifested without requiring that the reference to its groups of acts to which the meanings are bound should culminate in the organization of these groups into exhaustively defined systems. In other words, the positing meaning of an act *A* appears as the posited meaning of another act *B* without *A* and *B* being expressly related to two distinguished sets, but rather as immediately acknowledged parts of the general group of intelligible sequences, i.e., justifying themselves as such in their very realization. This applies to transitivity, the law of the syllogism of implication, to the properties of operations, to the general calculus of operations. The new operations which intervene bring the evidence of their fulfillment to bear upon the prior operations—or acts. Yet the intermingling of these operative groups of different essences, historically the confusions, the sources of paradoxes which they involve, in itself the internal appeal of their own unities, lead to their ordered reunion into separate systems which borrow nothing from the outside, which are closed, i.e., formal.

The definition of these systems is then external to them, i.e., the positing meaning of their constitutive acts is bound like the posited meaning to acts which are not only acknowledged as distinct from the first acts but situated on another plane. In fact, the thematic process is attached no longer to a particular act or a group of primary acts but to the total unity of a system, so that its own unity is articulated according to the organizing divisions of the system. In other words, the total character of the primary object—in admitting that it is authentic—the absence of bonds of mutual dependence with other objects, doubly transforms the positing meaning which on the one hand, in totally isolating it, permitted the representation of the passage as such and, on the other, owed its simplicity to the indeterminate utilization of prior relations. In the ordinary case, there is not really a description but a characterization through the very sequence of the secondary acts. Here the absolute of the beginning and of the end in some way obliges one to institute a basis for the setting, to the creation *ex nihilo* of an intelligible universe. Is that possible? Does it even possess a meaning? The logicists believe they have escaped the question by identifying the primary acts with their sensible representation, determinable objects for which, if not the totality, at least the modes of construction seem exhaustively definable. The starting point is a set of signs or of species of signs, the acts of regulated means for organizing them into groups of a determinate form. Semantics and syntax are, respectively, a description of initial structures and of results of operations and a regulation of operational procedures. The sign restores to secondary sequences the concrete base of certain primary sequences, in particular the familiarity of ordinary mathematical procedures which elaborate [themselves] in an analogous way, except for the absolute starting point. Formal logic becomes symbolic logic, i.e., mathematical logic.

In actual fact, the problem of description is not resolved to the same extent. The sign is not an object of the world, but if it does not refer to another thing that it would represent, it refers to acts which utilize it, the indefinite character of the regression being essential here. All the comparisons of mathematics with a spatial manipulation run afoul of this fundamental character of the mathematical symbol, cipher, figure, even a stroke of the pen, of simply being there as an integrating part or basis of application for an activity which is already mathematical. The symbol is internal to the act; it can neither be its starting point nor its actual result (which is a production of other acts). The definition of a complete formalism therefore cannot claim such a sensory barrier. What it assumes to be an absolute beginning is only the surreptitious recall of prior acts and sequences. Semantics must be explicitly recapitulated from their syntax insofar as the latter is organized into rules of employment, which are the only things that are significant for the system to be defined. The priority, the quasi-simultaneity of what this syntax brings is sufficient to justify a separation from the syntax which provides the rules of later sequences for progressive development. But then the totality of the formal system is not attained. The presence of a semantics which plays an actual role certifies the failure of the enterprise as an integral definition. Thus completed, the secondary system cannot therefore be complete. If it cannot discern its object, it cannot a fortiori close upon itself. Or rather the reference to the object here recovers the aspect of the mathematical thematization in which the properties of the primary act are elements in another process of sequence. But we cannot call this a description that would be a regression toward an immobile model. There is superposition for the acquisition of novelties, but not for the situation at the bottom. Since the secondary acts are not of an order differing from the primary acts, it is not a question of manifesting the essence of mathematics through them. As formalized, they are themselves mathematical. The theory of science can be clarified and specified through formalizations, but it is not constituted by them.

This is confirmed by the second difficulty of logicism, the problem posed by physics. The notion of coordination is not in fact more directly usable than that of description, but rather presupposes it. We coordinate only what by the same token is part of a higher system. There is a coordination of physics with mathematics only after a mathematization of physics, i.e., a descriptive effort that logicism is powerless to define. The "protocol sentences" invented by its naïve realism presuppose what is in question, namely mathematical relations which are a translation or reduction of physical experience. But the physical sequence, no more than the mathematical one, does not know an absolute beginning. On the one hand, as mathematical relations, the assertions assume their meaning only as elements in a system already posited and possessing an experimental meaning in a more or less precise fashion. On the other hand, the experiment itself as a system of acts is internally organized in a way in which it is impossible for its elaboration to be interrupted, except by a superficial abstraction. The experimental acts produce new ones by a sequence *sui generis* which, at least as such, is independent of the mathematical sequence, since it is of a different essence. The physical relation appears at the intersection of these two processes. From their more or less complete coordination, physical theory is born, for which the doctrine of science must determine the site and provide the meaning. But this a fortiori escapes all formalization. To say that "on such a page of such a book, a sentence composed of such and such signs is found on line n" has no relation with a physical proposition, since the book was designated as a definite copy situated in space and time and the other elements that enter in (line, sentence, composition) are cultural objects that no physical experiment can claim to reach. It is likewise totally absurd to "coordinate" physical experiment with the phrase materially written in an astronomer's notebook, "at such an hour such a star passed the zenith." The true experimental process is elsewhere, in the intentions, the utilizations, and actual constructions of instruments, the entire cosmic-technical system in which its meaning is revealed and whose unity as well as relation with the autonomous mathematical elaboration pose the fundamental problem of physical epistemology.

The traditional image of the internal emptiness of formalisms which an experimental matter comes to fill, thus alone giving them the solidity of true science, is not absent in the logicist solution of a choice imposed by physical experiment between parallel mathematical systems. The protocol sentences, by being placed in a definite way within the system privileged by their presence imparts to it as it unfolds the fullness of meaning that they draw from their sensory origin. We find the twofold prejudice that the mathematical theories, on the one hand, are juxtaposed systems without any necessary connection between them and, on the other, are not self-sufficient but assume a meaning only as an instrument for the knowledge of the world. But the possibility of justifying this subordination through the insertion of mathematics into the imaginative construction of experiments finds itself barred by the abstract character that formalism bestows upon them. It then hesitates between the naïve realism of Wittgenstein and the pragmatism of Schlick. The problem of the object poses itself in its full acuteness in every way. It is the world which is in question, the world that physics proposes to describe whose articulations are already given by logic. "The world is what is . . . logic is the architecture of the world." This reference to the object is significant for a theory whose initial intention was the exhaustive definition of the operational processes which were to be sufficient unto themselves. The object is an ideal pole toward which they can be said to converge, but it in no way intervenes in their elaboration and all of its reality is in them. But the descriptive intention of physics transforms everything: the object becomes not only determining, the point of departure for the theories, the basis of reference for their results, but also (in virtue of the subordination of mathematics) like an orienting instrument for the formal sequences themselves. The internal necessity of their development certainly stands, and the possibility of a choice among them gives them the same independence in relation to existing things as the understanding in the Leibnizian divinity had in relation to the will. But it is still a matter of virtual existence, therefore of a necessary affinity between these sequences and the characters of the existing object. With this, we are but one step away from positing that mathematics describes an object which is more general than the realized object, that syntax determines its conditions and therefore is itself also descriptive —and Wittgenstein takes this step. Even if we would want to reject his realism, the problem remains and through it the problem of the relations between mathematics and physics [is] transformed, as well as, by rebound, the problem of a theory of

386 / *Phenomenology and Science in France*

demonstration. The notion of object, an immanent necessity for the physical sequences, is *ipso facto* imposed on those of mathematics insofar as the latter at the same time constitute the framework of the former, and must be distinguished from them, i.e., situated on the same plane and polarized in a comparable fashion.

And so the attempt to found a theory of demonstration directly seems equally illusory. The difficulties of the relation between syntax and semantics as well as the system of sequences which they determine indeed show that the mere notions of intelligible sequence, of meaning dissociating itself into positing and posited sense, cannot suffice. The representation of the object, banished from one region, reappears elsewhere, even if this be only the object formal system or the object operational act, object in the sense of a reality sufficient unto itself and manifesting in some way or other a duality with the pure act which is immersed in the sequence which it develops. As soon as the direct theory of the sciences or of science refers to the theory of demonstration, the latter requires an ontology, a theory of objects that finally fixes the relative position of the authentic meanings and of the independent beings which either claim to found them or to which they are not related.

III

HUSSERL'S PHENOMENOLOGY claims to safeguard us from both acts and objects as irreducible elements. Thanks to the discovery, prepared by Brentano, of the intentionality of consciousness, because of the correlation that it establishes between noetic acts and noematic contents, it claims to be capable of simultaneously assuring the reciprocal independence between objects and the processes by which they are attained, and the higher unity in which both secure their source and signification. And so the doctrines for which phenomenology represents the deepening synthesis, logicism and the theory of consciousness— by a kind of reconciliation imitating Leibniz and Kant—would find their partial justification by being restored to their proper place.

Formale und transzendentale Logik begins with the problems of the relations between formal ontology and apophantic.

Apart from the logic of truth which terminates in the actual attainment of the object, the theory of apophansis in its fullest sense is divided into three branches. First comes a study of *forms* (or a purely logical grammar) which describes all the structures, the possible architectures of judgments, and finally their modalization. The classification is accomplished by the subsumption of particular forms under a primitive general form ("*Sp is q*" subordinated to "*S is p*") as well as by relating complications obtained by modifications to the initial simple form ("*If S is p*" related to "*S is p*"). This description acquires unity and necessity thanks to the notion of an operation subject to laws. Not only the modalizations but the transitions from categorial form to hypothetical form, the disjunctions and the conjunctions, even the fundamental form *S is p* "as a determination of a substratum of determination *S*," [28] can be considered the result of operations whose combinations and laws can be fixed a priori. Moreover, these operations are universally subject to the law of iteration, by which the indefinite extension of the system of forms is guaranteed. And so the Leibnizian idea of a combinatory as uniform source of the entire instrumental apophantic reappears in an enriched form. But Husserl in fact does not concern himself with the explicit demonstration either of the internal justification for the unity of the notion of operation thus extended, or of a principle of diversification which brings together under this single notion aspects as heterogenous as those of simple apophantic combinations (conjunction and disjunction) and of modalization. The very notion of logical form determined from this notion thereby remains with no precise content or justification of its delimitation other than the permanent possibility of referring to examples.

The *analytic of noncontradiction* comes next. Its task is to study the relations of inclusion, exclusion, and indifference relative to the judgments whose structure and combinations are already fixed by the theory of forms. The evidence which the latter theory claims is distinction, i.e., separation into articulations whose apophantic elements are correctly arranged, without necessarily procuring thereby a guarantee of noncontradiction ("Every *A* is *B*, among which some are not *B*" is a distinct

28. *FTL*, p. 46. Cf. the French translation by Suzanne Bachelard, *Logique formelle et logique transcendentale* (Paris: Presses Universitaires de France, 1957), p. 75.

judgment). Thus the notion of rational sequence surpasses the pure and simple description of structures. Contradiction and consequence, although they can be influenced by the form of judgments and are thus amenable to grammatical analysis, represent an advance in the direction of indicating a possible truth. No matter how radically the separation between logic of truth and analytic may be maintained, the development of analytic is a condition for the logic of truth, inasmuch as the sanction that it provides can be exacted from all of the elements susceptible to an examination of truth. But it is a one-way relation. The privilege conferred upon noncontradictory statements is not justified by an intrinsic property of these statements, and the analytic remains purely formal. In other words, it limits itself to isolating a particular species among all of the possible structures of the theory of forms, and its characterization is immediately realizable by the presence of negations and implications combined in a definite way. The fundamental entity here is the judgment in the broad sense, that is to say, the integrating parts which never appear as isolated, like the hypothesis in the hypothetical judgment, as well as the architectures of already complex judgments compounded into a single affirmation. "The question of pure analytic is . . . : when are any judgments, as judgments and in their simple form, possible within the unity of one judgment, and according to what relations?" [29]

Finally the *theory of systems* or theory of theories considers the groups of judgments which are characterized by a certain unity of sequence. Historically the works of Hankel and Riemann provide the initial notion of a *theory of manifolds* whose deductive closure permits a field of indeterminate objects to be defined exhaustively. The notion of formalism is rigorously maintained. The addition then posited is no longer a concrete operation but a relation characterized by the properties fixed in the axioms. These axioms do not possess a realizable content but are properly only forms of axioms, premises for forms of reasoning leading to forms of conclusions. The only things that matter are the behavior and the modalities of sequence between judgments, according to the properties which the two prior theories can recognize in them. But then the notion of theory assumes its full meaning only when it represents the system of all the judg-

29. *FTL*, § 18, p. 57.

ments which can be deduced from these initial axioms, i.e., when it is definite (or complete). The theory of theories is truly itself only as a nomology, as a determination of the types of theories for which it could first decide whether they are definite, that is, such that every judgment (form of judgment) constructed in a purely logico-grammatical way from the concepts (forms of concepts) which appear in it, is either true, i.e., an analytic consequence of the axioms, or false, i.e., an analytic contradiction: *Tertium non datur.*

The edifice of a formal apophantic is thus completed. From the elementary grammatical inflections to the architectures of axiomatized systems, it fixes everything which is constitutive and determining for a valid statement through form alone, prior to any relation to a concrete object. Accordingly, since the very knowledge of the objects is expressed in judgments, the apophantic already enunciates the indispensable preface to all knowledge; it is first ontology. Yet the connection is not easy to establish. On the one hand, what is aimed at here is not the object, but the judgment about the object. And since it is only a question of its structure, there is nothing to prove that we obtain anything but the extrinsic conditions of expression or at least of thought, which determines nothing in itself but the accidental character of its actualization in a consciousness; the proper theme is and irreducibly remains the pure apophantic entity. On the other hand, independent of all logical development, there exists a spontaneous general ontology, formal mathematics, expanded into a *mathesis universalis* by Leibniz, in which what is directly aimed at are the properties of any object whatsoever. What in fact is number, what are the higher order operations, however complicated their superposition may be, if not those determinations to which the modes of appearance of any object whatsoever are necessarily subject, with a necessity which is related to the very necessity of mathematical development? What does the mathematician do if not describe or fix that which concerns every object, as an abstract element of a manifold? True, the abstraction is generally specialized, in correlation with the operational system of a theory. But, on the other hand, the object thus obtained is not the indeterminate X which would represent the individual as an irreducible individual of the physical world, stripped of every particular qualification, but what Husserl calls a *categorial entity,* whose range of complications includes variable, function, set, and operation. Yet in and through the superposition of various levels, there is always the reference to "the universal empty *Object* or *Something in general*" [30] with its "derivative forms."

> From this is born the universal idea . . . of a formal mathematics in the full sense, whose domain is determined with precision as the range of the superior concept, *Object in general* . . . , with all the derivative forms which can be generated a priori in this field, which through construction always yields new forms. Besides the forms of set and number, these derivative forms are combination, relation, series, connection, whole and part, etc. This mathematics in its entirety is an ontology. [31]

Nevertheless, the "thematic separation" between *formal apophantic* and *mathesis universalis* should not mask their "actual solidarity." [32] Here an essential element in the Husserlian theory of judgment intervenes: the judgment is an expression of a "state of things" (*Sachverhalt*). [33] In other words, the role and the justification of the judgment is found not in the intelligible relation which it is in its immediacy, but in a relation, external and prior to it, which it is destined to express but which is directed through it toward another place, that of the world. The *Satz*, the position of any content whatsoever insofar as it is a judgment, dissociates itself into a position of judgment and a position of objects, of the *Sachverhalt* intended by the judgment and independent of it. The primacy of the *Sachverhalt* is a primacy of the object ("we are oriented toward the object"), and this manifests itself in all the stages of knowledge, even in that theory of knowledge which has the judgment as its term. "The syntactic transformations which are accomplished in the act of judging change nothing here," [34] in particular the operation of *nominalization* by which what was a property or an integral part of an asserted relation (therefore escaping the thematic field) becomes the theme of a higher reflection. For example, even plurality and singularity (the property of plural and singular

30. *FTL*, p. 68.
31. *Ibid.* [Husserl here actually describes the construction more fully, as "an ever new iterative construction."—Trans.]
32. All this is related to § 25: *Thematische Unterschiedenheit* . . . , *FTL*, pp. 68 ff.
33. *Ibid.*
34. *FTL*, § 42b, p. 100.

judgments) do not suppress the permanent and determining objective polarization through all the thematic levels. "No matter how many intermediate determinations of nominalized substrates there may be at the various stages, what matters ultimately are the lowest and primary substrates, in the sciences the objects of their domain; it is their determination which is intended through all the intermediate levels." [35] What emerges here is a kind of *principle of reducibility* by which, on the one hand, the scope and the true significance of every judgment are led back to a relation between primary objects and, on the other, homogeneity is reestablished between judgments from various levels. In fact "the syntactic operations have a double function": [36] they produce the categorial entities of whatever degree, and they introduce these entities to a syntactic role (subject, predicate) within new syntaxes. And so, due to nominalization, for example, a syntactic structure becomes a categorial object and what is intended and attained in it is always the primary object toward which every effort of knowledge tends. The categorial entities procured through syntax, "substrate, property, relation, species," [37] are qualifications of objects, and, since the superpositions performed here are necessarily actualized in the rational evidence of authentic knowledge, they are definitive for this knowledge and therefore for the object. They are essential elements of ontology.

Hence there is an equivalence of content between apophantic and formal ontology. Every element of the first is an element of the second and vice versa, since every object or every formal relation between objects is expressed by a judgment. There is nonetheless a difference of orientation between them. What apophantic fundamentally attains is in fact the judgment as such, with the property constitutive of its essence of being able to be true or false, or even suspended between truth and falsity and nonetheless retaining all of its characteristics as a judgment. To put it differently, it is the meaning of *Sachverhalt* which is in question here, a meaning in the sense of a relation whose actual validity is presupposed and which has import because it is presupposed and because it is actually true in reality. What is

35. *FTL*, pp. 100–101. [Husserl's phrase here is actually "the lowest and primary thematic substrates."—Trans.]
36. *FTL*, § 42d, p. 101.
37. *Ibid.*

important in the case of the formal judgment are thus its articulations, its fractions, the architectures into which it is inserted considered in themselves, although their signification requires that they be directed toward a possible object, without which determination, actually present at the moment when they are examined, they would be nothing. But there are still only possibilities of determinations here, and possibilities and determinations are the only two elements which are themes. By contrast, ontology must discern the object itself in its most general structure, the a priori conditions of its actual attainment. We can even proceed directly. Instead of following the natural line of the developments of abstract mathematics, we can immediately pose the problem of the properties of any object whatsoever. "What can we affirm within the empty region of the object in general? In this formal generality, the syntactic forms are placed at our disposal in a purely a priori way . . . the entire formal *mathēsis* springs from it." [38] But science as science, the system of the meaning of the relations between objects, is not in the thematic field. The *mathesis formalis* gives the determination of the possibilities of objects, while the apophantic gives the possibilities of the determination of objects.

And so the problem posed by the theory of science is resolved without sacrificing either the goal of objects whose being is presupposed independently of their attainment, or the autonomy of rational sequences. Moreover, the authority of logic over physics is thereby likewise explained. In fact, it is one and the same movement which, through mathematics, extends itself even to the realities of the world. There is no knowledge which can be halted in its course toward the self-enclosed intelligibility of a rational system. To know has only one meaning, and that is to attain the real world.

A mathematics constituting itself into a special science as an end in itself need not concern itself with the fact that it is a logic and a logical method, that it has to exercise a function of knowledge, that its products are called upon to serve as formal laws of indeterminate cognitive sequences for cognitive domains which also remain indeterminate. It need not bother with the fact that the relation to a possible application, indeterminate and always open, belongs to its proper formal-logical signification. . . . But the

38. *FTL*, § 54c, p. 132.

philosophical logician must concern himself with these matters. He cannot sanction a mathematics conceived *kata mēdemian symplokēn*, a mathematics which frees itself from the idea of possible applications, and becomes a subtle mental game.[39]

f applications are excluded, there is no such thing as mathematcal knowledge. Mathematics, conscious of its original meaning, f what it truly is, divides itself into two parts: applied mathenatics which is physics, and formal mathematics which is logic. t is only because he has forgotten his vocation that the mathenatician can claim to be self-sufficient. "Formal mathematics ecomes an art . . . one works with letters according to the rules f the game, as in cards or chess. The original thought which ives this technical procedure its proper sense is here bscured." [40] In fact, the application to the world dominates verything and unifies science, since formal logic in its ontologial correlation gives the most general laws according to which hings arrange themselves. "Formal mathematics is originally ogical analytic, so that to its proper logical meaning and based n the cognitive interest, there belongs a range of cognitive unction, i.e., of possible applications, which in all of their indeerminacy still belong to the mathematical meaning." [41]

In fact, the *principle of reducibility* guarantees that the most hysical physics is never out of sight. "If we trace its syntaxes, very real and possible judgment leads back to an ultimate ucleus. . . . It is a syntactical structure of elementary nuclei vhich no longer contain syntaxes." [42] The reduction leads us to ultimate substrates, absolute subjects (which are no longer ominalized predicates or nominalized relations), to ultimate redicates (no longer predicates of predicates, etc.), ultimate niversals, ultimate relations." [43] As a result, "every conceivable udgment finally has . . . a relation to individual objects . . .

39. *FTL*, § 40, p. 97.
40. *H* VI, p. 46. See also the review published in Belgrade in *hilosophia* by Arthur Liebert, Vol. I, pt. 1 (1936), p. 121. We are ndebted to Jean Hering for having been able to consult this article, nd we thank him for his kindness and for the suggestions which he ffered. Cf. also the French translation by Edmond Gerrer in *Etudes hilosophiques*, Vol. IV, nos. 3–4 (July–December, 1949), pp. 242–3.
41. *FTL*, § 40, p. 97.
42. *FTL*, § 82, p. 180.
43. *Ibid.*

therefore a relation to a real universe, a world or a region of the world for which it is valid." [44] Formal logic, *mathesis universalis* or a fortiori apophantic, absorbed in the complications of its own evolution, can forget this relation. The logic of truth, crown of the edifice, for which the rest is but a necessary though not sufficient preparation, reestablishes these perspectives. It is in arriving at knowledge that all the previous work is illuminated and that the respective values of the preliminary efforts—each tempted to take itself as an end in itself—assume their authentic sense relative to the one end being pursued. Formal ontology or apophantic logic represents the indispensable infrastructure in the architecture of science, one determining the most general categories of the object and the other the form of the meaning superimposed, in the sequence in which the object in general is pursued. But the object must actually be attained in order for there to be knowledge, mathematics in the end comes to completion in physics, there is only one movement and one knowledge for which the unity of the whole guarantees the validity of each of the moments and of their relations of subordination. Necessity is everywhere present and founded because it is unique.

It is thus the reference to the primacy of consciousness which in the end permits the difficulties to be overcome. As far as their being in relation to consciousness is concerned, the independence of the objects is not an affirmation of a heterogeneity which would involve subordination and, because of their diversity, a polymorphism of the corresponding knowledge. But consciousness is the totality of being; what it affirms is only because it affirms it, if it is truly what it affirms in full self-assurance. Since transcendental phenomenology is an analysis of all the claims and all the acts of knowledge, as in general of all the contents aimed at or intended by consciousness and of all the operations by which this aim is accomplished, it has to find in this correlation of the noetic and the noematic the means for resolving all the problems which are not false problems. There is no need searching elsewhere, since everything is only in its very life. And because its essence is truly conscious of itself, it permits an analysis that is an explanation. "Absolute being is being in the form of an intentional life which, whatever else it may be conscious of, is at the same time self-consciousness. The possi-

44. *FTL*, § 83, p. 181.

bility of self-reflection belongs to its essence, a reflection which discovers the original reality of its being under the veils of vague thought." [45] Habits, repetitions not actually justified of thoughts finding their meaning in their initial embellishments, thoughts muffled because they are rapid and confused—it is enough to raise these masks in order to bring to light a certitude of consciousness which does not admit of a beyond. It is the intentionality of consciousness, i.e., "the experience of having something in consciousness," [46] which explains and insures the duality between the intended object and the act which intends it, but the object is nothing but the pole of these acts and the system of contents, the pole of noeses, the unity of noemas. With its independence thus assured, knowledge is permitted autonomy of development and homogeneity of essence. In fact, since being is unique, there can be no unbridgeable gap between two domains of knowing. Sense experience or physical experiment are particular modes of evidence, but even if the diversity remains well-founded, it does not bring a barrier with it. Between the rational evidence of a mathematical demonstration and the sensory evidence of the historical perception of an object, there is the profound homogeneity of their both being the full insight of the same consciousness, so that relations of mutual conditioning are possible and justifiable through an analysis of the acts which secure both. Both the legitimacy of the relations and the means for their discovery are found in a coming to consciousness through the very consciousness of what it accomplishes. Truth is one in its many aspects because there is fundamentally only one knowledge, and this is consciousness. But there is no denying the variety of its manifestations insofar as it withstands the elimination of all that is confused and factitious. The role of transcendental analysis here is to recognize the genuine diversities and to establish their relationships. "It is only by a decisive return to subjectivity, to the subjectivity insofar as it establishes all the valid affirmations of the world with their content and in all prescientific and scientific modalities, as well as by a return to the What and How of the [productions] of reason that the objective truth can be rendered intelligible and that the ultimate meaning of the world can be reached." [47] The problem posed by

45. *FTL*, § 103, p. 241.
46. *FTL*, § 60, p. 143.
47. *H* VI, p. 70.

logic in particular will thus be resolved by bringing to light the role played by developments of formal ontology in the actual knowledge of the world. It is not a matter of asking how a priori categories can be applied to the real, nor how the form of physics, nomological or otherwise, can be described in an autonomous way by the theory of systems. It is sufficient to examine the point that logic and the theory of systems are in fact the indispensable preface for the actual thought of real objects. It is sufficient to describe their intervention and to bring to light the profound relations which make this necessary. The problem of phenomenology is a problem of *constitution*. In other words, it is a matter of "knowing, by scrutinizing all the strata and levels, the complete system of the configurations of consciousness constituting the original presentation of all the objectivities, and thereby making intelligible the equivalent in consciousness of the type of 'reality' under consideration." [48] The authority of logic has its foundation in its relation to the life of the transcendental subjectivity, which develops itself in internal necessity. It is here that the rules which logic asserts, as well as the general object which it considers and the products that it finally engenders, find their place as well as their relation with each other and with everything else. But it is not enough to have their assurance by decree. We must investigate and justify each of these by actually connecting them with the acts and the conditions of this life. Formal logic and the logic of truth find their conclusion and foundation only in transcendental logic.

Here we see the opposition to Kant, for whom the pure logic of the tradition retained an authority beyond critique, to the point of dominating it for the sake of guiding it. He in fact posed the critical problem too narrowly and from the outset too loftily. At first, it is the discovery of logical entities as independent objects possessing their own reality and still produced by the consciousness which is to initiate transcendental analysis. "How do ideal objectivities, which originate purely in our subjective activity of judgment and knowledge, and have original existence only as a manifestation of our spontaneity in our field of consciousness, acquire the sense and the being of objects [which exist] in themselves relative to the contingency of the acts and of the subjects?" [49] The answer comes close to asserting that the

48. *Ideen I*, § 152, p. 319. Cf. *Ideas I*, p. 390.
49. *FTL*, § 100, p. 233.

sense and the being of all objects can really be conferred only by a subjectivity which is their source and foundation. The problem posed by logic is transformed into a problem of the transcendental constitution of objective entities. It is only then, and parallel to it, that the problem of a nature attained and defined by science can be fruitfully examined. Even here the objects are tied in their definition to the transcendental subjectivity, and in a way more radical than with Kant, since the operation is already finished with regard to that which pertains to logic. But on the other hand, it is necessary for the same question to have been resolved in a preliminary way for prescientific intuitive nature. "It is only after the transcendental philosophy of nature, at first limited to intuitive nature, has been educed, that it will be suitable, through an incorporation of ideal realities, for motivating the development of a transcendental logic." [50] The abstract object of science has no more primacy than the object of sense intuition. The unity of knowledge demands a homogenization and a hierarchic sequence in the investigations which bring these transcendental dependencies to light. And so we once again discover the two driving motifs inherited from empiricist logicism and the philosophy of consciousness.

In the first place, experience remains the master of syntactic sequences, in the peculiar doctrine of the *relevance of nuclei*. "The syntactic materials which appear in the unity of a judgment must have something to do with each other materially," [51] through the internal interdependence of the contents which they join together. We cannot juxtapose just any syntaxes for a true judgment, simply limiting ourselves to following the laws of distinction and of noncontradiction. "This stems from the fact that the original genetic mode of judging (which is an eidetic genesis and not a psychophysical genesis) is the evident judgment in its most rudimentary stage [which is based upon] experience. Prior to every action of judging lies the universal ground of experience which is constantly presupposed as a harmonious unity of possible experience." [52] Whence the variety of a transcendental philosophy which starts directly from pure logic. The source and the justification of the apophantic unity must be

50. *FTL*, § 100, p. 235.
51. *Ibid.* On the relevance of nuclei, cf. § 87, p. 189; on the function of syntactic materials, cf. § 89b, p. 194.
52. *FTL*, p. 194.

sought in a preliminary affinity of the experiential contents which it organizes. It is thus important to examine this affinity first. "And so in its content every original act of judging," i.e., inasmuch as it no longer resorts to other judgments upon which to base itself, "has coherence through the coherence of things in the synthetic unity of experience, which is the terrain upon which it stands." [53] We see here once again the intervention of the *principle of reducibility*. For the categorial superstructures do not have definitive efficacy. In order to explicate the transcendental meaning of the judgment as it is really and truly posited (without allusion or symbolization), we must in the end go through them to reach the individuals, the brute singularity of the experiential ground. Hence the full value of evidence cannot be obtained on the categorial level. From this two consequences follow: on the one hand, the necessity of a transcendental aesthetic (in a larger sense than Kant's) which "treats the problem of a possible world in general as a world of pure experience" [54] prior to every categorial activity and defines the a priori conditions of unity *sui generis* which can be attributed to it and which will serve as a basis for the apophantic sequences studied by logic proper; on the other hand, the irremediable insufficiency of a universal analytic developing itself in autonomous fashion or, if you will, the superiority of "material" doctrines of science over the formal doctrine. Not only are they indispensable for the determination of the meaning of a positive science, fixing by means of eidetic variation (hence expressly without recourse to general formal ontology) the ontological categories of the objects which they attain, but also they have for their crown "the highest and most encompassing of all, the logic of transcendental phenomenological philosophy itself," [55] upon which both analytical logic and material logic depend. Now this second relation compromises, or at least transforms the very notion of logic.

Secondly, in effect, if traditional objective logic appears, like every science prior to transcendental analysis, as "a sort of philosophical infancy," [56] if transcendental logic is not a second logic but "the radical and concrete logic which can grow only at

53. *FTL*, § 89b, p. 194.
54. *FTL*, Conclusion, p. 256.
55. *Ibid.*
56. *FTL*, Introduction, p. 12.

the heart of phenomenological investigations," [57] it will not be developed within the empty abstraction of analytical logic but will itself be a material logic of phenomenological science. From the dissociation of this latter logic into superimposed branches comes the stratification of several transcendental logics. What characterizes phenomenological analysis is its "irremediable relativity, a provisional character" which comes from the fact that "at every stage it surmounts a naïveté but carries with it the naïveté" belonging to the stage to which it moves, making necessary in its turn a new deepening and the passage to the higher stage.[58] Now each stage is characterized by its own problems of evidence. Evidence cannot be prescribed once and for all but reveals itself each time in a mode of radical novelty through its immediate presence. Logic, the norm of truth, i.e., of evidence, is also new each time. If the logic of the positive sciences is oriented toward the world, "how does it stand with that logic under whose norms the transcendental investigations are realized? We forge concepts, we express judgments by drawing them from transcendental experience (from that which is given in the *ego cogito*) . . . we attain truths by adequation, we make inductions." [59] But these operations have only a homonymy with the corresponding operations of positive science, and the problem is to know to what new norms they must be subjected as conditions for the proper structure of their evidence. And so for the stages of egological phenomenology (through which *Ideen I* moves) "the notion of truth in itself no longer has a normal sense," [60] since there is no longer a relation to a "no matter who" but to the one possible subject. Truth is solipsistic here. We see "a peculiar transcendental discipline being developed . . . with essential truths, theories which are valid exclusively for me, the Ego [i.e., valid once and for all], without being able to vindicate a relationship with other subjects. Thus is posed the question of a subjective logic whose a priori has only a solipsistic value." [61] But there are higher stages, those of intersubjective phenomenology, where the truth and therefore the corresponding logic are defined differently. The subordination of analytic logic or the doc-

57. *FTL*, Conclusion, p. 256.
58. *FTL*, § 102, p. 239.
59. *FTL*, § 102, p. 238.
60. *Ibid.*
61. *Ibid.*

trine of the positive sciences to the transcendental logic which founds them is therefore not accomplished in a single stroke. In fact, "formal ontology as constituted by transcendental phenomenology is only a moment depending upon another formal ontology which is related to every being in every sense, to being as transcendental subjectivity and to everything that constitutes itself in it." [62] What is therefore needed is a logic to give norms not only for the constitution of the constituted being, but also for the constitution of the constituting being. Is this the same? Do the successive enlargements of ontologies corresponding to successive stages of phenomenological investigation come to the unique domain of an absolute formal ontology which absorbs and totally realizes the prior investigations? This is at least what Husserl affirms. But here it seems as if the course of the questioning has been arrested by a kind of violent truncation. One of the problems announced—and not examined—is to know how "it is possible to actualize the most general idea of a formal logic as formal ontology and formal apophantic on the absolute terrain where it constitutes itself within the framework of the absolute and ultimate universal science, transcendental phenomenology, as a necessary integral [layer]." [63] But [if] the absolute and ultimate science also requires a doctrine which governs it—ontology [and] apophantic—it cannot include this as part of itself. Perhaps we abuse the singularity of the absolute by withholding from it the coincidence between constituting moment and constituted moment. Besides, there is not really a coincidence but an insertion of the first in the second, since the norms of the constituting constitution are only one portion among the constituted constitutions. Now it seems that such an identification of planes is especially difficult to admit for phenomenology, where the motive of research and the foundation of objectivities are precisely the relation to a creative subjectivity. If this subjectivity is in its turn subject to norms, a new transcendental investigation would be needed in order to relate its norms to a higher subjectivity, since no content but rather consciousness alone has the authority to posit itself in itself. If transcendental logic really founds logic, there is no absolute logic (that is, governing the absolute subjective activity). If there is an abso-

62. *FTL*, § 102, p. 239.
63. *Ibid.*

lute logic, it can draw its authority only from itself, and then it is not transcendental.

Perhaps further phenomenological investigations will at least permit us to challenge a dilemma so bluntly posed. Yet it seems fundamental for the point of view of a philosophy of consciousness. If the *epochē*, in separating [the] transcendental consciousness from a consciousness situated in the world, removes the naïve aspect and somewhat scandalous aggressiveness of logical empiricism and psychologism, they still lurk beneath the surface of phenomenological development. We can recognize them by their fruits, especially in the two essential problems of logic and epistemology: the relation between mathematics and physics, and the role and the definition of logical entities.

We have already seen that Husserl divided mathematics in two: a formal part identified with general ontology, and an applied part integrated into physics. The formal part, in determining the general features of being, puts itself at the service of the knowledge which is nothing other than the attainment of the beings of the world. But can we say that physics itself is qualified for this end? Here again the internal exigency of the phenomenological attitude intervenes. On the one hand, mathematical physics in fact only represents a technical advance in relation to sense experience. It is an illusion dating from Galileo that the system of symbols and concepts of mathematical physics constitutes a cosmos more real than the world apprehended directly in intuition. "Through geometrical mathematization, we tailor for the vital world . . . a close-fitting garment of ideas." [64] But this is only a mask, a disguise under which the carnal body of things is alone important. There is no physical progress in the sense of a transformation of the landscape through the forward march of science. "The intuitive real world . . . remains as it is, invariable in its proper essential structures, in its concrete causal style." [65] Being is posed before science in the act which intends it; it is a constitutive character of its essence that both its reality and its internal structure are independent of the improvements and complications of this act. Since things are not in themselves but are founded as realities in the intentionality of consciousness, a

64. *H* VI, p. 51.
65. *Ibid.*

privilege must be granted to the primitive as well as permanent acts through which it manifests itself. The existing stable world demands perception just as perception demands the stable world, since in the end, even in a laboratory experiment, everything begins through it and everything ends in it. Physical theories are only an abstract interim, and their succession a play of shadows upon its immobile mass, always ready to intervene.

Also, on the other hand, their role from the start was exclusively technical. Only the sedimentations of traditions, the process of forgetting the primitive meaning of initiated habits could transform and inflate their importance. Physics is not a science but an art. "What we really do with it is prediction, a prediction extended to infinity. All life is based on prediction." [66] It is here that we slip toward the intuition of the vital. Physics is a speculation which is not alien to life but a moment of this life, a part of industrial technical activity, a part which can be isolated through abstraction alone or for the sake of a division of labor. It is only in this life that it finds its true meaning and its motive of progress. To predict is not to see in advance, to deny the event as radical novelty, to reduce it to something already seen like a regular manifestation of a permanent essence. The dialectic of prediction is that of regulated action. It involves both the refusal to abandon itself to time as dominant and situating itself within the rhythm of this time through which something takes place, across a necessary thickness of duration independent of conscious duration. It presupposes that the movement is irreducible, which therefore risks departing from itself in an adventure toward the Other, at once already there and not yet there, deceptive in anticipation and wont to move at its own pace. Its modality is probability and not necessity. Mathematization intervenes only as a coordination of spontaneous predictions, particularly in eliminating what is useless among them, through a process of infinite idealization. What does it mean to idealize, if not to smooth over the extrinsic, that which for the scientific mind is tied to the facticity (i.e., arising from the fact) of its present actualization and can make sense only in relation to it. Hence the invention of straight lines and perfect planes, the positing of an infinite and homogeneous space. The infinite is elimination of the arbitrary, the arbitrary in the choice of an example, in the

66. *Ibid.*

reputed obstacle to research and to construction. Measurement, a consequence of the postulate of homogeneity, is the domination of lived space through coordination and iteration of its actual apprehensions. Their synthesis, the exactness of relations characterizing Galilean physics, is simply the indefinite convergence of real operations and real contacts toward an ideal pole which before long will be substituted as their representative and conceived as more real than they are. Rather than genuine speculative moments, there is in all of this a methodic organization of a self-conscious and predictive action whose intermediaries and instruments can become thematic and take themselves as ends. If mathematics is in the service of knowledge, it is a service which accepts several masters.

But it is not a service which reveals itself only in its realization. We have seen that the categorial entities of ontology merely represent complications which can be suppressed at any time. But throughout this ontology, there remains the one object which is always intended, whose being is irrevocably posed, namely, the individual in the real world. And so we find again the thesis dear to empiricist logicism that mathematics does not have a proper content of knowledge. It is an organization or combination of what is already there, which alone matters, and we can undo and retie their interlacings without augmenting or diminishing the reality known. "What do the propositions of logic say? They all say the same thing, namely, nothing." [67]

Mathematics, the logicists of the neopositivist school repeat, is merely a tautology. Hence the short circuit from the idea of an abstract ontology to actual knowledge. We can ignore the progressive rational development and "pose the problem of a formal ontology to ourselves directly, without passing through the idea of a doctrine of science. . . . It is evident that the entire [formal] *mathēsis* will then emerge," [68] since such a *mathēsis* is a pure and simple combination which can readily be taken as complete. This is really the idea of a universal syntax as Carnap tried to describe it in a single stroke. We have seen what came of it. The mathematical sequence possesses an internal coherence which cannot be treated brusquely. Its progressive character is essen-

67. Wittgenstein, *Tractatus Logico-Philosophicus* (London: Routledge & Kegan Paul, 1922), proposition 5.43.
68. *FTL*, § 54c, p. 132.

tial and the decisions which neglect this lose themselves in the void.

A particularly clear example is Husserl's notion of *nomology*. It in fact characterizes for him the axiomatized theories of mathematics and mathematical physics. Only a *nomological* theory permits the univocal definition of the system of objects which constitute its domain. On the other hand, it can be incorporated into a larger theory without risk of contradiction and in preserving the permanent faculty of eliminating new elements in the results. With regard to the introduction of imaginary numbers, Husserl posed the following question: "When can we be sure that deductions which are obtained in working with the new concepts, but which yield statements in which these do not figure, are in fact . . . correct consequences of the axioms which define them? . . ." The answer: "If the systems are nomological the calculation with imaginary concepts can never lead to contradictions." [69] The advantage of a tautological conception of mathematics becomes apparent here. First, the entire content of knowledge is assembled in the enunciation of the axioms, so that the later deductions, the proper movement of the theory, merely make explicit what was already posited in advance as an independent and indispensable introduction to the mathematical labor. The progressive expansion of the theories is realized by juxtaposition, without any internal necessity or dependence of meaning between the restricted theory and the generalized theory. It can be halted at any stage. The domination by the thought which traverses and posits them is always present, since in instituting these systems of categorial entities what it is concerned with is only a technical apparatus which is to disappear, either at a single stroke or partially, once the statement relevant to real beings is obtained. It is indeed evident that for saturated theories, this condition is always fulfilled. Every proposition in terms of this theory is either demonstrable or refutable on the basis of the axioms. But then it is the utility of the detour which now poses [a] problem. Why is a demonstration simpler (unless the only one possible) because of the addition of ideal elements en route, which in the end disappear, e.g., complex numbers in ordinary algebra and real numbers in the arithmetic of whole

69. *FTL*, § 31, p. 85. [Husserl's word here is not "nomological" but "definite."—Trans.]

numbers? The reference to technique is a subterfuge. The success and value of simplification must be founded on an essential property. And so in the cases cited, the answer is not in doubt. Neither the theory of real numbers nor the theory of whole numbers are nomologies. The condition posited by Husserl for the expansion of a theory is indeed sufficient but not necessary. In the quasi-totality of the case, it is not realized.

The result of Gödel's work is well-known: every theory containing the arithmetic of whole numbers, i.e., practically every mathematical theory, is necessarily nonsaturated. A proposition can be asserted within them which is neither the consequence of the axioms nor in contradiction with them: *tertium datur*. On the other hand, the previous investigations have indicated the difference between the closure of the field of objects and the closure (or saturation) of its conceptual system. Abstractly considered, the two appear linked. In defining saturation, Husserl evokes the *axiom of inextensibility* introduced by Hilbert "for motives which go . . . essentially in the same direction, since it was in fact a question of closing the field of point-objects satisfying the axioms of geometry." [70] But the system of these axioms is not saturated despite the axiom of inextensibility (which for that matter has another end, to guarantee the continuity of the field: every convergent series of points defines a new point which by virtue of the axiom belongs to the field). Other simpler examples of nonsaturated systems and for an inextensible field have been given. Saturation evidently involves inextensibility but not vice versa. Here technique takes its revenge by subverting the constructions realized in an abstract realm that surpasses it. This surprising turn of events is particularly serious for the Husserlian conception of logic and mathematics. In the first place, the very notion of a theory which can be dominated and isolated cannot be maintained. If the nomologies are only the exception, it is impossible for the rest of the mathematical texture to isolate the prefaces (which are extramathematical) and to indicate the ruptures of dependence. Only the theories smaller than arithmetic, that is, the theories which may be called quasi-finite, can be nomological. Their development is indeed of a combinatory order, and their domination through the sole consideration of axioms is truly effective. But genuine mathematics

70. *Ibid.*

begins with the infinite. The incorporation of a theory into a larger theory is clearly subject to the sole condition of noncontradiction, but by virtue of the same result of Gödel, the noncontradiction of a theory can be demonstrated only within a more powerful theory. The demonstration retains its interest, which is to concentrate on a single procedure or a canonic system of procedures, the doubts being distributed over an indeterminate polymorphy of intertwined procedures. But there is no longer that apodictic assurance at the start. One must commit oneself to the canonic procedure, to the indefinite iteration of its employment. Thus the deductive sequence is essentially the creator of the contents that it attains. The possibility of assembling some privileged assertions at the outset is a source of illusion if we forget the operational rules which alone give them a meaning. Concrete axiomatics, like those of Hilbert for geometry, are in part responsible for the error by their reference to well-known notions. If we take away the indeterminate notions of point, straight line, plane, between, etc., the axioms still have a meaning, an aspect of assertion which would suggest the idea of exhaustive definition. Abstract axiomatics brings out clearly what is valid for both types, namely, that the only reality posited initially and constituting the unity of the system is the operation or the system of operations which are destined to simultaneously fix both assertions and rules. But here again the definition is not exhaustive, for it presupposes the constitutive operations of previous systems—with their characteristics and their results—and appeals as well to other operations which establish other theoretical unities. The body of a theory is a certain operative homogeneity—which the axiomatic presentation describes—but when the theory involves the infinite, the iteration and the complications furnish results and an intelligible system of contents which are impossible to dominate, and an internal necessity obliges it to surpass itself through an expansion otherwise unpredictable and which appears as an expansion only after the fact. There is no juxtaposition any more than there is an initial fixation. It is the entire body of mathematics which develops itself through the steps and in a variety of forms, and it is likewise this which in its entirety, technical devices included, accomplishes or does not accomplish the very function of knowledge. Knowledge, if secured by mathematics, can only be deduction. Second, the failure of an essential point renders the method doubtful. Neither objective logic—the analysis or combination of the formations already produced by spontaneous logic and presented for communication in a systematic aspect which can be extrinsic, because as a system it wants to be definitive and not what it is in reality, namely, a simple movement of the actual development —nor subjective logic—foundation of the first inasmuch as it relates its products to the activity of absolute consciousness— can account for either the actual progress or the structures and entities which mark it off. We have already seen this with regard to the pure theory of forms and the theory of noncontradiction. The content of the decisive notions of implication, deduction, negation is not questioned but simply presupposed for the definition of noncontradiction, which then remains an external consideration of forms. The same holds for the relation between noncontradiction and possible truth. It would no doubt be the role of subjective logic to examine all of this closely. But with the phenomenological method and its point of view, subjective logic is limited to analyzing the constitutive acts and intentions of the transcendental subjectivity, i.e., to unraveling the entanglement of motivations and elementary actions, but without questioning the logical entity itself. It is evident that it cannot be questioned since no consciousness is a witness of the production of its content by an act, since the phenomenological analysis will always move only in the world of acts or, for the corresponding noemas, be able to dissociate architectures of contents. But in both instances, it will stop before the simple elements, i.e., the realities of consciousness which refer to nothing which is other. And even more, in order to qualify them, it will have to utilize those same fundamental notions. Thus for implication: "he who has the thought of a judgment and . . . sees an analytic consequence of it . . . cannot do otherwise than to judge in this way." [71] And for noncontradiction: "of two contradictory judgments, only one can be valid if it is fully or distinctly actualized." [72] A lived impossibility or a distinct actualization are the ultimate instances for phenomenological analysis. And the meaning of consequence or of analytic contradiction is not made into a problem. Otherwise stated, what can be obtained will only be a distribution of realized sequences, with the critical purifica-

71. FTL, § 75, p. 168.
72. Ibid.

tion bearing exclusively on the alterations produced by the condensed or symbolic employment of a process which finds itself again only in its primitive profusion, or through ruptures between a method [and] the setting or the end which give it its meaning, so that it is no more than a habit or a technique. This is why historical investigations are important. History reveals authentic meaning to the extent that it permits us to rediscover lost links, first to identify automatisms and sedimentations as such, then to revitalize them by thrusting them back into their conscious actuality. It is a double necessity of time that the immediate act prolongs itself in habit and that the new act is weighted down and aided by the system of muffled traces of the past. But every simple position in its freshness is irrefutable. The return to the origin is a return to the original. We have seen that to make comprehensible in the phenomenological sense is not to change a plan or to reduce a content into something other than itself but to dissociate the entanglements, to pursue the referential indicators in order to bring out into the open the polished system of acts which "no longer refer to anything." In this sense, says Fink, phenomenology should be called an archeology. On the one hand, there is nothing to question beyond the act or the content in their immediate presence. On the other, the higher authority is this very presence or rather the impossibility of dissociating a single part or character from it through variation without losing everything. The foundation of all necessity is this "I cannot do otherwise" of eidetic variation which, however legitimate it may be, is an abdication of thought.[73]

We can see the difficulty for our problem: neither the illegitimacy for contents is reduced, nor the progress justified as such. If empirical history is used to reveal essential sequences, it is on the wrong side, not as a forward movement, but through the myth of the return of the past. "Before the geometry of ideal objects came the practical art of land measurement. . . . Its pre-geometrical results are a foundation of meaning for geometry."[74] But in what way? Is this not an arbitrary decree which adapts the origin of consciousness to a temporal pseudo-debut which appears to us as such only by virtue of the sequel as

73. *Ibid.:* "er kann nicht anders als so zu urteilen . . ."
74. *H* VI, p. 49. [*Leistung*, here translated as *résultat* by Cavaillès, is usually translated nowadays as *performance, production, work.*— Trans.]

well as by approximation? Husserl also speaks of an immanent teleology for the history of philosophy, for example, which illuminates through "a harmony finally full of meaning . . . the hidden unity of intentional interiority." [75] Here there is no longer a return to the origin, but an orientation according to the flux of a becoming which presents itself as such only by the intelligible enrichment of its terms. To be sure, because of its indefinite plasticity, phenomenology justifies everything even to the point of a hierarchy among the types of evidence. Yet the authority of these has only one source. At least the evidence which justifies the transcendental analysis is necessarily unique: if there is a consciousness of progress, there is not a progress of the consciousness. Now one of the essential problems of the doctrine of science is that progress itself may not be augmentation of volume by juxtaposition, in which the prior subsists with the new, but a continual revision of contents by deepening and eradication. What comes after is more than what existed before, not because it contains it or even because it prolongs it but because it departs from it and carries in its content the mark of its superiority, unique every time, with more consciousness in it—and not the same consciousness. The term "consciousness" does not admit of univocity of application—no more than does the thing, as the unity which can be isolated. There is no consciousness which generates its products or is simply immanent to them. In each instance it dwells in the immediacy of the idea, lost in it and losing itself with it, binding itself to other consciousnesses (which one would be tempted to call other moments of consciousness) only through the internal bonds of the ideas to which these belong. The progress is material or between singular essences, and its driving force is the need to surpass each of them. It is not a philosophy of consciousness but a philosophy of the concept which can provide a theory of science. The generating necessity is not the necessity of an activity, but the necessity of a dialectic.

75. *H* VI, p. 74 [The break in the quotation has been introduced by the translator—Trans.]

Suzanne Bachelard

SUZANNE BACHELARD, daughter of Gaston Bachelard and a professor at the Sorbonne, has made some remarkable contributions to the study of Husserl's philosophy as well as to the philosophy of science. In addition to preparing an excellent translation of Husserl's *Formal and Transcendental Logic,* she has written an important study of Husserl's logic and two absorbing works on the philosophy of science. She is undoubtedly one of the leading contemporary French phenomenologists working in the area of the philosophy of science.

The following selections are from the Preface and first chapter of *La Conscience de rationalité,* in which the author explains her conception of phenomenology and the contribution such a phenomenology wishes to make to the realm of philosophy of (natural) science.

16 / Phenomenology and Mathematical Physics

Suzanne Bachelard

THE ESSENTIAL GOAL of the present essay is to study the characteristic traits of apodictic knowledge by means of precise examples. I have chosen to place myself within the changing realm of scientific culture rather than to determine the bases of apodicticity in a purely abstract reflection. The latter task has often been envisaged: rationalism, from Kant to Husserl, has shed such light on this problem that, it seems, there would be some immodesty in returning to an examination of this fundamental rationalism. This is why I have decided to associate myself with *"applied rationalism"* and to try to follow science's power of rational assimilation in a new realm of examples.

In fact, in the different sciences "rationalism" and "application" are coupled in a more or less close way. Empirical receptivity is very different from one science to another. It is quite certain that a science such as chemistry is marked by a greater empirical receptivity than physics. Although chemistry is no longer in the state which justified Kant in removing it from every perspective of apodicticity,[1] it has nevertheless but a short past of deductive necessity. It seems, therefore, more in keeping with my capabilities to study a science which is more confident of its

This essay from *La Conscience de rationalité: Etude phénoménologique sur la physique mathématique* by Suzanne Bachelard (Paris: Presses Universitaires de France, 1958), pp. 1–12, has been translated by Joseph J. Kockelmans expressly for this edition.

1. Cf. Immanuel Kant, *Metaphysical Foundations of Natural Science*, in *Kant's Prolegomena and Metaphysical Foundations of Natural Science*, trans. E. Belfort Bax (London: Bell, 1883), pp. 137–49, esp. p. 141.

rationality. For this reason I have chosen to focus my investigation on mathematical physics. As far as mathematical physics is concerned, I had to face a less empirical prospective than does the rationalist activity of contemporary physics. That was an advantage for me in that the progress of rationality is founded here on a mathematical rationalism which was carefully constituted and clearly and discursively developed.

In this study which plans to follow mathematical physics in the positivity of its tasks, I felt that I would do well to adopt the principles of phenomenology. I did not forget, however, that Husserl stated that the sciences, by the mere fact of their development, have resolutely moved away from a thorough analysis of their bases and that their objective work has kept them from awakening to a genuine consciousness of themselves. As a matter of fact, the methodologies of the various sciences often appear as hypertrophies of positivism. In quite a number of sciences method has become a kind of training by means of which one economizes thought in one way or another. Subjectivity then manifests itself often, if one dares to say so, by means of its obscurities, by means of a more or less secret resistance to engage in the method and to "yield" to that method. Husserl has repeated time and again that even the preeminently theoretical science of mathematics is, all things considered, no more than a theoretical technique and that the only genuine theoretician is the philosopher. One may readily recall here the view of Kant as well, according to which "the mathematician, the physicist, the logician, whatever brilliant successes they may have had . . . are nevertheless only artists of reason." [2] All science risks degeneration into "cyclopic erudition" which "lacks the eye of the philosopher." [3]

But once it is admitted that the phenomenological conversion is well founded, it is still not without meaning, I believe, to speak of phenomenology where there is no longer a question of investigations which go back to an absolute origin. In fact, I think that the phenomenological dimension can be open to all phases of the *organization of a science*. If the development of a science is not the result of a contingent attainment or of an

2. Immanuel Kant, *Critique of Pure Reason,* trans. Norman Kemp Smith (New York: St. Martin's, 1965), p. 584.
3. Immanuel Kant, *Logique,* trans. J. Tissot (Paris: Ladrange, 1840), p. 65.

automatic procedure, if it truly results from a progress of thought, then an original power, which is implied in it, can reveal itself to a phenomenological interrogation. "Whatever is spirit witnesses its own birth" says the poet.[4] Every progress of thought is really an ensemble of *beginnings*. True, these beginnings certainly do not have the privilege of an absolutely first origin, but they nevertheless have the function of an inductive origin. And one cannot ignore the fact that an alert consciousness is in its own way a first consciousness.

Because I wish to give an outline of a phenomenology of the consciousness of rationality, no one will be amazed that throughout the whole book I adhere to the lessons of *applied rationalism*.[5] Science offers us a constant experience of the rational which continuously gives us new objects of rationality. But this supply of objects of rationality does not entail a simple extension of our domain of study. The central thesis of *applied rationalism* is that because of their novelty the objects of rationality react in depth on our consciousness of rationality. Rational knowledge does not increase in the same way as empirical knowledge, which does not change its structure even when it accepts the exoticism of the objects. The rational increases by reorganizing itself, by continually making new starts from enlarged bases as more and more complex rational structures establish themselves. In this way an original power is always active in the very development of rational science.

At the same time all rational science has an evident teleological power. A demonstration is always more than a result. It is always a stage on the road which leads us consciously toward a goal. Thus it seems that the teleology of science in a certain sense deepens the origin of it. Just as phenomenology, adhering to the fundamental property of consciousness, is fond of repeating that all consciousness is "consciousness of . . . ," so in the same way can one say particularly that all origin is "origin of . . ." Origin and teleology are the terms of a duality which has a phenomenological unity. And this unity manifests itself most vividly in rational science, where everything has an orientation.

But even if rational science, more than any other science, is

4. Joé Bousquet, *La Neige d'un autre âge* (Paris: Levis-Mand, 1939), p. 30.
5. Gaston Bachelard, *Le Rationalisme appliqué* (Paris: Presses Universitaires de France, 1949).

able to reveal its directive power, still it does not contain in itself a peaceful destiny: it is not, as it may seem to be at first sight, science in "linear" development. In fact, it might appear that rational science brings about an irreducible linear character by ordering reality according to an inflexible deductive line, whereas the real, on the contrary, presents itself naturally in a complex network of entanglements. In reality a rational science, at least a rich rational science such as mathematics, is a science which branches out. And it would be a mistake to think that one understands the growth of the tree because one knows its roots. In this simplified view, the origin of the rationality of science would determine the *nature* of science. But the productive dialectics are not yet visible in the elementary bases of knowledge. If it is a matter of following rationality in its development, the systematically elementary investigation of rational thought can lead to the fixation of false absolutes. Pascal said, "It is *not* a grave mistake to fail to ask for axioms in advance if one does not turn them down at the place where they are necessary." One can even go further and say that it is impossible to determine *in advance* all the "principles" necessary for the development of a science.

Owing to the fact that the further development of the rational contains something which is unforeseeable for a consciousness that is lucid but does not rise above the elementary, one can, I feel, in *the very heart* of the rational, legitimately speak of an "experience" of the rational which always contributes something new not yet *implied* in the elementary. It is in this sense that Jean Cavaillès talked about a "revenge" on the part of the technique which "subverts the constructions realized in an abstract realm which surpasses it," [6] whereas he precisely criticized the false absolutes at which Husserl's reflection on the essence of deductive theory had arrived. It is certain that notwithstanding the fact that Husserl did question the "natural" evidences which claim to be absolute, he never thought of doubting these evidences. As he himself says in *Formal and Transcendental Logic:* "Of these things which are self-evident we shall not abandon anything; they certainly have the rank of

6. Jean Cavaillès, *Sur la logique et la théorie de la science* (Paris: Presses Universitaires de France, 1960), p. 72. [See also above, p. 405.—Trans.]

evidences." [7] Once the natural evidences are unmasked as "prejudices," Husserl thinks himself justified in his analyses in assuming them *as prejudices*. But the greatest advantage of the unveiling of "prejudices" is still to thereby have the possibility of
breaking away from them. Poincaré stated that the "dangerous"
hypotheses are "above all those which are tacit and unconscious"; and he added: "because we make them without knowing
it we are unable to abandon them." [8]

But even if one succeeds in avoiding the misfortune of becoming attached to evidences which scientific technique in its
progress will reveal as revocable, then it is often the case that
the results of an absolute, reductive investigation are merely
trivial affirmations. Without a doubt the trivial has its patent of
nobility. Particularly, all those who have devoted themselves to
the practice of modern logic cannot deny the strange pleasure
which the mind experiences when at the end of rigorous exercises it finds again in all its purity the simplicity of a "natural"
evidence. The evidence becomes a novelty; the simple becomes
an object of attention. Even the most trivial affirmations of logic
retain the privilege of evoking interest. On the other hand, it
would be difficult for them to completely escape the reproach of
sterility. One must always take care to avoid the possibility that
lucidity will remain unproductive.

Thus, if one wants to account for the very *progress* of science, one cannot limit himself to the reductive investigations of
radical phenomenology. But by abandoning phenomenology's
radicalism, does one not at the same time abandon all possibility
of phenomenological investigation? Is it not a usurpation to
refer to phenomenology here? As a matter of fact, under these
circumstances one can lay claim only to a *phenomenological
epistemology*. But original phenomenology has introduced a specific type of analysis which has enough force to remain active in
a "weakened" form. And from the moment that a "phenomenological epistemology" does not claim to be the fulfillment of the
most absolute project of phenomenology, I do not see any danger
in installing myself on that level where one does not engage in
the ultimate interrogations characteristic of Husserl's phenomenology. On the whole, I do not feel that I am more unfaithful

7. *FTL*, p. 258.
8. Henri Poincaré, *Science and Hypothesis*, trans. W. J. Green-
street (New York: Dover, 1952), p. 151.

to "transcendental" phenomenology than those contemporary phenomenologists who, one can genuinely say, on their part are no more than phenomenological psychologists.

But even if one grants me the right to abandon the horizon of the transcendental investigations which marked the originality of Husserl's phenomenology, one can still contest the claim that an investigation which follows an "objective" science such as mathematical physics in the very development of its work could have any phenomenological characteristic whatsoever. When we perform an "eidetic variation" of all the possible forms of phenomenology, we see that among the invariant characteristics which remain during this variation, the following presents itself: a phenomenological investigation must be an investigation with a double orientation; it must have an orientation toward the subject as well as toward the object. But then a question emerges: unless one returns to the very origins of the constitution of a discipline such as mathematics—a project which we wish to avoid here—can one still hope to establish a subject-oriented investigation of such a discipline? In fact, each theorem of mathematics is a cell of clear and distinct thought. The mathematical results are accomplished truths. The difficulties of their constitution are no longer visible in them. And what is more, these difficulties are not even helpful for a comprehension of the accomplished truths. This situation is further accentuated by the distinctly difficult character of contemporary mathematical science. It seems that as far as mathematical consciousness itself is concerned, its difficult task becomes completely identical with the apparatus of its demonstration. The tension which the concatenation of the demonstration requires hampers the possibility of a reflexively conscious grasp of it. Consciousness ends by absenting itself from the very effort of its work. Does not the power of the operative ego annihilate itself before the perfection of its works? Maurice Blondel proposed to Jacques Paliard as a subject for a dissertation this theme of reflection: "Does consciousness at the limit of its perfection abolish consciousness?" [9] The mathematical situation, it seems, authorizes an affirmative answer to such a question. Jean Cavaillès was inclined to accept

9. Jacques Paliard, *Profondeur de l'âme* (Paris: Aubier, 1954), p. 32.

such an answer: "There is no consciousness which generates its products or is simply immanent to them. In each instance it dwells in the immediacy of the idea, lost in it and losing itself with it, binding itself to other consciousnesses (which one would be tempted to call other moments of consciousness) only through the internal bonds of the ideas to which these belong. . . . It is not a philosophy of consciousness but a philosophy of the concept which can provide a theory of science." [10] I nevertheless believe that the object-oriented investigation of mathematics can be doubled by a subject-oriented investigation and that the latter can be a starting point for a study of the consciousness of rationality. True, first-hand material for a psychology of the mathematician is rare and poor. Moreover, one can hardly hope that the actual psychology of the mathematician will be clarified by questionnaires drawn up by psychologists. The establishment of such questionnaires would imply that the epistemological situation characteristic of mathematics has already been mastered. But such a state of affairs is not prejudicial to our project: an investigation of phenomenological epistemology has nothing to do with psychological inquiries. To orient oneself phenomenologically toward the "mathematical subjectivity" is to determine an *attitude of mind* which *each* mathematician *must* have, and this does not mean to search for the particular motivations of this or that mathematician. In the first part of this work I shall show that in order to differentiate certain *closely related* disciplines, the merely objective inquiry proves to be an insufficient means of analysis and that only by taking into consideration the attitude of mind which corresponds to these disciplines is one justified in arriving at an explanatory differentiation.

If a phenomenological epistemology cannot expect any help from an inquiry by static psychology, neither can it rely on a *genetic* inquiry, if it is to account for a rational science. The psychologist who has engaged in the tasks of genetic epistemology may certainly say that "from the very start the genetic method escapes reproach for having ignored the normative, because from the effective action to the most formalized operations

10. Jean Cavaillès, *Sur la logique,* p. 78. [See also above, p. 409. —Trans.]

it follows step by step the constitution of norms which are constantly being renewed."[11] But, in this case, the norm is studied as *fact* and not as *norm*. And to hold that "one can describe the whole system of norms in terms of 'normative facts,'"[12] is—to take up again an expression of Husserl—"to level the difference between logical and natural thought."[13]

The term *origin* which I used a moment ago could in this respect lend itself to ambiguity. Usually, in fact, this word refers precisely to a horizon of questions of a genetic order. But it seems to me that Husserl's phenomenology, by stripping this notion "origin" of all chronological references, has given a genuine meaning to it. To think in the chronological mode is a schema of natural thought which, however, often adapts itself poorly to the rational sciences. In these sciences one must most often cease thinking in terms of the schema *earlier-later;* one must rather think in terms of the schema of condition and conditioned and resist the transposition (which is so natural) of relations of implication into temporal relations. Understood in this way and free from all reference to chronology, the notion "origin" receives an explanatory value; the expression "original concept," for instance, designates a *determining* concept which allows us to account for the theoretical development which it evokes.

Moreover, one must underline the fact that even when one orients oneself toward the history of the sciences—of the sciences in the strictest sense, that is to say, of the rational sciences —one cannot pattern this history after the model of history in the current sense. When one follows the history of an elaborated science a bit further, when one goes from its *prehistory*, where it formulates its knowledge in terms of sensible qualities, to its *history*, where experimentation takes the place of observation, when one finally arrives at those periods where science, suddenly dominating its historical development, constitutes itself as a rational doctrine, then one cannot fail to recognize that the history of the sciences is finally a history *where contingency has been eliminated.* As soon as one approaches the truly scientific

11. J. Piaget, *Introduction à l'épistémologie génétique* (Paris: Presses Universitaires de France, 1950), I, 34.
12. *Ibid.,* p. 30.
13. *LU,* Vol. I, § 56, p. 209.

ages, the history of science more and more clearly becomes the history of the rational institutions of our knowledge. It must unfold itself by following the lines of rationality and by becoming conscious of the necessity of well-concatenated thoughts. The historian of the sciences who wishes to pursue his history up to the flowering of science in the modern ages enters, therefore, a domain of *judged history*.[14] He must designate as *errors* thoughts which have been given currency but *should not have been*. Without a doubt, the historian of the sciences, just as any other historian, can be interested in the spirit of an epoch; in a given epoch he may bring to the fore a certain coherence between the governing theses. But if he pushes his inquiry toward the ages of science and becomes a historian of modern science, the historian of the sciences understands that a new task is allotted to him: that of determining the lines of normalized scientific thoughts.

But how is one to appreciate the historical contingency of the unproductive remnant, in a word, how is one to "judge" the past if not by starting from the present? The history of science must then be a *recurrent* history, constantly enlightened by the present of science. The temporal mode in which it expresses itself is therefore not the past, but the conditioned past. In an essay devoted to the "origin" of geometry, Husserl, too, could present his project of study in this way: "The question concerning the origin of geometry, such as we wish to ask it here, is not an external philologico-historical question. It does not seek to know who were the first geometers, those who in fact were the first to express purely geometrical propositions, demonstrations and theories. . . . We seek the sense in which geometry appeared for the first time in history, in which it *had* to appear, even though we know nothing about the first inventors and even though we in no way seek to know this."[15] But, without "returning to the original hidden beginnings of geometry," let us rather think about the tasks of more recent "history" and follow Leibniz who insisted on the difference between "the method which has led to the discovery of the sciences" and that "which one employs to

14. Cf. Gaston Bachelard, *L'Actualité de l'histoire des sciences*, Conference du Palais de la découverte (Paris, 1951), p. 8.
15. Edmund Husserl, "Die Frage nach dem Ursprung der Geometrie als intentionalhistorisches Problem," *Revue internationale de philosophie*, II (1939), 203–25, esp. p. 207. Cf. *H* VI, pp. 365–86.

teach science," that is to say, the method which follows normalized knowledge:

> Sometimes chance has given occasion for discovery. If we had noticed these occasions, and had preserved the memory of them for posterity (which would have been very useful), this detail would have been a very considerable part of the history of the arts but it would not have been proper to make systems of them. Sometimes also discoverers have proceeded rationally to the truth, but by extended circuits. I find that in matters of importance authors would have rendered service to the public if they had been willing sincerely to indicate in their writings the traces of their experiences; but if the system of science should be built upon that foundation, it would be as if in a finished house you wished to preserve all the apparatus which the architect required in building it. Good methods of teaching are all such that by their means science could certainly have been discovered. . . .[16]

But if the history of science which can be incorporated into epistemology as an integral part is to be an "empirical" history, it must not for that reason purely and simply project the present realizations of science into the forms of the past; it must not indulge in rationalizations which see precursory attempts at modern theories in discoveries of the past. And this imperative is all the more pressing when the historian turns toward a more distant past. Is it, for example, a question of studying the applicability of geometry? One will gain nothing by recalling that geometry began in land surveying. Reflection on the etymology of the word "geometry" would similarly be of little value. By taking pleasure in easy examples where the applicability of mathematics seems to have immediate success, one often devalorizes the task of rational thought. One rapidly comes to the conclusion that geometry drapes itself over the empirical forms like a "garment." How much more instructive would a method be, for instance, which would make the problem of applicability evolve from the measuring of a field to the cartography of a continent. The triangle of the land surveyor is ill-suited for the terrestrial sphere. It applies only locally. Complex problems arise if one is to find a total applicability for what applies so well on a partial basis. The complete rationalism of cartography is *imme-*

16. G. W. Leibniz, *New Essays Concerning Human Understanding,* trans. A. G. Langley (Chicago: Open Court, 1916), pp. 475–76.

iately impossible. One must cut and recut the "garment." The philosophers led to this "critical point" in the relations between land surveying and cartography could, according to their philosophical optics, either say that cartography generalizes land surveying or that the different methods of cartography "dialectize" the one method of land surveying. But in any case applicability *causes a problem* here, whereas it did not really cause a problem in simple land surveying or, at least, no longer causes any problem for all educated men. For the thinking of the educated man of our time land surveying is a *dead origin*. Leibniz said in the *New Essays* that the only ones who can content themselves with "receiving in geometry what the images tell us" are "those who trouble themselves only about practical geometry such as it is" and not "those who desire to have the science which serves indeed to perfect the practical. And if the scientists had been of this opinion and had relaxed their efforts on this point, I think they would have made but little advance, and would have left us only an empirical geometry such as that of the Egyptians apparently was, and such as that of the Chinese seems still to be: this would have deprived us of the most worthwhile physical and mechanical knowledge which geometry has caused to discover, and which is unknown wherever our geometry is unknown." [17] Even if in the vicissitudes of the dialogue Theophilus, the spokesman of Leibniz himself, comes to grant to his interlocutor that the geometry of the Egyptians has after all a little more dignity than that of an empirical geometry, his conclusion is still no less decisive: "For if the Babylonians and the Egyptians had anything more than an empirical geometry, nothing of it at least remains." [18] It is still a dead origin.

On the contrary, the more history focuses on a past which is closer to us, the more it will have to take interest in epistemological issues. Particularly when it is a matter of determining the meaning of the results of a highly developed science such as contemporary physics, one finds himself before the difficult problem of giving a *fundamental* meaning to the nuances which have nevertheless only appeared recently in the course of history. Thus the notion of historical "filiation" loses all explanatory force and in certain cases even leads us to erroneous judgments.

17. *Ibid.*, pp. 522–23.
18. *Ibid.*, p. 416.

In fact, our project of examining a science such as mathe matical physics from a phenomenological point of view encoun ters a difficulty which we do not underestimate. Mathematica physics is a very recent science which, therefore, supposes quite a long past of knowledge and which accordingly is more remote from the experiences of our daily world. In order to be able to equal the minuteness and perseverance of Husserl's analyses, a phenomenological study would require a very profound regres sive analysis. We are aware of having "solved" this difficulty only at the cost of lowering our standards.

But if original phenomenology, like any philosophy at its beginning, had the advantage of starting with the first task namely, the study of what offers itself most immediately to our experience, it has on the other hand had to face the "naturalist" danger which dominated the "natural" domains of inquiry. Phe nomenology requires a psychological de-conditioning. This de conditioning is seldom well performed, seldom complete. On the contrary, when there is a question of a mathematical science this de-conditioning is a matter of course. But as I shall not cease to emphasize, mathematical physics is a mathematical science In the problems studied by mathematical physics the mathemati cal spirit does not limit itself to placing our empirical knowledge between brackets. There, as in all mathematics, the mathemati cal spirit absolutely bars psychologistic explanations and tha empirical primitivism which ill-advised pedagogies try to reestab lish in the elementary education of geometry. It was not with out a motive that Husserl, in order to dispense with all naturalis tic interpretations of the phenomenological investigations of essences, showed the analogy of this investigation to the method of mathematical idealization.[19] One cannot go halfway in an attitude of mathematical rationality. For at that moment shielded from all empiricist temptation, the specifically phenom enological inquiry will have a free field.

But if the advantage which we find in the study of mathe matical physics is connected with the fact that this science is a mathematical science, why then did I not, in order to determine an authentic attitude of rationality, choose pure mathematics as my domain of inquiry?

On the one hand it seemed to me instructive to try to grasp

19. Cf. *Ideas I*, § 70; *EU*, § 90.

ıe efforts made by rationality where it finds itself faced with
ıfficulties which are not merely difficulties to the rational
phere itself. In mathematical physics the real will propose prob-
ems to a thinking which could develop in an autonomy which is
ıdifferent to these "obstacles." The "challenge" of the real per-
ıits mathematical physics to be able to assure itself completely
f its explanatory power.

On the other hand, in relation to the physical sciences, math-
matical physics represents a genuine *conversion* of attitude.
Vhat is more revealing for the phenomenologist than a conver-
ıon of attitude? Mathematical physics transforms the infer-
nces of a physical order into foundations from which the math-
matical deduction can take its departure. It ends by giving a
tatus of demonstrative evidence to facts revealed by experience.
t is a re-information of an experimental knowledge which is
lready strongly established. In a word, it materializes a *conver-
ıon from the a posteriori to the a priori*. It is quite remarkable
ıat mathematical physics operates at the borderlines of reason
nd experiment without adulterating its requirements of rigor
nd its rational methods. Although not a "mixed science," it is a
cience with a double interest and a double theme. It wishes to
ssure itself of its rationality, *and* it wishes to account for the
eal. In its *demonstrations* its activity is purely mathematical.
ut, the length of the discursive processes of its demonstration
otwithstanding, mathematical physics maintains a power of
ffirmation which has a bearing on reality. The security based on
ıe guarantee given by the real joins here the formal beauty of
ure mathematics. The following dialogue between the physicist
)ppenheimer and the mathematician Leray pointing to such a
onvergence is on record:

R. OPPENHEIMER: I am not interested in that; this is not physics.
J. LERAY: It is so beautiful that it should be.
R. OPPENHEIMER: This time we agree.

One might say that mathematical physics is the asymptotic
mbition of all sciences of the real.

17 / The Specificity of
Mathematical Physics

Suzanne Bachelard

THE FACT that mathematical physics may at first sigh
seem to stand between physics and mathematics asks for a
discriminating enterprise which engages in a phenomenologica
investigation of double orientation. In fact, one would have a
great deal of trouble in defining mathematical physics exclu
sively by means of its object. What really matters first of all is t
make its spirit felt. One can truly speak of the "spirit" of a
theory; and this spirit cannot be characterized by the mere refer
ence to the methods employed—which would still belong to a
purely "objective" investigation. It is because of this appreciation
of epistemological nuances that Oliver Costa de Beauregard car
write: "One knows that wave mechanics is relativistic in the
sense that one has not been able to constitute it and to keep it in
harmony with experience, except by respecting the new kinemat
ical variants, but *it does not really have the genuine spirit of the
theory of relativity.*" [1] This is an important text because it shows
that the use of relativistic formulas does not necessarily imply a
modification of the teleology of a science. The "spirit" of a doc
trine is a type of intentionality, an intention which is as precise
as it is specific.

This essay from *La Conscience de rationalité: Etude phénoméno
logique sur la physique mathématique* by Suzanne Bachelard (Paris:
Presses Universitaires de France, 1958), pp. 15–28, has been trans
lated by Joseph J. Kockelmans expressly for this edition.
    1. Oliver Costa de Beauregard, "La Relativité restreinte et la
première mécanique broglienne," *Memorial des sciences mathéma
tiques*, CIII (1944), 2.

[426]

If one succeeds in grasping this specific spirit, if one can indicate the special teleology which guides the thought of the modern mathematical physicist, it will appear then that mathematical physics is by no means a doctrine standing between physics and mathematics, but that henceforth it specifies a particular mode of *rationalistic information*. The notion of the applicability of mathematics will then be dominated by the notion of information, taken in the traditional style of philosophy. In order to establish the particular status of mathematical physics we will have to ask that the philosopher refrain from any verbal definition. In this expression "mathematical physics," the word "mathematical" is not a simple adjective which particularizes the noun "physics." Instead, one must confer upon the expression "mathematical physics" a unitary signification.

Thus one understands the necessity in which I find myself of determining as explicitly as possible the specificity of mathematical physics in order to avoid the confusion which comes from philosophical points of view which are too general.

Is there any need to say that, for all scientists engaged in the investigations of mathematical physics, the specificity of this doctrine does not raise doubts, does not pose problems? The best guarantee of the specificity of mathematical physics is probably its modernity. Lamé could write in 1886:

Mathematical physics in the strict sense is a wholly modern creation which belongs exclusively to the geometricians of our century. Today this science really contains only three differently developed chapters which are treated rationally, that is to say which are founded only on unquestionable principles or laws. These chapters are: the theory of static electricity on the surface of conducting bodies, the analytic theory of heat, and finally the mathematical theory of elasticity of solid bodies. . . . Without a doubt, it will not be long before analysis will embrace other parts of general physics such as the theory of light, and that of electro-dynamic phenomena. But one cannot repeat too often that genuine mathematical physics is as rigorous and exact a science as rational mechanics. It is thereby distinguished from all its applications which are founded on dubious principles, on gratuitous or convenient hypotheses, on empirical formulas.[2]

2. G. Lamé, *Leçons sur la théorie mathématique de l'élasticité des corps solides* (Paris: Gauthier-Villars, 1866), Preface.

II

IN THE FIRST PLACE, one must separate mathematical physics from the thesis which is so often evoked by philosophers who are accustomed to considering mathematics as a *language*. A language expresses something, it presupposes a thing which calls for expression. Here, there is a great temptation to say that in mathematical physics, mathematics *expresses* physics. And as a matter of fact this temptation can be explained as long as one has not realized the unitary conception of mathematical physics. Once one understands this unitary conception, one has to say in a tautological way: mathematical physics expresses mathematical physics. As soon, in fact, as one comes to a philosophy of mathematics which stays close to actual mathematical thought, one cannot separate mathematical expression from mathematical thought. Thought and language are inseparable.

In fact, in isolated examples there is some foundation for this "expressionism." But isolated examples where mathematics expresses a physical law do not yet belong to the domain of mathematical physics, given that mathematical physics is essentially a coordination of rational information, a coordination which cannot be given by isolated examples.

Let us nevertheless discuss an isolated example and follow an epistemological path by means of which one feels able to justify the thesis of "mathematical expressionism." Let us study the pressure of a gas in a Mariotte tube. We note the volume and pressure in a series of experiments. We record the values of the pressure on the abscissa and the values of the volume on the ordinate axis. In this way we get a graph which summarizes efficiently a series of actually performed experiments. This graph implies very reasonable interpolations which do not call for objections. We posit as self-evident a "continuity of the law." The curve we have drawn summarizes experiments which we did not perform, but which we could have performed. The mind acquiesces thus to the idea of a continuous induction. We recognize then that the graph has the shape of an equilateral hyperbola. We can then conclude that the mathematical notion "equilateral hyperbola" *expresses* the physical law of Mariotte. From this time on there is evidently only a difference in language between the expressionist who understood immediately that the volume of the compressed gas varies in inverse ratio to the pressure, and the mathematician who says that the two variables of the phenomenon (volume and pressure) are connected with the mathematical function known under the name "equilateral hyperbola."

But this expressionism which succeeds here does not say it all. The summary, at first graphic and then algebraic, of an indefinite sequel of physical experiments is very far from exhausting the power of thought held in reserve in the mathematical expression; with the mathematical formulation of the law the activity of mathematical physics begins. From now on deductions and inferences are possible. Mathematical physics has its own inductive value which governs the simple properties of experimental induction. When we speak of the *inductive* value of mathematics we think of the fecundity of mathematics which leads us ever further in the rational development of our thought. This fertility does not come to it from a thought process which is comparable to physical induction; on the contrary, it comes from its *constructive* deductive power. Moreover, mathematical physics underpins a set of hypotheses in order to discover in the physical law of Mariotte the mathematical law in its essence, and then to prepare generalizations from it. One must therefore note well that the inductivity of rational mathematical thought reinforces, as it were, the confidence in the inductivity of nature which Husserl rightly described as one of the most important characteristics of the sciences of nature. Mathematical physics comes in a way to increase the inductivity of nature and begins, as it were, to put to work a *continued expression* which corresponds to continued rational thought. Later, where I shall follow some lines of development in mathematical physics, we shall see that the mathematical formula which summarizes Mariotte's experiment is not a *final* formula but rather a *point of departure*. In various and more complicated forms, such formulas will be established under the head of *state equation*, in the sense of thermodynamics, as genuine postulates for a large sector of mathematical investigations. We shall have to shed light on this notion of a postulate *which becomes more explicit in an algorithmic representation*. In several of its chapters mathematical physics takes its point of departure from a *table of equations*. But naturally such postulated equations are already thought-laden; mathematical physics contributes a coefficient of initial coherence to the act of postulating. Thus in mathematical physics the mathematical organizations brought into play initially have a consistency which clearly surpasses the level of conventionalism. This thesis concerning the consistency of the algorithmic hypotheses of mathematical physics will become clearer when we have been able to give some examples of it. But even now one can see that a simple "expressionist" conception of the philosophy of mathematical physics is a confusion of epistemological values.

Thus we shall have to show the properly mathematical action of mathematical physics as well as its informative value in regard to phenomena. In mathematical physics there is a kind of mutual induction on the part of two inductivities: the experimental inductivity and the inductivity of mathematics. One can properly say that the language of mathematical physics is a language which "thinks." We shall even see that it thinks on two levels. The mathematical physicist is creative in the mathematical as well as in the physical domain. If he is creative in the domain of experimentation, then this is so *because* he is so in the mathematical domain, and he is creative in the latter domain because he *aims at* explaining experiments. Mathematical physics in itself alone presents an arsenal of objections to the skeptical thesis of pure expressionism in regard to mathematics. These skeptical theses, which have been generally current in the last century, appear quite clearly to be surpassed. At that time mathematics had come to be considered as an ensemble of utensils. George D. Birkhoff reacted negatively to such an attitude and reports these words of a physicist which are highly indicative of this attitude: "It is not so many years ago that a distinguished physicist, after I had just answered a question which he had asked me, said to me: I wish I had a mathematical slave. Today, however, it is scarcely possible to consider mathematics exclusively as a useful tool, given the fact that for almost four decades the most important progress materialized in theoretical physics has been due to mathematical insight and has implied ever larger sectors of mathematical knowledge." [3] Thus the coupling of mathematics and physics from now on is so tight, and the

3. G. D. Birkhoff, "The Mathematical Nature of Physical Theories," *Science in Progress*, IV, no. 4 (1947).

intuitions between theoretical and mathematical physics so correlative, that one can no longer think physically without thinking mathematically.

In addition, generally speaking, in all that is related to a science which more or less remotely aims at reality, one must object to the simplifying theses which put the stress exclusively on the formal manipulation of symbols. They do not describe the plurality essential to the levels of consciousness in the work of a thought which must follow different modes of concatenations in the double coherence of the experimental organizations. These simplifying theses—expressionism, conventionalism—lead rather, provided they may be pushed to their limits, to replacing actual scientific thought with a pure automatism. If this were the case, by dint of bringing about "thought economies," one would no longer think. At least one would have to compensate for the ease with which these thoughts are materialized in an economy of thought by the *consciousness of this economy*. But precisely, each time the mathematician realizes an economy of thought, he is "at the same time" conscious of this economy; and this economy is for him merely a means of liberating thought. Our inquiry will show, I hope, the diversity of the mental attitude of the mathematical physicist.

III

A SECOND FALSE ORIENTATION would be to confuse mathematical physics with a geometrical organization similar to Cartesian physics. One must in fact state that the physics of the mathematical genius which Descartes was, is not a mathematical physics. With the exception of some sectors such as that of his dioptrics, where recurrent history can find certain themes which prepare mathematical physics, Descartes' physics does not contain any trace of an algebraic thought. There is not a single equation in the entire book on the *Principles,* but only geometrical figures. Descartes, who used algebra in order to elucidate geometry, does not use it in his physics.

In fact, Descartes' cosmology is a doctrine of the absolute solid. The heavens themselves are an arrangement of large or small solid bodies. The reference to a process of wear which takes the edges off the corners is only a weak connective in regard to the absolute character of the geometrical forms assigned the task of explaining the phenomena. In summary, Descartes' explanation of the phenomena is dependent upon simple geometrical intuition. From this fact an eminent privilege is attached to Descartes' universal geometrization: this geometrization *immediately* satisfies our intuition. That is why the book on the *Principles* can be presented in short paragraphs. Each of these paragraphs has its own evidence, a hastily presented evidence. Each tends to legitimate a general explanation. Sometimes this legitimation is long-winded, built up of isolated pieces.

As a counterpart to this privilege of a hastily presented and multiple explanation, one must recognize that geometrical intuition cannot penetrate so simply and without discursiveness into the internal phenomenality. It lacks precisely an essential discursiveness. In this respect—as Husserl has noted in *Krisis*—it is to Galileo that the glory for having given the impulse to mathematical physics belongs. The problematic of Cartesian physics is always very brief. But when the problem is short, when the intuitions associate too hastily, one is never quite certain that the phase of *description,* that is to say, the phase which remains preliminary and preparatory in relation to a genuine explanation of the phenomena, is surpassed. In that phase of Descartes' description, time (which is so deeply implied in a complete study of phenomenality) does not intervene. One cannot even say that time is really integrated in the doctrine of the Cartesian vortices. Descartes' physics is, as it were, atemporal. It is truly geometrical.

The doctrine of the absolute solid is so clear in Descartes' physics that one can rightly say that the solid bodies are impenetrable for reasons connected with pure exteriority, for reasons which are solely geometrical. They are not impenetrable because of an intrinsic hardness. What argument in Descartes' opinion is satisfactory enough to prove that hardness is not an attribute of the material substance? It is this, that if a body moves away from us as fast as we are approaching it, the contact we would make with it would be completely geometrical, "we would never experience its hardness." Therefore, because the hardness can be cancelled out by a movement, it does not belong to the substance of the object. In the final analysis the hardness of a solid body does not have any "cement" other than the relative repose of the parts of the solid substance (Part II, section 63). If our hands are not able to break this cement which is the relative repose of two parts of a "hard body," this is "because our hands are very weak, that is to say because they participate more in the nature of liquid bodies than in that of solid bodies; and this is the reason that all the parts of which they are composed do not work together against the body which we want to separate, and that these are none other than those which, in touching it, rest jointly on it." One sees the trick in the argument to which Descartes resorts in order to establish his pure geometrism, that is, his will to limit all physical investigations to geometrical characteristics. This universal geometrization is in a way purely visual. Descartes' solid bodies are *seen* rather than *touched*. If the hand is "soft," the eye is "clear." It is not necessary to interfere with the world in order to comprehend it. Seeing with the eyes of a geometer suffices to understand the world.

By pondering this example—one could easily give others— one sees that the reference to exteriority characterizes Descartes' physics. Cartesian physics corresponds to the description of a world of objects and not to a description of phenomena, and even less to an intimate determination of phenomena in their temporal development. It is a spatio-temporal determination which is the task of mathematical physics.

In fact it is very remarkable that the true physics of the *phenomena of solidity* presents itself only late in history. One has to go to the twentieth century for such a science to be constituted.[4] But in Descartes' time the domain of inquiry toward the solidity of solid bodies, toward the interior of bodies had not yet opened up. In Descartes' time the interior of bodies, a domain in which mathematical physics will have to develop inferences, was a region prohibited to an inquiry of rational thought. And by some of its aspects, the absolute universal geometrization characteristic of Descartes' physics serves to record this prohibition.

In fact, if one places Descartes' physics in its time, one must not fail to point to its eminent polemic aspect. The doctrine of absolutely solid bodies is an *exteriorism* which, with particular bluntness, forbids all reference to internal qualities. And since the internal, through lack of positive experiences, is the occult,

4. See, for instance, among many other textbooks, the book by Wilhelm Seitz, *The Modern Theory of Solids* (London & New York: McGraw-Hill, 1940), (particularly chap. XIII, where the five types of solid bodies, the five types of "solidity," are presented.)

434 / Phenomenology and Science in France

one sees the philosophical importance of Descartes' physics for a scientific position of our knowledge of the real. Descartes' physics has played the useful role of a genuine psychoanalysis of objective knowledge. When we shall have to study the phenomenology of discursive knowledge, we shall have an opportunity to recall Descartes' physics as one of the types of barriers against any projection of sensible knowledge, which is more or less colored by affectivity and still carries the sign of sensibility. In Cartesian physics the act of becoming aware of rationality is simple, clear, and distinct. The realism connected with this act of rationality is undoubtedly concise. More complex detours are necessary in order to follow with mathematical physics the complication of the rational as well as the multiplicity of experience. But on a number of occasions we shall have to draw attention (along the road we are following) to points of departure for a rationality of the Cartesian type which proceeds by barring all sensible qualities. For example, all the efforts of the mathematician to constitute a mathematical physics of electrostatics will start by establishing theorems in regard to the well-defined geometrical surfaces which do not make any reference to the sensible qualities of electricity.

But the rationalist positions facilitated by Descartes' universal geometrization merely bar the irrationalism of substantive qualities. Descartes' rationalism does not proliferate as does the discursive rationalism of mathematical physics.

There is still another element which has hindered Descartes' engagement in geometry from developing in the direction of a genuine mathematical physics. This is the mobility of explanation which Descartes adopts. Strictly speaking one cannot say that in Descartes' physics deduction proceeds more geometrico. There is no question of a strict geometry. Descartes' physics is an illustrated geometry. The images of extension are offered freely and indifferently. They are many, and the reader is left, as it were, with freedom of choice. There is pluralism of figuration.

The abstraction which must remove all the properties of a body takes place by referring to clashing examples. When there is a question of showing that the nature of a body consists merely in its extension, Descartes says: "Let us take a stone and remove from it all that is not essential to the nature of body." One may remove its hardness because if the stone were reduced to powder, the stone would no longer be hard. The *color* does not belong to it because there are stones so transparent (rock crystal) that they have no color. *Weight* does not belong to the stone either "because we see that fire although very light (bereft of weight) is yet a body." [5]

Thus I grant myself the right to cut out from the experience which the stone positively gives me the characteristic of being heavy because I know of another body, fire, which seems to be without weight.

The induction which a moment ago in the case of color allowed us to go from a colored stone to a colorless one accelerates to the point of going from a stone to fire. This skipping induction could not profit from that *inductivity* about which Husserl speaks and which he already sees at work in the algebraism of Galileo's physics. This inductivity will determine long lines of arguments in the problems of mathematical physics. My general aim in this study is to give an outline of a phenomenology of this inductivity. Descartes' physics is of no help to us in such a task. In fact, it seems that the dogmatism of the geometrical intuition in Descartes is accompanied by a kind of skepticism in regard to an experience which is discursively pursued. The "experiments" to which Descartes refers are more thought experiments than realized experiments. These thought or imagined experiments take place in the atmosphere of possibility. In his physics Descartes appears in a number of ways as a precursor of the philosophy of the "as if," a philosophy whose lack of engagement Husserl has often stressed. Because of the fact that Descartes always adheres faithfully to his universal geometrization, his "world of fiction" is, generally speaking, a coherent fiction. But if one enters into the details of his arguments, if one follows the apparatus of his proofs in his incongruous examples, one sees that this fictive world is in reality a mosaic of fictions. Descartes' physics dwells in a geometrical rationality which does not have an effective hold on reality. It can certainly not give us the basis for reflections which are related to the mutual inductivity of experimental and mathematical physics. Descartes' physics is not a mathematical physics.

5. René Descartes, *The Principles of Philosophy*, trans. E. Haldane and G. Ross (New York: Dover, 1955), I, 259.

IV

IN THIS PRELIMINARY CHAPTER my intention is to dismiss certain aspects of the problem of rationality which could come to mind and obscure the very precise discussions which I wish to institute in order to define the value of the rational induction of mathematical physics. In the preceding pages I have therefore dismissed, as precisely as possible, the philosophical theses which devalorize mathematical organization in the extreme and make of it a simple organization of a language and the theses which exaggerate the value of a purely geometrical intuition such as that which illuminates all of Cartesianism.

We would be more at a loss if we had to judge the general inspiration of Newton's thought with the same rapidity. After all, Newton's philosophy really faces that double requirement which will always remain the dual condition of scientific progress: it wishes to extend the realm of experience, and it wishes to rationally coordinate experience. In order to make allowance for empiricism and rationalism in Newton's philosophy, a lengthy book would be necessary. But this book has been written: in 1908 in his admirable dissertation Léon Bloch analyzed the interweaving of reason and experiment in Newton's thought.[6] He showed how the impulse toward an experiment, always aiming toward refined precision, and the impulse toward an increased rationality relieve one another throughout the long development of Newton's science. The historical study of this double progress which Léon Bloch undertook makes fully clear not only the importance of Newton as a physicist and mathematician but particularly the entire new forms of the close cooperation between experiment and mathematics. With Newton's scientific thought we are in a complex situation. With Newton, in fact, a transaction factor of immense importance has been introduced: the calculus of fluxions, infinitesimal calculus. At this point in the history of ideas the human mind systematically and methodically integrates the notion of the infinite and applies this notion to the real. The word "fluxion" concentrates in itself a number of experiments and thoughts. Undoubtedly one can certainly find

6. Léon Bloch, *La Philosophie de Newton* (Paris: Alcan, 1908).

antecedents for the calculus of limits. In this connection one may properly recall the genius of Archimedes. But a usage of the calculus of limits which is wholly geometrical, however precious it may be, does not give a complete idea of the possibilities of the applicability of the rationalism of the infinitesimal.

By its application to the real, infinitesimal calculus gives an unexpected structure to the "nearly." The "nearly"—a case which deserves the attention of the phenomenologist—no longer exclusively refers here to a consciousness of failure in the pure organization of thoughts. It has become a solicitation to well-determined and precisely regulated approximations. Without a doubt the doctrine of approximation receives a greater depth in the science which springs from Newton's science. Relativity theory even denounces Newtonian mechanics as a doctrine of first approximation insufficient to inform us about phenomena which can be apprehended through a mathematical organization in second approximation only. But in Newton's start one feels at work a kind of autoapproximation of rational thought in its application to astronomical phenomena.

Newton's law of attraction will allow us to account for—and to foresee—perturbations which escaped Kepler's *description*. Kepler's laws can be rigorous only if one takes into account the sun and a single planet; they are therefore rigorous only for the two-body problem. They *become* approximate when one considers them by starting from the problematic of Newton's law of attraction, a law which through its rational information provides the approximation with a rigorous rule. One does not abandon the perturbations as if they fell within the realm of the "nearly," of that "nearly" which is the inevitable margin between the rational and the real. Léon Bloch correctly says: "One of the original characteristics of the law of universal gravitation is this successive improvement to which it is susceptible. Before Newton there was no known law which could complete itself in this way. Descartes' theorems concerning the celestial movements are necessarily false or necessarily true. They cannot be admitted as first approximations, except in order to explain the inequalities of our observation by an application of the same theories." [7]

It is apparent that in quite a few respects Newton's philoso-

7. *Ibid.*, p. 303.

phy is a privileged domain for studying the relationship between mathematical thought and our knowledge of reality. So it seems that one can subscribe to this judgment of Léon Bloch: "One can say with exactness that the *Principles of Natural Philosophy* is the first treatise on mathematical physics." [8]

However, I do not believe that I had to go so far back in the history of mathematical physics. I prefer to establish my philosophical commentary on themes which arise when mathematical physics is already truly constituted, when mathematical physics is established in its maximal specificity.

In order that the specificity may come clearly to the fore, even in regard to Newton's philosophy, let us therefore at the conclusion of this introductory chapter point to the difference which exists between Newton's science and the doctrine characteristic of contemporary mathematical physics.

In fact, the remarkable success of Newton's mathematical information has been materialized on the basis of celestial phenomena. If one considers Newton's science a mathematical physics, he must affirm that the master chapter of his mathematical physics is astronomy.

Certainly, anyone who wishes to come to grips with the rationalism of scientific prevision will always profit by following the emergence of applied rationalism as materialized in Newton's philosophy. Then the difference between a prevision which merely and simply registers the regular return of a star and a prevision which builds upon a mathematical organization becomes clear. It is in fact a matter of giving this difference all of its phenomenological meaning by living, as an emergence of consciousness, the passage from fact to norm, the passage from the assertoric to the apodictic. Once one has realized the *level of apodicticity* which Newton's mathematical information materializes, he is able to realize a kind of condensed prediction which is rooted in a domain which is very close to astronomical observation. Concerning the prevision of the return of a comet, Louis Figuier wrote that to foresee the return of an event which occurs only once is the work of a prophet or a fool. One must, however, recognize that Newton's rationalism is able to foresee the whole trajectory on the basis of a segment of its path. The observation of the return of a star passes then to the simple rank

8. *Ibid.*, p. 127.

of the verification of a law. The rationalism of the law of attraction is obviously the dominating epistemological mark.

However, mathematical physics does not claim that Newton's astronomy is a sector of its investigations. Or, more exactly, mathematical physics has taken up again the problem of Newton's attraction by *spatializing* this attraction even more through the theory of potentials to which I shall devote a chapter in the second part of the present work. In Newton's astronomy stars are *points*. Kant, too, emphasizes this "punctualization." [9] If the celestial bodies are considered in a spherical approximation, they can be reduced to points, and even rigorously so; in fact, according to a well-known Newtonian theorem, the motion of the center of a spherical mass is the same as when all of its mass is concentrated at its center. Under the form of punctual and linear determinations such as the movements of a star in its orbit, determinism teaches us clear lessons, but in the final analysis these lessons are too easy. The rationalism which springs from it is too hastily satisfied. This simplified rationalism falls into banality and thus is often absorbed by an empiricism which abandons all concern for epistemological structure. All phenomenological inquiry must take into consideration this trivialization of the rational. It seems that science cuts itself off, that its relief wears away. Empiricism then grants itself the rational as a habit; it receives it passively as a lesson without ever living in its emergence. It is thus of some importance to determine the philosophical values of our rational explanation on the basis of examples taken from a more advanced science such as mathematical physics. Then one does not limit oneself to rational explanations which are enfeoffed to a single domain of physics. One may properly say that mathematical physics receives its full meaning only when it acquires an explanatory power which is polymorphous. Certainly, Newton's theory has the merit of providing a rational explanation, but this applies only to one single type of physical field. In fact, the progress made in regard to the notions related to "attraction" came from the study of electrical attraction, particularly after mathematical physics had undertaken the mathematical organization of electrostatics. Then a great number of theorems which imply the

9. Immanuel Kant, *Metaphysical Foundations of Natural Science,* in *Kant's Prolegomena and Metaphysical Foundations of Natural Science,* trans. E. Belfort Bax (London: Bell, 1883), pp. 161.

electric distribution in fields of varying forms presented themselves. From then on one was able to envisage a kind of spatial analysis of attraction.

These theorems would be scarcely useful if one studied only a *center* of attraction, a "point" in the Kantian sense, which has been provided with a numerical coefficient translating an intensity of attraction. All the space around this point becomes intuitively analyzed into a series of concentrical spheres and discursively analyzed into a set of quasi-immediate theorems. We would have no way of transcending the isotropy of space in order to materialize the schemes of the anisotropy of space. In order to follow the conceptual enrichment of thought and intuition one must, therefore, come to considerations concerning extended mediums whose study is one of the major occupations of mathematical physics. Here mathematical physics meets Newton's astronomy, encompasses his astronomy. In any case one may say that the mathematical organizations which render explicit Newton's hypothesis of an attraction which is in inverse ratio to the square of the distance reappear in numerous sectors of mathematical physics.

Jean Ladrière

JEAN LADRIÈRE was born in Nivelles, Belgium, in 1921 and received his doctorate (1949) and *maître agrégé* (1956) from l'Institut Supérieur de Philosophie at the University of Louvain, where he has been a professor since 1959. In addition, he has been a visiting professor at Duquesne University in Pittsburgh, Lovanium University in the Congo, and the University of Paris at Nanterre. The courses he has taught range from mathematics and the philosophy of nature and the natural sciences to social philosophy. His published writings include numerous articles, as well as one book on the implications of Gödel's theorem and related theories in their role of manifesting the limitations of formalism.

The following two selections from Ladrière's work serve to complement each other. The first serves to introduce the second. More general in scope, it begins by adapting the notions of "project" and "horizon," terms suggestive of a hermeneutical phenomenology, to the general tasks of a philosophy of science and continues with an outline of the specific tasks of a philosophy of mathematics, among which is the problem of the relations between mathematics and the natural sciences. The second essay moves in the opposite direction, beginning with the nature of mathematical reality and concluding by placing it in the larger context of the life of reason. The nature of mathematical being is situated in the reciprocal involvement of two opposite and yet complementary tendencies, abstractive formalization and concretizing intuition, the one emphasizing the system and the other specific problems. Such a view represents a *rapproche-*

ment between formalism and realism and suggests a balance between logicism and phenomenology as well as a regard for the dynamics of mathematical existence. Contrary to Husserl, the abstraction of formalization is viewed not as a *Sinnentleerung,* but as an apprehension of the most original nucleus of a hierarchy of theoretical layers, their singular essence. But while mathematics strives for the comprehensive structures that formalization can yield, it necessarily continues to receive its nourishment from the intuitive origins to which it must perpetually return. The fulcrum of the twofold movement that the progression of mathematics describes is to be situated neither in the mind nor in reality but in the concept, the intentional reality that mediates them. It is in this intermediate space that mathematical being is situated, where its movement traces a dialectic in which each term generates the next, fulfilling it by giving meaning to it, in a regulated progression whose trajectory assumes a privileged direction and indicates a necessity according to which no step can be skipped. This essay thus sketches the details of that dialectic of the concept which Jean Cavaillès, in the last lines of his last work, identified as central to the life of science. What is said of mathematics here is applicable by analogy to mathematical physics, which in its own way is suspended between the formalizing and intuitive tendencies, and involved in the dialectical tension between formal and material a priori.

18 / Mathematics in a
Philosophy of the Sciences

Jean Ladrière

Is A PHILOSOPHY of the sciences possible? Just to ask this question is to enter into the movement of philosophical reflection. For the question of the possibility of philosophical knowledge belongs to philosophy itself, insofar as it resolves to be radical.

Before approaching one or another region of experience, a position with regard to experience as a whole must be taken, and an objective, a method, some tools must be forged. And by a sort of a circle, every question of method presupposes the final result toward which it moves. For the movement of philosophical reflection cannot be linear but represents a deepening, a process of radicalization, involving halts, backtracking and resuming again and again. The method can become clear to itself only in the very act by which it affirms its mastery over its field of application. There is no ideal of explanation present in advance, which one then strives to realize through a progressive execution. It is not just a matter of passing from an abstract point of view to a concrete undertaking. It is rather the way in which a question is asked which seems decisive. Every question carries with it not only the hope of an answer but also a horizon of comprehension within which the answer can be elaborated. The answer is not only the positing of a new term within the discourse, by virtue of which the question finds itself suppressed, but it is also the

Theodore J. Kisiel has translated this article by Jean Ladrière, originally entitled "La Philosophie des mathématiques et le problème du formalisme," *Revue philosophique de Louvain,* LVII (1959), 600–22.

process of making the horizon of comprehension explicit. It might even be said that this latter operation is the primary one, for the mind is rendered capable of formulating the content of the answer only insofar as the dimension of the answer becomes explicit for it. Properly speaking, no new term is created. There is only an acknowledgment of what was already inscribed in the very first moment of questioning. And when we come to a question which bears on the very foundation of experience, we can no longer expect to illuminate it on the basis of some preceding discourse. Here the question itself sheds the light in which it can be seen. The horizon which this question institutes defines the ultimate dimension of comprehension. This horizon is the foundation of all comprehension, in the sense that it is necessarily present in any effort to elucidate experience.

If this is true, the primordial philosophical movement consists in asking that first question which must give meaning to the whole endeavor, or to put it another way, in conquering that dimension of reflection in which such a question, with all of its implications, becomes possible. To say that philosophy begins with a first reflection does not state a banality but affirms the necessity of a conversion of thought and already indicates the style of a certain kind of inquiry.

Once this style is mastered, thinking can develop by a continual deepening which is at the same time a recovery of its original movement. It can thus overtake, in a twofold sense, the totality of experience. For if the philosophical ambition tends to radicalize itself in the unveiling of an ultimate aporetic horizon and to thus reabsorb every possible question within the unity of a final encompassing dimension, it can receive full satisfaction only in a procedure which reunites the different sectors of experience in a way which illuminates both the singularity of each and their mutual connections. There is thus a movement which carries itself beyond every particular in order to open the absolute space of comprehension and another movement which flows back in some way from this absolute space toward the different subspaces which it includes. It is in this backflow that the particular regions of experience can be illuminated. Just as it is necessary, in order to arrive at an ultimate point of view of interrogation, to encompass not only every actual experience but also every possible experience in order to transcend it towards its foundations, it is also necessary, in order both to illuminate the detail of experience and to manifest the fruitfulness of the encompassing principle, to restore in its illumination everything which the first movement had provisionally dispelled from its field of attention. To a regressive operation which returns experience to its source and thus permits it to be illuminated through and through must be conjoined a constitutive operation which shows how the totality of experience deploys itself from this source in the diversity of its contents and the multiplicity of its regions. But it is not as if we can conceive these as integrated into a kind of universal container according to a spatial relation of inclusion. The ensemblist language would only betray reality here. It is rather a matter of successive layers of comprehension that philosophical analysis must make apparent in dissociating them from each other.

Experience is not a chaos; it is not a pure and simple juxtaposition of disparate elements, nor is it a simple elaboration of internal states or external situations. It is the name of an encounter between the human existent and what is given to it; it is the constitution of a certain world. It necessarily involves a unity, an organization, a structure. It is articulated; it involves a logic. Experience is not a repetition of the homogeneous but includes diversity and heterogeneity, discontinuity and rupture. But in each of its moments, it can be realized only on the ground of a precomprehension of its object, which in some way opens the space in which experience can come to the encounter of its content. It is this precomprehension that constitutes the horizon in relation to which experience performs the reading which is proper to it. And so each type of experience has its characteristic horizon. To the term *horizon*, the term *project* can be made to correspond. The first connotes an attention to objectivity; it indicates the way in which the world gives itself to man; it signifies a mode of revelation of that which manifests itself. The second connotes an attention to subjectivity; it indicates the fashion in which the human existent approaches the encounter of the world; it signifies a characteristic initiative of the consciousness, a way of forming the given. In reality, the two terms overlap. As soon as one tries to make their content precise, one sees them pass into each other. For they are only different names for one and the same reality, which is the encounter of an interiority and an exteriority, of a consciousness and a world, of a subjectivity and an objectivity. The encounter is always singular and in a strict sense ineffable, in which the two terms can be distinguished only by a kind of violence which bursts the concrete unity of experience into an abstract duality in which the original character of the lived experience is lost.

If we project ourselves toward the world in this manner, it is because it was thus offered to us. And if it manifests itself to us under such a form, it is because we possessed the wherewithal to so grasp it. The structure of a horizon thus refers to the structure of the project and vice versa. Everything occurs as if the consciousness already possessed within itself the objective structures that the detail of experience will have it progressively retrieve, and as if the world were in advance totally permeated by the categories of the consciousness, ready to let itself be overtaken through the actual initiative of consciousness. Hence the world is in the consciousness and the consciousness is in the world. There is not only a preestablished harmony, a mysterious or providential correspondence between two parallel terms but also a reciprocal interiority, a circumincession, perpetual passage from one into the other. The two vocabularies of horizon and of project, corresponding to a unique reality, simply constitute different tools of description. One could say that it is the project that opens the horizon and that the horizon constitutes itself in the light of the project.

And for each particular type of experience, there will accordingly be a corresponding characteristic constitutive project. If experience is not a chaos, it is not only because its data are organized according to a well-determined polarity, but also and more profoundly because the different polarities themselves, which correspond to different layers of experience, are tied to each other according to hierarchical relations. Not that one raises oneself from region to region toward ever greater syntheses by a process of increasing generalization. The synthesis is possible only by continually referring to a principle of organization or of comprehension. It is only the increasing specification of a certain horizon. The process of synthesis belongs to the execution of the project within its characteristic region. There is no continuity between the various planes of experience; hence there is no indefinite process of synthesis. But certain regions can be constituted only on the basis of other regions which are already constituted. The passage from one region to another cannot be made in any direction whatsoever. There are among the regions relations of necessary priority. When an experience is realized according to its own type of clarity and evidence, it includes within itself other experiences which have already been realized and which in turn depend on other types of evidence. It includes them not as constituents or parts but as a ground which must necessarily be present if the actual operation is to be achieved. We are trying to evoke a relation of presence rather than a relation of inclusion.

This presence is not and cannot be explicit. When one or another project is actualized, it occupies the consciousness completely, so that the project, in a nonexplicit way, in its very exercise, refers to an anchorage in something preconstituted. Each project presents itself as an absolute initiative. It is always a new beginning of the world, proceeding from an original astonishment and establishing an absolutely new type of bond with the things themselves. The presence which is operative here is accordingly nonthematic or still structural, in the sense that it necessarily belongs to the structure of the experience which it makes possible and which it efficaciously sustains.

Furthermore, the project is hidden from itself during the course of its actualization. It is likewise given to the consciousness in nonthematic form, as an invisible and effective presence, as the point of escape of a perspective, or more exactly, as the style of a certain movement. It is totally in the acts through which it realizes itself. The consciousness in operation does not survey these operations like a power which is always attentive to itself even in its most external manifestations. It is as if it were immersed in its act, alienated in its gesture, lost in its products. Its project is not given to it as a preexisting term, in the manner of an ideal, an avowal, or a decision. It reveals itself in the movements through which it realizes itself.

Moreover, the horizon of an experience is not a scene in outline which is simply to be filled out. It is rather the style of the liaisons by which the acts are linked in a way that constitutes, not an incoherent landscape but a universe endowed with meaning. It is at once present and absent. It is absent in the sense that it is never overtaken, always escaping every attempt of retrieve and always beyond every realization. It is present in the sense that it is always given, not only at every stage of the progression but at the very origin of it, at the moment when nothing as yet was, when the project still hovered above the void in the tentative groping of its first initiatives. This presence is therefore not a full, effective, and saturating presence. It is an absent presence. Everything is already there, but nothing as yet is. Nothing ever is, but everything already is. The mode of revelation proper to the horizon corresponds to the structure of the manifestation and is based on the very nature of human experience in all of its extension and all of its depth.

The project truly belongs to consciousness precisely because there is presence in absence. It belongs not to the domain of the unconscious but to the order of the nonthematic consciousness. It is the object of what might be called a lateral regard. If it is correct to say that the consciousness inhabited by the project (which is always the case) is, as it were, lost in its products, it must also be said that it is never imprisoned there. It is always beyond what it realizes, precisely because it bears a project, precisely because it is consciousness. Its mode of progression is that of both inherence and transcendence. It buries itself in its acts and loses itself in objectivity, but at the same time it always retrieves itself, perpetually surpassing its objects and the very objectivity which it constitutes, which is moreover why it can truly act. This permanent movement of recovery is precisely the life of the project which, so to speak, colors all of the objects upon which it deposits its efficacy, to which it delegates its light. The object is never a pure reference to itself but is also a revelation of the project. This revelation is at once partial and total: partial because it cannot of itself exhaust that which essentially presents itself as inexhaustible, total because the project is indivisible and completely present in each of its manifestations. Hence the consciousness always has the wherewithal to turn back in some way toward its initial project. It can forget or revive it according to the occasion, insofar as the evidence holds up or trails off. As soon as the perspectives become confused or the clarity wavers, the consciousness can provisionally abandon the detail of its procedure and detach itself from the constituted objectivity, in order to return to the origin and there to rediscover the initial impulse which set everything in motion. It can do so because the impulse was always there, because it suffices, in order to restore its entire force, to capture the trace of it that is operative at the very moment of doubt. Moreover, it is due to this permanent action that the doubt itself is possible, inasmuch as it already prompts the return to the original evidence. Because it is never totally absorbed in its productions, consciousness is capable of doubt and of separating itself at times from its exteriority in order to question it and to turn from it to the fundamental questioning upon which this particular question necessarily depends. Once again, this return does not consist in referring to a preconstituted ideal which would be present before the consciousness as an image ever available for contemplation. The return is realized in new acts and new gestures whose entire meaning is precisely to furnish an actualization more adequate and more certain than that which was inscribed in the moment of incertitude.

The project is thus present to experience only in nonthematic form. But even here, it is not an absolute epiphany. The referential structure which it constitutes is itself based on other underlying structures, according to relations which can moreover be quite different from one case to another. More and more the different projects whose union defines the extension of the field of experience refer back to a fundamental project which is the primordial bond by virtue of which there is experience, and which in this sense is the primary constituent of all the particular projects. Otherwise stated, the different horizons through which experience is articulated are themselves articulated among themselves and refer finally to an ultimate horizon which makes all the others possible and defines the very possibility of the life of consciousness.

It is the act of reflection which reveals these different structures and their articulations in an explicit way, bringing the nonthematic elements of experience into thematic view, freeing the project and the horizons which outline the shape of the whole of experience from the contents in which they are implicated. Reflection is possible because these elements are not situated in an inaccessible realm, because they are really part of the given, even though in a more or less hidden form. It is a kind of recovery of the living flux, a return to the origin. Reflection merely executes the movement which perpetually primes itself in the concrete life of consciousness, in which the consciousness continually reappropriates its project at the very moment in which it constitutes this project externally.

But such a recovery can be carried out only because of a transcendence. In relation to a certain sector of experience, the act of thematization is itself carried out in a characteristic horizon which is necessarily beyond the horizon which is to be retrieved. The effort of reflection is an effort of comprehension, which aims to clarify an experience that in its initial manifestation in the dispersion of its duration could seize itself only in an obscure way. To comprehend a datum is to explicate its relation with the shape of the whole in which it is inserted or to make apparent that by which it truly belongs to the life of consciousness, to explicate the structure of intelligibility which it involves, to show its inclusion within the illuminating horizon which determines its place in the network of terms and of relations in which it takes part.

There are several modes of comprehension, several levels of thematization, bound to each other according to the law of hierarchization of horizons. It is therefore possible to resume a given endeavor of comprehension within a larger endeavor which, transcending the first, illuminates its movement by relating it to a more profound realm of comprehension. The different sciences are so many modes of thematization of naïve or immediate experience as it is realized in perception and spontaneous praxis. The sciences themselves are integrated within a general mode of comprehension which defines the scientific enterprise as such. Nevertheless, none of these endeavors claims to exhaust the intelligibility of the given. Total in their order, they are not totalitarian. Philosophy on the contrary presents itself as a totalitarian enterprise. It proceeds from a radical requirement for comprehension, claiming to overtake the ultimate horizon in relation to which all the others can be illuminated. This implies that it is capable of accounting for itself, of comprehending its own enterprise in the very act in which it tries to comprehend the whole of experience.

In this sense, the ultimate horizon has to be radically different from all the others, having within itself its own light. It is the supreme principle of intelligibility from which all the others take their power of illumination. It is that by which there is clarity and by which human existence is spirit. Its role is therefore not only to give a more radical foundation to what was already partially founded, hence to produce a more perfect knowledge, but also and above all to found experience itself, to establish that "there is" experience, dialogue between man and the world, life of a consciousness, becoming of spirit.

Philosophy is an attempt to conquer such a horizon, and,

insofar as it can be launched and developed only under the motion of this last horizon, it is an attempt to comprehend itself. It is the questioning which radically places itself under question. In this sense, philosophy is at once circular and integrating. What it strives to conquer was already given to it in its very first act. And in the act by which it founds itself, it at once founds the totality of experience. Furthermore, it is never finished, both because experience never ceases to enrich itself, so that each new conquest demands elucidation, and because the regressive movement through which philosophical reflection thematically grasps its working dimension is never at its term. The work of establishing foundations calls for continual resumption through an incessant process of deepening.

Yet as soon as this reflection is launched, it permits a return to already constituted experience and already realized efforts of comprehension. From this moment, there is room for a philosophical comprehension of the particular regions of experience. The return to the type of evidence proper to each region ought to include a triple operation: it should uncover the project-horizon structure proper to that region, show how this structure could constitute itself from other regions previously constituted (here of course the question of the original region which supports all the initiatives of consciousness will be asked), and then show how this structure is inserted in the broader horizons of comprehension within which it is thematized and finally in the last horizon which defines the properly philosophical explanation.

II

THESE BRIEF INDICATIONS of a purely abstract nature should permit us to pose the problem of the philosophy of the sciences a little more clearly.

The scientific enterprise constitutes a particularly important region of experience. It possesses its own light and its own types of evidence. In developing itself, it has itself produced the type of comprehension which belongs to it and continues to make this precise to the degree in which its conquests multiply. By its very existence and its claims, it places philosophy under question, at least implicitly. We can in fact ask whether science is not the only possible type of comprehension, at least at some distant date. Should we not expect that a future development of science will completely eliminate philosophy, by revealing its illusory character? We might think so, if it were not for the fact that science and philosophy right from the start present themselves from radically different perspectives. No doubt the problem of their relations is especially difficult, since in each case it is a matter of an enterprise of comprehension and of knowledge. No doubt the question opened by the development and increasing effectiveness of modern science retains all of its poignancy. But every attempt at reduction would be arbitrary and would correspond to the abandonment of an essential dimension of the life of consciousness.

It is moreover not a matter here of justifying philosophy but only of indicating the possible function of philosophy with regard to science. The latter is developed in a horizon of comprehension which is not presented as final, for it at least lacks the pretension of founding itself. The scientific project itself can be resumed in a more profound comprehension, which could manifest its articulation in the totality of experience and assign a place to it in the becoming of man.

It cannot be a question, for philosophy, of interfering in the work of science, of assigning methods to it, of criticizing its results, nor even of appropriating these results in order to make them the object of its own examination. If philosophy is an integration of existence, it is so not in the sense of the totalization of a content but in the sense of an operation of foundation. It does not legislate on what does not belong to its own order but is content to explicate the structures underlying other orders.

Philosophy, moreover, is not first in the chronological sense. It is not philosophy which fixes the program for science. On the contrary, science has won its autonomy and has established its rights by opposing philosophy. Philosophy makes its entry only at the moment in which experience is already constituted, when science is already done. It can comprehend only the acquired. Every attempt at prediction on its part would go beyond its possibilities. Only the scientist can get an idea of the future of his science, to the degree in which he lives the project which produces it.

What philosophy can endeavor to do is to comprehend how there is science, indicating the meaning and the nature of the scientific project. And this it can do only by showing both on what ground this project is built and what teleology it implies. For science itself is not the first layer of experience; it is not an absolute beginning. It constitutes itself in starting from perceptual experience, thanks to a thematization of a special type. On the basis of the primordial datum, which always presents itself in the actuality of the singular, it establishes a world of truth by means of an ever more complex hierarchy of concepts. It breaks the unity of the perceptual consciousness and the kind of complicity which ties it to its world, in order to manifest a new world in the old, which is like the effigy of the old, but where abstract entities have replaced the living flux of the concrete life.

This thematization is never achieved. As the scientific project develops itself, it extends its field of action and continually draws from the perceived the wherewithal to nourish its constructions. At the same time, the intention which bears it is itself directed toward the perceived, to which it returns through the intermediary of the theoretical body that is fashioned. The world of perception is therefore doubly subjacent to the theoretical world of science, at once in the moment of genesis and in the moment of application. Science never operates in a void. It starts from the concrete and returns to it, and it is in this that it is truly knowledge and knowledge of reality.

But between these two terms of the movement science describes a trajectory which obeys its own laws of generation. Once constituted, the notional universe possesses an autonomy by virtue of which it can proliferate indefinitely by extension, generalization, and integration. Along this entire trajectory, the scientific project hardens into an objectivity which appears as the visible body of science, upon which the mind can support itself in order to perform new generalizations.

Finally, the entire process has deferred itself to the realization of an end of the whole which always presents itself as unfinished, but which nevertheless truly dwells in each of the terms of the development and which realizes itself gradually as the enterprise succeeds and extends itself in efficacy.

Comprehension of the scientific project necessarily involves the explication of these three moments of its execution and their mutual relations. We must at once explain the passage from the perceived world to the world of science, the internal development which characterizes science in general (and each science in particular), and finally the general finality which governs the genesis of the movement as well as its effectuation. For the scientific project resides in each of these three moments. As it is in each of them in its entirety, they are related to each other in a necessary fashion, such that any description of one ought necessarily to lead to a description of the other two.

But the scientific project in its turn has to be located in the total movement which defines the life of consciousness. The horizon of comprehension to which it corresponds is inserted within a broader horizon, which is that of the rational. Scientific reason, the modality of consciousness through which the project of scientific knowledge is realized, is itself only a part of reason in general, through which experience tends to retrieve itself integrally upon the pure given in order to construct itself according to principles, conforming to a plan of intelligibility. This horizon of reason, which simultaneously manifests itself in many regions of experience, accounts for the existence of science and explains the close relations that exist between science and other regions that appear to be quite remote from it. Thus one can speak of a history of reason and can disengage a guiding thread in the confusion of facts and the multiplicity of interactions which concrete history describes for us among the different sectors of its development.

If the role of philosophy is to extricate the idea of reason from the experience in which it was born and in which it continues to develop itself, it is not within its power to fix the form and the functioning of reason. Reason constitutes itself in the concrete detail of the life of spirit. We can come to recognize what reason is only by becoming conscious of the project that traverses the history which is already realized. To each epoch it reveals something of itself and specifies the law of its evolution. Because it is given not in the form of an explicit term but only in the form of an intention which is actualized gradually as concrete gestures complete it, it presents itself as a reality in becoming, in which there is always something unpredictable and new. It is at once the product of spirit, when considered under its form of exteriority, in the visible results of the cultural life, and the motor of its activity, when considered under its form of interiority, insofar as it is immanent to the activities which it inspires. The initiative of spirit is thus total and nil. The world presents the face it has today because such and such gestures were once made. But these gestures were governed by a requirement which from the very beginning was inscribed in the very law of human existence.

The detail of the life of science must therefore be investigated in order to know something of the nature of reason and of its becoming. From this point of view, nothing is in vain. The hesitations, detours, failures, errors, and denials have as much significance as the most assured successes. The destiny of reason is outlined in the complex frame of these interactions, in the incessant comings and goings that define the life of science. It is in the patient advance of its history that its finality reveals itself. In the techniques of its elaboration are announced the hopes that it carries within itself, as well as the dangers that it dimly conceals.

But the thematization of the scientific project involves not only the consideration of science as an integrating moment in the over-all project of the life of spirit but also the investigation of the meaning of the objectivities which are constituted in its achievement. Science is not only an act and an enterprise but also a visible body which tends to constitute, alongside the natural world given to the perceptual project in its most immediate character, a cultural world which is like a transposition of the spirit on the plane of the in-itself, a naturalized spirit, or a humanized nature. Over and above the reality of the primordial world, the scientific endeavor constructs new layers of reality, from the purely abstract creations of the formal sciences to the technical paraphernalia of the sciences of application. The meaning of these new objectivities must be examined. They should, moreover, not be considered independently from the project, since they are structurally bound to it. For the project exists only in the objects that it institutes, and, inversely, these objects take their meaning only in relation to the project which evokes them. It should simply be noted that the life of spirit presents a double aspect: an aspect of interiority in which spirit is nothing other than a movement polarized by nonobjective ends, and an aspect of exteriority in which spirit is "supported" by the visible forms in which it manifests itself and apparently extenuates itself.

Reason is not only the style of a certain institution of the world; it is also a system of objects (real or ideal). It is at once teleology and sedimentation. Only in the interaction of these two aspects is its concrete becoming carried out.

The horizon of the ultimate question should accordingly make it possible for us to explain all of this at the same time. It should illuminate the different projects not only in their becoming but also in their stabilized products. It should account for this duality and explain its genesis. But to explain this genesis is to show how the scientific, aesthetic, and social objectivities come to be founded on the primary objectivities of natural experience, by virtue of the projects and of the fundamental movement which defines the life of spirit.

Just as there is a hierarchic production of projects, there is a hierarchic production of the objectivities which manifest them. And the entire life of spirit finally comes back to the immediately given world. Hence the final question is to know how there is a world in general. On the basis of this question, all the others can be illuminated, so that we can then comprehend how there is a scientific world, a technical world, etc. This final question can be posed only in the ultimate horizon of all comprehension, under the final intelligible light, precisely in virtue of which a world can be given to us. This ultimate horizon is that of being. The ultimate problem is that of a fundamental ontology, on whose foundation can be elaborated the different regional ontologies which will have to account for the different worlds constituted by the diverse projects and which will have to explicate the structure of the different regions of being that existence makes apparent at the heart of the primordial datum, that is, in the ultimate horizon of Being in general.

The general project of reason itself has to be related to this horizon. The problematic of *logos* is inseparable from a problematic of Being.

III

It is within such a schema that a philosophy of mathematics could be integrated.

The fundamental problem that it must confront is that of the nature of mathematical being. To pose such a problem is to pose the problem of the mathematical project or of the horizon of mathematical comprehension.

The striking thing about mathematical being is that it seems to be constructed and given at the same time.

Mathematical thought provides itself with its own object. In the laws of construction, the definitions and the axioms which it expresses, it brings into existence the very entity whose nature and properties it proposes to study. The objects with which it is concerned possess characters of ideality which radically separate them from the objects of immediate experience. The only existence that they seem to have is that which the acts that produce them impart to them, and this remark could found a pragmatic theory of mathematical being. But, at the same time, it seems that mathematical thought only recognizes what already was. It explores a field which has already been constituted. Mathematical being possesses existence prior to any activity of thought, and if it is not of the same nature as the data of sense intuition, that is because it belongs to some ideal world whose objectivity is as total as that of the world of sense.

On the other hand, mathematical being is given to us only in a development. What we know of it is coextensive with a certain history. There is neither a linear unfolding of consequences by starting from a principle posited once and for all nor an increasing explication of an original intuition, but a progressive manifestation within extremely complex laws of sequence, whose details identify themselves with the concrete development of the history of mathematics from Greek geometry to the present day.

There is in this development not only an increasing extension of theories but a creation of new theories, either by generalization, or by mutual fertilization of prior theories, or by a discovery of still unknown structures in starting from domains already explored (a discovery which moreover may have a bearing either on the properties of the entities themselves or on the operations used in these various domains) or finally by the invention of new procedures of production.

Not only is the development not linear, but the very discontinuities that occur in it may correspond to radical difficulties which demand a total reexamination and which can be resolved only by a creative act. There are crises in the history of mathematics.

Yet even though it includes a dynamic element, mathematical being is presented to us in a certain state of objectification. It expresses itself in an appropriate symbolism whose role appears as necessary. Creation in mathematics is necessarily accompanied by the invention of a certain symbolism, which is not a simple transposition of natural language but tends to constitute a language of a new type. Every mathematical theory is fulfilled in a formalism.

But even though formalism, once it is constituted, can develop on its own level, it does not have the wherewithal to transcend itself. There are moments when it becomes inadequate and when a new initiative of thought is necessary in order to forge a more adequate formalism. These readjustments occur under the pressure of problems that appear in the course of development. There is thus a give and take between the realm of problems and that of formalization, the one constituting the living milieu in which the impulse of creation continually nourishes itself, the other providing the necessary framework in which the latter can be realized and in which the problem itself can be posed.

Finally, though mathematical being seems to be situated in an ideal sphere of which the formalism is only the visible manifestation, it can never be totally divorced from experience. It holds to experience both in its origins and in its prolongations. It comes from experience and returns to experience. By starting from the most elaborate theories and following the entire chain of problems which led to them, it is possible to draw nearer and nearer to the initial gestures through which the world of ideality was constituted on the basis of perceptual experience, in which mathematical experience is always involved. Because it is a thematization of the perceived, it always refers to the ground upon which it constitutes itself. That is why mathematical being is an effective tool in the knowledge of the world. Pure theory leads to applications and through these it is in fact the real world of ordinary experience which is intended. To be sure, the relation is not immediate. Application is possible only when the scientific project has already mastered the datum in a way which readies it for calculation. And it is from this point of view that we will have to comprehend how the mathematical project, the physical (or biological or sociological) project, and the world of perception articulate with each other.

Be that as it may, a reflection on mathematical being will have to account for all of these characteristics and at the same time explain why mathematical being is neither purely constructed nor purely given, why it presents itself in a development which has its own laws, why it tends to be realized in a formalism but at the same time always overflows already constituted formalisms, and finally how it relates to the perceived world, both in its genesis and in its utilization.

It will be necessary to show how it takes its place in the whole of the scientific project and in the life of reason and thus to link its interpretation to the totality of the life of spirit.

Finally, we must show how it is illuminated in the perspective of a fundamental ontology and by what modalities the most general metaphysical problems are manifested in it.

The announcement of such a program can evidently only have meaning as a question. Even before undertaking its execution, we must confront its suggestions in a critical way in order to test how well-founded they are and above all to establish the very possibility of its realization.

Yet there are humbler tasks which must constitute the preface to such a reflection. Before undertaking a descent into the foundations, it is necessary to listen to science, to know what it affirms of itself, to perceive how it comprehends itself. If a fundamental reflection is possible, it is precisely because it is already broached by science in the course of its realization. In science, the moment of creation is inseparable from the moment of reflection, and there comes a time when the latter becomes primary. Science at a certain stage of its development tends of necessity to found itself. It is obliged to do so by certain profound difficulties which it encounters, tied to the very meaning of its enterprise. In order to surmount them, it is obliged to criticize not only the methods or the scope of this or that particular result but also the primary objectives which it claims to pursue. And the work of criticism necessarily deepens into the work of founding.

Therefore before making the attempt on the properly philosophical level, we must try to enter that reflective dimension which belongs to scientific procedure, both because it already traces the itinerary over which philosophical reflection will have to pass and because it is not possible to comprehend the phenomenon of science without accounting for this recovery of its own acts that science itself performs.

Superimposed of necessity onto the problem posed by science is the problem posed by the theory of foundations. Each science possesses its reflective level and places itself under question to a certain extent. Yet this questioning has nowhere else been pushed so far as it has in the case of mathematics. Here the critical operations have transcended the level of first approximation and have constituted themselves into an autonomous technique whose rigor cedes nothing to the best established branches of classical mathematics. The new discipline which has thus been constituted is the science of formalism. Following Hilbert, it is also called metamathematics, inasmuch as it appears as a kind of higher demand responsible for assuring the coherence of the mathematical edifice itself.

But this appellation is much too restrictive, first because it is more and more evident that the science of formalism tends to transcend the domain of mathematics and to extend to the entire domain of science. It has absorbed the classic role of logic as a general canon of reason. But it has assumed a content that classical logic did not have, for it not only furnishes the procedures of admissible reasoning and the frameworks of possible edifices, but it also furnishes the basic notions upon which these edifices are constructed. It thus becomes a kind of general formal ontology.

Next, metamathematics tends to be identified with mathematics itself, which thus takes on a new sense. It is no longer the science of numbers, nor of extension, nor of abstract manifolds, nor of the most general operations. It becomes the science of formal systems. Thus the discipline which was charged with the control of mathematical activity progressively absorbs the latter, the frontier between mathematics and metamathematics disappears, the operation of foundation is fulfilled in a reunification which suppresses the opposition between the founding and the founded. This opposition has only a historical meaning and is merely relative to a certain stage of development. Thus the progress of science profoundly modifies its direction and meaning. The result of what has been called "the crisis of foundations" is to make the scientific edifice in its entirety pass to a higher stage of organization, where the reflective dimension is in some fashion rendered homogeneous with the objective acquisitions. There is thus a kind of thematization of the project which is realized within the project itself.

In the initial stages, the project remains dissociated from its productions. It belongs only to a lateral, nonthematic consciousness.

At certain times crises of a partial order occur, in the form of local obstructions which momentarily curb the development of this or that sector. These crises are most often resolved through acquisitions obtained from other sectors, which bring new methods of solution into view. The blocked sector is then integrated into a larger sector, which corresponds to the liberation of more profound structures. A case in point is the passage from Euclidean geometry to analytic geometry.

Such evolutions already realize a reorganization of types of evidence, since they are based on a modification of the ideals of demonstration. Thus the evidence of the purely formal manipulations of algebraic calculation replaces the evidence of spatial construction.

Every crisis affects the criteria of evidence, the conditions of mathematical existence. Their reverberations are even more intense when the structures which they affect are more profound. Some day we might expect a crisis so radical that it would threaten to topple all that has been acquired, because it would question not the legitimacy of this or that procedure or the existence of this or that object but the very coherence of mathematical thought as a whole, hence its fundamental project. The crisis could be surmounted only by a recovery of the project, by an accentuation of the reflective moment. The very idea of mathematics would have to be submitted to a rigorous critique, and the notion of mathematical existence would have to receive a more specific content. The project would have to be objectified to a degree, for it is only in the data of a concrete and actual procedure of verification that a criterion can find a content and hence a real bearing. The most natural procedure evidently consists in superimposing this objectivity of criteria upon that of existing demonstrations. But this could only be a transitional step. Once objectified, the project would once again have to master its demonstrations and make them over according to a new style.

One could not be content with developing two disciplines along parallel lines and simply performing the verifications of one by means of the other. One would have to go further and place the demonstrations under the direct control of the newly disclosed criteria. It is precisely through formalism that this transformation could be initiated. The use of a formalized method seemingly only introduces a greater precision in the proceedings. But in reality it corresponds to a radical deepening. The intuitions which dominated the prior developments find themselves criticized and transcribed into a perfectly controllable mechanism of proof, which more and more permits the elimination of contingent aspects of the demonstration in order to give it the demeanor of a rigorously canonic process. At the same time, the procedures become much more powerful, capable of directly attaining an entire category of results. A calculus which only had a bearing on objective entities is progressively replaced by a calculus which bears directly on the operations, thus providing the key to the most fundamental sequences by permitting the study of the properties of entities in their genesis.

The creative intention is thus renewed at two levels. On the one hand, the criteria of demonstration are made explicit and integrated into a symbolic edifice. On the other hand, the thematization focuses within this edifice on the very acts of construction and of mathematical demonstration. In objectifying itself in this way, the project transforms and reduces itself, becoming a project of integral formalization. In this sense, a duality could continue to exist between the formalism itself and the generating intention which bears it. But this duality itself tends to disappear. The formalism aims to absorb not only the criteria of existence and of demonstration but its own idea and strives to retrieve the integral field of reflexivity. At the limit, the constitution of an absolutely closed system should be reached, in the sense that it would be perfectly reflected within itself. Such a system would be completely divorced from thought, constituting, as it were, an objective transposition of it. In it mathematics would be achieved. Undoubtedly new developments would always be possible, but they would be made under the motivation of the reflective principle established at the base of the system. To perform new deductions or even to extricate new theoretical levels, it would no longer be necessary to base oneself on some intuition prior to the act of formalism. It would be enough to let the mechanism function according to its own laws. At this stage, the project would be entirely absorbed in its product or, more exactly, it would be completely fused with it. Mathematics would then coincide with its own genesis. There would no longer be any distinction between the generating intuition and the acts which realize it, nor even between these acts and their concrete traces. The system would at once be the description of intuition, the sequence of acts, the construction of products. In one and the same movement, the intention would manifest all of its fruitfulness and would retrieve itself. Creation would be identified with reflection, the elaboration of the system would be both its own description and its own justification, comprehension would no longer have to be achieved by going over to another horizon. There would be some sort of telescoping of horizons, with the horizon of comprehension coinciding perfectly with the horizon of execution.

Of course such an ideal remains a limit. Nothing indicates a priori that it cannot be more and more closely approximated. Even though a duality persists, though the formalization is never complete, though the reflexivity cannot be completely translated into objectivity, though the structure of a horizon continues to impose itself on mathematical experience, it is still this limit situation which gives the progressive movement its meaning and direction, thereby polarizing it. An experience which elaborates itself on the basis of a horizon, and which accordingly presents itself as always unachieved, is defined by the hope of an achievement. It carries its own negation within itself, tends to suppress itself as a projective movement in order to retrieve itself under the form of a reflexive movement, and thus tends to replace inadequateness with saturation. It is precisely this negating element in it which gives it the character of perpetual transcendence and of involving a horizonal structure, just as it is this horizonal structure, with the infinite that it entails, which gives it the character of possessing an element of negativity. There is a horizon because there is never a stabilization in the actual, and there is negation because there is never complete identification. Such a structure is evidently the proper character of finitude, and if it is not only a general character of human existence, if it is found again in each of the dimensions in which human existence elaborates itself, even the most abstract, it is because finitude is really a constitutive element that penetrates categorial thought itself and reappears even in its most purified products.

The description of the formalist enterprise should bring us very quickly to a metaphysics of finitude. But this very passage obliges us to pose the problem of manifestation in a radical way, in order to comprehend how the most fundamental structures of existence diffuse into its actual appearances in order to establish its truly concrete mode of operation.

Now, the real surprise in the history of the theory of formalism is that this ideal of complete formalization is inaccessible not only in fact, as a term which always recoils before the gesture that wishes to possess it, but also by law. And it is the theory itself which has assigned itself its own limits.

The reflexivity thus attains its culminating point in the moment in which it discovers its own boundaries. In formalism, the project retrieves itself but it indicates just to what point. And the extreme point of this recovery is precisely the point at which the recognition is made. If there can be total reflection in the system, it is in this sense: the limit is capable of recognizing itself.

It follows from this that a duality never ceases to exist between the project and its products, or in other words, between the plane of formalism, where the objectification of the project and thus the reflection is realized, and the plane of intuitions, where the thematizing acts which organize the fabric of the mathematical world on the trace of the perceived world are realized.

Hence the enterprise of formalization itself reveals this character of incompleteness and of openness, a characteristic of our experience which qualifies the actual becoming of reason.

In and through the incarnations of the theory of foundations, it is really the figure of reason which specifies itself in transforming itself. For the audacious image of an ever victorious reason, more and more master of the world and of itself, is substituted the humbler image of an uncertain reason, always militant and always contested. For the idea of a total integration into the homogeneous is substituted the idea of a progressive and discontinuous movement obliged to secure its steps one by one and to continually adapt itself to the unforeseen necessities of the terrain. For the ambition of a total reflection is substituted the acknowledgement of an always necessary duality. Reason preserves its value as capable of attaining something certain, but on condition that it continually control its proceedings, returning unceasingly to the intuitive ground upon which it is obliged to support itself. It operates no longer under the sign of the definitive but under the mark of the precarious. It turns away from the system and holds close to the concrete. It ceases to surpass the given toward fixed a priori intentions and to harden its project into ideal ends. Instead, it turns back toward the very life of the project and toward its sources, accomplishing itself in the realizable, step by step.

What science thus permits us to attain in these moments of greatest reflexivity is the general figure of an evolution by which reason, provisionally hardened in the assurance of an indefinite success, acknowledges and integrates its own failure in order to prepare for a new phase of the history of the idea.

19 / Mathematics and Formalism

Jean Ladrière

CONTEMPORARY MATHEMATICAL THOUGHT seems to be developing on a double level, that of mathematics proper and that of metamathematics. On the one hand, we see the elaboration of old problems and the creation of new theories (either by axiomatic and thus analytic means, as in the case of topological algebra, or by synthetic means, as in the case of Schwarz's theory of distributions); and on the other, a veritable proliferation of logico-mathematical formalisms.

This duality of levels corresponds to Hilbert's distinction between mathematics and the theory of demonstrations: on the one side, conquest of new results, and on the other, integration of classical theories (arithmetic, algebra, calculus) into appropriate formalisms and examination of the properties of these formalisms by means of finitist methods. This Hilbertian distinction was based on a certain conception of mathematical being. For Hilbert, mathematical reality is that of the sign. "In the beginning was the sign." From this point of view, the constitution of a formalism represents neither the passage from a concrete to an abstract mathematics nor a reduction of mathematical being to a particular representation, but the extrication of the proper reality of mathematical being. The theory of demonstration does not simply shift us to a higher level of analysis but constitutes a genuine deepening of mathematical procedure. By

This translation of "Mathématiques et formalisme," *Revue des questions scientifiques* (Louvain), October 20, 1955, pp. 538–74, has been done by Theodore J. Kisiel expressly for this edition.

[466]

permitting us to penetrate to a more fundamental layer of phenomena, it gives us the key to all previous efforts. And besides, this simply manifests a fairly evident methodic necessity: how to assure oneself of a rigorous foundation, without reinvoking the very essence of that which is to be founded?

If we examine the matter more closely, this distinction, apparently quite clear, seems to branch off in such a way that it finally trails off into a distribution of levels which is really more of a continuity than a heterogeneity. Mathematics thus presents itself at different levels of abstraction: there are theoretical and applied mathematics, axiomatized theories and those which are not, pure axiomatics and intuitive axiomatics. Of course, these different levels are arranged according to a hierarchy, which is moreover of a dynamic character. It is a matter not simply of a superposition but of a movement which transposes the theories to a more and more advanced state of abstraction. (It should be noted here that generality and abstraction do not necessarily coincide. Axiomatization can bear on a very particular theory, and such a theory can be generalized without the aid of axiomatics.) This movement introduces a temporal dimension into the relation between theories and an aspect of becoming within each theory, since a single theory can be resumed at different levels of elaboration. The meaning and direction of this movement is evidently not arbitrary and reveals something of the profound nature of mathematical being to us. (We shall have to return to this point.) But as it graduates the levels of formalization according to a privileged direction, the movement maintains an effective alliance among them, thus preventing the sacrifice of any one of them to totalitarian claims which would be too geometrically rigorous. For each level is nourished by the one which precedes it and at the same time provides the previous level with something like the exemplar image of a coherence which already regulates its course and introduces, in the very concrete matter of this prior level, the negative imprint of the articulations which it is called upon to actualize. If there is a movement, it is accordingly not only in the sense of an ascent marked by successive halts but also in the sense of a reciprocal exchange which assures the very continuity of the whole and prevents each of its components from being hardened into an autocratic totality.

On the other hand, formalism hardly presents itself in a uniform way. It also involves a display of diverse moments which represent something more than simple technical improvements. Here also there is movement: on the one hand, construction of formalisms which are ever more encompassing and ever richer in their possibilities of representation; on the other, construction of ever simpler formalisms which avoid artificial procedures, the multiplication of conventions, and reduction to a very small number of fundamental data. Hence we have, on the one hand, increasing totalization, and on the other, increasing simplification. These two aspects of research are relatively independent, but there are profound connections between them. The effort of simplification should be understood not simply as a purely aesthetic enterprise, for it corresponds to some truly new acquisitions. The ascent toward the simple is always an ascent toward the universal. Here the most significant phenomenon is the development of combinatory logic, which succeeds in creating a remarkably simple formalism in which many of the difficulties of the old formalisms are avoided. In reality the gain is not primarily of a technical nature. Combinatory logic realizes a transgression of the perspectives opened by the *Principia Mathematica*, by taking its starting point no longer from the idea of object but from the idea of operation and even, finally, from the idea of level of operation (axioms of functionality). Thus, at the very heart of formalism there is a progress in the direction of abstraction.

Finally, and this is perhaps more decisive, the frontier between mathematics and metamathematics is becoming more and more blurred. From a certain point of view, all is formalism. The most elementary algorithms, e.g., those given in geometrical constructions, already constitute a formalism. It cannot be a question of opposing a nonformal to a formal stage; it is only a question of indicating the variations which are introduced within the nature of formalism. And from this point of view, the distance which separates intuitive geometry from the theory of abstract groups may seem as great as that which separates classical algebra from the theory of demonstration. Hilbert has persistently emphasized that the formalization demanded by *Beweistheorie* must integrate the procedures of reasoning. It would in short be a matter of passing from a mathematical formalism to a logico-mathematical formalism. But can this be considered as essential? There is to be sure a merger of concerns. What interests the formalist is no longer the solution of a mathematical problem but the internal coherence of a theory considered in its entirety. But this can only reinforce the accidental character of the distinction. The passage under question signifies nothing less than a reorganization of the formalism according to new criteria, in line with the demands of a new research program.

And from another point of view, everything is mathematical. The constitution of a logico-mathematical formalism for the theory of sets adds nothing to the content of this theory. Such a formalism is situated entirely on the level of representation, while the reality of the formalism reduces itself completely to that of the content which it expresses. And insofar as we elevate ourselves to a pure formalism, it is no longer even possible to distinguish between logic and mathematics. For example, the very same system can be interpreted as a theory of propositions, a topological system, an algebra of classes, or as a lattice. Needless to say, this does not by-pass the problem of the criterion of distinction among the different representations of a system, but in any case we are obliged to acknowledge that the distinction between mathematics and metamathematics does not correspond to the distinction between mathematics and logic.

Finally, the distinction established within the theory of demonstration between a formal system and a theory of this system is in its turn blurred, for since the work of Gödel, what one calls metamathematics appears only as a part of arithmetic. And as soon as a theory is large enough to include arithmetic, and if it does not force us to go beyond the realm of elementary formalisms, it itself contains its own metatheory. The theorems of a Gödelian type certainly do not signify an irreducibility of metatheory to theory but only manifest certain internal limitations of the theory itself. In forcing us to resort to a hierarchy of formalisms, they reveal certain structural conditions which pertain to the very essence of the formal method and articulate themselves around the paradox of the diagonal. But in no case do they provide us with a criterion of distinction between mathematics and metamathematics. Hence everything comes back to a question of interpretation. It is possible to interpret a certain part of the formalism under study either as a part of arithmetic or as its own metatheory. And even if we adhere to the intuitive sense of the concepts of the metatheory, we could in the end view it only as a new form of algebra whose originality comes from the nature of its object, which is an already constituted system. We would then have a sort of algebra of the second degree. But this passage to a higher level of manipulation is classical in the history of mathematical theories and certainly does not force us to depart from mathematical reality itself.

II

THIS TRIPLE SERIES of remarks thus invites us to reconsider the distinction introduced by *Beweistheorie*, at first sight so clear, and to suspect its basis. This is not to challenge the fact that *Beweistheorie* has added a new chapter to mathematics, but it would be an error to insist on any particular discontinuity between this chapter and the preceding ones. All formal investigations appear rather to be in line with the oldest investigations. The movement which began at the level of applied mathematics leads to the level of *Beweistheorie*, but in fact it is one and the same movement. What must be accounted for is not a duality of points of view but the internal demand which leads every axiomatic theory to conclude in metatheoretical considerations which guarantee its soundness. Mathematics, therefore, does not have to seek its justification outside of itself by appealing to new intuitions or by finding support in a reality other than itself, whether it be that of the physical world or of the mental world. It is only by returning to itself that it can be given its full coherence. Furthermore, there is nothing which guarantees the existence of a term to this movement of regression which completes and deepens the movement of progression, nor does the actual state of this regression in any case mark its definitive limits. (The efforts of combinatory logic indicate on the contrary that we must guard against interpreting the theorems of limitations in this sense.)

The investigations of foundations thus belong to mathematics just as much as algebra and calculus. Without suppressing any of their moments and without making their methods superfluous, they continue the previous investigations, from which they draw the material for their own operations, while at the same time giving meaning to them. The last step of the movement is both the result of the preceding ones and that which integrates them. For it is not a simple translation but corresponds to a very precise polarization of thought. Each step recapitulates the preceding step and realizes it in a purer and more profound manner, manifesting its essence with greater truth. By adding to it, it carries the preceding step to a more perfect realization.

To comprehend mathematical reality is to grasp both its present actuality and its progressive realization within a movement which indicates not only an increasing enrichment on an always identical plane but also a successive deepening and the opening up of new realms of actualization, of which the theory of demonstration, in making the reflexive character of the mathematical procedure explicit, today marks the most advanced point. The mathematical project is thus articulated in perspectives arranged in a hierarchy, which are like a priori forms of its development. Not that the form is given before the content, for it can be given only in and through the content. But the mind, in reflecting on what it has already accomplished, becomes aware of a new type of rigor which concretizes itself in a new layer of theories.

Yet while one emphasizes that an overly radical distinction between mathematics and metamathematics can be somewhat unrealistic and insists on the essential continuity of the mathematical undertaking through the interruptions of levels which it involves, it should be noted that within this continuity there nonetheless exists a tension which must be of great significance. And after having shown how Hilbert's distinction is progressively blurred, it must be shown that it corresponds to a fundamental phenomenon linked to the very nature of mathematical being. This is the opposition which manifests itself within mathematical thought between the formalizing tendency and the problematizing tendency, or between the abstractive tendency and the concretizing tendency. It is undoubtedly not possible to give a rigorous criterion permitting us to discern exactly where these two tendencies separate, and it is because of this that the frontier established by Hilbert seems blurred. But that is precisely because this duality of tendencies underlies the constitution of theories, and we cannot expect that a formalism which is essentially encompassing should itself describe that which remains irreducible for it.

In speaking of tendencies, we place ourselves at a level which is not yet that of an elaborated mathematical thought but that of a groundbreaking and exploratory activity still close to a real datum in the brute state and somewhat removed from a truly satisfying expression. In examining the constituted theories, we can only grasp the trace of this duality, provided moreover that we do not restrict ourselves to the sole consideration of a definite level of elaboration but take into account the whole of mathematical science at the different levels of its evolution. So if we wish to grasp the point at which these two tendencies articulate themselves and to comprehend the necessity of their opposition, we must go back to a state of thought which is still undifferentiated, to the point of origin of the theories, as well as the veritable style of their actualization.

For the formalist, what counts is the rigor, the thoroughgoing exposition of the means of demonstration, the reduction of operations to the simplest acts which are closest to an elementary intuition, the manifestation of procedures of fertilization either in the laws of the construction of expressions or in the rules of deduction, the conquest of coherence. What he aims at is the transparency of the system. And the system appears as an object from which the living thought has been extracted, where only the rules of manipulation still testify to its antecedent efficacy. It is an object in which everything has become explicit, where everything is stabilized in the definitive evidence of noncontradiction.

Through the detour of abstract axiomatics, the formalist elevates himself to the general theory of formal systems and succeeds in constituting systems in which the structure has completely eliminated the content. While abstract algebra still preserved a concrete anchorage by the reference which it includes to operations directly exemplifiable in more elementary theories which are closer to calculation, the formal system becomes a self-sufficient reality whose internal possibilities of deduction can be completely isolated from the power of representation. There is, of course, no radical heterogeneity between these two steps. As already emphasized, it is rather a single movement which realizes itself, a single tendency which purifies and confirms itself. But pure formalism, by carrying to the extreme the promise borne by every effort of axiomatization, by revealing its intentions in a particularly efficacious purity, isolates at the heart of mathematical thought a component which at the level of incompletely formalized axiomatic theories was still associated with rival and at once compensating components. By making the system self-sufficient and isolating it from its exemplifications, it eliminates the concretizing intuition which remained within less elaborated systems. By reducing itself to its single appearance, it empties itself of that hidden dynamism which carries a theory toward its possible fields of application and at the same time reveals its origins. While an axiomatic of the classical type can be understood only within a perspective of a totality which fixes its scope and its limits, a pure formalism cuts itself off from every alien reference. And when it comes to its interpretations, it is a matter of a completely extrinsic procedure which nothing within the system demands or even facilitates. While classical axiomatics is elaborated by beginning with well established theories which are to be unified or whose structures are to be clarified, the formal system is presented to thought as a sort of enigma which is to be elucidated or, more exactly, as an unknown instrument for which the best usage is to be found. The relation between the abstract and the concrete is inverted. We no longer ascend from the particular to the general but descend from the general to the particular.

But what is most significant in this tendency thus isolated in its pure state is not the reversal which it effects in the internal movement of the generation of theories but its professed claim to disengage the true nature of mathematical being, as though this purification of an epistemological ideal were at once a conquest in the order of essence. Mathematics becomes the science of formal systems. It is this conception which the identification established by Hilbert between mathematical being and the sign already proclaimed. But in Hilbert it remained much too rigid, for the formal system is by no means reducible to the reality of the sign. It possesses a proper reality which manifests itself in its properties of coherence and in its internal fruitfulness (either on the level of deduction or on the level of representation), for which the sign is only the material carrier, that which presents.

If we go beyond the materiality of the presentification in order to get to the internal reality of the system, the reduction of mathematics to the theory of formal systems, which at first sight seemed to empty it of all content and to exaggerate one of the levels of its actualization at the expense of all of the others, now appears much more natural. For the system, far from identifying itself with an empty and somewhat extenuated scheme in which the reality of the symbol is the sole support, reveals a structural essence whose manifestation is only mediated by the symbolism, and which at a single stroke brings about the comprehension of all of the subsystems which interpretation allows to be brought together. The abstraction, precisely because it is perfect, gives us what is most unique in incompletely formalized theories, the uniqueness by which they are mathematical. At first this uniqueness is given to us only in an impure state, blended with elements of representation which belong to other categories of experience, from which mathematical thought must progressively extricate it. This purification is accomplished through a series of steps which realize the elimination of successive levels of intuition, including that of number and that of content. This leads us not to the most general scheme of every possible theory but to the most original nucleus of all of the theoretical layers. The ascent toward the universal is at the same time a regression toward the individual. The transcendence is a deepening. The movement of transgression which raises us from one level of theories to another is identical with the movement of envelopment or of concentric approach which brings us to discern more and more exactly what is common to these different levels, which is the foundation of both their continuity and the dynamism which generates them one upon the other in a perpetual ambition of radical elucidation.

If there is abstraction, it is not in the sense of an elimination of contents, of the institution of an increasing emptiness, but in the sense of an isolation, purification, and grasp of a hidden essence. We then comprehend the sense and direction of this formalizing tendency. It does not correspond simply to an intention of clarification and explicitation but is founded in the more profound dynamism of mathematical thought. For this thought can be developed only within a constant attention to that which, constituting its initial project, renders present to it, at the heart of each of its procedures and through each of its particular objects, the very essence of mathematical being. Within this attention is situated the implicit aim which makes the particular acts possible, assuring their continuity, effectiveness, and polarization. Every new conquest is at the same time an elucidation of this aim. We can say neither that such a result precedes the aim so as to make it clear to itself nor that the aim precedes the results so as to secure them in deductive fashion. There is rather a rigorous simultaneity between the results and the aim. The philosophy of mathematics cannot precede mathematics. There is no explicit preconception of mathematical being from which its properties could be deduced. The form of their bearer is progressively revealed in the patient and difficult exploration of these properties. And, strictly speaking, it is even inaccurate to speak of a bearer, since the properties here are identified with what they manifest. If there is a preconception, it is only in the form of a nonthematic aim, a preliminary openness which deploys for the mind the space in which it will be able to execute the encounter with its object.

Because mathematical thought is based on the reality of this global aim, the movement toward pure formalism constitutes a deepening in the comprehension of mathematical being, and this is what founds the claim of pure formalism to present itself as mathematics itself. It could be said that this progress of comprehension corresponds to the opening of a privileged subspace within the primitive space of comprehension. Here again we could find that image of the concentric approach of which the analytic method of nested intervals or the topological concept of filter give us a particularly suggestive formal equivalent.

III

AND YET this totalitarian claim of formalism does not avoid arousing a vehement protest on the part of another tendency of mathematical thought which could be called the problematizing or concretizing tendency, or the realistic tendency, inasmuch as it opposes the reality of problems to the abstraction of systems. Closer to the initial data, it applies itself above all to the solution of problems left open by the old theories or manifested by the newly created theories (often in order to try to resolve precisely the old problems). It thinks that the true fertility of mathematical thought is not on the level of axiomatics but rather on the level of the concrete questions posed by the theory of functions, the theory of equations, or the study of the properties of different spaces. Axiomatics is certainly of interest, for it can be useful in elucidating the structure of a theory, in manifesting certain relations between theories sometimes far removed from each other. In its turn, it poses problems that should not be neglected. But the sole criterion of its interest is its concrete effectiveness. Thus the establishment of a kinship between two theories often permits the solution of an unresolved problem by means of a method of analogy, as in the algebraic utilization of geometry. Or again, the extrication of an abstract structure, by purifying the data of a problem or by generalizing its field of application, can provide a solution or extend partial solutions, as in the completion given to the theory of algebraic equations by the theory of groups. The metamathematical problems (in Hilbert's sense) are of interest, for it is obviously indispensable to be assured of the rigor of our instruments and of the coherence of our procedures of reasoning. But this can only be a tangential concern here. What is important is to obtain new results. Besides, the efforts of formalism are often disproportionate to what can be expected from it. The greater part of mathematics, that which is the most useful from the point of view of concrete results, can be constructed without going beyond relatively elementary levels of formal means. This point of view, moreover, reverberates at the very heart of the theory of formal systems. The effort bears less on the constitution of an encompassing system, such as that of the *Principia Mathematica,* whose metamathematical properties one must after all acknowledge, than on the progressive constitution of partial systems, corresponding to one or another established theory (for example, to a certain sector of calculus) and whose metamathematical properties are established in the very act of construction. This corresponds to a gain of generality in the metatheoretical method but at the same time manifests the presence of the realist perspective at the very heart of the formalist perspective. There is thus a reciprocal presence of one perspective in another, but according to a different polarization. While the formalist tendency gives priority to the system, the realist tendency gives priority to the problems. In either case the system is present, but in the one we go from concrete problems to the system, in which we perceive the truth of the problems, and in the other we go from the system to the concrete problems, in which we perceive the truth of the system. It is this inversion of polarity in the movement of coming and going between problem and system which marks in the most exact fashion the opposition between the two perspectives.

As we see it, this opposition is not total. If in a first approximation (which itself corrected whatever was too radical in the Hilbertian point of view) we could insist on the continuity of investigation from the stage of closest application to physical reality to that of the most complete formalization, it is precisely because the opposition whose importance we must now emphasize is not immobilized by a completely defined surface of separation but rather corresponds to a displacement of the center of gravity of research. This center oscillates between two extremes from which each realizes the total absorption of the opposite point of view, not by simple exclusion but by assimilation. And it is susceptible of occupying a whole series of intermediate positions, whose spectrum must be considered as in principle continuous, where each position corresponds to a well-determined state both of actual research and of the history of mathematics (for each historical layer remains present within the larger body in which it finds itself included by the progress which actualizes its potentialities and fills up its gaps). But what gives this oscillation its full weight is that the multiplicity of lines of research which it makes possible covers a duality in the conception of mathematical reality.

While for the formalist mathematics is identified with the theory of formal systems, for the realist mathematics is identified with that concrete proliferation of problems which are generated from one another, beginning with the most elementary problems of arithmetic and of geometry, according to an ineluctable succession with respect to which the role of mathematical thought is not to fix a priori the law of development but to recognize the rigorous sequence. Formalism thinks of itself as a concretizing abstraction, as an ascent toward the truly concrete, which is revealed by the universality of the system. For it, mathematical reality is found when the system ideally comes to cover the entire edifice of mathematics and to disclose its essential substructures, and thus takes on a proper consistency which henceforth isolates it from thought, forcing thought to acknowledge an autonomous essence there, the very essence that it sought to extricate in the course of previous stages of its enterprise and upon which the efficacy of its effort obscurely supported itself. The passage from the concrete to the abstract is in reality the conquest of a concrete of the second degree which was present in the first as that which gave it its proper specificity and prevented it from being swallowed up into the reality of the physical world or into the ideality of a pure construction. Mathematics is neither a physics nor a poetics. It is the act which constitutes an autonomous reality in the very movement in which it explores it. And it is precisely formalism which revives its most proximate image for us.

Formalism is neither a pure inclusive synthesis nor the system of the possible modes of appearance of theories, neither an a posteriori schema nor an a priori structure. It is the body in which is manifested a reality which was already present in the first outlines of geometrical mathematics and which is present at every step of the history of mathematics (and in this sense we could speak of an a priori). But the work of centuries and the progress of abstraction were necessary to extricate it in its purity (and in this sense we can speak of an a posteriori). There is ascent, exhaustion, encompassing, not within the undifferentiated totality which is the place of evanescence, but within the rigorously determined singularity which is the node of concretization.

Realist mathematics, on the contrary, considers itself as a permanent return to the differentiated and multiform concreteness of mathematical experience. It is in effect more attentive to the act of generation which inaugurates a theory or to the operation of elucidation which inspires the solution of a problem than to the rigorous objectivity of the system in which thought is transformed into an operative mechanism regulated in all of its details. Formalism, at whatever level one envisages it, is always only an aspect derived from a fundamental reality which is given in a movement and not in the definitive stability of a system. Formalism guarantees the coherence of a whole, assures the soundness of reasoning, presents a synthesized harmonious view of a plurality of data. But the requirement of coherence is secondary. It corresponds to an ordering which must indeed intervene at a given moment, but only when everything is already played out. The act of discovery necessarily precedes that of precision. It is certainly necessary to eliminate the superfluous elements and to dispel the causes of ambiguity, but this is only a labor of refinement which no longer belongs to the order of creative thought. What remains, what constitutes the true acquisition, is the initial ore. We can be sure in advance that an absolutely pure material can finally be extracted from it. It will take ingenuity and patience, but it is only a matter of the choice of an adequate method of treatment. What matters to us is not the axiomatics of the theory of sets but Cantor's theory itself. That certain antinomies manifest themselves cannot shake our confidence in the initial creation. We will have to assure ourselves of the proper means to eliminate them, but that adds nothing essential to the very content of the theory.

What has been said of the content can be repeated with regard to the procedures of reasoning. It is certainly useful to forge a tool which is more and more precise and to present it in a particularly manageable form. But, after all, mathematical reasoning has always been done, and no one has waited for symbolic logic to elaborate theories whose subtlety cedes nothing to that of present theories. Once more, the formal method adds nothing to the arsenal of procedures of thought but only effects a precision whose interest will always be relative. The truly creative act is that which opens up new possibilities of demonstration and not that which fabricates greater or lesser formalisms from which one could never expect anything but convenient representation. What initiates a new impetus for mathematical thought is the invention of procedures such as the procedure of exhaustion used by the Greek geometers, the procedure of passage to the limit of the seventeenth-century founders of calculus, or the procedure of the diagonal of Cantor. The act of creation in the order of procedures of reasoning overlaps the act of creation in the order of objective contents and in the end coincides with it. And it is because of this latter creation that the formalist has after all something to formalize.

Finally the unification performed by formalism remains artificial. For it corresponds simply to the search for a framework large enough to encompass a certain manifold, or more exactly, one large enough to lend itself to sufficiently differentiated interpretations. The true unification is not the integration of a diversity into a general scheme which recovers the diversity only by sacrificing the singularity of the elements to the impoverishing universality of a common structure. It is rather the creation of new concepts which include the preceding ones as particular cases. It is thus really an enrichment, for the diversity is recovered not by adding particular properties to a general scheme but by a restriction of the conditions of validity which define the field of application of the new notion.

Furthermore, the system cannot transgress itself. Once a framework is established, it is not permitted to depart from it without having recourse to procedures which do not belong to it. We could certainly try new interpretations, but we would thereby only come to a concrete dimension which constitutes the true reality of the system and gives it its sole authentic consistency. Contrariwise, the truly prospective procedures, those which make us enter new realms of mathematical reality, are articulated upon concrete problems which, moreover, very often are rather furnished by physical reality than by theoretical mathematics itself.

It is in fact the necessities of the analysis of the physical datum which oblige mathematical thought to create new tools. Thus geometry was born from the problems of land surveying, calculus from the study of movement, the calculus of probabilities from the study of phenomena of chance, statistical analysis from the study of collectivities, the recent theory of games from the examination of phenomena of competition. The close ties which exist between physics and mathematics have been sufficiently emphasized. This relationship is not a one-way street. It is a matter not only of the application of already constituted theories to the analysis of observed phenomena but also of the production of new mathematical structures which seem to be preformed in certain structures of the physical world (as in those of continuity and of chance) and required by them as instruments of manipulation. Today this exchange between mathematics and experience is being extended and diversified. It is not limited to physical experience but is valid for every category of experience from the moment in which it presents a degree of elaboration sufficient to lend itself to a rigorous analysis. This extension, moreover, corresponds to a displacement of mathematics from the quantitative to the structural. It is thus only by a permanent attentiveness to these solicitations of experience that mathematical thought will be able to develop itself. It is there that it finds the concrete ground from which it must build itself and in which it must find the permanent nourishment for its effort. To detach itself from these roots would in reality be to condemn itself to asphyxia, to enclose itself in a kind of mortal solitude which would result in the emptiness of a system void of all content.

This fertility which mathematical thought draws from the contact with problems related to the interpretation of experience is propagated at a more elaborated level of problems where it is no longer a matter of drawing the prefiguration of mathematical structures from the intuition of an external reality but of responding to questions posed by these structures themselves: thus in the theory of numbers, the problems related to the distribution of primary numbers; in algebra, the extension of the theory of equations to more and more general sets; in calculus, the solution of differential equations; in combinatory topology, the establishment of systems of invariants, etc. . . . It is when we penetrate into this category of problems that we touch on what is most specific in mathematics and are closest to the reality of mathematical being.

For the contact with external experience was only a point of departure, a launch pad, like a necessary, but at the same time an accidental, support: necessary in the sense that thought needed this external pressure against which to lean its intuitions; accidental in the sense that the theory, once elaborated, can be developed without returning to its place of origin. It is when this divorce from physical reality occurs that mathematical being is truly constituted. The fact that thought takes its support in an intuition of a nonmathematical kind should make us alert to the presence of mathematical structures at the very heart of structures which are more pregnant of apprehension. But at the same time the fact that it conquers its own style of progression by rigorously isolating mathematical intuition from the richer intuition in which it was placed obliges us to recognize the autonomy of mathematical being and to emphasize its irreducible originality. Thus in the very moment in which we most resolutely rebel against the overly purist pretensions of a radical formalism, we are obliged to acknowledge, in the very dynamism of our movement, what gives the formalizing ambition its point of departure and its justification. Once again we are led back to that reciprocal interiority of the two tendencies which we are trying to circumscribe. We thus find ourselves invited to comprehend their mutual opposition only in the irreducibility of an exchange which accounts for both their apparent exclusivism and their mutual fertilization.

But before coming to an over-all interpretation which strives to maintain this double attention, to the duality of a movement and to the reciprocity of its moments, we must indicate more precisely what constitutes the original bearing of the realist perspective.

If it is true that every effort of mathematical thought is centered around an implicit aim which actualizes an original precomprehension of its object, the problematizing style should involve an original conception of mathematical being perceptibly different from the formalizing conception. What appears as primary to a thought which dwells on the sequence of problems is the internal dynamism of the investigation, a dynamism which is not only that of a prospective thought, but more profoundly, and moreover founding this dynamism, that of an autonomous reality which is no more given in the still too qualified intuition of the diversity of experience than in the quasi-extenuated reality of the totally formalized system. If it is in none of these terms, mathematical reality is in the development which leads from one to the other, and in this sense it is also in the terms which unite this movement.

There is therefore, underlying the constitution of formalism, something like an internal life of mathematics of which the mechanism of calculation or procedures of representation only manifest the outcrop with regard to the intuition of signs. Mathematical being is conceived not as the comprehensive essence which reveals itself in an appropriate formalism but rather as the conquering dynamism which underlies the production of theories and continually poses new problems to the degree to which we furnish solutions to the old problems. This dynamism is not founded at a precise point where it would be possible to localize its expansive power but is present in each of the moments of the development. And if at certain moments it draws from the intuition of an external reality the wherewithal to pursue its inventions, it is at the moment in which this intuition is forgotten for the sake of an internal coherence which relies only on its own possibilities that the reality of its efficacy manifests itself. Mathematics is not an effort to overtake the singularity of a universal structure by means of an abstractive operation but the progressive revelation of virtualities inscribed in a concreteness which it is never a question of abandoning. Indeed, there is no abstraction, no passage from a concrete of the first degree to a concrete of the second degree, no ascent toward the universal, and no conquest of singularity. But there is an elaboration, in the historical duration and in the theoretical manifold, of what was given from the beginning in that moment of fulfillment which marks the institution of the properly mathematical experience and, as it were, its conquest of physical experience.

We never relinquish the concrete; we only actualize its inexhaustible content. Insofar as there is formalization—and as we have seen, it always ends up reintroducing itself as a necessary component—there is impoverishment and loss of contact with the truly concrete which alone sustains mathematical thought and prevents it from perishing in a universality without content. The concrete is not reconquered on a first level of reality still in highly roughhewn form but is reconquered on the abstract. Yet the abstract is not first. It is by a perpetual return to its intuitive origins and to the reality of its problems, by a close fidelity to the imperatives of this hidden life which traverses theories like a fertilizing sap, that mathematical thought reconquers, through the inevitable snares of a necessary abstraction, this original concrete which is always present at the core of its movements and which manifests in most characteristic fashion its permanent activity in the highest moments of creation. The creativity of thought is in effect one with an internal dynamism which owes nothing either to the undifferentiated reality in which it was plunged before the intervention of mind or to the power of initiative of this same mind, but which is the very law of a reality whose different moments can only be given successively, according to a rigorous succession of productions, whose living physiognomy, necessary connection, and minute mechanism it is precisely the role of mathematics to describe. The mind acts here not in the manner of a liberty of invention which draws its efficacy only from itself and knows of no limitation other than that of its own refusal but in the manner of a revealer who, in expressing to himself the mechanism of a genesis, provokes its objective accomplishment while he is himself borne by it.

And if there is a necessity which manifests itself at the heart of this realization, it is not an external translation, solidified in formulas, of a proper necessity of thought, binding the terms of its creations by decree, nor that evanescent necessity of a deductive system in which everything is submitted to the rigorous rules of a canonic demonstration; it is a necessity which is founded in a need for realization in virtue of which each term evokes the following as that which completes it and gives meaning to it. Mathematical reality thus constitutes itself as an untearable fabric whose traverse is not constituted in an arbitrary way but rather imposes on the thought which wants to seize it a rigorously regulated course, in which no step can be skipped nor can come before those which must precede it.

The concrete development of mathematics obliges us to speak of a dialectic which is neither that of the mind nor that of reality but is really that of the concept—that is, if we truly want to consider the concept in its own right, in its most radical state of objectification, in that moment of its existence when it is no longer the place of exchange between mind and reality, like the fringe along which their mutual penetration is achieved, but instead constitutes itself in objectivity and outlines between the mind and physical reality a neutral space which mediates their encounter and becomes reality in its turn. But it is now an intentional reality through which the horizon of the experience from which it has been drawn and to which it unceasingly returns is always announced.

The life of the concept is that perpetual coming and going between the horizon from which it breaks away, and which invests it with its content, and that supreme objectification in which it cuts itself off from its horizon and empties itself of its content in order to constitute itself as a pure form with respect to mind. To grasp it in only one of these terms is to miss its proper state of reality. To attain it for what it is, we must place it back in that movement with which it identifies itself and in which are correlatively and simultaneously present the horizon which provides it with its anchorage in reality and the status of autonomy which makes it the proper food for thought.

Just as it would be an error to consider it only in this status, where it takes on the inconsistency of formalism, it would be a mistake to consider it only in its intuitive ground, where it is dissolved into the opacity of the pure datum. Mathematical reality is situated in that intermediate zone which cannot be characterized in a direct way but which can at least be circumscribed by a series of approximations which end up by indicating its entire interval of existence. To draw mathematics from the side of intuition would be to deny its structural aspect and to absorb it into the undifferentiated, where all is given and hence nothing is understood. To draw it from the side of formal objectivity would be to deny its intuitive components and, under the pretext of transporting it to the highest level of understanding, to suppress its moment of givenness.

If the concept is thus in this movement, and even more is identified with that very movement, to say that there is a dialectic of the concept is to say that this movement is articulated according to a necessary progression in which each term generates the following by its own power and without having recourse to some external agent or some surplus force. But if each term thus includes, with the indication of its own insufficiency and the avowal of its own indigence, the force of appeal which makes of this insufficiency a demand for fulfillment and the power of generation which is capable of filling this indigence and of responding to this demand with a new production, it is because it is the place of a teleology which goes beyond it and of which it is only the ephemeral and transitory bearer. The term is, to be sure, nowhere given but only brings itself to actualization in each of the moments. But these exist only through this term which they bear in them as that which dynamizes and fertilizes them. The term does not appear at a given moment, by virtue of some internal unpredictable event or some external fortuitous intervention. It is given from the beginning, in the very moment in which mathematical experience is inaugurated at the heart of intuition. It is nothing other than that horizon to which the concept belongs. In this sense, if a complete system were conceivable, it could only be as a total explication of this horizon. But precisely because it is a horizon and because it always transcends that which actualizes it, it cannot be attained in an adequate manner. The total system is therefore unthinkable if not in the form of a regulative idea whose reality is nothing other than that of the horizon, but whose prospective character adds to the antecedent (but at the same time always present) reality of the horizon the necessity of an explicit articulation. It can then be said that this term, present in each particular concept, is the complete system where the plenitude of comprehension would recover the totality of the given, or again, where the universality of the structure would make the totality of the initial horizon explicit.

IV

WE ARE THUS LED to acknowledge at the heart of mathematical thought a duality of tendencies which, in seeming to mutually exclude each other, are in a certain way interior to each other (each including, by virtue of its very demand, something like a trace of the other), and which in reality correspond to two different ways of envisaging mathematical being.

We could obviously force the opposition and summon the mathematician to choose between two styles of thought. We could even see in the necessity of this choice the manifestation of a progress of thought rather than the exclusion of two simultaneous points of view. Formalism would then appear as a conquest against which there is no possibility of turning back and which gives mathematical reality the most adequate transcription in the present state of research. But this would be to lose sight of the reciprocal interiority of the two perspectives and to sacrifice a component of thought whose significance seems extremely important.

Enclosing themselves in a point of view which appears to be the only one truly justified, all the more so as it permits the other to be situated within its own view, each of the perspectives presents itself as exclusive and claims to take over the truth of mathematical being all by itself. But if, in returning to a movement of thought already elaborated and hardened into its own creations, we try to rediscover a more primitive and more undifferentiated zone of the mathematical process, it becomes possible to grasp these two perspectives simultaneously and to perceive that we cannot account for mathematical reality without taking this duality into account, not only in its very existence but in the content of its terms.

In reality, the two perspectives which we have distinguished should be considered as complementary. What must be understood is how mathematical thought necessarily articulates itself according to this duality of aims, where each indeed seems to manifest an irreducible demand. Each of these two demands is rooted, with the same necessity, in mathematical reality; each obliges us to perform a double reading of it, as if it were not possible to exhaust this reality through a simple procedure and according to a unitary dimension.

In the same way that we have described our two perspectives, we have tried to inspire this larger understanding which should make their necessary complementarity apparent. On the one hand, we have indicated how formalism acknowledges its concrete rootedness, but in order to surmount it in the seizure of an essence which constitutes the genuine reality internal to the different levels of the elaboration of mathematics. On the other hand, in the movement which elaborates the reality of the concept and displays its internal dialectic on the plane of objectivity, we have shown the necessary presence of formalism as bearer of that exteriority which alone can bring the confusion of the initial intuition to pass to the explicit state; as frontier of the interval of oscillation within which the dynamism proper to mathematical reality develops itself; and finally, under the form of the total system, as the term immanent to each of the moments of the life of the concept, as the principle of its living teleology.

We are thus led back to the double reality of an essence and of a movement. Just as the essence can be conceived only as that which is at the extremity of a movement of abstraction and which manifests its truth, the movement can be conceived only as that which is finalized by an encompassing structure to which it is indeed permitted to give the name of essence. Perhaps it is only by a misunderstanding, due to the narrowness of a particular perspective, that formalism underestimates the reality from which it draws the matter for its own construction and that realism in its turn underestimates the reality of the system within which it tends, almost in spite of itself, to be realized.

We now see the terms passing into each other. That essence which had appeared to us as the reality most interior to the structures not yet totally formalized in fact ends up by being identified with the regulative idea which unifies the movement by which these structures are substituted for each other according to a privileged direction. And the conceptual dynamic which unfolds the initial intuition into newer and newer problems ends up by being identified with the movement of abstraction by which this singular essence is progressively conquered. In reality, this essence is never given to us explicitly. Even in the purest formalism we only come in contact with a deficient manifestation of it. For the initial intuition is never exhausted, as the problematizing tendency sufficiently emphasizes. And here it brings a useful correction to the temptation to which formalism is always subject, of presenting itself as the truly adequate expression of mathematical reality and as the total manifestation of the essence which constitutes it. This manifestation would in effect be total only if there were a coincidence between this essence and the formalism which expresses it. But then there would no longer be a manifestation, but only pure and simple presence. If there is manifestation, it is precisely because this coincidence is not yet realized and indeed because it is in principle impossible to ever attain it. For that, formalism would have to cease to be itself; the display of a discursive structure would have to cede it to the saturating simplicity of an intuition which would overtake, but in a totally transparent purity, the initial intuition in which our encounter with the world is inaugurated. Thus, this essence whose inaccessible character has been exposed by the realist perspective now appears to us, from the point of view of the formalist perspective itself, as a finalizing term more than as a reality given in a totally thematized form.

And, on the other hand, the essence really constitutes the truth of the problematizing movement. Formalization corresponds to an actual progress of mathematical thought. While it always remains necessary to return to the primitive intuitions and to replunge oneself into the ever moving life of problems, it is nonetheless true that mathematics finds its realization only in the constitution sufficiently powerful to manifest all the richness contained in the intuition but, at the same time, sufficiently autonomous to tear mathematical being away from the initial hold of the intuition in order to give it its proper consistency. It is only in the system that the concept finds its true objective reality and that its dynamism blossoms forth in all of its purity. The formalist is right in underlining, against the realist, the eminent value of the system and in noting emphatically that only in the system does the mathematical movement attain the plenitude of its expression. He thus saves the realist tendency from the temptation which threatens it, in minimizing the thrust of formalism, of dissolving the objectivity of the concept into the fluidity of intuition. In reality, formalism is not an empty framework in which the content of the concept finds itself evaporated.

The inconsistency is not on the side of the system but on the side of intuition. For formalism gives the concept its indispensable support and its complete independence with regard to the initiative of thought and the prestige of intuition. The deductive sequence which makes up the internal life of the system and seems to reduce itself to a mechanical production of theorems in which the creative act of thought is effaced before the stereotyped operation of the calculating machine is only the manifestation (at a level of objectivity which, in order to mask its unpredictable fertility, nonetheless bestows upon it its genuine autonomy) of that internal life whose moving reality we have tried to describe in the dialectic of the concept.

V

BUT IT IS NOT ENOUGH to show how, by slipping one into the other, the two perspectives correct each other and in a certain sense reciprocally annul each other. We must try to found this double reality of the opposition and of fusion in more fundamental structures which make us understand their necessary character and deepen the description into a genuine theory of thought and of mathematical reality. Now the description almost immediately imposes a double problematic on us: on the one hand the problematic of dynamism and on the other that of manifestation, a dynamism which plays at the same time on the level of thought and on the level of reality, and a manifestation which is as much in the movement of problematization as in the conquests of formalism.

Thus, the opposition between a realist and a formalist perspective is deepened into an opposition between a double dynamism, which makes us grasp being in the single reality of its development, and a manifestive structure, which makes us grasp it in the irradiation of a presence of essential type. Whether we have gained in this transposition depends on the extent to which it now becomes easier for us, because we have taken over a more fundamental layer of comprehension, to show the mutual implication of two perspectives which are not only complementary aspects of a single reality but which are only two descriptions, finally identical, of that reality. And we shall have to show how the opposition which we first grasped on the plane of a description of mathematical reality is inserted into a metaphysical perspective which manifests its truly fundamental character. If mathematical being is only given to us according to this duality of perspectives, this pertains not to its singular structure but to a much more fundamental law which rules the encounter of our thought with being. For it is evidently in relation to the ultimate horizon of all comprehension that we must understand and thereby resolve the antinomies which can appear in the very actualization of this comprehension.

We see on the one hand that mathematical being is not given to us at a single stroke but is revealed to us in a series of approximations whose regulated sequence outlines a continuous movement stretched between pure intuition and pure formalization. In a certain way, all is given in that first contact with the reality from which the mind draws the intuition of a structure whose exact nature and properties are left to the scrutiny of later research. In another way, nothing is yet given, for mathematical being is always present only as a limit which manifests itself in each of the particular conquests through which we strive to overtake it but which can never be actually seized.

Mathematical research is thus deployed between a double horizon, that of an intuition in which it incessantly nourishes itself, and thanks to which it really participates in that reality of the world which is at the origin of every genesis, and the horizon of a total actualization toward which it always directs itself, and thanks to which it really participates in that reality of the objective spirit which is at the term of every creation. If these two horizons are related to each other, it is not in an arbitrary way or by virtue of an external synthesis which would bear the stamp of an absolute initiative of spirit but in truly necessary fashion, by virtue of their very constitutive structure. For they are inscribed within each other and appear to us in that mutual connection from the first moment of their discovery. The intuitive horizon is grasped from the start as a task. At the same time as it offers an infinitely complex matter to our powers of appropriation, it presents itself as an indefinite demand of elucidation. Precisely because it is a horizon and not a brute datum, it includes within itself the indication of an enterprise whose horizon of objectification constitutes the finalizing principle. The datum of intuition not only gives itself as a compact mass for understanding but already includes an internal articulation which outlines in it, as in a stipple drawing, the itinerary of comprehension, marking in advance its necessary circuits. It thus already includes, in the form of an inviting rough draft, that other horizon which polarizes the research and which, if not present in a thematic grasp, is nonetheless present from the start as the secret soul of all comprehension.

And reciprocally, the horizon of objectification refers necessarily to the datum which it permits us to penetrate, to the ground from which it scaffolds its moving constructions, to the matter from which it composes its provisional actualizations. It presents itself not as a pure task but as a principle of organization, as the structural essence of a datum without which it would no longer be anything. We can comprehend it neither as an a priori dynamism coming from the outside to animate terms independent of it nor as a pure form coming to bestow the consecration of universality on a concreteness always in danger of returning to the opacity of some irreducible in-itself. It is present in the datum as that which offers itself to comprehension, though not in the immediate transparency of a completely constituted rationality but in the demand of an indefinite deepening and the promise of an inexhaustible harvest. Once again the image of the filter can be evoked here to supplement the inadequacy of the description, both because it evokes an operation of purification which corresponds well with that ascent toward the rational included in every movement of explicitation and because it is the most exact mathematical expression, at the level of general topology, for the classical notion of limit. The horizon of objectification is inserted into the intuitive horizon as the limit point which is to be overtaken by a series of concentric approaches. It is like the point of escape of an increasingly precise effort. Just as the limit is actually given in topology, not in a serial law as in calculus but in the structural characterization of open subsets of the set considered, so the horizon of objectification is not the last evanescent term of an infinite series but is actually given in the very deployment of the intuitive horizon.

The dynamism of which we were speaking is then only the translation on the level of explicit determinations of that internal demand of comprehension given with the intuitive horizon as the nonthematic principle of rationality which inaugurates the mathematical act and polarizes its successive moments. And if there is a dialectic of the concept, it is because the concept is precisely the instrument of this actualization. Furthermore, it is this in a radical sense, not because it would be its bearer but because it is its actual place, so that it must be said that it is in and through the concept that the movement which we were evoking works itself out. There is not a movement first, and then an accidental expression in which it comes to be embodied, as in a deficient matter external to it. There is from the start the reality of the concept as that which realizes the passage between the two horizons that define the space of comprehension. A horizon is nothing in itself but exists only in relation to an actuality whose mode of production and of achievement it specifies. If we speak of horizon, it is precisely to avoid any allusion to an exteriority of terms which would come to ruin the original relation which is constitutive of the concept and, in assigning to the concept boundaries of a spatial type, to render incomprehensible the dynamism which the description still obliges us to recognize in it. This structure of the double horizon belongs to the concept itself. And after having tried to describe it in an independent manner, it must be restored to that which constitutes its unity. Moreover, it cannot be otherwise understood how the mutual implication of the two perspectives is founded and how their mutual fertilization works.

VI

BUT AT THE SAME TIME as we describe the objective face of this dynamism, we must grasp its subjective face again, under pain of missing an essential moment of it. Already the mechanism of exchange between the horizons has obliged us to speak of comprehension, and this shifting of vocabulary announces the complementary aspect of the description to which we must now come. It is in fact only through the mediation of spirit that the dialectic of the concept can work itself out. The structure of horizonality which it involves in effect necessarily returns to a thought which is, so to speak, at the intersecting surface of two subspaces.

What has been described in terms of horizon can and should now be repeated in terms of openness. Just as there is in the intuitive horizon a kind of preliminary sketch of comprehension which indicates the trace of categorial operations in it, there is in thought a preadaptation to its object, an original schema of seizure, a genuine precomprehension which alone makes its effort possible. Just as there is in the horizon of objectification a polarizing finality which takes over the primitive demand of the given, there is in thought a conquering dynamism, an immanent end idea, which takes over the initial initiative of comprehension. Just as finally the two horizons are included in each other, the internal dynamism of thought is included in its inaugural perspective. The act which opens the comprehension of a certain domain at the same time outlines an ideal which will be the permanent soul of the investigation. To give oneself a certain mode of comprehension and thereby to open oneself to a certain domain of reality is in the same stroke to assign oneself an infinite task of exploration and of deepening, for it is a manner of giving oneself the things which is not yet thematic, the installation of an original relation with the world which is still only a style of thematization and not yet the explicit shaping of a content. It is at once like a matter to be organized and like a form to be filled. The nonthematic datum of a reality necessarily presents itself as an ideal to be actualized. Moreover, it is through this that a temporal structure whose necessity the history of mathematics objectifies is introduced into the act of rationalization.

We see that the description of the initiatives of thought brings us back to evoking the horizons of which we spoke above, when we were basing ourselves solely on the testimony of phenomenal objectivity. This manifests the essential connection of the two themes of our description and obliges us to acknowledge the intimate solidarity of thought and of the world which it gives itself. This solidarity is so profound that it finally becomes an exchange, and the shifting which occurs on the level of the description between the vocabulary of project and that of horizon symbolizes the real passage in virtue of which one perspective comes to blend itself into the other, the trace of a comprehension into the openness of a zone of rationality, the limit point of a horizon into the end idea of a constitutive project. Mathematical reality is thus not a pure datum and by no means represents the place of a passivity, just as mathematical thought is no longer a pure activity and by no means represents the place of a creation. There is neither pure registration nor pure creation but rather a reading, explicitation, development, revelation, disclosure of what is. In a certain way, mathematical reality exists only by virtue of the initiatives of thought, being constituted in mathematical activity. In another way, it belongs to a trans-historical objectivity whose enigmas mathematical thought always only partially deciphers. To separate these two aspects would be to betray both reality and thought. We must rather hold on to both simultaneously by showing in what way they mutually correct and finally pass into each other.

But if it is false to reduce the structure of horizon to the dynamism of thought, we must nonetheless note the necessary role of its initiative. For the preliminary openness of a certain domain of reality is needed to constitute the intuitive horizon from which the development begins, and the implicit aim which extends the original precomprehension into the present act of thematization is needed to constitute the entelechy which finalizes the development and gives it the wherewithal to perpetuate itself. Thought is thus mediator of the concept. In it occurs that transmutation by which the concept is continually being torn from the primitive confusion of the intuition, where it is still completely caught in a shell of alienation, in order to be oriented toward that total objectification which would mark the definitive victory of a perfectly closed system. Place of elaboration and of passage, thought is that medium through which the concept comes to itself but from which it afterwards divorces itself in order to place itself before it in the historicized reality of the objective spirit. The dialectic of the concept is not the dissipation of a creative force in a world of objectification but the advent of an objectivity by way of an active receptivity, a revealing power and an indefinite capacity for transmutation. To accomplish the progressive disclosure of mathematical being, to fulfill the initial project of science, to realize the ideal which presents itself as the term to be overtaken, is identically to reveal the concept to itself and to make possible that internal life which fills history with its inventions and its failures.

It is this activity which constitutes both the docility to problems, which we have seen to be an indispensable condition of enrichment, and the ambition of formalism, which we know represents the supreme integration in which science in its actual state is realized. We see that the relation of thought to the concept is thus reciprocal. For if it is true that the concept is the

mediator of thought, when we envisage it as the detour by which
mind is made explicit to itself and reconquers itself over all that
denies it, then thought is also the mediator of the concept, insofar as the concept appears as the place of a genesis which
reveals, in the encounter of spirit and the world (or more exactly, of man and the world), a new layer of reality which is at
once included in every thematization of this encounter and totally autonomous.

VII

INSOFAR AS THIS AUTONOMY is constituted in the form
of a system which symbolizes its reality, the problematic of
dynamism is transformed into a problematic of manifestation.
When mathematical being is no longer grasped in the instability
of a movement but in the permanence of a system, this is
because it appears to us no longer as a reality on its way to
constitution but rather as an essence in the act of revelation.
And in order to truly account for the opposition from which we
have begun, we must show how these two aspects come to be
reunited.

As indicated above, to say that there is manifestation of a
structure in the system is to say that the system is not itself this
hidden structure and also that the latter is given to us only in it.
What is proper to manifestation is precisely a revealing in a
hiding, or again, a dissimulation in the very act of revelation.
This cannot be interpreted in a quantitative way, as though only
a part of the reality were accessible to us while another part
remained concealed from us. In fact, the entire reality is given to
us, but according to an imperfect mode. Through its body of
manifestation it is indeed reality which we come to know, but
without being able to overtake its complete actuality. Every manifestation tends to overtake the manifested, but the distance
between the two is insurmountable because it is of the nature of
the manifested to reveal itself not in person but only through
delegations of itself, none of which can be identified with it.

Yet we must guard against introducing a radical heterogeneity between the two terms. The manifested is truly present only
in its manifestation, and the latter draws its reality only from
the former. There is no term situated somewhere in an inaccessi-

ble region of reality which would come to correspond to an expression attainable in the actual movements of intuition. There is, on the one hand, a body of appearance whose meaning transcends immediate appearance and, on the other hand, a reality which gives itself to be known only through the mediation of this appearance. We must therefore exclude a purely empirical interpretation which, by magnifying the significance of the sign, would reduce being to its appearance, just like a Platonic interpretation which, by magnifying the significance of the distance between being and its appearance, would conjure both into a duality of terms quite incomprehensible for philosophical apprehension.

If mathematical being tends to give itself to thought in the form of a system, and that from the start, so that the constitution of pure formalisms only marks the last step of a necessary progression, this is because it is precisely its nature not to give itself in person. In a certain way, we could consider the foundation of this structure to be the dynamic aspect which we have tried to characterize. Because mathematical being is not given in a thematic way but has to be overtaken in the very act which constitutes it, according to a movement polarized through the finality of the system, it cannot appear to us in the evidence of a total revelation but only in the vicariousness of a partial delegation. The manifestive structure simply expresses the necessity of a deployment for which none of the terms are given, except in the form of horizons inserted at the very heart of conceptual reality. The inadequation which always separates being from its manifestation and prevents it from ever being reduced to an objectified datum expresses the temporality of the movement which strives to complete it, or again, that internal dialectic of the concept in which the aspect of perpetual incompleteness is united with that of an ever efficacious plenitude which prevents the movement from being halted.

But perhaps it would be equally exact to found the dynamic structure on the manifestive structure. If we can overtake mathematical being only through the mediation of an ever unachieved movement and with a permanent attention to an objective sequence whose entire law is never given to us, this is because it is of its nature not to manifest itself as a totality. It is given in its totality neither at the beginning of the movement, in a way which would make of it the simple enumeration of a set of properties that are present a priori (and this bestows the character of horizonality on the intuitive anchorage), nor at its term, in a way which would make it into the progressive generation of a synthesis that is recoverable a posteriori (and this bestows the character of horizonality on the objectifying aim).

In reality, if it is possible to found each of the perspectives on the other, it is because neither of them possesses absolute primacy; they are only different descriptions of the same reality. This reality is that of the encounter of our spirit and the world at the core of a constituting project which here is that of rationality. In order to account for it, we must situate it in the totality of the projects which articulate the life of consciousness, from the innocence of perception to the restlessness of the metaphysical quest.

Mathematical reality is inscribed in our initial contact with the world, at the very heart of the most immediate perception, but it is the role of a particular project to extricate it for its own sake. And as we have seen, the extrication is complex, for it is based not only on the immediacy of perception but equally and perhaps more so on already more elaborate intuitions which correspond to the activation of the scientific project. The properly mathematical project then appears as a specification of the scientific project and this implication, while it already manifests itself in the fertility of the applications of theory, blossoms forth nowhere better than in the generality of the formal system which constitutes, as it were, the ideal framework of every scientific systematization and which subordinates calculation to itself in the same way as any axiomatizable reality whatsoever. In purifying itself, mathematics extends the field of its validity. In returning to itself in the most rigorous fashion, the mathematical project tends to mask the scientific project completely, and it is in this form that it exercises a sovereignly regulative role on the whole of the rational economy. Not only the paradigm of really fruitful procedures but also the integrator of truly successful procedures, it tends to constitute, in tearing the datum away from the confusions of a still tangible intuition, the canon par excellence of reason. Neither a priori framework nor a posteriori synthesis, it is as it were the most vital element of research, its surest guiding thread, its most invariable objective. Formalism, inasmuch as it corresponds to a certain achievement of the mathematical project, and through it of the scientific project, is like the invariant of pure reason.

But once the conquest hardens into formalism, the initial encounter of perception is transformed into an encounter of the rational, in which the inexhaustibility of the primary world becomes the inexhaustibility of a project of objectification. The same structures are rediscovered, reflecting on a second level what description permitted us to discover on a primary level. And undoubtedly more extended descriptions, rediscovering modalities of consciousness quite removed from that of rationality, as for example in the affective and voluntary structures, would rediscover the same fundamental categories of experience. Here critical prospection must be held in abeyance in order to be integrated into a truly metaphysical perspective. Just as there is a first horizon of disclosure, that which outlines the space of our first encounter with the world, there is an ultimate horizon of comprehension, that in which all of our procedures are inserted and where their aspirations are consummated at the same time as their signification is illuminated. This ultimate horizon, that of the encounter of the existent and of Being, gives us the key to structures which we could have discovered at the level of more particular encounters which are realized in science, in artistic creation, in moral initiative, and in political action. These different categories of experience then appear as so many manifestations of a fundamental encounter which exists only through them at the same time as it founds their profound mechanism.

Once again, things can be taken here just as much from the side of the existent as from the side of Being, and we will be able to describe experience in its totality either as a conquest, which is the point of view of the life of spirit, or as a gift, which is the point of view of the life of Being. Do we not find again here, but transposed to a more fundamental and, to tell the truth, ultimate level of reflection, the opposition which we have tried to establish from the start between formalism and realism, as though our enterprise of the elucidation of experience could never escape this duality which is grounded in the very nature of our condition, at once devoured by contingency and charged with necessity, given over to passivity and traversed by a creative desire, hardened into objectivity and mobilized by a perpetual drive?

What we must perceive is how this condition has repercussions on each of the levels of our behavior and even permeates the apparent impossibility of the purely rational. For the mobility of the life of spirit does not admit of limits and bursts forth into the very act by which the latter tries to surmount it in the most radical way, by exhausting itself in the objectivity which it has itself set up. We are speakers but also listeners, conquerors but at the same time besieged; we receive as much as we give, and if our experience seems to us like the inexhaustible gesture of a spontaneity ever on the alert, that is because it is only the response to an appeal which unceasingly tears us away from our own resignation and always gives us the wherewithal to respond to its solicitation. The last word of philosophy is perhaps the evocation of that generosity which is in us only because it is in being and which, much more than a property or an act, is really the name of that encounter in which our vocation is consummated.

Selected Bibliography

GASTON BACHELARD

I. Works by Gaston Bachelard

Etude sur l'évolution d'un problème de physique: La Propagation thermique dans les solides. Paris: Vrin, 1928.
La Valeur inductive de la relativité. Paris: Vrin, 1929.
L'Intuition de l'instant. Paris: Stock, 1932.
Le Pluralisme cohérent de la chimie moderne. Paris: Vrin, 1932.
Le Dialectique de la durée. Paris: Presses Universitaires de France, 1933.
Le Nouvel Esprit scientifique. Paris: Presses Universitaires de France, 1934.
La Formation de l'esprit scientifique. Paris: Vrin, 1938.
La Philosophie du non. Paris: Presses Universitaires de France, 1940. English translation by G. C. Waterston. *The Philosophy of No.* New York: Orion Press, 1968.
Le Rationalisme appliqué. Paris: Presses Universitaires de France, 1949.
L'Activité rationaliste de la physique contemporaine. Paris: Presses Universitaires de France, 1951.

II. Studies on Gaston Bachelard

Dagognet, François. *Gaston Bachelard: Sa Vie, son oeuvre, avec un exposé de sa philosophie.* Paris: Presses Universitaires de France, 1965.
Hyppolite, Jean. "Gaston Bachelard ou le romantisme de l'intelli-

gence," *Revue philosophique de la France et de l'Etranger*, CXLIV (1954), 85–96.
Quillet, Pierre. *Bachelard: Philosophes de tous les temps*. Paris: Seghers, 1964.

SUZANNE BACHELARD

I. Works by Suzanne Bachelard

La Logique de Husserl: Etude sur logique formelle et logique transcendentale. Paris: Presses Universitaires de France, 1957. English translation by Lester E. Embree, *A Study of Husserl's Formal and Transcendental Logic*. Evanston, Ill. Northwestern University Press, 1968.
Logique formelle et logique transcendentale: Essai d'une critique de la raison logique. Paris: Presses Universitaires de France, 1957.
La Conscience de rationalité: Etude phénoménologique sur la physique mathématique. Paris: Presses Universitaires de France, 1958.
*Les Polemiques concernant le principe de moindre action au XIII*ᵉ *siecle*. Alençon: Imprimerie alençonnaise, 1961.

OSKAR BECKER

I. Works by Becker

"Beiträge zur phänomenologischen Begründung der Geometrie und ihrer physikalischen Anwendungen," *Jahrbuch für Philosophie und phänomenologische Forschung*, VI (1923), 385–560. This treatise has recently been published under separate cover by Max Niemeyer Verlag, Tübingen.
"Mathematische Existenz: Untersuchungen zur Logik und Ontologie mathematischer Phänomene," *Jahrbuch für Philosophie und phänomenologische Forschung*, VIII (1927), 439–809.
"Die Philosophie Edmund Husserls," *Kantstudien*, XXXV (1930), 119–50.
Einführung in die Logistik, vorzüglich in den Modalkalkül. Meisenheim a.d.G.: Hain, 1951.
Untersuchungen über den Modalkalkül. Meisenheim a.d.G.: Hain, 1952.
Grundlagen der Mathematik in geschichtlicher Entwicklung. Freiburg and Munich: Alber, 1954.
Das mathematische Denken der Antike. Göttingen: Vandenhoeck & Ruprecht, 1957.

Grösse und Grenze der mathematischen Denkweise. Freiburg and Munich: Alber, 1959.
Dasein und Dawesen: Gesammelte philosophische Aufsätze. Pfullingen: Neske, 1963.

JEAN CAVAILLÈS

I. Works by Cavaillès

"L'Ecole de Vienne au Congrès de Prague," *Revue de métaphysique et de morale,* XLII (1935), 137–49.
"Logique mathématique et syllogisme," *Revue philosophique* (1937).
Méthode axiomatique et formalisme: Essai sur le problème du fondement des mathématiques. Paris: Hermann, 1938.
"Du Collectif au Pari," *Revue de métaphysique et de morale,* XLVII (1940).
"Mathématiques et formalisme," *Revue internationale de philosophie,* III (1949), 158–65. Includes a complete bibliography of Cavaillès' works.
Sur la logique et la théorie de la science. 2d ed. Paris: Presses Universitaires de France, 1960.
Philosophie mathématique. Paris: Hermann, 1962. This collection includes: *Remarques sur la formation de la théorie abstrait des ensembles* (originally published in 1938); *Transfini et continu* (1947); and *Briefwechsel Cantor-Dedekind* (edited by Cavaillès and originally published in 1937).

II. Studies on Cavaillès

Dubarle, D., "Le Dernier Ecrit de Jean Cavaillès," *Revue de métaphysique et de morale,* LIII (1948), 225–47, 350–78.
Granger, G. G., "Jean Cavaillès ou la montée vers Spinoza," *Les Etudes philosophiques*" (1947), 271–79.
Morot-Sir, Ed., "La Théorie de la science, d'après Jean Cavaillès," *Revue des sciences humaines,* L (1948), 154–59.

MARTIN HEIDEGGER

I. Works by Heidegger

Sein und Zeit. Tübingen: Niemeyer, 1927. English translation by John Macquarrie and Edward Robinson, *Being and Time.* London: SCM, 1962.

Was heisst Denken? Tübingen: Niemeyer, 1954.
Vorträge und Aufsätze. Pfullingen: Neske, 1954.
Holzwege. Frankfurt a.M.: Klostermann, 1957.

II. Studies on Heidegger

Astrade, G., Bauch, K., et al. *Martin Heideggers Einfluss auf die Wissenschaften.* Berne: Francke, 1949.
Kockelmans, Joseph J. *Martin Heidegger: A First Introduction to His Philosophy.* Pittsburgh, Pa.: Duquesne University Press, 1965.
Pöggeler, Otto. *Der Denkweg Martin Heideggers.* Pfullingen: Neske, 1963.
Richardson, William J. *Heidegger: Through Phenomenology to Thought.* The Hague: Nijhoff, 1963.

EDMUND HUSSERL

I. Works by Husserl

Philosophie der Arithmetik. Psychologische und logische Untersuchungen. Vol. I. Halle a.d.S.: Pfeffer, 1891.
Logische Untersuchungen. 3 vols. 3d ed. Halle a.d.S.: Niemeyer, 1921–22.
Ideen zu einer reinen Phänomenologie und phänomenologischen Philosophie. 3 vols. The Hague: Nijhoff, 1950–52. The first volume has been translated by W. R. Boyce Gibson. *Ideas: General Introduction to Pure Phenomenology.* New York: Collier, 1962.
Formale und transzendentale Logik: Versuch einer Kritik der logischen Vernunft. Halle a.d.S.: Niemeyer, 1929. Cross-paginated English translation by Dorion Cairns. *Formal and Transcendental Logic.* The Hague: Nijhoff, 1969.
Die Krisis der europäischen Wissenschaften und die transzendentale Phänomenologie: Eine Einleitung in die phänomenologische Philosophie. Edited by Walter Biemel. The Hague: Nijhoff, 1954. English translation by David Carr. *The Crisis of the European Sciences.* Evanston, Ill.: Northwestern University Press, 1970.

II. Studies on Husserl

Farber, Marvin. *The Foundation of Phenomenology: Edmund Husserl and the Quest for a Rigorous Science of Philosophy.* Cambridge, Mass.: Harvard University Press, 1943.

————. *Philosophical Essays in Memory of Edmund Husserl.* Cambridge, Mass.: Harvard University Press, 1940.

Gurwitsch, Aron. "Comments on the Paper by Herbert Marcuse" ["On Science and Phenomenology"]. In *Boston Studies in the Philosophy of Science*, edited by Robert S. Cohen and Max W. Wartofsky, II, 279–90, 291–306. New York: Humanities Press, 1965.

————. "Galilean Physics in the Light of Husserl's Phenomenology." In *Galileo, Man of Science*, edited by Ernan McMullin, pp. 388–401. New York: Basic Books, 1967.

————. "The Last Work of Edmund Husserl," *Philosophy and Phenomenological Research*, XI (1956), 370–99.

Kockelmans, Joseph J. *A First Introduction to Husserl's Phenomenology.* Pittsburgh, Pa.: Duquesne University Press, 1967.

————, ed. *Phenomenology: The Philosophy of Edmund Husserl and Its Interpretation.* New York: Doubleday, 1967.

————. *Phenomenology and Physical Science.* Pittsburgh, Pa.: Duquesne University Press, 1966.

Lauer, Quentin. *The Triumph of Subjectivity: An Introduction to Transcendental Phenomenology.* New York: Fordham University Press, 1958.

Osborn, Andrew D. *The Philosophy of Edmund Husserl in Its Development from His Mathematical Interest to His First Conception of Phenomenology in Logical Investigations.* New York: International Press, 1934.

Spiegelberg, Herbert. *The Phenomenological Movement: A Historical Introduction.* 2 vols. The Hague: Nijhoff, 1960.

Thevenaz, P. *What Is Phenomenology? And Other Essays.* Translated by James M. Edie. Chicago: Quadrangle Books, 1962.

JEAN LADRIÈRE

I. Works by Ladrière

"Mathématiques et formalisme," *Revue des questions scientifiques* (Louvain), October 20, 1955, pp. 538–74.

Les Limitations internes des formalismes. Louvain: Nauwelaerts, 1957.

"Philosophy and Science," *Philosophical Studies*, VII (1958), 3–23.

"La Philosophie des mathématiques et le problème du formalisme," *Revue philosophique de Louvain*, LVII (1959), 600–22.

"Hegel, Husserl, and Reason Today," *The Modern Schoolman*, XXXVII (1960), 171–95.

"Les Limitations des formalismes et leur signification philosophique," *Dialectica* (Neuchatel), XIV (1960), 279–320.
"Le Symbolisme comme domain operatoire," *Cahiers internationaux de symbolisme* (Geneva), no. 3 (1963), pp. 29–46.
"Objectivité et realité dans les sciences mathématiques," *Dialectica* (Neuchatel), XX (1966), 215–41. Also published in *Revue philosophique de Louvain*, LXIV (1966), 550–81.
"Les Limites de la formalisation." In *Logique et connaissance scientifique*. Paris, 1967.
"Sens et systeme," *Esprit*, CCCLX (May, 1967), 822–24.

Maurice Merleau-Ponty

I. Works by Merleau-Ponty

La Structure du comportement. Paris: Presses Universitaires de France, 1942. English translation by Alden L. Fisher. *The Structure of Behavior.* Boston: Beacon Press, 1963.
Phénoménologie de la perception. Paris: Gallimard, 1945. English translation by Colin Smith. *Phenomenology of Perception.* New York: Humanities Press, 1962.
Le Visible et l'invisible. Edited by Claude Lefort. Paris: Gallimard, 1964. English translation by Alphonso Lingis. *The Visible and the Invisible.* Evanston, Ill.: Northwestern University Press, 1968.
"Phenomenology and the Sciences of Man." In *The Primacy of Perception and Other Essays*, edited by James M. Edie, pp. 43–94. Evanston, Ill.: Northwestern University Press, 1964.
"The Metaphysical in Man." In *Sense and Non-Sense*, translated by H. L. and P. A. Dreyfus, pp. 83–98. Evanston, Ill.: Northwestern University Press. 1964.
"Einstein and the Crisis of Reason" and "The Philosopher and Sociology." In *Signs*, translated by Richard C. McCleary, pp. 192–97 and 98–113. Evanston, Ill.: Northwestern University Press, 1964.

II. Studies on Merleau-Ponty

Bannan, John F. *The Philosophy of Merleau-Ponty.* New York: Harcourt, Brace and World, 1967.
De Waelhens, Alphonse. *Une Philosophie de l'ambiguïté: L'Existentialisme de Maurice Merleau-Ponty.* Louvain: Publications Universitaires, 1967.
Langan, Thomas. *Merleau-Ponty's Critique of Reason.* New Haven: Yale University Press, 1966.

EUGÈNE MINKOWSKI

I. Works by Minkowski

La Schizophrénie. Paris: Payot, 1927.
Le Temps vécu. Paris: d'Artrey, 1933.
Vers une cosmologie. Paris: Aubier, 1936.

II. Studies on Minkowski

May, Rollo; Angel, Ernest; and Ellenberger, Henri F., eds. *Existence: A New Dimension in Psychiatry and Psychology.* New York: Basic Books, 1960.
Tymieniecka, Anna-Theresa. *Phenomenology and Science in Contemporary European Thought.* New York: Noonday Press, 1962. Pp. 139–55, and *passim.*

WILHELM SZILASI

I. Works by Szilasi

Wissenschaft als Philosophie. Zurich: Europa, 1945.
Macht und Ohnmacht des Geistes. Bern: Francke, 1946.
Einführung in die Phänomenologie Edmund Husserls. Tübingen: Niemeyer, 1959.
Philosophie und Naturwissenschaft. Bern: Francke, 1961.

HERMANN WEYL

I. Works by Weyl

Die Idee der Riemannschen Fläche. Leipzig: Barth, 1913. English translation by Gerald R. Maclene. *The Concept of a Riemann Surface.* Reading, Mass.: Addison-Wesley, 1964.
Raum, Zeit, Materie: Vorlesungen über Allgemeine Relativitätstheorie. 5th rev. ed. Berlin: Springer, 1923. English translation by H. L. Brose. *Space-Time-Matter.* London: Macmillan, 1922.
Gruppentheorie und Quantummechanik. Leipzig: Barth, 1928. English translation by H. P. Robertson. *The Theory of Groups in Quantum Mechanics.* New York: Dover, 1931.
"Philosophie der Mathematik und Naturwissenschaft." In *Hand-*

buch der Philosophie, ed. Alfred Baeumler and Manfred Schröter. Munich: Oldenbourg, 1926–30. No. 4, pp. 1–64, and no. 5, pp. 65–162. English translation by Joachim Weyl, revised by Hermann Weyl. *Philosophy of Mathematics and Natural Science.* New York: Atheneum, 1963.

II. Studies on Weyl

Newman, M. H. A. "Hermann Weyl." In *Bibliographical Memoirs of Fellows of the Royal Society*, 1957.

Index to Names

[509]

Index to Subjects

Absolute subject, 115
Abstraction, 474
Anthropomorphism, 264–65
Apophantic, formal, 15, 45, 351, 386, 391, 400; its branches, 5, 16, 17
A priori, 158, 205, 264, 359; vs. a posteriori, 314; formal, 18; material, 22; as vague and inexact, 25
A priori realism, 207–8
A priori sciences, 10–13
Atom, 214–15
Axiomatics, 21, 470; abstract, 406; classical, 473; concrete, 406; as a nomology, 351. *See also* Nomology
Axiomatization, 473

Being, xiii, 149, 200; as *das Frag-würdige*, 185; dimensionality of, 272; experience (happening) of, 208, 216, 229, 231; history of, 176, 231; interpretation of, 169; mathematical, 457, 471, 486, 496; modes of, 209; as reality, 149–50; and science, 193–95; "traits" of, 272; as ultimate horizon, 456
Being-in-the-World, 152, 274, 307
Be-Sinnung, 77, 167–73
Biology, 168–70, 211–12, 217, 223–25, 261, 263, 278

Body: as absolute nonobjectifiable here, 38; as ego, 280; lived, 29, 35; and meaning, 278; in Merleau-Ponty and Sartre, 276–79; as mine, 38; and perception, 279–80; proper, 267; role in perception of, 275; as system of anonymous functions, 289

Calculus: differential, 370; infinitesimal, 371, 437
Causal laws, 126–29, 143
Causality, 33, 78, 99, 113, 120–25, 140, 142, 218, 220, 325, 365; in Galileo, 60–62; "general style" of, 57; as inductivity, 60; of the laws of nature, 125; in prescientific life, 28, 56; vs. probability, 222
Cause, 7, 28, 61
Certitude, 164
Classical epistemology: and Heidegger, 149–51
Cogito, 199–200
Community of scientists, 36, 70–72, 339
Complementarity, 226
Concept: critique of, 81; development of, 484; dialectic of, 86, 348, 352, 368, 409, 442, 489, 492, 496; fundamental (basic), 12, 23, 71, 167–70, 258, 344; as intentional reality, 442; intrinsi-

274; as a mathematical manifold, 52; as mathematically idealized, 36; objective, 35–36; ontology of, 13, 21, 32, 67; in philosophy, 165; prescientific conception of, 52; as presupposition of presuppositions, 41; in science, 51, 165, 280; of science, 35, 48; to be constructed, 344; "total-meaningfulness," 274; totality of, 213

World eidetic, 32

World-forms, 35

World-picture, 196–99